EDITORS: Nancy Couling & Carola Hein with contributions from Nancy Couling, Carola Hein, Reinout Rutte & Yvonne van Mil, J. M. Ledgard, Claudia Bode & Lizzie Yarina, Christian Schmid, Stephen J. Ramos & Jan Derk Diekema, Serge F. van Gessel, Lennert J. Goemans, & Jan Matthijsen, Susan Dunne, Maarten Hajer & Dirk Sijmons, Taneha Kuzniecow Bacchin, Niccolò Bassan, Elisabetta Manea, Alberto Innocenti, & Francesco Musco, Artists' Collective Satellietgroep, Medine Altiok, Milica Topalović, and Rania Ghosn & El Hadi Jazairy.

COPY EDITING & PROOFREADING: Molly Mullin
DESIGN: Bureau Mondial, bureaumondial.com
PRINTING: Wilco Art Books
PAPER: Fly 05, 115 gr
PUBLISHER: Marcel Witvoet, nai010 publishers

This publication is published in collaboration with the Chair History of Architecture and Urban Planning, TU Delft, PortCityFutures/LDE centre and TU Delft Open/BK Books

This publication was made possible by financial support from the Creative Industries Fund NL, the Swiss National Science Foundation, PortCityFutures/LDE Centre collaboration, the EU Horizon 2020 programme (Marie Skłodowska-Curie Grant No. 753882) and the Chair History of Architecture and Urban Planning, TU Delft

Photography: p. 229 François Bruneau, Photography in visual breaks, Nancy Couling

nai010 publishers is an internationally orientated publisher specialized in developing, producing and distributing books in the fields of architecture, urbanism, art and design. www.nai010.com
nai010 books are available internationally at selected bookstores and from the following distribution partners:

NORTH, CENTRAL & SOUTH AMERICA
Artbook | D.A.P., New York, USA, dap@dapinc.com

REST OF THE WORLD
Idea Books, Amsterdam, the Netherlands, idea@ideabooks.nl

For general questions, please contact nai010 publishers directly at sales@nai010.com or visit our website www.nai010.com for further information.
Printed & bound in the Netherlands

ISBN 978–94–6208–593–0
NUR 648 + 900
BISAC ARC010000 + ARC000000

The Urbanisation of the Sea is also available as e-book: ISBN 978-94-6208-594-7 (pdf) and open access through: https://books.bk.tudelft.nl/index.php/press/catalog

THE URBANISATION OF THE SEA: FROM CONCEPTS AND ANALYSIS TO DESIGN

Edited by Nancy Couling & Carola Hein

nai010 publishers

PREFACE

Philip Steinberg, Whitley Bay, UK

Every now and then, when I peer at the North Sea from my home on the northeast coast of England, I spot barges, topped by tall yellow structures, turning northward out of the River Tyne. A quick look at my ship-finder app reveals that these towers are not destined for land but for the sea itself. Produced in Hadrian Yard in the Tyneside community of Wallsend, these are wind turbine foundations headed for the Beatrice Field, an area of shallow continental shelf just off Wick, at the northern tip of Scotland. Once they reach their destination, the foundations will be implanted in the sea bed to support what is planned to become the fourth-largest offshore wind farm in the world.

The voyages of these wind turbine components, and that of the energy they will produce, exemplify ocean urbanisation. If urbanisation is defined as an intensified transformation of nature, and thereby a transformation of place, then the transportation of these steel scaffolds and their placement on the sea bed will turn the sea into a space of social relations, an *industrial* site, an arena of logistics and production. But the turbines will do more than this. Not only are they urbanising the ocean, they are also making urban complexes increasingly marine. Sea bed transmission wires tether these regional ocean energy complexes to the land, locking in a relationship that is not so much symbiotic as co-constitutive. With the placement of wind turbines, the offshore becomes something more than a resource extraction zone, or a surface across which goods are transported. It becomes a part of the urban industrial-energy complex, a part of the *urban*.

At one level, none of this is new. On their northward journey along the English and Scottish coasts, the turbine foundations will pass countless lighthouses and navigation buoys. For centuries, these infrastructural objects have been urbanising the ocean, turning it into a space supportive of habitation, even as the settlements they were supporting were rooted on land. Likewise, firms based at what was to become Hadrian Yard, the Wallsend industrial park where the turbine foundations were manufactured, have a long history providing components for the Tyneside shipbuilding complex. Since the 1990s, shipyards along the Tyne have been repurposed to serve the offshore energy industry, building on a long history of ocean-orientated urbanisation.

Nonetheless, there is something different in the current wave of ocean urbanisation. In their heyday, the shipyards, and the ships they produced, provided connections with far-off cities. The sea was always crucial for the region's survival, but the sea was a locational *resource* for the riverside shipbuilding economy, not a *part* of it. In his musical *The Last Ship*, Sting, who grew up in Wallsend, dramatizes the decline of the Swan Hunter Shipyard, which was adjacent to Hadrian Yard (and for which Hadrian Yard's Wallsend Slipway and Engineering Company produced engines). In the play's title song, the "last ship" produced at Swan Hunter is described as "a mountain of steel [that] makes its way to the sea." As it disappears beyond the mouth of the Tyne, it takes with it hope for the livelihoods of countless men and women dependent on Tyneside's shipbuilding economy. Sting's Wallsend exists *by* the sea, but it is not of the sea. Once the last ship leaves, the distant maritime connection that pumps life into the riverside community, bringing the "outside" "in," is gone. Indeed, once the play's protagonist, Gideon Fletcher, goes to sea, he too leaves Tyneside behind (at least until his prodigal return).

Today, however, the bright yellow "mountain[s] of steel" that depart the Tyne for the North Sea never really leave. Implanting towers in the sea bed, tethering them to land, and fuelling production and consumption far beyond the banks of the Tyne (or, for that matter, the North Sea coast), this wave of urbanisation brings the sea to the city and the city to the sea through a revolutionary transformation of maritime and coastal nature and space. As the chapters in this book reveal, the urbanisation of the sea is not a story unique to the North Sea. Nor is it an entirely new story. However a focus on the North Sea and the ways in which ocean urbanisation is occurring at an unprecedented scale there, to unprecedented effects, can tell us much about the changing shape of what the editors of this volume call our increasingly "viscous" world.

CONTENTS

THE NORTH SEA: NEW PERSPECTIVES ON THE SEA-LAND CONTINUUM

Nancy Couling & Carola Hein

The North Sea region has been the nexus of northern European technological, cultural, and economic advancement. According to historian Michael Pye, "this cold, grey sea in an obscure time made the modern world possible."(1) Together with its neighbouring coastal areas, the North Sea is also an exemplary case of intense interactions across the land-sea threshold. The "commons" of the North Sea has long been central to the region's climatic and ecological balance, but also to its economies. After centuries of shared use, maritime and industrial processes have led to international border regulation, uninterrupted traffic along major transport corridors, intensified offshore capture and distribution of energy, and the erection of a multitude of structures. Related transfer sites have also created important nodes in coastal and hinterland areas. The sea itself has been so transformed that it has become an enigmatic urbanised space, charged with the task of increased economic production both from traditional and new maritime sectors while at the same time it has been emptied of imaginative narratives and cultural significance.

International laws and national institutions have divided the North Sea into seven parts based on national maritime borders attached to seven different countries, wholly consuming what was once a shared, fluid space. Each of the countries bordering the North Sea follows its own legal, planning, and policy approaches in order to manage extraction, green energy generation, and other areas of "blue growth" potential. Contemporary urgencies, such as flooding and other extreme weather events, ecological degradation, and predicted sea level rise, are increasing. These effects highlight the vulnerability of a continued industry-led sectorial approach to the North Sea and have drawn public attention to the unstable status of the sea itself. While collective policies and plans are needed, and EU Directive 2014/89/EU requires that all EU maritime areas must have strategic management plans in place before 31 March 2021, it is not clear whether such a transnational approach will be established at a time of dissolving European collaboration as signaled by Brexit.(2) To meaningfully address the challenges raised by the urbanisation of the sea, to avoid further overexploitation and to ensure foresight in management and stewardship, we need a comprehensive approach with collaboration among diverse stakeholders and disciplines. Such an approach could make the North Sea the epicentre of a paradigm shift of spatial considerations, from conceptualisation to design.

The urbanisation of the sea and its relation to land-based developments cannot meaningfully be studied or undertaken through the lens of a single discipline or from a single national perspective. It requires a long-term historical and large-scale understanding of the space we are studying. It requires different tools and new perspectives that help us bring together diverse sources and languages. To initiate conversations, the editors present voices from many disciplines and geographic positions. The book builds upon discussions that took place during the Marie Curie Fellowship held by Nancy Couling in the Chair History of Architecture and Urban Planning from 2017–2019 at Delft University of Technology and brings together selected contributions from the 2018 TU Delft conference "Viscous Space: The Offshore Physicality of the North Sea between Solid and Liquid." This conference, convened by the editors, used thickness and resistance to flow as fundamental conceptual guidelines to link thematic sessions on representations, narratives and projections, infrastructure and heritage, and legal and theoretical constructions.(3)

The contents of the book are heterogeneous, combining artistic research, urban design projects in maritime contexts, and speculative proposals as well as academic papers, essays, contemporary and historic maps, photographs, and contemporary fiction. Presenting plural starting points offers potential for cross-fertilisation and opportunities to rethink cultural positions, spatial history, and practice. An excerpt from a novel offers a sense of ocean depth through an account of a physical descent into the deep ocean. The reader's experience of the ocean's interior differs from that of maritime planners who must weave conflicting economic and ecological threads together from above the surface. Policymakers are apt to view their task in the sea space as a battle against time. Researchers and designers report on the findings of specific studies, including artistic projects, where the investigation of sea sites has produced unexpected findings. This variety is intended to capture the richness and complexity of the topic, to facilitate different points of entry for readers who can then follow journeys from concepts through analysis to the design of possible futures. Together, these multiple perspectives present an illustrative overview of some of the ways that we can think of, think with, and represent the sea as an urbanised space.

Our aim is to encourage understandings of shared land-sea spatial histories that go beyond the traditional exploration of development in the framework of nation-states or land-based entities. Employing a perspective *from the sea*, we aim to draw the sea-land continuum into discussions of urban and territorial development by investigating selected sites of critical interactions. These are sites that have been imagined, occupied, planned, and represented mostly by private actors, some of which have long operated autonomously, outside of classic land-based national and urban planning and policy frameworks that did not take the sea into account. Increasing in frequency and force, the effects of climate change have made the sea potentially more dangerous and unpredictable—conditions that neither directives nor technology are able to control. Our approach therefore promotes a three-dimensional understanding and calls for a trans-disciplinary investigation that is focused on space, society, and culture. The book argues that such an approach can help develop new directions in representation, design, and planning along the sea-land continuum and help dislodge inherited binary assumptions.

The geographic focus on the North Sea is not exclusive: we include perspectives from the Mediterranean, the Singapore Strait, the Pacific, the Barents, and the Baltic Seas. This allows us to gain a better understanding of what a paradigm shift from a land-based logic with fixed spatial and legal delineations to a more fluid, integrated, sea-based approach can mean for research, representation, and ultimately policy-making, planning, and design. In the next part of this introduction, we introduce two fundamental concepts to support our approach: the urbanisation of the sea and the port cityscape. We then offer a glimpse into the historiography of the North Sea, followed by a presentation of the issues at stake and the key analytical approaches. Finally, we provide a brief overview of the book.

URBANISATION OF THE SEA AND THE PORT CITYSCAPE: THE CONCEPTS

Inspired by the influential work of Henri Lefebvre and his understanding of urbanisation as a multi-dimensional process including material structures and practices, regulations, and the modalities of everyday interactions, the theory of planetary urbanisation offers a comprehensive framework with which to conceptualise and critically appraise processes unfolding around us.(4) In particular, extended urbanisation draws attention to the logistical, infrastructural, and legislative systems that transform space outside of familiar urban environments, thereby restructuring vast areas, frequently causing social upheaval and environmental degradation. Such areas, including the world ocean and seas, serve vital functions for urban agglomerations, yet the direct links and interdependencies between them have mostly been neglected in the "city" focus of urban studies discussions.(5) Today, what was previously considered rural or natural has been engulfed by networks, dedicated structures, and forms of labour that serve the requirements of what Lefebvre called a fully urbanised society, and the city must be differentiated from the processes of urbanisation extending far beyond it.(6)

In addition to material forms of its manifestation, urbanisation has many immaterial dimensions of social and cultural exchange that have been extensively researched by Manuel Castells and other scholars in the social sciences.(7) This land-based, city-focused approach has led to research in urban studies that occasionally looks out to sea, but either focuses on abstract economic dimensions or logistic flows, or on select and limited spaces of network structures, for example, in relation to port cities.(8) With the notable exception of Fernand Braudel, researchers have rarely explored people and infrastructure in the sea space—the foreland—or reflected on how they are directly linked to the hinterland.(9) Land-side decision-makers, often working in capital cities away from the coast, exert a profound influence on the sea, shaping its spaces and practices often with land-based tools. Institutions and scholars studying the North Sea region also often have a land-centred bias and study ports, cities, and their regions through select lenses. The port cityscape—that is, the network of port-related spaces in a larger port city region—is a conceptual framework that aims to overcome these divisions through a focus on the sea-land continuum.(10)

Developing from these two perspectives, this book provides an analysis of the sea as an urbanised space of transformed nature in relation to resources and not in relation to existing urban nodes. It also analyses expanding urban development from port cities encroaching further into the sea. These two spheres of inquiry are dealt with unsystematically in current literature.(11) Addressing this absence, we set out to investigate how the urbanisation of the sea is reshaping our regional economic, social, cultural, and human environments at sea, through the spaces of the coast and to the hinterland. In particular, we draw port city regions into the analysis of the sea-land continuum, providing a diversified context for a networked approach. We also aim to identify tools, methods. and frameworks that can help reconceptualise the sea space as an integral part of our historical urban realm and restore its *cultural* relevance, thereby testing the role that narratives and representations play in such a reconceptualisation. The urbanisation of the sea requires multiple perspectives and has yet to be specifically defined. This book opens up a range of possibilities and calls for further discussion, using the North Sea as a point of departure.

THE NORTH SEA: A BRIEF HISTORICAL INTRODUCTION

The North Sea—a complex topographic space characterized by a unique combination of natural and cultural features—provides the book's central case study. It is a relatively shallow "shelf" sea, with a maximum depth of around 70–80 metres, and, in the southern half, there are large areas of only 40 m deep or less. Scientific evidence points to the southern part of the North Sea being a fertile plain during the mesolithic period from 12,000 BC to 6,000 BC, and settled by large numbers of people, until it was finally flooded around 8,000 BC.(12)

Cities around the North Sea developed through a rich legacy of trade and cultural exchange, where before the rise of the nation-state, dynamic inter-regional influences were readily absorbed into local culture. The similar warehouses of the Hanseatic cities of Hamburg, Amsterdam, and Bergen are one architectural example. Knowledge and cultural practices were connected across the water and, around the sixteenth century, literacy rates were higher on the coasts than inland.(13) Michael Pye argues that in the formative period between 700 and 1700, people were constantly migrating around the North Sea and identities were not based on a notion as abstract as race.(14) Anglo-Saxons originated from Germany and Denmark in the fifth century and the Vikings settled all around the region. The Shetland Islands were Nordic for 600 years.

During this period of continuous exchange and maritime activity, the North Sea began to be modified and "constructed." Its sand has been extracted, it has been used as a dumping site, and, for hundreds of years, it has been dredged and trawled. In the mid-nineteenth century, highly developed areas on the North Sea's southern shore, where port cities like Amsterdam, Antwerp, and London served as nodes on the sea-land continuum, began attracting growing numbers of residents, industries, and technologies, particularly related to the transport and transformation of petroleum.(15) The discovery of oil in the North Sea in the 1960s led to the growth of techno-logistical activities for oil and gas infrastructure in and around the sea. Today, the southern region of the North Sea boasts the highest population density in Europe. The densely populated areas, in conjunction with the existing maritime infrastructure, make it particularly attractive for development of the offshore wind energy sector.

The influence of the energy transition is evident in the offshore territories of wind parks, energy ports, empty sub-sea hydrocarbon formations, and left-over hydrocarbon infrastructure. This transition presents a challenge to planning and society as a whole, but also an opportunity to reimagine the on- and offshore energy landscape, which, as several contributions point out, will be no less "invasive" than the inherited landscape of fossil fuel—the petroleumscape.(16) Currently around the North Sea, the transition to, for example, wind energy, is concentrated, large-scale, and state-led. Because it is developing in the tradition of the older oil-based energy landscape, it is characterised by dedicated zones, fixed infrastructure, and a continuous circulation of components, capital, and labour. Energy and communication infrastructure has been extended into the sea over the past 150 years, but we have failed to conceptualise this extension, instead allowing planning decisions to follow inherited notions of temporary structures and a visually open horizon.

The ongoing physical modification of the North Sea—like many seas—has been paradoxically accompanied by the upholding of inherited conceptual binaries: sea and land, urban and rural, nature and culture. Sea spaces have become sites of intensive activity for logistics, the extraction of food and energy, which also feed production processes downstream. Public access to the North Sea is limited and large areas are dedicated to security zones around industrial installations. As a result, these binaries have not only persisted but they have enabled a particular type of industry-led urbanisation to take hold within a space otherwise perceived as "natural."(17) These binaries have also, until recently, prevented the sea from being perceived as an urban realm. From a cultural perspective, northern European society has also withdrawn from the sea. In his photography and film essays, Alan Sekula has poignantly documented the "disappearance of the sea" brought about by container shipping.(18) Seafarers on the North Sea now lead a marginalised existence and contemporary maritime workers in other sectors are hired for their experience in steel, not the sea. Recent proposals, such as the creation of a giant dam across the North Sea, speak to a long-standing trust in technological solutions.(19) The need to change human patterns and perceptions has become urgent.

CARTOGRAPHY, NARRATIVES, AND DESIGN

Investigating the sea as an urban realm resonates strongly with the current call to recalibrate inherited concepts of "nature" and "culture."(20) It also challenges the notion of the "urban" as a discrete, bounded site.(21) The sea is a critical protagonist and partner to urbanisation processes. It,is paramount to the ecological well-being of the planet and to the emotional and economic well-being of the human population. Novel approaches that combine culture, imaginaries, and non-industrial narratives are needed to fully understand the North Sea and other oceans.

One language with which to tell this story is cartography. Cartography boasts a rich tradition on land and at sea, and is a useful way to communicate across disciplines, to identify gaps and common concerns, and, most importantly, to propose new perspectives. Cartographic representations help us see patterns and outliers, read critical territorial relationships, power structures, understandings, and belief systems, and derive meaning from huge, complex territories. But there can be no such thing as an objective map reproducing a pre-existing reality. Choices must always be made about what to represent and how, and what to exclude.(22) Mapping is therefore also an act of design: orienting, navigating, and in a state of becoming. Contributions to this volume show how cartography can capture both activity and desire and how it can narrate stories as well as delineate property and relate scientific facts.

Narratives are another way to rethink the North Sea. Author Tom Blass describes the North Sea as "too substantial, too terrible, to be glamorous,"(23) yet the sea's magnetic pull, a sensation felt by many Europeans, has not diminished, rather it has perhaps intensified, but has been channelled into specialized views, sites, and events. The sea is thick with activity and desire. We tell ourselves stories about the sea that fuel human emotion. These stories include those that assert myths of unlimited space and resources, those that build new cultural relations to the sea, for example, around oil, and those that question our place in the world and our aesthetic interpretation of it. In each case, narratives can exert a powerful force.

The book takes a spatial view and is particularly interested in the formulation of speculative design proposals rather than purely theoretical reflections. Both cartography and narratives, sometimes working together, are used as design tools to reimagine relations between land and sea, and to reassert the public dimension. Design enables new forms of access to areas that, through industrialisation and privatisation, have become illegible, invisible, or impenetrable—frequent characteristics of the offshore spaces of the North Sea, and other seas, as well as multiple coastal and hinterland sites. Artists and designers are able to break down physical and conceptual barriers, to reconstruct dialogues between separated fragments, and to explore the design potential of the sea's spaces, rhythms, materiality, and intangible qualities.

OVERVIEW

Our approach is reflected in the structure of the book. Consisting of four parts, it is organised to assist the reader in establishing a perspective from the sea to the land, to gain a sense of what is at stake in the space of the North Sea and in imagining future possibilities. The book progresses from preliminary methodological foundations in Part I to explorations of concepts of the sea in Part II. Extensions across the land/sea threshold are discussed in Part III, with a particular focus on the North Sea. Possible future orientations are presented in Part IV, "Cultivations," which offers examples of art and design projects that have traced new pathways of understanding and representation. An introduction to the individual chapters is provided at the beginning of each of these parts.

The visual orchestration of maps and photographs between these sections sets the atmosphere for the ensuing topics and creates a pause in the on-going narrative. These elements intend to present the central contradictions of the urbanisation of the sea: on the one hand, the scale of industrial processes can be vividly portrayed and, on the other, the aesthetic qualities of selected seascapes around the North Sea capture the imagination and instantly communicate a common sensual and cultural experience. Throughout the book, maps convey what is otherwise invisible to the public, and sometimes the maps convey a sense of what has been lost. Historic North Sea maps present a different sea—more populated, displaying more diverse types of maritime knowledge—than the North Sea we observe today. The ocean and seas comprise a sophisticated planetary system that exerts a sense of wonder. The book includes discussions on how the use of the stars in traditional navigation methods linked the sea directly to the cosmos, thereby connecting mystery and spirituality to the practical task of sailing from place to place.([24]) Quantitative evaluations of the economic potential of the sea should not replace awareness of the sea's intangible qualities and its connectedness to interscalar natural forces.

Several contributions argue that our current ecological crisis is accompanied by something potentially more acute: *a crisis of the imagination*.(25) Hence, as an interwoven collection of episodes, this book aims to retell the story of our relationship to the space of the sea. Together, the encounters in these chapters lead us to imagine a multi-dimensional urbanised sea; deep, thick, layered, viscous, emergent, partially anchored to port cities and partly connected to temporary sites of offshore development. This urban sea demands new governance systems and more complete forms of representation, adapted to planning with time, understanding grades of permanence and the dynamics of tides, currents, and seasons. But the urbanisation of the sea is not a laissez-faire option. While the congestion and degradation of the North Sea clearly emerges through many contributions, this book argues that to urbanise the sea must also mean practicing a form of *cultivation*: we must take care of commons, ecologies, and synergies for the long-term and acknowledge deep cultural and spiritual ties. This represents a paradigm shift in current practices and demands an urgent cross-disciplinary effort. Current marine planning is faced with a myriad of complex issues and dynamic parameters that defy land-based planning tools. Spatial and environmental reserves are reaching critical limits.

As a place that has absorbed, facilitated, and forged divergent histories, the sea also offers us a place for creative futures. Therefore, we focus on ways forward for designers regarding questions of the sea space and issue a call for greater involvement from the creative industries in collaboration with complimentary experts. The book aims to inspire such involvement and encourage further collaborations in this emerging field.

(1) Michael Pye, *The Edge of the World : How the North Sea Made Us Who We Are* (London: Penguin Books, 2015).
(2) European Parliament and the Council of the European Union, "Directive 2014/89/EU Establishing a Framework for Maritime Spatial Planning" (European Union, 23 July 2014), https://eur-lex.europa.eu/legal-content/EN/TXT/PDF/?uri=CELEX:32014L0089&from=EN.
(3) The conference was held 20-22 June 2018. See the website for details: www.viscousspace.com
(4) Neil Brenner and Christian Schmid, "Planetary Urbanization," in *Urban Constellations*, ed. Matthew Gandy (Berlin: Jovis, 2011). See also chapter six, this volume.
(5) Hillary Angelo and David Wachsmuth, "Urbanizing Urban Political Ecology: A Critique of Methodological Cityism," *International Journal of Urban and Regional Research* 39, no. 1 (2015): 16–27, https://doi.org/10.1111/1468-2427.12105.
(6) Henri Lefebvre, *The Urban Revolution* (Minneapolis: University of Minnesota Press, 2003).
(7) Manuel Castells, *La question urbaine* (Paris: François Maspero, 1973).
(8) Carola Hein, "Port Cities and Urban Waterfronts: How Localized Planning Ignores Water as a Connector," *WIREs Water* 3 (2016):419–38.
(9) Fernand Braudel, *The Mediterranean and the Mediterranean World in the Age of Philip II*, vol. 1 (New York,: Harper, 1972).
(10) Carola Hein, *Port Cities: Dynamic Landscapes and Global Networks* (London: Routledge, 2011).
(11) Carola Hein, "The Port Cityscape: Spatial and Institutional Approaches to Port City Relationships," *PortusPlus* 8 (2019).
(12) Laura Spinney, "Searching for Doggerland," *National Geographic Magazine*, December 2012.
(13) Blass, *Naked Shore*.
(14) Pye, *Edge of the World*.
(15) Carola Hein, "Oil Spaces: The Global Petroleumscape in the Rotterdam/The Hague Area," *Journal of Urban History* 44, no. 5 (2018):887–929.
(16) Hein, "Oil Spaces."
(17) See chapter 7.
(18) Allan Sekula and Noël Burch, *The Forgotten Space: A Film Essay Seeking to Understand the Contemporary Maritime World in Relation to the Symbolic Legacy of the Sea*, 2010, http://www.theforgottenspace.net/static/notes.html.
(19) Jon Henley and Alan Evans, "Giant Dams Enclosing North Sea Could Protect Millions from Rising Waters," *The Guardian* (12 February 2020), https://www.theguardian.com/environment/2020/feb/12/giant-dams-could-protect-millions-from-rising-north-sea.
(20) Timothy Morton, *Ecology without Nature : Rethinking Environmental Aesthetics* (Cambridge, MA: Harvard University Press, 2009).
(21) Neil Brenner and Christian Schmid, "The 'Urban Age' in Question," *International Journal of Urban and Regional Research* 38, no. 3 (May 2014): 731–55, https://doi.org/10.1111/1468-2427.12115.
(22) Geoff King, *Mapping Reality: Exploration of Cultural Cartographies* (Basingstoke: Macmillan Press, 1996); Mark Monmonier, *How to Lie with Maps*, third ed. (University of Chicago Press, 2018), https://www.press.uchicago.edu/ucp/books/book/chicago/H/bo27400568.html.
(23) Tom Blass, *The Naked Shore: Of the North Sea* (London: Bloomsbury, 2015).
(24) See chapters 5 & 8, this volume
(25) See chapters 14, 17, 20, this volume

Part I FOUNDATIONS

Part I presents the book's research origins at the École Polytechnique Fédérale de Lausanne (EPFL), Switzerland, and at the Chair of History of Architecture and Urban Planning, TU Delft. In chapter 1, Nancy Couling explores the urbanisation of the sea from a maritime perspective, and proposes a methodology for analysing and representing the sea as a regional territory. Couling makes the case for considering the sea as a cultural product formed through relations between its geophysical, biological, and socioeconomic attributes. It is thereby relational, and a space central to the region, rather than a domain peripheral to land. Using the Barents and Baltic Seas as case studies, she proposes two co-existing urban formats for each sea, which are derived from urbanisation processes interacting with the sea's inherent dynamics. This chapter summarises Couling's research in nine principles of urbanisation in the Barents and Baltic Seas, contributing to an understanding of the urbanisation of the sea foundational to this book.

The Delft cartographic method promotes research through mapping. It aims at gaining an understanding of a territory's long-term developments using geo-spatial historic mapping. Building on a study of the Netherlands in the period 800–2000 through the lens of landscape, infrastructure, and habitation patterns, in chapter 2 Carola Hein, Reinout Rutte, and Yvonne van Mil describe how they adapt the method to North Sea port city regions in the period 1300–2000 with a focus on the Rotterdam, London, and Hamburg areas and on the spaces shaped through the presence of the port, the port cityscape. Taken together, the two investigations showcase the potential of geo-spatial mapping as a tool for understanding the impact of long-term development on the present and how the technique can form a foundation for design decisions of the future. The investigations also highlight the need for a new conceptualisation of the spaces of sea and land as a shared, common, liquid territory and the need to develop a comprehensive theoretical framework for port city regions as nodes of distribution and the sea-land continuum as a developmental axis.

Chapter 1 OCEAN SPACE AND URBANISATION: THE CASE OF TWO SEAS*

Nancy Couling

Through her analysis of the Barents and the Baltic Seas, Nancy Couling reveals initial insights regarding the urbanisation of the sea as well as findings specific to these two territorial contexts.

Currently Assoc. Prof. at Bergen School of Architecture, Norway, Nancy was awarded a Marie Skłodowska Curie Individual Fellowship at the Chair of History of Architecture and Urban Planning, TU Delft 2017–19 with the project "Oceanurb: The Unseen Spaces of Extended Urbanisation in the North Sea." Trained as an architect at Auckland University, New Zealand, she completed her PhD at EPFL in 2015 after much international practice experience and cofounding her own interdisciplinary practice in Berlin 1995–2010. Co-editor of the prize-winning "Barents Lessons-Teaching and Research in Architecture" (2012. Zürich: Park Books), she frequently publishes and lectures and is a member of the research group "Territories of Extended Urbanisation," led by the ETH Zurich, & FCL Singapore.

* This chapter includes excerpts from Nancy Couling's doctoral thesis,"The Role of Ocean Space in Contemporary Urbanization" (Lausanne, EPFL, 2015), http://infoscience.epfl.ch/record/212706. Partly funded by the Swiss National Science Foundation (SNSF), PI Prof. Harry Gugger, Grant nr: 146457.

Although many scientific fields investigate the ocean, research about ocean space is scarce. To begin filling this research gap, this chapter discusses case studies of the Barents and Baltic Seas. The research discussed establishes a methodological foundation for the study of the North Sea presented in this volume, and presents preliminary conclusions about the urbanisation of the sea. The investigations of the Barents and the Baltic Seas looked at—from an urban perspective—possible ways of addressing the quantum shift in scale and intensity of spatial demands on the sea through energy production, the extraction of resources, and infrastructural and logistical development. While these developments are ephemeral in relative spatial terms, often remote and hard to decipher, they also carve out vast territories and leave lasting physical legacies. The ocean has become a site of spatial and environmental convergence, a type of "hinterland" to urbanised territories at the same time as the urban has become more diffuse, porous, and far-reaching.

History is rich in examples of fluid forms of urbanisation that engaged the ocean as a network agent, without claiming territorial rights. Intensified activities, however, have led to the territorialisation of the ocean through the establishment of fixed Exclusive Economic Zones and the implementation of land-based planning tools within these zones. A fundamental contradiction between open ocean systems and bounded space becomes apparent. When boundaries have been established in the ocean, the outcome has been not spaces of human settlement, but rather specialist spaces with a range of purposes—both productive and protective—permitted for limited periods of time. The lack of settlement qualifies these spaces to become either mono-functional, semi-industrial landscapes or protected areas for important ecosystems—to name two extremes. In both cases, further planning processes have been unleashed through Marine Spatial Planning.

The lack of settlement has meant a lack of habitual interaction with ocean space. Since the ocean does not contain places of dense human occupation, offshore spaces appear increasingly autonomous, incomprehensible in terms of scale and similarly inaccessible in both visual/conceptual and physical terms. Their specialised nature and distance from settlement areas prevents organic contact. Our relationship is mediated and technicised. Specialist knowledge and skills are required to enter these realms on an individual basis, and therefore the ocean takes on an abstract, remote status that fuels the imagination but also, in the majority of cases, further determines the sequence and form of development.

In 1974, Henri Lefebvre wrote that "natural space is disappearing" and described how such spaces have become compartmentalised for a form of consumption subordinate to the dominant strategic modes of production.(1) In their essay "Planetary Urbanization," Neil Brenner and Christian Schmid describe the end of the wilderness as "one of the four most marked and far-reaching worldwide socio-spatial transformations of the last thirty years."(2) If natural space has disappeared, we are challenged to find appropriate terminology and conceptual references for a volumetric environment geared toward the natural laws of flow and a physical body constantly in motion as it interacts with territoriality, fixity, and human-produced flows. For these reasons, contemporary urban conditions demand an expanded view of architectural relations, including geographic, geological, and hydrographical dimensions, since urbanisation processes now involve places that previously were buried, inaccessible, or that remained "natural."

Our two case study seas are coherent territories within which specific forms of urbanisation can be identified. I take a holistic, cross-disciplinary approach, departing from the geographical sea as a central relational space and draw on theory and literature, technical reports, GIS data, and fieldwork. While interactions with the coast are a constant occurrence in these two seas, the search for traces of urbanisation processes here is specifically focused on the sea space itself, and aims not to examine the littoral condition per se or the wealth of existing literature concerning the meanings of the coast. The chapter aims to find out what contemporary offshore phenomena could bring to a discussion on ocean urbanisation. Seas are cultural products, the result of intersecting relations between geographic properties and sociocultural activities. The analysis presented here of the Barents and Baltic Seas reveals specific territorial profiles. These maritime regions are each unique, and in each case I draw conclusions about the specific relations and dynamics of the urbanised sea. However, the analysis aims to shed light on recurring components and common processes, and to this end, I propose nine principles of ocean urbanisation.

OCEAN TERRITORY

Stuart Elden argues that territory has a series of culturally and historically specific meanings, which are "produced, mutable, and fluid."(3) One meaning is a politically contested and controlled space, depending on techniques of land surveying and cartography, which Elden calls "political technology."(4) According to Elden, fifteenth–sixteenth century spatial understandings are "still the overriding geographical determination of our world."(5) As a cultural product, ocean territory is comparable to land-based territory: each sea is the result of a unique combination of historical, political, cultural, and environmental forces. However, its dimensions are multiple. To understand these forces requires a holistic approach capable of reconciling poles of interest that are even farther apart than those on land.

To serve the interests of sailors and mariners, in 1952, the International Hydrographic Organisation took on the task of delineating the world's oceans and seas.(6) Their limits were roughly based on bathymetry, had no political significance, and are still frequently referenced. The Barents Sea, for example, occupies a shelf of an average 230 metres in depth, which drops down to the Atlantic Ocean to the west and the Arctic Ocean to the north. The Baltic Sea is a semi-enclosed, relatively shallow sea with an average depth of 54 m, internally divided into fourteen parts by a series of gulfs and sub-basins.(7)

Primary oceanographic spaces and topographical limits therefore exist outside of political demarcation. Topography, flora and fauna, geological formations, and water flows are landscape characteristics shared by both land and sea, but which relate mostly to the surface condition. Not only is the sea more topographic than the land, (8) but it is deep, composed of different masses in constant flux according to seasons, currents, temperatures, salinities, and densities. Compared to land, the surface condition is inverted to the sea bed, and a new "surface"—the abstract ocean plane—takes its place on the horizon. Within this fluid volume, multiple exchanges create spaces and conditions that support the ocean's richness of life. These resources, including topographic features such as natural harbours, wind, and water currents, have then structured human interaction with the sea.

The spatial entity of a bathymetrically defined sea can be conceived of as territory, even if the Latin *terra* means land. However, the sea has a history of territorialisation distinct from land. The political technology Elden describes has only partially and recently been applied at sea, therefore the concept of ocean territory has yet to be accurately defined. Geometry, politics, and concepts of bounded space are not the only determining characteristics.

As an alternative to a definition based on contained space, French geographer Bernard Debarbieux, pursuing the line of thinking established by Claude Raffestin, defined territory as "the arrangement of material and symbolic resources capable of structuring the practical conditions needed to support the existence of an individual or a social community."(9) Ocean space—sparsely populated yet continually traversed, harvested, and tapped for energy—would seem to be better represented by this idea. Territorialisation can then be seen as the result of several forces: superficial (on the surface) legal boundaries, networks of human interests, communities of marine life occupying different zones at different times, and natural oceanographic events.

DEFINING OCEAN TERRITORY: A PROPOSAL

Rather than a territory defined by political borders, I propose an integrated, kinetic definition of ocean territory based on oceanography and biological thresholds with which urbanising forces interact. Both the ocean's inherent spatial properties and cultural interventions become active components. The fundamental physical characteristics—the inherently spatial oceanography that forms a differentiated, dynamic, interconnected habitat—and a range of both organic and inorganic forces are active in this space to form an elastic territory with porous edges. This can be summarised as the interactions between the geophysical territory, the biological territory, and the socioeconomic territory [Fig. 1, p. 45].

The biological territory is closely connected to the geophysical base and together these spaces define the range of oceanic ecosystems, however edges are open and characterised by zones of transition. The socioeconomic territory, on the other hand, creates political borders, areas of resource extraction, and static systems of order that are used to define protected areas or to organise extractive or productive activities such as fishing, oil and gas exploration, and other forms of energy production. I used this understanding of territory as the analytical basis for urban research in the Barents and Baltic Seas.

TWO SEAS

Covering an area of 1,405,000 km^2, the Barents Sea is vast, remote, pristine, and rich in resources. Yet, its geographical location on the edge of the Arctic, the effects of climate change, and the discovery of significant offshore fossil fuel reserves have swiftly made the Barents Sea the focus of international attention. Urbanisation processes have accelerated. Easier access to the Northern Sea Route from Europe to Asia across the northern Russian coastline due to the receding ice front could save shipping companies valuable time and transport costs.(10) The Barents Sea holds an estimated 30 percent and 25 percent of the world's untapped gas and oil reserves respectively and exploration activities have intensified, but it is also "one of Europe's last large, clean and relatively undisturbed marine ecosystems," one of the most productive in the world, and among the most biologically diverse in the Arctic.(11) These interests steer the development of the Barents Region—a geographic entity, an ecosystem, and a political-economic construct created as recently as 1993 to "mark the end of the cold war and the beginning of something new."(12)

The Baltic Sea and the Barents Sea are very different—spatially, culturally, and geographically. The prosperous period of Baltic trade through the exploits of the Vikings and the Hanseatic League left a legacy of cultural achievement expressed architecturally in urban centres. Extensive maritime interaction continued with the Danish Kingdom, the Swedish Empire, and the contemporary post-Soviet collaboration among the Baltic States of Estonia, Latvia, and Lithuania. Centrally located in Europe, the Baltic Sea straddles geographic, cultural, and political boundaries in both an east-west and a north-south direction and is accessible to a large population, although at 393,000 km^2 it is only one-third the size of the Barents Sea. Development pressures indicating the Baltic Sea's levels of urbanisation include some of the world's busiest maritime transport routes and the expanding wind-energy sector. Due to its brackish water and its ongoing transformation from lake to sea, it is ecologically unique and hosts a range of unique species specifically adapted to this change. The combination of a sensitive oceanographic predisposition and the intense coastal exchange bring the Baltic Sea to a tipping point where the sea as a resource in the broadest sense is endangered. As the focus of its nine surrounding countries, many efforts have been mobilised, in particular from the EU, to economically unite and strengthen this realm, while addressing the sea's pressing environmental issues. Hence the Baltic Sea is also a strategic political project.

I analyse the two seas in relation to their geophysical, biological and social-economic territory. I also consider networks, seascape, technology and ecology—the most prominent types of use of ocean space as well as subjects of important literature in urban studies.(13)

URBAN FORMATS IN THE BARENTS SEA

Territorial analysis of the Barents Sea reveals two urban formats: firstly the loose, flexible mesh of activities oscillating with the extreme seasonal changes in the region and tied to the seascape resources, and secondly, the strategic geometries which harden into marine highways and technical sites of extraction.

The first format is made up of interactions that set up patterns of settlement and trade liaisons which have been mediated by the sea itself. This form of urbanisation is not based on density, population numbers, or centrality, but rather on the double periphery of the littoral zone—both peripheral to the northern European continent and to the geographical sea itself—and connections presiding over large, dispersed areas of small settlements. Apart from the city of Murmansk, which was established during World War I within the Russian governmental policy of deliberately populating the north, the fringes of the Barents Sea have traditionally never given rise to dense urban areas. Instead, since the end of the last ice age, many small, widely dispersed settlements developed along the coast at natural harbours. Ocean trading routes were the vehicle of exchange between settlements and with international partners. Today, the towns that grew out of earlier settlements are connected through coastal services, are economically reliant on diverse forms of ocean production, and are remote and detached from nationally centralised modes of organisation. The density of ocean activities is comparable to activities on land [Fig. 2, p. 46].

The resulting spatial system embraces diverse forms of movement and exchange, which consolidate relationships and define the territorial dimensions: fishing, the seasonal transhumance of the indigenous Sami culture, seasonal population fluctuations, and border crossings. The Barents Sea is an extensive region of negotiation, exchange, and flux. Since the shores of the Barents Sea are not suitable for commercial agriculture, the specialised crop cultivation and surplus food production that has been a decisive factor in urban history and increasing settlement density did not apply here. Instead, the urban morphology of the Barents region describes its own singular relationship between settlement and territory, mediated through the agency of the sea. Urban systems operate in a loose, shifting mesh across land and sea—a strategy seemingly well suited to an environment of extremes.(14)

The second urban format, overlaying the first, is comprised of strategic geometries. While exerting a powerful force on a map, these formats are still to be verified. They constitute a pre-urban phase of speculation, a phase the Barents region well understands from its history of "boom and bust" resource exploitation including coal mining on Svalbard, the Kirkenes and Kiruna iron-ore mines, and nickel-mining in Nikel. The establishment of offshore exploration grids, rigs, and pipelines represents an extension of this preliminary resource infrastructure as it developed first on land. Since the cycles of these industries are out of tune with natural cycles, and carry on year-round, the offshore Barents Sea environment holds them in check due to the difficulty and expense posed by deep, rough and cold waters. Its double periphery is a receptor for visions of extended urbanisation, always in a state of becoming: "the region is a complex field of unrealised dreams and visions."(15) In the Barents Sea, resistance to an urbanisation of strategic geometries confirms a co-relation between urban activities and oceanography, which is stronger than the co-relation of topography to the urban on land. On land, topography and the forms of organic organisation that adhere to it have largely been overtaken by efficient geometrical patterns of primordial order [Fig. 3].

URBAN FORMATS IN THE BALTIC SEA

Borders and enclosures in the Baltic Sea are abstract fixtures, some of which define operational systems such as zones of marine planning or traffic routes, and some of which are projections of competing activities not yet reinforced by law [Fig. 4, p. 47]. The zones earmarked for wind park developments and marine protected areas, which appear scattered and small in scale compared to the scale of environmental degradation, are examples of the latter. The result is a complex, fragmented series of singular but frequently overlapping spaces. Traversing the sea, a deep-water shipping route forms a central backbone of transit.

The bathymetric and morphologic division of the Baltic Sea into fourteen parts is exacerbated by the overlay of anthropogenic borders described above. In addition, the Exclusive Economic Zones of the nine surrounding countries create eleven zones that do not correspond to natural divisions, but which generate national and sometimes trans-

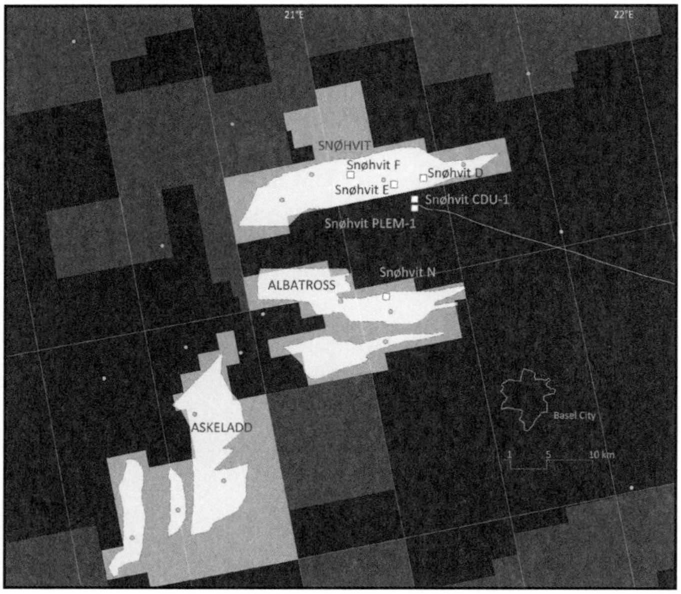

Fig. 3
Plan of Snøhvit extraction area, Barents Sea (Couling)

boundary planning efforts to organise the space. Superposing these layers, the combined shipping passages describe a space of perpetual movement irrespective of borders. The history of the Baltic Sea demonstrates a persistent network component, which has accelerated interactions and created an interconnected space, which one study has called the "sea common."(16) This is reinforced through the relative proximity of ports and shorelines—a ship in the Baltic Sea is at no point more than 130 km from land.(17) [Fig. 5, p. 48]. Intersecting all of these spaces is the movement of species between important natural habitats. Combined, these manifold relationships create a dense network of spatial claims in the Baltic Sea that are inherently contradictory. On the one hand, borders describe increasing forms of static control applied to both the commercial/productive and the environmental spaces of the Baltic Sea. On the other hand, networks of linear connections define a common, fluid, periodic space, and over time the networks appear, appear to wholly consume the space [Fig. 6, p. 47]. The environmental capacity is close to saturation.

Urbanisation in the Baltic Sea is therefore characterised by the complete interpenetration of spaces of movement, both organic and inorganic, with an increasing number of fixtures and artefacts. Technological seascapes are forming through wind parks, with the leisure seascape and bird resting areas located nearby. All kinds of boating activities use the space periodically and the sea is characterised by a high degree of human interaction. This interaction, both physical and virtual, has created a common referential space that unifies the region. It is a complex realm of cohabitation hanging in a delicate (im)balance.

URBANISATION IN THE BARENTS AND BALTIC SEAS

Urbanisation in the sea can be the result of a chain of interdependencies originating in oceanic features which produce habitats, followed by life forms attracted to these habitats that then become a resource utilised in production processes. The Barents Sea fishing industry is one example, originating in plentiful phytoplankton production at the marginal ice edge. However, the two seas demonstrate intensified interactions which go beyond this logical chain, such as in the offshore energy industries. The emerging energy seascape has a highly technological component and is spatially dispersed yet tightly connected through networks. Urban indicators are periodic, diffuse, unevenly dispersed over vast areas but embedded in abstract ordering systems, and are aligned to specific locations with absolute technical precision. These factors all contribute to the apparent unfamiliar and radical nature of urbanisation processes operating within the Barents and Baltic Seas.

Contemporary urbanisation processes have been able to link into "habitats" provided by the legacy of interactions facilitated by, and in connection with, these seas. The intensification of urbanisation processes has bought such habitats into relief, and enabled us to recognise their urban characteristics over the territorial scale, which until now, had remained unfamiliar. The radical nature of ocean urbanisation is also due to one further critical characteristic. The space outside of territorial waters but within an Exclusive Economic Zone, is, according to the Law of the Sea, both a common, fluid resource and a potential site for national production and extraction. Therefore, this space is a site of continual negotiation.

NINE PRINCIPLES OF OCEAN URBANISATION IN THE BARENTS AND BALTIC SEAS:

1. The seas are vital producers.

Economic activities, and shipping in particular, dominate the use of both seas. Environmental aspects are either completely integrated into production through research and technology, as in the Barents Sea, or tentatively outlined through "soft" legislation and therefore largely ignored, as in the case of the Baltic Sea.

2. Production activities create new seascapes.

Energy production, which has not traditionally been located offshore, such as wind in the Baltic Sea or fossil fuel in the Barents Sea, is creating new seascapes. These technological seascapes are replacing the seascapes on which the fishing profession has traditionally relied. In the Baltic Sea, millions of ferry and cruise passengers experience the sea annually and the new seascapes are well-integrated in the urban imagination. In the Barents Sea, the new production sites are further offshore, characterised by less surface infrastructure, and they will not be experienced by the public.

3. Urbanisation is supported by specialised technology.

The space of the sea is integrated into systems of monitoring, control, strategic forecasts, and economic programmes. The acquisition of knowledge is a primary step in urbanisation processes. Vast amounts of research data exist for the Baltic Sea—the most intensively urbanised of the two seas. Oceanographic scanning and monitoring require specialist technology and equipment and large-scale financial investment. The Barents Sea still contains large areas about which little is known, but the knowledge-base for both environmental purposes and petroleum-production are completely integrated; extensive scanning has been carried out in the areas deemed most promising for fossil fuel production. This knowledge is then translated into grids of potential exploration licences, which represent one of the most extreme urban typologies in the sea.

4. The seas are a common referential space.

The cultural and historical context, combined with current political forces, determines the form in which this common space emerges. In the Baltic, manifold crossings and connections, both historical and contemporary, have constructed this space and they are currently being reinforced by political efforts to create a stable Baltic region on the EU border. In the Barents region, the ocean is richer in resources than the land. Regular interaction with the sea, and its connecting role between small scattered settlements, makes it a common referential space. Identity has developed under local conditions, since the northern districts are distant from central government control in both Norway and Russia. While the political efforts to reinforce this space under the title of the Barents Euro-Arctic Region have met with local scepticism, they are proof of the mounting strategic importance of a region with the Barents Sea as the central point of reference.

5. Both regional and international urbanising forces are exerted on the seas.

In the Baltic Sea, relatively evenly distributed urban forces issue predominantly from the regional coastline to structure different spatial strata—pipelines and cables on the sea bed, shipping movement across the surface, and wind-energy capture in the air space. In the Barents Sea, the two dominating forces of urbanisation issue from different sources: the local fishing industry and the international interests of the oil and gas industries.

6. Spatial and ecological budgets are closely linked in the sea.

Ecological systems require a spatial budget. In the Barents Sea, marine life makes use of generous, uninhibited habitats over large areas and depths, further enhanced by the open oceanographic borders to the Atlantic and Arctic Oceans. However, the long-range transport of pollutants poses environmental threats.(18) In the Baltic Sea, species suffer habitat loss and displacement due to spatial competition with wind farms, large transport vessels, and coastal development.(19) The same habitats are often favoured by both organic and “inorganic” species, such as shallow sandy bottoms for wind farm development, fish spawning grounds, and bird resting areas.

7. Urbanisation patterns are characterised by dispersed intensities.

Urbanisation patterns in the Barents and the Baltic Seas are comprised of loose, diverse, shifting fragments that are widely dispersed, but connected by precise, specialised trajectories —more numerous and more frequent in the Baltic Sea. Rather than characterised by density, the seas are characterised by situations of periodic intensity, manifest as the technological link to a resource exploited for a defined period. While the intensity itself may be localised, singular, and of short duration, it relies on sophisticated, large-scale spatial systems that have been constructed on the basis of extensive research, coordination, and investment and are centrally controlled. Such a dispersed intensity can align networks, seascape, technology, and ecology within one single operation.

8. Infrastructure is the hardware of ocean urbanisation.

The large-scale maritime spatial systems are mostly of an abstract nature, but extended urbanisation in the Barents and Baltic Seas is materialised through infrastructure. Infrastructure utilises linear arrangements that have an apparently negligible spatial impact in one direction, but are of a territorial dimension in another. Infrastructure fulfils the function of transferring forces, therefore the spatial implications of forces are also transferred, giving rise to oscillating spatial expansions and contractions.

9. Natural conditions support urbanisation processes.

Extended urbanisation is anchored in systems utilising the natural properties of ocean space. Ice conditions, marine life forms, deep-water harbours, winds, currents, and bathymetry all support urbanising activities to varying degrees. Oceanic forces increase the efficiency of transportation methods and the common status of the space itself outside unilateral control allows for an enhanced freedom of exchange.

CONCLUSION: FROM URBANISING TO CULTIVATING THE SEA

This research is based on the notion of seas as cultural products related to their respective geophysical territories, which are relational, in flux, and constantly transforming. Hence, what we understand as the entity of the “Baltic Sea” or the “Barents Sea” is more than a fluctuating geographical outline; these seas have been occupied, imagined, and cultivated through a long process, involving both direct interaction in the sense of farming resources and negotiations to create diverse geopolitical units over time. The seas possess potential that draws them into socioeconomic relations with their inhabited littoral zones.

In the years since World War II, under accelerating urbanisation processes, not only have seas been drawn into the urban sphere by corporations and planners, but this urbanisation has been of an overwhelmingly industrial, infrastructural nature. Closer attention to the sea as an urbanised realm is a call to engage with the legacy of these interventions, including how they are now partially integrated into ecological systems and therefore part of what we must now nurture and cultivate.(20) As urban systems weave more extensively through sensitive, dispersed, fluid territories, practices must be adapted to ensure parallel cultivation of the material maritime world, and to reclaim public responsibility for this cultural territory.

(1) Henri Lefebvre, *The Production of Space*, trans. Donald Nicholson-Smith (Oxford: Blackwell, 1991), 30.
(2) Neil Brenner and Christian Schmid, "Planetary Urbanization," in *Urban Constellations*, ed. Matthew Gandy (Berlin: Jovis, 2011).
(3) Stuart Elden, *The Birth of Territory* (Chicago: University of Chicago Press, 2013), 330, https://press.uchicago.edu/ucp/books/book/chicago/B/bo15506915.html.
(4) Stuart Elden,"Land, Terrain, Territory," *Progress in Human Geography* 34, no. 6 (1 December 2010): 799–817, https://doi.org/10.1177/0309132510362603.
(5) Stuart Elden, "Missing the Point: Globalization, Deterritorialization and the Space of the World," *Transactions of the Institute of British Geographers* 30, no. 1 (2005): 8–19, https://doi.org/10.1111/j.1475-5661.2005.00148.x.
(6) International Hydrographic Organization, "Limits of Oceans and Seas," Special Publication (Monégasque, Monte-Carlo: International Hydrographic Organization, 1953).
(7) Matti Leppäranta and Kai Myrberg, *Physical Oceanography of the Baltic Sea* (Berlin: Springer, 2009).
(8) Ocean depths exceed the highest mountains: height Mt Everest = 8,848 m, depth Challenger depth in the Mariana Trench= ca. 11,000 m.
(9) See chapter 6 (Schmid) this volume, Vincent Kaufmann, *Rethinking the City: Urban Dynamics and Mobility* (Lausanne: EPFL Press, 2011:50). Originally published in Jacques Lévy and Michel Lussault, eds., *Dictionnaire de la géographie* (Paris: Belin, 2003).
(10) Bjorn Gunnarsson, "Future Development of the Northern Sea Route," *Maritime Executive* (18 February 2016), https://www.maritime-executive.com/editorials/future-development-of-the-northern-sea-route.
(11) World Wildlife Fund, "The Barents Sea Ecoregion: A Biodiversity Assessment" (Oslo: WWF, 2004), http://d2ouvy59p0dg6k.cloudfront.net/downloads/barentsseaecoregionreport.pdf.
(12) Morten Andreas Strøksnes, "The Inner Space of Barents," in *Northern Experiments. The Barents Urban Survey 2009* (Oslo: 0047 Press, 2009).
(13) Nancy Couling, "Formats of Extended Urbanisation in Ocean Space," in *Emerging Urban Spaces- a Planetary Perspective*, eds. Philipp Horn, Paola Alfaro d'Alençon, and Ana Claudia Duarte Carduso (Springer International Publishing, 2018), XII, 219.
(14) Harry Gugger, Nancy Couling, and Aurélie Blanchard, eds., *Barents Lessons. Teaching and Research in Architecture* (Zürich: Park Books, 2012).
(15) Espen Røyseland and Rø Oystein, eds., *Northern Experiments. The Barents Urban Survey 2009* (Oslo: 0047 Press, 2009).
(16) Jan O. Lundgren, *The Transformation of a Geopolitical Space into a Tourist Space: The Case of Passenger Shipping in the Baltic*, Les Cahiers Du Tourisme. Série C, no 186 (Aix-en-Provence: Centre des hautes études touristiques, 1994).
(17) Monika Stankiewicz, Hermanni Backer, and Nikolay Vlasov, "Maritime Activities in the Baltic Sea—An Integrated Thematic Assessment on Maritime Activities and Response to Pollution at Sea in the Baltic Sea Region," Baltic Sea Environmental Proceedings (Helsinki: HELCOM, 2010), http://www.helcom.fi/Lists/Publications/BSEP123.pdf.
(18) Royal Norwegian Ministry of the Environment, "Meld. St. 10. Report to the Storting (White Paper)First Update of the Integrated Management Plan for the Marine Environment of the Barents Sea-Lofoten Area," 3 November 2011, http://www.regjeringen.no/en/dep/md/documents-and-publications/government-propositions-and-reports-/reports-to-the-storting-white-papers-2/2010-2011/meld-st-10-20102011.html?id=682050.
(19) Environmetal Group, "Danish Offshore Wind. Key Environmental Issues- a Follow-Up" (Danish Energy Agency, 2013).
(20) See chapter 11, this volume.

Chapter 2 NORTH SEA CROSSINGS: HISTORICAL GEO-SPATIAL MAPPING AS A TOOL TO UNDERSTAND THE LOCAL DEVELOPMENT OF PORT CITIES IN A GLOBAL CONTEXT

Carola Hein, Reinout Rutte, & Yvonne van Mil

Researchers at the Chair of History of Architecture and Urban Planning, TU Delft, Carola Hein, Reinout Rutte, and Yvonne van Mil use geo-spatial mapping methods to reveal patterns of urbanisation on land and around the North Sea coastlines, over long historical periods.

Carola Hein is Professor of History of Architecture and Urban Planning (Delft University of Technology). Her books include *Adaptive Strategies for Water Heritage* (2019), *The Routledge Planning History Handbook* (2017), *Port Cities* (2011), *The Capital of Europe* (2004), *Rebuilding Urban Japan after 1945* (2003), and *Cities, Autonomy and Decentralisation in Japan* (2006).

Reinout Rutte is Assistant Professor in History of Architecture and Urban Planning at Delft University of Technology. He focuses on long-term development of Dutch cities and has co-edited *the Atlas of the Dutch Urban Landscape* (2014)

Yvonne van Mil is researcher spatial history and cartographer, affiliated with the TU Delft. She co-authored *Driven by Steel: From Hoogovens to Tata Steel 1918–2018* (2018) and contributed chapters to *the Atlas of the Dutch Urban Landscape* (2014).

The North Sea has long been a hub of maritime flows. A relatively flat sea, for many centuries it has facilitated exchanges among people living on its shores. An analysis of medieval road systems seems to connect places in the Netherlands with those in Great Britain. Antwerp, Amsterdam, London, and Hamburg have been leading trade centres in Northern Europe since the medieval period, as part of the Hanseatic League, for example. Hamburg's trade and culture was more closely connected to London than to its hinterland as the joke suggests: "When it rains in London, Hamburg puts up its umbrellas." From the sixteenth to the eighteenth century, cities around the North Sea grew into colonial and global hubs. Since the Industrial Revolution, they have become industrial and transportation hubs as well as decision-making centers. Additional port cities have grown around the North Sea, including several of Europe's largest container ports, such as Rotterdam and Bremerhaven. Each of these ports and cities have responded in their own fashion to global flows of goods, people, and ideas from sea to hinterland. A comparative analysis speaks to the ways in which maritime flows and ocean urbanization have shaped coastal regions, port cities, and hinterlands.

As port cities around the North Sea became part of nations and then as industrialisation led to urban expansion and a land-based approach to planning took hold, the cultural power of the sea declined. Nonetheless, for centuries its extensions—the rivers and deltas that serve as connectors with and extensions of the sea—have featured prominently in representations of port cities.(1) References to shipping and the sea have also been part of the imaginaries, cultures, and maritime mindsets of many port cities.(2) Today in port cities, an awareness of the importance of water remains evident in mental maps and the experience of everyday citizens.(3) This awareness can be used to help revive or develop planning and design approaches that acknowledge the importance of the sea in general and the North Sea in particular.

To address contemporary urgencies like climate change, energy transitions, or sea-based migration we need to understand ocean urbanisation. We need to do something other than extending land-based planning or translating hinterland planning to the maritime foreland. Rather, we need to reimagine ocean space as a spatial, social, and cultural complex. Such an approach involves acknowledging coastal and port cities not only as extensions of land-based infrastructures and plans, but as maritime access points and almost as extensions of the sea. It also requires multidisciplinary collaboration and agreement and coordination of effort among port and city professionals as well as local citizens and maritime specialists. There is a need for information about the physical reality on sea and land in which human life and work take place in port city regions. The Leiden-Delft-Erasmus PortCityFutures (portcityfutures.nl) research group has taken on this challenge as its mission. It argues that comprehensive development of port city regions as ecosystems, including the maritime foreland, can benefit from a methodology built on the analysis of spatial and cultural patterns. We are exploring how to complement the excellent data produced in economic geography on maritime flows with a space-based methodology and whether it is possible to create a new form of abstraction that allows us to consider the spatial, temporal, and functional elements of port, city, and region in a geographic context.

Academics in separate disciplines have tended to study maritime flows and port-city relationships independently of each other, with different goals, focused on separate values and different scales. The study of ports and port cities is dominated by quantitative and abstract data-based approaches that often fail to consider qualitative aspects and local particularities. Other research has explored the individual development of these cities, their architectural and urban history, mostly within their national context. There is a need for analytical links between the two types of literature.(4) Scholars have written comparative histories, but these writings do not illuminate how port cities translated global demands or hinterland challenges into spatial transformations.

Studies of hard values need to be aligned with a study of soft values, including in the spatial and social sciences and the humanities. Such collaboration requires a methodology that connects currently disparate sectors and types of knowledge and understanding. We argue that the scale of such an investigation should be that of the port city region, including the sea space, and not just that of the port city, the area where port activities leave their footprint. An assessment of conflicts and opportunities at the intersection of port and city interests warrants consideration of spatial, social, and cultural factors.

Examining the challenges and opportunities of geo-spatial mapping, this chapter calls for a methodology that parallels abstract quantitative economic modeling of port city regions and their networks with historical investigation of individual port city regions—sea and land—with their specific local challenges and opportunities. Quantitative mapping, while informative for ports and shipping, remains without scales and features, and lacks the topographical aspects that are key to spatial, social, and cultural experience. These aspects can be captured in historical geo-spatial mapping, revealing how diverse governance structures have created policies, laws, and administrative borders as well as physical spaces.

Building on the Delft geo-spatial method presented in the journal *Over Holland*, we aim to establish a socio-spatial and cultural approach focusing on maritime connections and their impact on port cities to better understand their historical evolution over time, and to highlight how practices of the past shape the present and the design of the future. The studies of port cities around the North Sea serves as our first case study. Following an explanation of the geo-historical mapping developed at TU Delft for the western Netherlands, we present visualisations of the historical development of three port city regions that have developed in relation to each other around the North Sea and that we are using as pilot studies: Rotterdam, Hamburg, and London.(5) We conclude that this type of geo-spatial analysis can connect quantitative and qualitative approaches and help identify historical forms, spatial structures, and governance patterns with lasting importance for decision-making in port city regions.

Historical geo-spatial mapping is a research tool that provides an opportunity to connect diverse data in space and over time. To make this research meaningful, a number of decisions have to be made relating to scale, time, and research perspectives. Identifying scales at which data is available and can be meaningfully presented, determining moments in time that capture moments of change, and identifying the most relevant information are key challenges of mapping. The decisions are relevant for a specific location and are only partly transferable as, for example, ports and cities exist and grow at different scales, as the introduction of new technologies or energies is picked up at different moments in time. For our research on port cities around the North Sea we use the findings and decisions made for mapping the Netherlands as a starting point.

THE DELFT HISTORIC GEOSPATIAL MAPPING METHOD

In 2011, researchers of the Chair History of Architecture and Urban Planning and the Department of Architecture at Delft University of Technology published with the University of Amsterdam's historical research group "Twelve Centuries of Spatial Transformation in the Western Netherlands in Six Maps."(6) We used geo-spatial mapping to study the urbanisation process in the area now known as the Randstad, the so-called Rim City in the western part of the Netherlands. Changes in landscape, habitation patterns, and infrastructure are shown in six maps that indicate the situation in AD 800, 1200, 1500, 1700, 1900 and 2000. These "snapshots" provide an overall picture of (a) the history of habitation and the urbanisation process and (b) changes in landscape and infrastructure. The six maps showing the spatial transformation of the western Netherlands focus on the landscape on a regional scale [Fig. 1, p. 49]. We reconstructed unknown situations using a series of comparable maps. While we did not depict the sea separately, it is possible to see the relation between sea and land and the ways in which land reclamation and urbanization pushed back the sea.

In the spatial disciplines, drawings, including cartography, are valuable both as research tools and research output. Research output can be recorded pictorially as well as text. At the same time, drawing is itself a way of analysing source material, creating links that may lead to new insights. Not only is the drawing methodology exact and substantiated, but the design and analytical skills of map-makers enhance the impact of the final drawn result.

The series of six maps was created using a set of interrelated information. Within the specific area of the western Netherlands a patchwork of maps (or map sections) was used for each of the six years, together with written source material and sketches showing relative changes in the landscape. We used a retrogressive approach to reconstruct a number of earlier maps. We analysed and compared spatial structures to fill in missing pieces of the puzzle. We used elements from later dates, for example habitation patterns, to reconstruct earlier ones, and in some cases vice versa. As the study progressed, the results of the various maps were compared, and this in turn led to new insights. The drawn material—the series of six maps—thus became a new source of information.

To what extent can a study such as this provide a representative picture of the situation in each of the years chosen, indicating processes of urbanisation and features that remain unchanged? Can the long-term development of the western Netherlands be divided into periods on the basis of spatial transformation?

In 800, we can see a very thinly populated natural landscape in which sand, peat, clay, and water were the predominant features. By 1200, many of the peat and clay areas had been reclaimed and dyked and the urbanisation process had begun. Three centuries later, the western Netherlands was a cultivated landscape full of towns connected by a dense network of waterways and by unpaved roads. By 1500, the distribution of towns over the landscape was fixed. By 1700, some of the towns had expanded into cities, the water infrastructure had become denser and overland roads had been improved. At the same time, peatland areas had been substantially altered by peat dredging and land drainage. The main features of the map for 1900, apart from a number of major polders, were infrastructural changes and renewed urban expansion: railways, paved roads, new urban districts, and suburbs. A hundred years later, in 2000, the most striking features were large-scale urbanisation associated with the motorway infrastructure.

We can conclude that the sand, peat and clay subsoil that formed before 800 determined the structure of what is today the Randstad. Another crucial factor was the wet infrastructure in the watery delta from the eleventh to the fifteenth century, when Holland emerged as a region in its own right and experienced its first period of growth. The same period determined the distribution pattern of cities and towns in the Randstad. From the fifteenth to the seventeenth century, the landscape was partly transformed, and a clear urban hierarchy developed during the Golden Age. After more than 150 years of stagnation, urbanisation resumed in the western Netherlands beginning in the late nineteenth century. At first, this growth was mainly within the spatial framework that had developed earlier, but later the new infrastructure played a greater role—at first the railway system, but after the Second World War, increasingly the motorway network.

The series of six maps shows that existing spatial structures, such as reclaimed peatland, habitation patterns, and infrastructure, tend to be remarkably persistent in the long term. This phenomenon, often referred to as inertia, implies that large-scale spatial interventions do not occur easily. The term also indicates that existing infrastructure and habitation patterns have a major impact on the continuity of spatial distribution of economic activities in a given area. It is easier to bring about a change of function within an existing physical structure than to make substantial alterations to a spatial pattern. Such spatial pattern alterations usually come about as a result of external factors such as a flood disaster, war, or a change of position on the international political and economic stage.

Finally, it should be noted that large-scale government intervention in the spatial planning of the Randstad area during the second half of the twentieth century was exceptional. If we look at the design and spatial transformation of the landscape in the western Netherlands over the long term, we can see that this was mainly due to private initiative and largely the result of mechanisms that are today referred to as "project development," such as the dykes in the south-western delta and many of the major polders. In some cases, such as the mediaeval reclamation of the peatlands, a local ruler, a count or a bishop played a leading part, in what we might now call a public-private partnership. Substantial changes were usually made in times of economic prosperity. One of the main prerequisites for prosperity was closely bound up with the landscape and its cultivation: the water infrastructure. There was not usually much planning, let alone central management. The new railway infrastructure in the nineteenth century was also largely the result of private initiative; the central government was forced to take a hand in its development simply to ease bottlenecks notably of mobility. Only in the cases of the IJsselmeer polders, the Delta Works, the motorway system, and post-war urbanisation up to the 1990s does actual or attempted government intervention—rather than interaction between economic potential, private interests and geographical conditions—appear to have been the predominant factor.

This Delft geo-spatial method shows how it is possible to understand the present by mapping long-term developments. Making a series of uniform maps with uniform legends we can reconstruct the past to gain new insights in the present and to design a just future. For Dutch cities and landscapes, the discussion of how to deal with sea-level rise and increased flooding is clearly one of survival.(7)

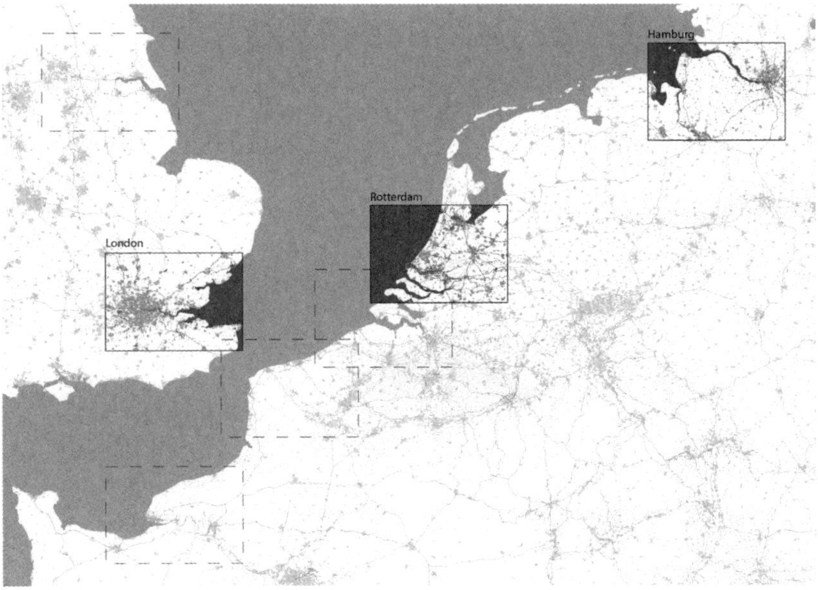

Fig. 2
Research area of North Sea studied in the Chair History of Architecture and Urban Planning, with case study of London, Hamburg, and Rotterdam with other potential port city areas framed with a dashed line. (Yvonne van Mil)

COMPARATIVE GEO-SPATIAL MAPPING OF PORT CITY REGIONS ROTTERDAM, HAMBURG, AND LONDON

The methodological and content-related findings of the mapping of the Randstad have the potential to be further developed through the lens of ocean urbanisation and port city relations. We think that the findings offer a foundation for historical geospatial mapping of ocean urbanisation and port city regions, allowing us to compare and analyze their spaces and institutional structures in the context of other port cities around the North Sea.

Selecting a shared body of water—the North Sea—as the foundation for a comparative research program on port city regions allows us to establish and test a methodology for historical and spatial analysis [Fig. 2]. For our pilot study, we have chosen three port city regions on which we have already worked and for which we have sufficient data. The port city region of the Nieuwe Waterweg, around the port of Rotterdam, serves as an example of the challenges and opportunities that large port city regions face worldwide. In our current areas of investigation, Hamburg and London provide examples of other planning challenges for port city regions of past, present, and future. Each of these three case studies shows different historical interactions between port and city in the larger region. The continued importance of Rotterdam, Hamburg, and London as port city hubs confirms their relevance as key places to begin.

In accordance with the mapping method used for the 2011 *OverHolland* project, we reconstructed the historical settlement of the three port cities, based on current European data sets, historical maps, and written sources. For a comparative study of port city regions, we used geo-spatial mapping (GIS), overlaying different data layers with a similar level of abstraction and a uniform legend. While the approach is similar to that of *OverHolland*, the research question and associated layers as well as temporal and spatial frameworks are different. To better understand port city region relationships and their connection with the hinterland, we opted to show port and city areas, important infrastructures and political boundaries as a foundation for a comprehensive sea-land historical analysis [Fig. 3]. Rather than analyzing the spatial development of a pre-defined area (as we did with the Randstad), we aim to systematically identify and map the extent of the port city region. We therefore need to understand the scale at which port cities operate. The relationship between the size of a port, the size of the metropolitan area, and its location in relation to the hinterland has changed over time. In the case of Rotterdam, Hamburg, and London it is therefore necessary to analyze the port cities not only on the scale of the medieval city at 1:10 thousand or 1:25 thousand, but also on a regional scale at 1:100 thousand and 1:150 thousand.

The remaining section focuses on methodological implications of geo-spatial mapping and the representation of data for the analysis of three port cities that are interconnected by shared maritime practices. Our aim is to get a preliminary sense of what historical geo-spatial mapping can add to economic modelling-based research in terms of spatial, institutional, and cultural development. Details of the history of these three cities can be found in two published articles.(8) The maps presented here are aimed at exemplifying the challenges and opportunities of mapping port and city space and regional governance at four moments in time: 1300, 1700, 1900, 2020 [Fig. 3].

The series of maps from 1300 show the estuary, the morphology of port and urban areas, and the infrastructure. The fledgling cities controlled dykes and dams, intersections between rivers (Rotterdam and Hamburg), and bridges (London). In general, the cities developed alongside the river. Urban spaces and buildings were dense and multifunctional. There was no clear distinction between dedicated port areas with fixed infrastructures nor any specific identification of multifunctional spaces. In 1300, Hamburg and London ware already well-established North Sea cities, but the urbanization of Rotterdam had only just begun. The city of Rotterdam is therefore many times smaller than the other two, although the port of the three cities is almost the same size.

The relation between ports and cities changed around 1700, as shown on the maps. In Rotterdam and Hamburg, the ports expanded considerably through reclamation and the formation of new port islands in the rivers Maas and Elbe. New settlements grew also on the estuary near the main cities: Delfshaven near Rotterdam and Altona, the Danish port, near Hamburg. The form and function of urban areas was closely aligned with the needs of their local geographical, political context. Rotterdam provided—with neighboring port

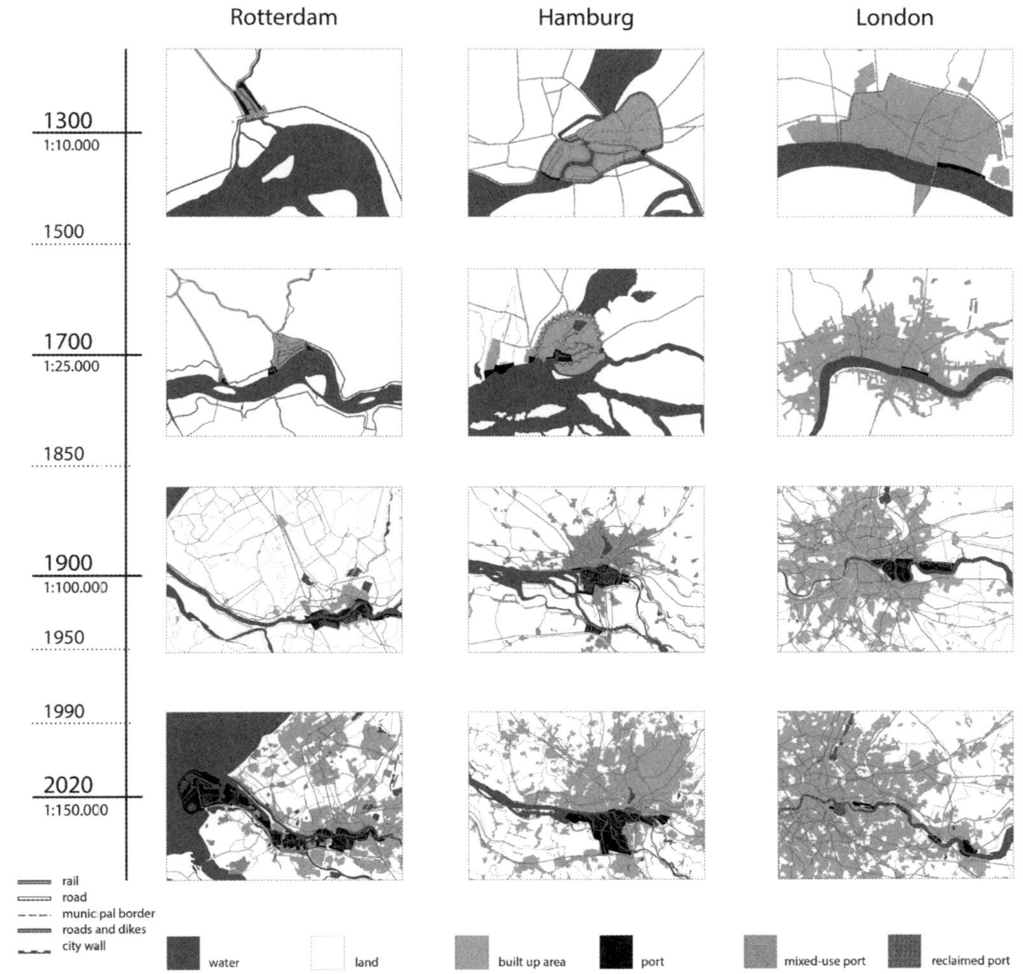

Fig. 3
First draft for comparative geo-spatial mapping methodology, case study of London, Hamburg, and Rotterdam. (Carola Hein, Yvonne van Mil, Blanka Borbely, and Batuhan Özaltun)

cities Delfshaven and Schiedam—access to inland transportation via Delft and Leiden to Amsterdam. Hamburg, a city-state without its own rural areas, surrounded itself with strong walls and a dense spatial pattern as another port city, Danish Altona, grew just outside its walls. London, a capital on an island did not need that kind of protection and instead spread along the river.

Beginning in the early nineteenth century, enormous port areas were carved out of the land and facilitated shipping and warehousing. With industrialisation and new forms of transport, private actors, port companies, and some city governments created dedicated port areas separate from the urban spaces in all three cities. Water access was a privilege largely reserved for trade. Rapid growth of trade, the emergence of petroleum as a fuel, and urbanisation required port and city expansion. Extensive landside route and rail infrastructures connected the port to the hinterland. Specific patterns varied, but in every case, port spaces expanded dramatically and started to occupy land in the estuaries. In Rotterdam, the port expanded and merged with the port of Schiedam and in 1886 annexed Delfshaven. The ports of Altona and Harburg grew next to Hamburg, and would be integrated into the city state in 1937. In London, the port grew beyond the administrative boundaries of the city.

As the maps of 2020 show, the scales of decision-making have shifted over time and no single institution can compete with or control the region, which has grown beyond the scale of a single government entity that depends on is influenced by the port. To adjust to contemporary needs, new ports have been built and historic ports left behind as heritage. Containerisation played an important role in the separation of port and city as less and different work was available in the port. The arrival of larger and often automated port terminals pushed the industrial ports away from the city. In Rotterdam, the port authority has consciously built the port toward the sea, creating new boundaries with rural instead of urban areas (see Dunne, this volume) where fewer citizens are affected. In Hamburg, port and city are still intertwined in the same city-state, but the river itself has become a barrier. In the case of London, private actors moved the port beyond the boundaries of the city where environmental, infrastructural conditions are less restrictive. New multifunctional spaces have emerged, where heritage ports serve urban and often non-maritime functions, such as dwelling and leisure.

CONCLUSION

Ports have a foreland that is now global and a hinterland that extends often beyond national borders. They are crucial elements of economic flows and shipping movements and they are physical entities and socio-spatial constructs. Models and maps offer a means to show similarities and patterns in a world of differences and make it possible to understand the complexity and diversity of port cities within their context. Historical contexts can be difficult to compare. Cultural aspects are not documentable in a way that lends itself to visualisation based on widely agreed upon facts and used for comparative purposes. Any attempt to understand the spatial extent of shipping requires an examination of the spatial footprint of the port beyond its legal or administrative boundaries. Additional conversations are needed to theorize ocean urbanisation in relation to port city regions through in depth study, including around the North Sea.

A first conclusion regarding the development of the three cities around the North Sea can be drawn to show that a single maritime system—like the North Sea—can generate a range of diverse and complementary port city spaces and governance systems, each with their own particularities. Such analysis can provide an opportunity to understand, but also to influence and design. The goal is to identify how ports and cities have evolved spatially in relation to each other and to understand the role that private and public actors, political interests, economic opportunities, or social preferences play in the implementation of these challenges. This will allow us to identify areas that will be under pressure due to competing port and city interests. Port cities around the world experience the same type of challenges, but local responses vary in line with political, economic, geographical, historic, social, and cultural conditions.

The methodology introduced here for the North Sea region can be used to gain a better understanding of many other regions with shared waters, such as the Mediterranean, the Black Sea, or the Gulf of Mexico, and provide a better foundation for decision-makers.

(1) Carola Hein, "Hamburg's Port Cityscape. Large-Scale Urban Transformation and the Exchange of Planning Ideas," in *Port Cities: Dynamic Landscapes and Global Networks*, ed. Carola Hein (New York: Routledge, 2011).
(2) Hilde Sennema, "Experience Port City Cultures from Your Couch," PortCityFutures, https://www.portcityfutures.nl/news/experience-port-city-cultures-from-your-couch; Sabine Luning, "Port City Culture - Culture(S) and Cultural Practices," https://www.portcityfutures.nl/news/port-city-culture-cultures-and-cultural-practices; Yvonne van Mil et al., "Mapping Maritime Mindsets: Towards a Shared Methodology," PortCityFutures, https://www.portcityfutures.nl/news/mapping-maritime-mindsets-towards-a-shared-methodology.
(3) Maurice Harteveld, "Mapping Maritime Mindsets: Mental Maps," https://www.portcityfutures.nl/news/mapping-maritime-mindsets-mental-maps; Sarah Sannen, "Maritime Mindsets of Rotterdam's Port Communities," https://www.portcityfutures.nl/news/maritime-mindsets-of-rotterdams-port-communities-0.
(4) Carola Hein, "Port Cityscapes: Conference and Research Contributions on Port Cities," *Planning Perspectives* 31, no. 2 (2016).
(5) Carola Hein and Yvonne van Mil, "Towards a Comparative Spatial Analysis for Port City Regions Based on Historical Geo-Spatial Mapping," *PortusPLus* 8 (2019).
(6) G Borger et al., "Twelve Centuries of Spatial Transformation in the Western Netherlands, in Six Maps: Landscape, Habitation and Infrastructure in 800, 1200, 1500, 1700, 1900 and 2000," *OverHolland* 10/11 (2011).
(7) Rolf Schuttenhelm, "In Face of Rising Sea Levels the Netherlands 'Must Consider Controlled Withdrawal.'" https://www.vn.nl/rising-sea-levels-netherlands/.
(8) Carola Hein and Dirk Schubert, "Resilience and Path Dependence - a Comparative Study of the Port Cities of London, Hamburg and Philadelphia," *Journal of Urban History* (2020); Carola Hein and Paul van der Laar, "The Separation of Ports from Cities: The Case of Rottterdam, Springer," in *European Port Cities in Transition*, eds. Angela Carpenter and Rodrigo Lorenzo (Springer, 2020).
[Fig. 1] G Borger et al., "Twelve Centuries of Spatial Transformation in the Western Netherlands, in Six Maps: Landscape, Habitation and Infrastructure in 800, 1200, 1500, 1700, 1900 and 2000," *OverHolland* 10/11 (2011).
[Fig. 2 & Fig. 3] Copernicus, "Corine Land Cover. Version 18.5. Copernicus," (2016); Eurogeographics, "Euroglobalmap. Version 10.0. Eurogeographics,"(2017); Global Administrative Boundaries, "Gadm Data. Version 36–2018. Global Administrative Boundaries," https://gadm.org/download_world.Html.

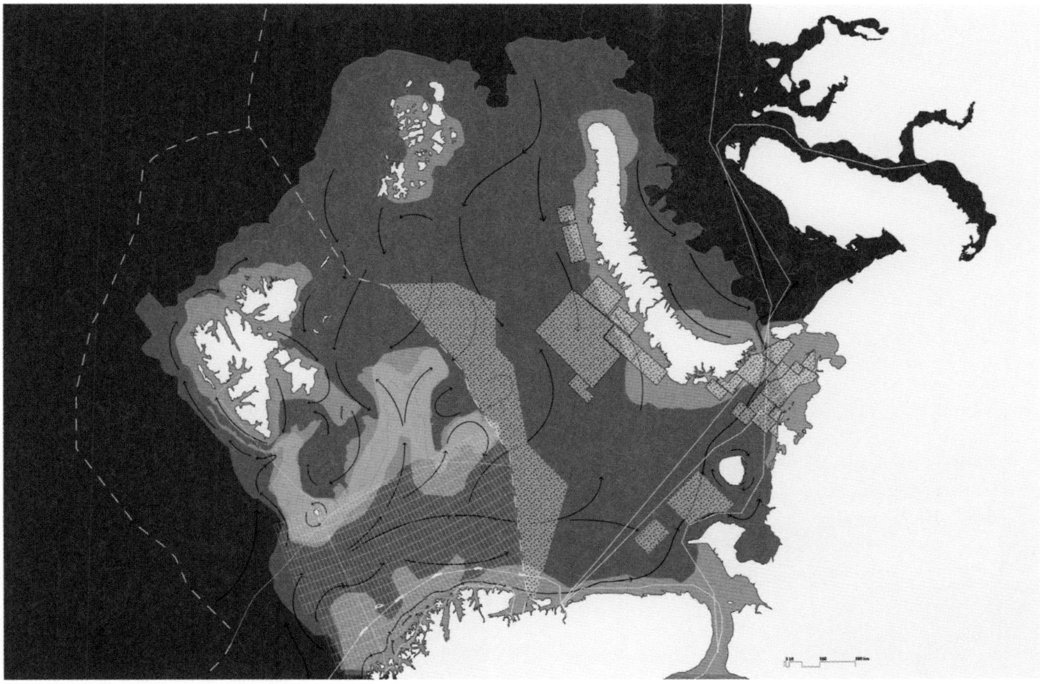

Fig. 1
Barents Sea: the socio-economic territory superimposed over the geophysical and the biological territories (Couling)

Fig. 2
Barents Sea: a loose, dispersed mesh across land and sea (laba, EPFL).

Fig. 4
Borders and enclosures, Baltic Sea (Couling)

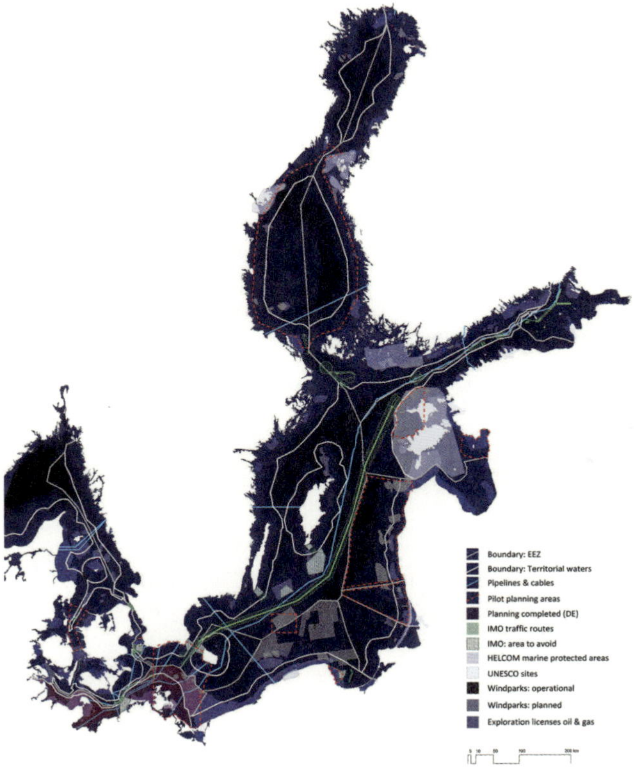

Fig. 6
Baltic Sea: a saturated sea of shipping movement (Couling)

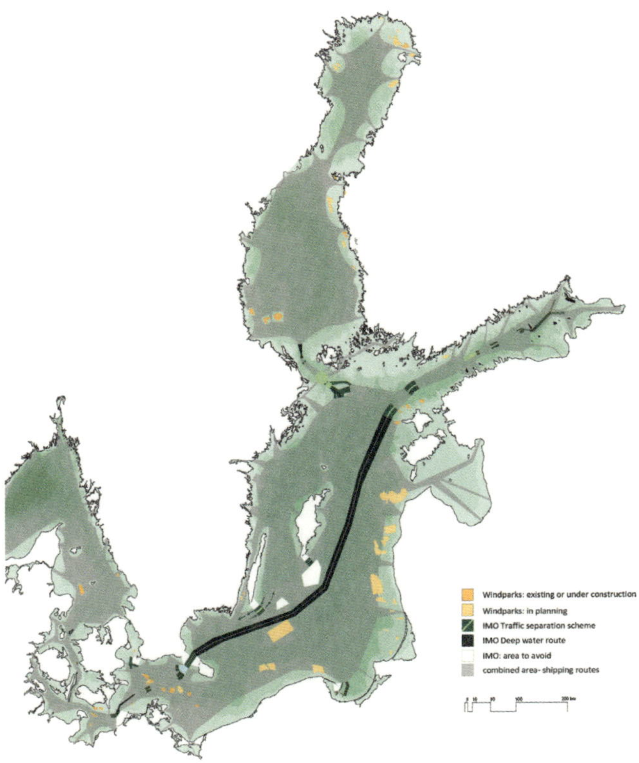

Fig. 5
Sea Common,
Baltic (Couling)

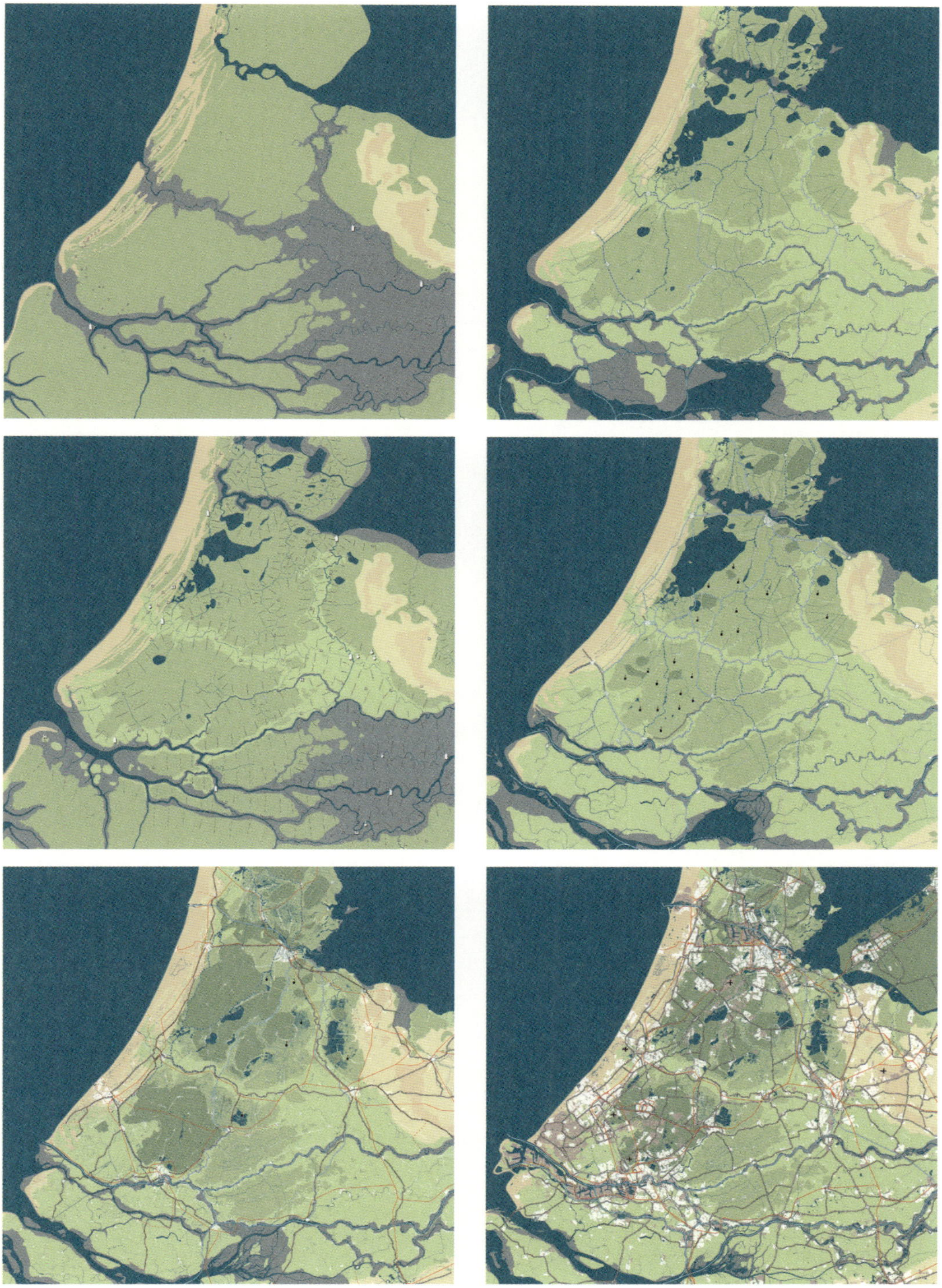

Fig. 1
Series of six maps showing the transformations of the western Netherlands in AD 800, 1200, 1500, 1700, 1900 and 2000.

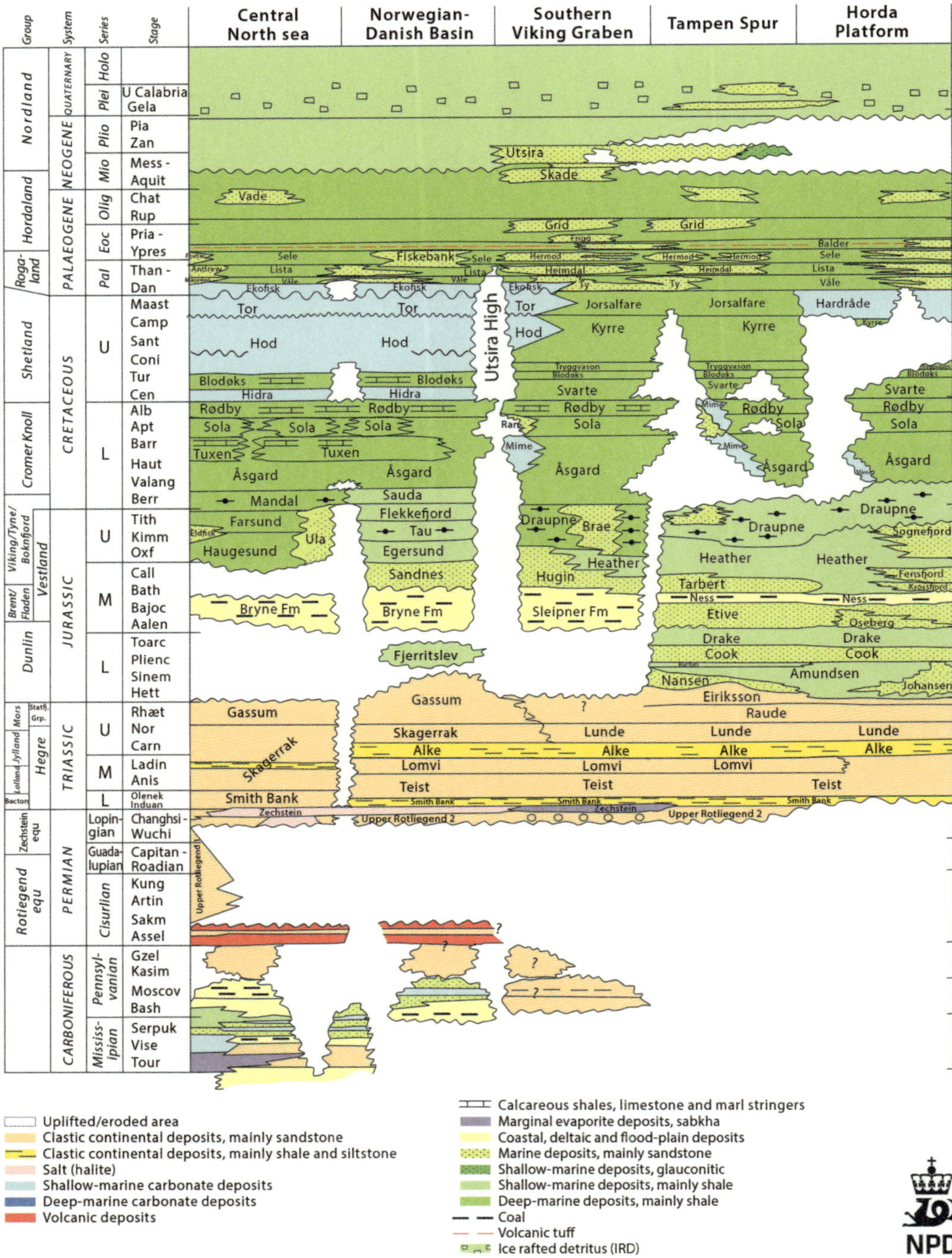

Fig. 1
Lithostratigraphic chart of the Norwegian North Sea (Norwegian Petroleum Directorate)

Fig. 2
Brent Delta topside arriving at Able Seaton Port, Hartlepool 2017 (Able UK)

Part II CONCEPTIONS

Developing a sea-to-land perspective requires a recalibration of inherited perceptions. Industrialised nations have adopted an attitude to the sea that corresponds to land-side development characterised by rationalisation, commodification, and static Cartesian coordinates. This approach ignores the inherent fluid properties of the sea itself and the historical socio-spatial and cultural engagement of people with the sea—a relationship that is still present in more traditional seafaring communities around the world.

The chapters in this part of the book investigate fundamental differences in thinking about, representing, and intervening in the sea-land continuum. Consideration of these differences should be the first step toward necessary change. The volume of the sea is vast, thick, deep, dark, and kinetic—and mostly still foreign to humans. These contributions interrogate the potential of embracing expanded spatial dimensions that distinguish the sea from land and illustrate shortcomings of current conceptual approaches to the sea.

Viscosity is discussed by Couling and Hein in chapter 3 as a property of the sea that defies the binary assumptions of solid and liquid. Considering viscosity demands approaches that straddle these categories and provide space for material transformations.
J. M. Ledgard explores the deep sea in chapter 4 through extracts from his novel *Submergence*. Beginning in the third of five ocean layers where there is no light, adjacent to the most mysterious parts of

the earth's crust, the deep sea operates on different scales of space and time and has yet to be fully explored. It comprises the majority of the biosphere—where life in our world takes place. In relation to the volume of the deep sea and the length of its existence, we are reminded that humans occupy a thin space, only briefly.

Fluid, volumetric, and contingent properties of the sea pose challenges for representation and also for planning: how we conceive of the sea space determines how it is mapped and spatially organised. In chapter 5, Claudia Bode and Lizzie Yarina discuss shortcomings of current maritime planning methods, alongside alternative ways of conceptualising human relations to the sea, drawn from current cultural and theoretical perspectives which do not "flatten" or simplify its complexity.

Urban theorists argue that the understanding of urbanisation has also been simplified, in that it has been restricted to cities, while urban transformation processes determine entire territories. Christian Schmid presents methods that more accurately reveal the specific dialectical relations between centres and peripheries in chapter 6. Understanding the urban as "open zones"—differential rather than bounded spaces—represents a fundamental conceptual shift that enables territories along the sea-land continuum to be interpreted in their full relational dynamic.

Considering the implications of these propositions on the space of the sea, Nancy Couling and Carola Hein propose the concept of "blankness" in chapter 7, to reveal the convenient conceptualisation of the sea as a void to be heavily exploited for logistical purposes, which in the case of the North Sea, has been closely related to the development of the petroleum industry.

In chapter 8, Stephen Ramos and Jan Dirk Diekema introduce a historical division in classical geography between Ptolemy's quantitative, Cartesian methods of "mapping" and the cultural, ethnographic approach of Strabo, suggesting that the sea could be better served by the latter method. Today, the invisibility of operations in sea space continues across the threshold to land, with a scale and technological force that overrides all earthly dimensions of land and sea, and is finally directed to the task of observing the multiverse.

Such conceptualisations are an essential foundation for the rethinking of sea spaces and their land-side extensions in concrete situations, such as the North Sea.

Chapter 3 VISCOSITY*

Nancy Couling & Carola Hein

Nancy Couling and Carola Hein explore the physical and metaphorical viscosity of two North Sea liquids–oil and seawater. Thickness and resistance to flow cause friction in planning and in the petroleum industry but installations erected to enforce the flow of petroleum, create unexpected viscous conditions in the North Sea as a whole.

Nancy Couling is Assoc. Prof. at Bergen School of Architecture, Norway and an independant researcher in Switzerland. She investigated the urbanised sea as a Marie Skłodowska Curie Fellow at the Chair of History of Architecture and Urban Planning, TU Delft 2017–19 and in her PhD at the EPFL (2015). She taught at the TU Berlin and co-founded the interdisciplinary practice cet-0/cet-01 in Berlin 1995–2010.

Carola Hein is Professor of History of Architecture and Urban Planning (Delft University of Technology). Her books include *Adaptive Strategies for Water Heritage* (2019), *The Routledge Planning History Handbook* (2017), *Port Cities* (2011), *The Capital of Europe* (2004), *Rebuilding Urban Japan after 1945* (2003), and *Cities, Autonomy and Decentralisation in Japan* (2006).

*Part of a previously published essay: Nancy Couling and Carola Hein, "Viscosity," *Society & Space*, Volumetric Sovereignty, no. Part 3: Turbulence (March 2019), http://societyandspace.org/2019/03/17/viscosity/.

Viscosity refers to a fluid's resistance to flow. Fluids with a naturally high viscosity are thick and frequently valuable (oil), precious (honey), or essential to life (blood). Viscosity is inherently relational, depending not only on the composition of the fluid but also on temperature and environment. At high enough temperatures, even solid gold, steel, and sand become viscous fluids and can be poured into molds to take on new solid shapes. Viscosity disrupts assumptions of a clear boundary between solid and liquid.(1)

Spaces that resist binary assumptions are frequently transitional or intermediary. In the simple, material example of littoral zones where land meets sea, a viscous space of rich exchange exists where terrestrial and marine ecosystems intertwine and land- and seaborne urban systems converge. Port cities are located at this land/sea intersection, producing a specific type of friction which is discussed more fully in chapter 2. The port cityscape provides one possible perspective from which the urbanisation of the sea can be conceptualised. These are challenging places for planning and design, since viscosity is always changing but also volumetric and therefore requires space to maneuver. Planners have not always ceded space to viscous processes: in the interests of efficiency, security, and real estate values, they have encased waterways in concrete channels and drained estuary marshes to create new developable sites. In the process, they have tended to prioritize the binaries of fixity or flow, and in doing so have negated the inherent volumetric sovereignty of viscosity. On the other hand, principles of fluid dynamics—the flow of liquids and gases—steer innumerable urban services. Traditions have seeped into our contemporary behaviors, laws, and thinking, effectively creating viscous governmental structures and policies: despite the pressure to flow, our institutions themselves move slowly, clog, and stall. Hence, viscosity is all around us but seldom discussed.

To discuss the volumetrics of viscosity, the laws and principles by which it is shaped, and the spaces produced by interactions with viscous materials, it is necessary to consider both its physical and metaphorical properties and meanings. To explore the spatial potential of viscosity is to consider that in changing their state, viscous materials demand negotiation, temporal considerations, and tolerance for heterogeneity. Within the inherent thickness of viscous conditions, multiple unlike entities that are not easily separated or filtered out can potentially co-exist and adhere to each other in different ways. The ways in which viscous relations characterise urbanisation processes in the North Sea are explored more thoroughly in chapter 12 of this volume.

THE PHYSICAL PROPERTIES OF VISCOSITY, OIL, AND SEA

Within the North Sea, the organisation of the viscous materials of oil and the sea itself are closely linked and mutually transformative. Oil is a thick and coveted liquid which does not easily flow, but the petroleum industry has managed to convince the public that it is contained within a simplified, effortless, and flowing linear system of impenetrable pipelines, vehicles, and containers. The industry has promoted this impression largely to avoid debate over the ownership of oil and the environmental damage caused by extraction and production. The relations between water, oil, and land are characterized throughout by malleable policies favouring the oil industry and systems set in place to overcome the inherent friction.

At a distance of 280 km from the Norwegian mainland stands what the Norwegian Directorate for Cultural Heritage calls one of the "largest and most complex cultural monuments of our time,"(2) descending through 75 m of the North Sea to subsea formations 2,900-3,250 m below the sea-floor and rising around 100 m above the 30m extreme wave threshold: Ekofisk City,(3) a production hub and center of field operations for this extreme south-eastern corner of the Norwegian continental shelf. At its peak in the 1980s, this vast machine represented the greatest concentration of infrastructure on the North Sea, comprising eight oil and gas fields, thirty-two platforms, two flare stacks, and an oil storage tank the size of a city block.(4) Ekofisk City was constructed for the purpose of extracting petroleum—the driving force of our contemporary societies and perhaps the most characteristic viscous material of our time.

Sprawling North Sea agglomerations such as Ekofisk City have transformed the sea into a viscous space in ways that are quasi-independent from littoral port cities, thereby presenting an alternative starting point for reflections on the urbanisation of the sea. These installations are designed to force petroleum to flow—from the sophisticated injection of high-pressure liquids into reservoirs deep under the sea-floor, pressing hydrocarbons up to the preliminary processing stations on makeshift steel settlements high above the waves to the pumping of oil through pipelines and into the global supply networks downstream. All of these actions require powerful machinery, complex infrastructure, multinational investments, purpose-built legal frameworks, and a constant workforce that circulates around the North Sea (each person on rig tours of two–three weeks). Brent crude, one of the five major international oil benchmarks against which oil is evaluated and priced, initially referred to oil from the North Sea Brent field, but has since been expanded to include the Forties, Oseberg, and Ekofisk fields, also in the North Sea. It is a sweet, light crude with a dynamic viscosity of 16 mPa.s (5), which is less than crude from the Opec Reference Basket and easier to pump, transport, and refine—and hence more valuable. Transported by ship until the late twentieth century, crude oil is now mostly delivered through pipelines that criss-cross the bed of the North Sea. Minimizing viscosity and maximizing flow through these lines is an industry priority.

Compared to petroleum, water is fluid, but compared to freshwater, the sea is viscous. Although both the public and institutional perception of the sea is overwhelmingly focused on the surface (literally superficial), the body of the sea is a volume composed of distinct water-masses differentiated by currents, salinity, temperature, and atmospheric pressure. Stratification occurs when bottom currents and salinity differ from those of the surface, creating saline boundaries and temperature gradients that vary seasonally. So, in the North Sea, denser, saltier water of a higher viscosity flows seasonally below less saline surface water in an arc through the North Sea from the Atlantic to the Skagerrak and the entrance to the Baltic Sea.

Compared to land, however, the sea has a low viscosity.(6) At sea, border and ownership conditions that create resistance on land are reduced and subject to interpretation. Subsea pipelines and cables hold a privileged position in international law—their installation cannot be prevented by bordering states. Public and corporate actors can achieve undisputed large-scale interventions and companies can simply drop cables into the sea from vessels in open waters.(7) The sea is therefore a favored site for network infrastructure, and companies steer valuable flows through fibre-optic cables, (8) gas- and oil pipelines.

METAPHORICAL PROPERTIES

In relation to oil, the sea's volume is ruled by viscous sovereignty. The United Nations developed the 1982 Convention on the Law of the Sea (9)—the comprehensive legal framework for ocean space—largely in response to pressure from the post-war oil industry and to President Truman's claim that the US had sovereignty over resources on its continental shelf.(10) The resulting Exclusive Economic Zone rule stipulated that littoral nations have the right to exploit resources up to 200 nautical miles offshore, in what are still legally international waters. Governments license surface blocks to oil companies, temporarily "renting them out,"(11) but those blocks are merely abstract outlines far above the space of true interest—ancient geological formations thousands of metres below the seabed [Fig. 1, p. 50]. Measuring 9 km in width × 12 km in length and 300 m in height, the Ekofisk reservoir is only one of many within the Ekofisk formation; it in turn is part of the vast Mandal-Ekofisk system of sedimentary rocks, an area below the central North Sea of around 90 × 280 km.

The volume of a surface block's water column—its composition, currents, temperature, and marine life—is of no relevance to companies' interests in either the two-dimensional 200 nautical mile border extensions or the grid of licensing blocks. Oil platforms are either fixed directly to the sea-floor by steel or concrete foundations, or they are floating vessels connected solely by anchor lines and risers delivering oil from wellheads attached to the sea bed. They are connected to submerged land, as if the viscous sea did not exist and the waters that swept in to flood "Doggerland" in the central North Sea roughly 10,000 years ago had again retreated.(12)

The North Sea has the world's largest agglomeration of drilling rigs (13) which are up for decommissioning as mature wells run dry. Over the last fifty years, this infrastructure has filled up the North Sea floor, water column, and surface and increased the sea's overall resistance to flow—a process currently being continued in the wind-energy sector. Other North Sea artefacts are being removed; in April 2017 after ten years of preparation, the "topside" of the Brent Delta—a Shell-operated platform located 115 miles north-east of the Shetland Islands—was removed and transported to the UK port of Hartlepool for dismantling and recycling. Brent Delta weighed 24,000 tons, was 131 m tall, provided accommodation and recreational facilities for 161 workers and included drilling equipment and a production plant: "all the facilities that were needed to produce and export oil and gas."(14) [Fig. 2, p. 51]. Trawlers have systematically swept the once stony sea-floor of the southern North Sea bare, leaving only sand, and marine life has colonised petroleum and wind-energy hardware, infiltrating metal surfaces that provide a diversification of habitat.(15)

These evolving relations of infrastructural and habitat construction and decay are exemplary of viscous conditions that, while frequently contradictory, are potentially rich and emergent. They offer important opportunities to develop more inclusive, comprehensive, adaptive, and spatial understandings of the "cultivated sea"—a unique cultural product formed over time through the interactions of a multitude of agents and events; human and non-human, organic and mineral. In her reflections on Hurricane Katrina, Nancy Tuana points out the impossibility of drawing lines between the natural and the human-induced, arguing instead for the "viscous porosity" of these categories: "We must attend to the porosity and to the in-between of the complex interrelations from which phenomena emerge."(16) In the chapters that follow, authors present their different contributions to this challenge, based on specific sites and experience.

(1) Andrew Barry, "Petrochemical Zones" (Viscous Space- the offshore physicality of the North Sea between solid and liquid, TU Delft: TU Delft, 2018), http://viscousspace.com/. Presentation at the Viscous conference, TU Delft 2018.
(2) "Kulturminne Ekofisk," accessed 7 May 2017, http://www.kulturminne-ekofisk.no/.
(3) Stig Kvendseth K, *Giant Discovery. A History of Ekofisk through the First 20 Years* (Norway: Phillips Petroleum Company, 1988).
(4) H. D. Trotter, 'The Ekofisk Tank—A Concrete Gravity Structure In The Norwegian North Sea' (Annual Meeting Papers, Division of Production, American Petroleum Institute, 1974), https://www.onepetro.org/conference-paper/API-74-B001.
(5) millipascals/second at 0°C. Sweet crude has a lower sulphur content, and light crude is less dense than water.
(6) The dynamic viscosity of seawater at 0°C and 35 g kg^{-1} salinity is 1.88mPa.s. (http://www.kayelaby.npl.co.uk/general_physics/2_7/2_7_9.html)
(7) Nicole Starosielski, *The Undersea Network* (Durham, NC: Duke University Press, 2015).
(8) See chapter 8, this volume
(9) UN, "UNCLOS 1982," 1982, http://www.un.org/Depts/los/convention_agreements/convention_overview_convention.htm.
(10) Keith Chapman, *North Sea Oil and Gas: A Geographical Perspective*, (Newton Abbot a.o: David & Charles, 1976).
(11) See chapter 7, this volume.
(12) Laura Spinney, "Searching for Doggerland," *National Geographic Magazine*, December 2012.
(13) Statistica, "Number of Offshore Rigs Worldwide as of January 2018 by Region," Statistics (London ; New York: Statistica Ltd., 2018), https://www.statista.com/statistics/279100/number-of-offshore-rigs-worldwide-by-region/.
(14) David Wilkes, "How Do You Dismantle 'the Mother of All Meccano Sets'?," *Daily Mail Online*, 10 May 2017, http://www.dailymail.co.uk/~/article-4493586/index.html.
(15) See chapter 11, this volume.
(16) Nancy Tuana, "Viscous Porosity: Witnessing Katrina," in *Material Feminisms*, eds. Stacy Alaimo and Susan Hekman (Bloomington: University of Indiana Press, 2008), https://www.academia.edu/12103511/Viscous_Porosity_Witnessing_Katrina.

Chapter 4 EVERYTHING HAS ITS DEPTH*

J. M. Ledgard

J. M. Ledgard plunges the reader into the deep sea, describes its unique characteristics through his protagonists, and opens up the unanswered question of our present and future relations to this space.

J. M. (Jonathan) Ledgard is a writer and a thinker on near future risk, technology, and nature. His writing often contrasts the steady state of nature with the flux of the lived life. He is considered a leading proponent of planetary writing. His novel *Submergence* was a New York Times Book of the Year and has been adapted into a Hollywood film by Wim Wenders.

*Extracts from the author's novel *Submergence* (2011), published by Jonathan Cape, UK.

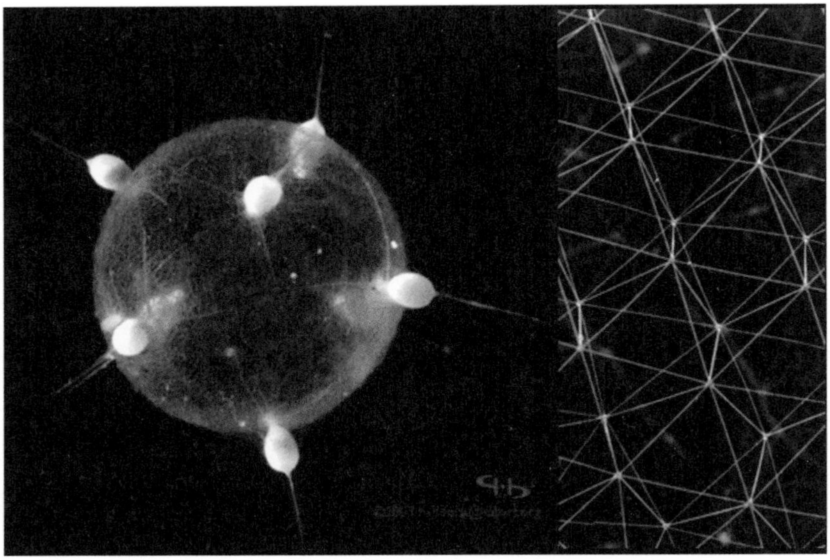

Fig. 1 Tuscaridium cygneum, a single-celled bioluminescent radiolarian. (Stephen Haddock)

It is the largest and most stable living space in our biosphere. It challenges us to understand life without light, life in three-dimensions, under crushing pressure, more slow-moving and ancient than anything on the surface. We will sooner exist on Mars, or some asteroid at pace, than we will set ourselves in the deep.

HOW THEN SHOULD WE PLACE IT IN OUR IMAGINATION?

I think our appreciation of it will have to be mediated by artificial intelligence sentinels, whose patience and fidelity will outstrip what we are capable of.

Our first task will be to define and build these sentinels and set them at depths of over 3,000 metres. Suspended there in absolute blackness, drifting on nameless underwater rivers, these cubes will be upgraded into half-consciousness over the next decades, and will deliver us beauty and meditation, a truer understanding of time and dimensionality for all of us living out our lives on the sunlit surface.

THE DIMENSIONALITY OF THE OCEAN

"The Cuviers," she continued, "have learned to dive deeper over a million year evolution. They edged further in from one mutation to the next. Thinking about the way a beaked whale dives is a good way to think about the dimensionality of the ocean." She selected a softer lead pencil and drew in thick lines on the paper she used for her calculations: a cross section of the planet from its stratosphere to its molten core.

"The oceans cover 70 percent of the planet surface. You know that. It has five layers. The first is epipelagic… That's wrist-watch depth. It contains all the plant life and coral reefs and all the shipwrecks that can be dived with aqualungs; all of Jacques Cousteau. Whatever memory we have of baptism or any other form of submersion is here in blue water.

The next layer is the mesopelagic. This is the twilight zone, into which blue and all the other colors and light vanish." She drew more lines. "Everything under the mesopelagic is night. First the bathypelagic zone, then the abyssopelagic, finally the hadopelagic."

She looked up. They both did.

"The hadopelagic is what interests me. Hadal from the Greek hades, meaning unseen. This," she said, shading it in, "is the other world in our world. The only light is the bioluminescence of fish that move under the weight of a thousand atmospheres."

She drew circles representing the inner parts of the planet.

"There are 3,481 kilometers of molten rock and 2,690 kilometers of mantle. No one knows much about the mantle. It has no life and therefore no possibility of reanimation and so is without scientific interest. I disagree. I'm studying what I think is the living bit of the mantle, the first few kilometers underlying the Hadal deep. I believe the fissures on the sea floor into the mantle are filled with microbial life."

Her pencil lingered on the core and mantle.

"The biosphere is the dermis. All life and regeneration in our world belongs to it. Thick as it seems to us, with our histories of evolution and extinction, exploration and colonization, the abiotic mantle is several hundred times thicker." She drew another scale showing how nearly all the biosphere was in the ocean.

"We exist only as a film on the water," she said. "Of course, this goes against the religion of the Garden of Eden and the canon of political documents ending with the international law of the sea, which promote the primacy of man on the planet. Just take a look at it," she said, running the pencil again over the lines and curves. "We're nature's brief experiment with self-awareness. Any study of the ocean and what lies beneath it should serve notice of how easily the planet might shrug us off."..."Let's say the Atlantic is 160 million years old," she continued. "It might be older. We appeared less than one million years ago. We walked in yesterday. It's not much of a claim. Yet somewhere in the Atlantic right now and in the other oceans, some man, I'm sorry, it's always a man isn't it, some man is smashing up a seamount more ancient than any greenwood on land, which he can't see and refuses to value."

A JOURNEY INWARD

What the hell is down there? 91 percent of the planet's living space, 90 percent of the living creatures. For every flea; nine sea fleas. No dogs, no cats, but so many other creations with eyes and thoughts, moving in three dimensions. It needs to be explored. With what?

There are only five submersibles in the world capable of diving deeper than 3,000 meters. These tiny submarines can spin on a coin, yet have trouble braking in the water column.

Their operating depth ranges to 6,500 meters, or 680 atmospheres, putting 96 percent of the ocean within reach of man (including most of the Hadal deep), but none of these submersibles are capable of matching the feat of bathyscaphe Trieste, which in 1960 touched down on the Challenger Deep of the Mariana Trench; at 11,034 meters, the very bottom of the known world.

An aquanaut is someone who explores the ocean in the same way an astronaut explores space. The first aquanauts were dangled on a cable in a steel ball to depths only those buried at sea had previously plumbed. There were trays of soda lime in the ball to absorb the carbon dioxide the aquanauts breathed out.

"I felt like an atom floating in illimitable space," one said.

Space flight is a journey outward... Space is about weightlessness and speeds never before achieved by machines and that can scarcely be felt; the discharge of aerosol is enough to propel a vessel forward, a nudge of a pencil sets its course, and all the while the air inside of it presses against the void outside. Ocean flight is, by contrast, a journey inward, toward blindness. It is about weight, the stopping of the craft on thermal layers, the pressure of water pushing in, and the discomfiting realisation that most of the planet you call your own is hostile to you. There will never be a Neil Armstrong moment in the ocean. There is nothing to light the way, no prospect, no horizon; even encased in a metal suit the human body is too liquescent to contemplate stepping out onto the deep sea floor.

It is easier for human beings to push outward than it is for them to explore inward. The wind that carries you away like a kite will blow you on your back if you turn to face it.

Millions and millions of years ago we lived in the ocean. When we emerged we had to move in two dimensions, instead of three. That was painful at first... The lack of a third dimension is one explanation for our need to head out over the horizon. Another explanation is that we were raised up from chemosynthetic life in the deep ocean to become photosynthetic life at the top. Having ascended from the eternal night we cannot stop ourselves from heading toward the light. We are moths in the thrall of the sun and the stars, shedding off darkness. That is our instinct, but our conscious nature is also to be drawn to the unknown. We want to know what is in the sky and what is behind the sky. These have been our obsessions since our beginnings, yet the curiosity does not extend to the ocean...We know the tides, because they cover the edges of our countries and swell our river mouths and fill our fishing nets, but the connection with the ocean has been lost. If it is described at all, it is as a tomb or a hiding place.

To push inward is hard, to descend even more so; it challenges our sense of who we are and where we came from. This is why, even though we are inundated with seawater, the advances of our oceanographic agencies do not match those of our space agencies.

THE HADAL DEEP

They had left Iceland behind, Akureyri, with its fjord and green hills and glaciers, and steamed north into the Greenland Sea, Grønlandshavet. She was bound for the largest uncharted hydrothermal vent field in the world, far below the plunging icebergs and the blue-black top, in a part of the Hadal deep whose unlit clock ticked at an incalculably slower speed.

She stood at the railings. The air was raw. *The Pourquoi Pas?* Was approaching Jan Mayen Island. She wanted to see it.

Gulls wheeled above cold rich swells. There were pieces of ice and icebergs. There were pilot whales riding the bow wave. It was beautiful to watch them. A killer whale cut loops under migrating geese. It went in and out of the water. It sparkled. She could see from its dorsal fin that it was a male, old and tired. It appeared troubled by the thrumming of the ship. It made her think of the changes that had occurred in the Greenland Sea in its lifetime. When it was birthed there were hardly any ships. There were no submarines. There were no engines, klaxons; no man-made noises. There were many seals and fish then, whereas now there was such a competition the killer whale was forced to trail geese in the hope that one might fall from the sky.

The ocean was being fished out, poisoned and suffering acidification. Quite apart from the vessels there were sonar arrays and other electronics that ruptured the orientation of sea mammals. And if sea mammals could become so disorientated as to beach themselves, so could man exterminate himself. Man had hardly taken breath from the Stone Age and yet was altering the flow of rivers, cutting up hills and discarding the materials that would be easily identifiable to future geologists. The anthro-pocene: a geological age marked by plastic.

She believed manned submersibles were vital. They provided the necessary leap of imagination, the human connection to the deep. Machines could complement them. Hundreds of drones could fly far under the sea, quietly, at all hours, providing a constant flow of information to the surface.

Then there was the biological revolution. It was possible to
Then there was the biological revolution. It was possible to see creatures that had never been noticed before, the living matter of the minestrone, of which only one recently discovered species of picophytoplankton in the upper layers of the ocean was reckoned to have a biomass equivalent to the insect life in the Congo River basin. The diversity was overwhelming.

There were microbes in the sea that were deliberately rare. These microbes were waiting for conditions to change so they could become abundant. She found this a very powerful thought. It changed her idea of what a lifespan meant. A microbe waiting a million years, holding to a different rhythm through those many sunrises and sunsets. What was that rhythm?

They passed through the fog bank and Jan Mayen appeared then with the clarity of a photograph taken with the highest-quality camera; thin beaches, blues and grays of augite and pyroxene. The volcano looked like Mount Fuji, only more spectral. The cone coughed up cinders. The fire inside of it glimmered on the underside of the clouds. The iron ore on the slopes, the snowfields and shreds of mist about the rim were the sulphurous way in.

HYDROTHERMAL VENTS

It was the French polar explorer, Jean-Baptiste Charcot, who, on his many voyages to the Greenland Sea, discovered that the temperature of the Hadal deep is a uniform four degrees Celsius around the world. Its sole virtue is constancy. Its processes are uniform. Cold water percolates into the rock, is superheated, and spurts from the chimneys of hydrothermal vents. It dissolves minerals and metals in the rock and, in this way, provides the ingredients for chemical life in what would otherwise be a deathly night, visited only by matter from above.

Until the discovery of hydrothermal vents off the Galapagos Islands in 1977, scientists assumed that life on Earth was photosynthetic and belonged to the surface. It was the other way around: photosynthetic life came later, when cells strayed to the top where they were cooked for millions of years before evolving a way to absorb the light, and all the while the chemosynthetic life in the abyss was evolving a stability we cannot hope for. The hydrothermal vents are only a small part of it. In the fissures, crevices, clefts, and cracks; in the volcanic pus, in all the amazing lattices of the deep, are heat-loving or hyperthermophile protists, archaea, fungi, and especially bacteria, which together constitute the earliest life on our planet. They are chemosynthetic, with no need of the sun. They live off hydrogen, carbon dioxide, or iron. They excrete methane, or eat it. Some breathe in rust to produce magnetic iron.

The microbial life of the deep exists in the queerest plane, where worms live in scalding pools and keep fleeces of microbes on their backs that are even more extraordinary than those that live on the timbers of our eyelashes.

In the white night of the fourth day out of Iceland, the *Pourquoi Pas?* Dropped anchor over the underworld they sought. Enki was the northernmost hydrothermal vent field yet discovered, with some of the largest recorded sulphide deposits. The water that poured from its chimneys was 399 degrees Celsius. There was proof

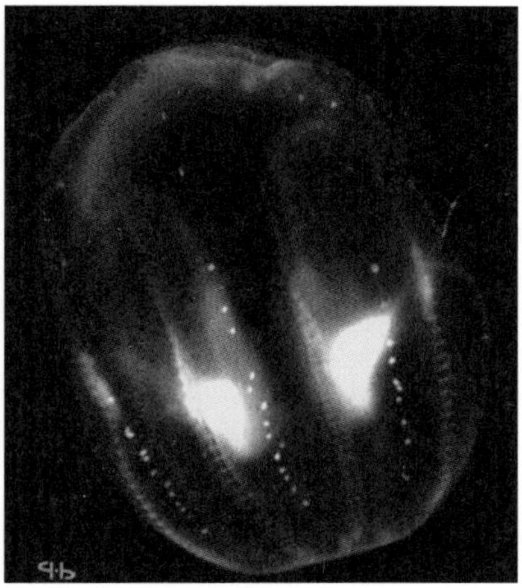

Fig. 2 Bathyctena, a bathypelagic ctenophore typically found deeper than 2000 metres. (Stephen Haddock)

of a chemosynthetic life cycle, with acid-feeding bacteria at its foundation, working up to tube worms, white clams, and other bivalves. It was extraordinarily large and ancient. More than that was unclear. The 2011 expedition had discovered the field near where the Knipovich and Mohn undersea ridges joined after weeks of dragging a CTD (where C was conductivity, T was temperature and D was depth) sensor behind the boat in saw-tooth patterns. The sensor looked for anomalies. When it found them, it took a sample of vent water, which could then be analyzed for telltale levels of dissolved hydrogen and methane oxidized in the water column by microorganisms. Her challenge for 2012 was to scrape from a fissure some richer material, of mathematical consequence.

Microbial life was tenacious. It swarmed even in mineshafts and caves. Seen from up close, the cracks in the sea floor were like the cross-hatching on a metalplate engraving. She believed that some of them went down eight kilometers into the mantle, and were carpeted with a density of microbial life that, taken together with the deep biota, was more than all the photosynthetic life on the surface of the planet combined. To prove her thesis she had to come up with methods of counting the methanogens, the hyper thermophilic autotrophic iron reducers, and the peculiar states and leagues of archaea and bacteria. She had also tried to identify the boundary that separated the living part from where there was no life and to understand the percolation between existence and nonexistence.

THE DESCENT

It was a clear morning. The sea was calm. The pilot climbed in first, then the other scientist, then her. Two men, one woman.... She went up the ladder and dropped down through the hatch. It was a thick nickel sphere. There was no need for decompression: the pressure inside was a constant one atmosphere. The walls were covered in dials and switches. There were three viewing windows and three padded benches. The smell was of bleach and behind it of sick. The carpet was very thin, brown, shiny; of the kind you might find in the entrance to a prison or a military installation. She put on her ski hat. The hatch was closed above them and sealed.

The *Nautile* was winched down over the side and into the Greenland Sea. There was a clanging of chains, final checks, and then they sank. The colors coming into the craft changed like the color of the sky seen by a rocket when it blasts into space, although of a different density: school ink, blue, blueblack, black. She saw charr, starfish, and little whirring shrimps. The craft began to breathe. Oxygen was pumped in and the carbon dioxide they expelled was scrubbed clean by a lithium-hydroxide filter. The biggest window was for the pilot. Her window was the size of a laptop screen. She pressed her face to the thick quartz pane. She wanted to feel the trembling on the other side. She could not see much, the monitors from the cameras were a truer guide. Even so it was important to look with her own eyes. She gazed into the deep and the deep gazed back.

Nuclear submarines went windowless in the wristwatch shallows, without a care to look out—only listening, making no sound. A submersible was just the opposite. It was a seeing device: from the Nautile people had observed the hull of the Titanic.

…

They sank, sank, sank. All the waters closed over their heads. 607 meters… 634 meters… out of the mesopelagic layer… into the bathypelagic. There was a time when the dominion of countries ended at five fathoms, the keel of a ship, the run of an anchor. Enki was at 3,133 meters, 1,741 fathoms.

The sphere was too small to stand up in; after an hour, her legs became numb. She wiped away their condensed breath from the window and stared out. There was another hour of descent to go.

Everything that belonged to them disappeared, except the light on the switches and on the emergency lever. The water was alive with bioluminescent fish and eels. The salp and jellyfish gave themselves in disco lights when the Nautile brushed them. Down there everything spoke in light: it was the most common form of communication on the planet. The puniest fish had the brightest lanterns. There were fish who wore a cape of silver chain mail to reflect light. Transparency was another form of protection. So was casting a red light to appear black and so invisible. Or to fill one's belly with ink and so disappear, as surely as slipping on a magic ring.

They sank deeper.

"Can we turn up the lights now?" Peter asked.

"Certainly," said Étienne.

Everything was illuminated…The sphere creaked. The microphones picked up ghostly whining, knocks, moaning, shrieks, wailing, and firing. The walls grew cold. They were wet to the touch.

She began to smell the men; they might have begun to smell her.

She wiped away more condensation from the porthole with her elbow.

921 meters… 1,043 meters….

“Starboard. Jeweled squid!” exclaimed Peter. They hovered to get a better look. She zoomed in with the video camera. The squid were white and appeared to be encrusted with emeralds and amethysts. They had a massive sapphire eye for looking about them and a tiny eye pushed into their bodies like genitalia. They swam at a forty-five degree angle to make use of both eyes.

1,830 meters… 1,832 meters. They were covered up. All of Britain could be sunk over them, the peak of Ben Nevis would not see any trace of daylight.

There were strings of bell-jar jellies with numerous transparent stomachs, all of them pulsing. The ocean was hungry. It was a mouth, and a grave.

She saw a fish with a deathly pallor whose face was like a sponge with holes pushed into it by a pencil. Each of those holes was a sensory pore detecting the slightest movement nearby.

The Nautile stopped in a cold layer of the water. It keeled over, righted itself, shuddered, and continued to sink. The thermal layers were like a staircase going down. She said thermal layer and a lithograph presented itself of her slave ship halted on such a layer, not able to sink any deeper, instead carried forever on the North Atlantic Drift, its fire doused, its souls intact, in irons, their lungs full of water.

LANDING

3,088 meters… 3,120….

They went slowly toward a column the size of an office block. The chimneys on it billowed like so many Turks setting back their heads and expelling cigarette smoke through their nostrils.

It was in the style of Gaudi; pitted, knobbly, rust-colored from oxidation, black in places, in others mottled white with mats of bacteria. Amphipod danced at the edge of the vents. Tubeworms swayed like heavy cocks. There were mussels and other bivalves. Blind fish circled. The Turks sat very still, smoking, regarding them.

After some time at the base of the column Étienne lifted the Nautile and piloted it to where the floor of the earth was cracked. There was no fire, no hearth. The magma was glassy and cool. The light broke against heavy drifts of marine snow; it was useless to think the abyss could be illuminated by thallium iodide. She was excited, intent, but at the same time thought, the places we will have to dwell as a species are terrible. We will have to accommodate ourselves to realms for which we are not evolved, to lodge ourselves in them, to articulate our bodies from inside a suit of titanium and the other materials. She felt the metal hollow inside the submersible acutely—the stale air, the sweat of Peter and Étienne, the smell of vomit, bleach....

With great care Étienne set the Nautile down at the edge of a crack. They extended the robot arm to scrape bacteria from its interior. She adjusted her weight on the bench and the craft in turn settled on the fine silica mud, on the diatomaceous ooze of dead creatures that on land was used as scouring powder.

It was tranquil, in a way. There were no storms, no swells, the water was very calm. Did the abyss sing of itself? Seen from below, the surface looked like heaven. Seen from heaven, she thought, it was a roiling sea, a darksome air infernal. Human beings were between worlds, they were in-betweeners, who did not know where light dwelt or where darkness had its place.

[Fig. 1 & Fig. 2] Bioluminescence Web Page https://biolum.eemb.ucsb.edu/

Chapter 5 THICK REPRESENTATIONS FOR OCEANIC SPACE

Claudia Bode & Lizzie Yarina

To represent is to provide the basis for a plan. How the ocean is represented therefore fundamentally influences not only power relations but future possibilities. Claudia Bode and Lizzie Yarina explore a range of alternative ways of capturing ocean space that avoid compacting its thickness and stifling its contingent vitality.

Claudia Bode is a practising architect and an affiliate researcher at the MIT Urban Risk Lab as well as the Habitat Unit at TU Berlin. She is a member in the German Scientific Advisory Council for Marine Spatial Planning at the Federal Maritime and Hydrographic Agency (BSH). Claudia holds a Master of Architecture degree from MIT.

Lizzie Yarina is a PhD student in the MIT Department of Urban Studies and Planning and a Research Fellow at the MIT Leventhal Center for Advanced Urbanism. Her research explores the spatial politics of climate change adaptation. Lizzie holds a joint Master of Architecture and Master of City Planning degree from MIT.

The sea is a thick space, characterised by depth, movement, and change over time. Yet planning for marine space often uses tools more suited to solid ground than fluid seas. Planning and urbanising this viscous space thus requires moving away from fixed and bounded conceptions of space to ones that are deeper, richer, multifaceted, and dynamic. This chapter explores alternative conceptual and representational strategies which move toward "thick representations," reflecting richer approaches to planning for marine space.(1) By building on visual systems from disciplines and epistemologies beyond conventional, horizontal planning, thick representational tools can better communicate the viscosity and depth of oceanic space, forming a more comprehensive base from which to envision marine futures.

TO REPRESENT IS TO SIMPLIFY

Marine research reveals an astonishing array of sensory tools through which aquatic animals negotiate the underwater world —organs that detect and interpret electromagnetic fields, temperature, salinity, vibration, odours, very high and low frequencies of sound, light polarisation as well as many non-visible (to us) wavelengths of light.(2) In contrast, our species is simply not equipped to survive in marine space, much less to fully understand its fluidity: without the assistance of bulky technology, we last mere minutes underwater. Our comparative blindness makes it difficult to comprehend the extent to which the seas are in fact shifting and dynamic *volumes* shaped by a sea-floor as varied in terrain as its terrestrial counterpart, in places so deep that the bottom is more alien to us than the surface of the moon (see chapter 4). Characterized by significant flux—in salinity, temperature, currents, tides, extending or retreating sea ice, atmospheric conditions, and ecosystems—today's oceans are also shaped by the immeasurable influence of humans. Since we cannot directly access this oceanic space we rely on representations, as mediators, to understand it.

Despite its mysteriousness, we are actively and quickly territorialising the sea. In the interest of coordinating the construction of offshore energy infrastructure and shipping lanes, nation-states are launching ambitious plans to map, regulate, and categorise their offshore zones, producing marine spatial plans (MSPs) that represent approved uses of the sea almost as if they were land-use plans. MSP development has greatly accelerated in recent years and was enabled through international treaties, in particular the United Nations Convention on the Law of the Sea (UNCLOS)—an agreement that defined the limits of territorial waters and Exclusive Economic Zones (EEZ) as extending 200 nautical miles from the coast of a nation-state.(3) The "viscous sovereignty" of UNCLOS set the stage for more intensive usage of the ocean through the establishment of more universal rules; the deployment of these uses, however, has produced a situation in which multiple actors—fish, fishers, wind turbines, container ships, coral reefs, whales, oil platforms—struggle to share increasingly crowded waters.

Political scientist and anthropologist James C. Scott argues that new planning frontiers have, in the past, produced deterministic projects that attempted to strip the unknowns from complex situations with the aim of achieving *legibility*. In *Seeing Like a State*, Scott describes how top-down planning requires simplified representations of the world: maps and other documents that enable bureaucrats to compress complex realities into a legible package.(4) The results can be seen in planning examples as varied as the design of the city of Brasília, nineteenth-century industrial forestry, and Soviet agricultural collectivisation schemes. The messiness of the world is reduced to something easily drawn or entered into a ledger, entailing, in many cases, a loss of deep traditional knowledge. Maps and other forms of representation play a critical role in this process, since they both record and participate in an attempt to make legible a complex reality.

Attempts to tame or territorialise unruly places are deeply intertwined with the question of (planetary) urbanisation. If the entire planet is urban, we can no longer rely on easy representational shortcuts that flatten large, messy areas: wilderness, rural areas, ocean, desert. The relevant question for those concerned with global urbanism is no longer "where does the city end and nature begin?", but rather how increasingly the entire planet, climate, and beyond are human-constructed "second natures."(5) Viscous littoral zones at the boundaries of city and not-city, difficult to categorize or even comprehend, demand a particularly nuanced understanding not only of physical space, but of the myriad invisible networks, objects, and relationships that produce an "extended" form of urbanization.(6)

The oceans pose a particularly complex problem. As we plan our way further and further from solid land are we appreciating the richness and complexity of marine space as a unique facet of our urban planet, or are we simply attempting to bring it under control? Lacking pre-existing models and working literally in uncharted terrain, marine spatial planners are at risk of falling into the trap described by Scott, flattening the ocean's depth, fluidity, and complexity in the interest of rationality and legibility.

Existing planning processes were developed for a solid, Euclidean space. The seas could, however, provide an opportunity to explore different methodologies toward planning for an expanded understanding of the urban, whether dry or wet: approaches rooted in dynamism, multiscalar and overlapping boundaries, and relational ontologies. "Soft" planning approaches, for instance, move away from land-based views of territory, in which "each unit is thought to be a container, a view inherent to the classic notion of territory as an area that has been reappropriated, with borders marking the limits of control."(7) Given the difficulty of inscribing boundaries on liquid space, soft planning takes into account flows, connectivity, and change, while decentering the human in the presence of non-human and material actors.(8) The space of the sea—inherently fluid—could be seen as the prototypical "soft" space, an opportunity to rethink planning theory and practice.

Scott's argument critiques how we represent the world to ourselves. The simplification inherent to representation irons out reality, and ultimately extends from the plan into the planned world. The form of a planner's drawings is a central component of the plan, and yet one that is often entirely overlooked as a mere technical skill. Most (if not all) MSPs adopt terrestrial tools for planning and representation that sit uneasily on the ocean's fluid surface, and rarely dive down into the depths [Fig. 1]. If marine spatial planning (and, more broadly, marine urbanism) is to break out of an overly rationalistic paradigm to embrace the richness and complexity that is inherent to the space of the ocean, it will be necessary to develop representational techniques that better comprehend this reality [Fig. 2, p. 85].

WET ONTOLOGIES AND SOFT TERRITORIES

Human understanding of marine space is mediated by biological limitations and cultural constructs. For oceanic cultures that co-evolved with fluid waters, traditional fluid understandings of time, material, and space were suppressed by colonially imposed dry ontologies. Tongan/Fijian writer and anthropologist Epeli Hau'Ofa has argued that Pacific island nations are not "dry surfaces in a vast

Fig. 1
German MSP document for the North Sea 2009 (BSH)

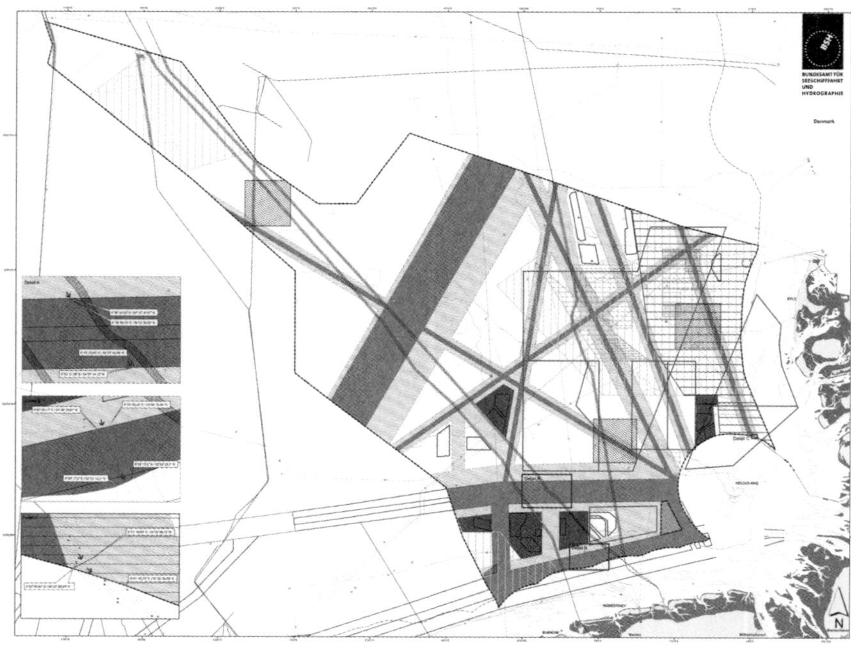

ocean far from the centres of power."(9) Indigenous understandings of Oceania as a "sea of islands" reflect an enduring ontology where wetness contributes to the potency of oceanic space, defined not by land but by water and the interconnectedness it facilitates and represents.

In his discussion of wet ontologies, geographer Philip Steinberg uses surfing to grasp the fundamental *material* interconnectedness of the sea: the surfer is propelled by waves, which, despite their force, can never be seen, contained, or reduced to a Euclidean point.(10) He calls for this volumetric complexity and mysterious fluidity to wake up call planners who, as if on autopilot, are insisting on extending flat, static, dry ontologies into the space of the sea, reflexively extruding a two-dimensional map into three-dimensional space.(11) In a similar vein, Nancy Couling and others call for design and planning strategies that acknowledge interlinkages, feedback loops, and larger contexts of natural as well as anthropogenic factors.(12) Within planning, the term "ecosystem-based planning" addresses the failure of typical tools to acknowledge the complexities of the marine environment, and demands a "wetter" or "softer" approach focused on evolving relationships rather than hard boundaries.

The EU's push for "Territorial Cohesion" is marked by initiatives—for example, comprehensive planning for the Baltic Sea region, involving many countries—which often span across boundaries, both national and international.(13) These projects necessitate a softer planning that grapples with multiscalar, overlapping territories, while embracing flexibility [Fig. 3]. The space of the sea—featuring overlapping and layered governance structures—is a natural prototype for this approach: it is contingent, relational, multiscalar, and fluid.(14) In his analysis of the BaltSeaPlan Vision 2030, developed between 2009 and 2012 for the Baltic Sea region, geographer Stephen Jay presents six descriptors of such "softness": *flexing, teeming, connecting, re-configuring,* and *anticipating.*(15)

The territorial understanding found in the BaltSeaPlan implicates an equally foundational rethinking of representational techniques. As geographer Stuart Elden notes, "cartography does not just represent the territory, but is actively complicit in its production."(16) If maps are a political technology used to define and enforce territories, then a fundamental reorientation of how we understand territory—from static and dry to contingent and wet—would imply an equally radical shift in how these spaces are represented. As regions begin to develop tools to represent, and ultimately plan, marine space, cartographic simplifications manifest in real-space planning actions.

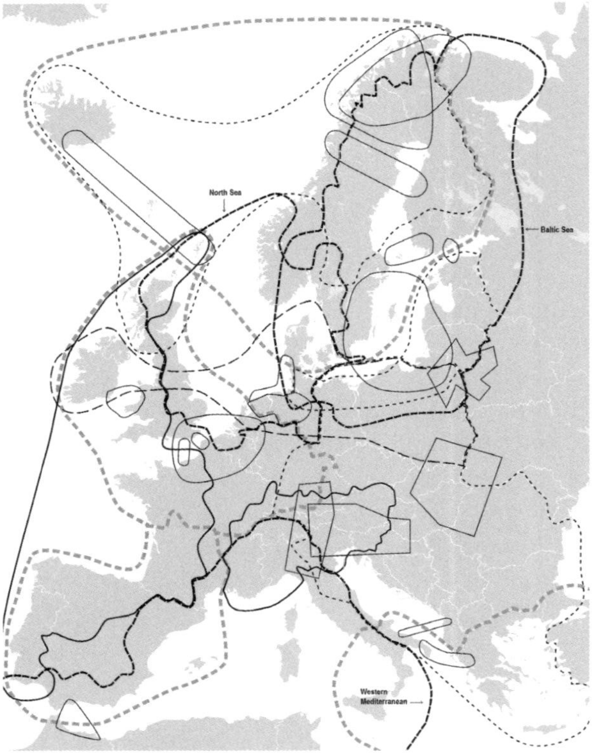

Fig. 3
Overlapping territorial projects in Europe. (Claudia Bode).

REPRESENTING AND PERCEIVING: HOW DO WE SEE THE SEA?

Incomplete cartographic and other representations shrink the realm of possibilities for planning. How do we capture the complexities and contingencies that define marine space? Representation is critical in at least two ways: first, as a form of *understanding*—we represent information to ourselves in order to process it and act on it. Secondly, representation is also a form of *projection* that enables us to actively create future visions. If we do not actively imagine alternative futures that are appropriate for the space of the sea, planners inevitably return to known terrestrial templates.

This section explores relational, subjective, narrative-, time-, and volume-based representations that suggest alternative tools for understanding a space that we can't physically inhabit—with different implications for various human and non-human actors.

MAPPING VOLUME AND TIME

The thinness of existing representations and resulting plans for the ocean delaminate them from reality. Elden notes that "we all too often think of the spaces of geography as areas, not volumes. Territories are bordered, divided and demarcated, but not understood in terms of height and depth."(17) Although, for the majority of its inhabitants, the space of the sea is experienced in three dimensions (see chapter 4)—with significant vertical differentiation in terms of light penetration, salinity, temperature, and ecology—cartographic tools used by planners to represent territories are almost universally plan-based, flattened drawings that locate fixed borders and landmarks.

EEZs are differentiated vertically in that free movement is allowed across the surface while nations retain economic rights to seabed resources below. However, these thinly layered distinctions fail to fully conceptualise the ways in which the ocean might operate as "vertical territory."(18) The seafloor hosts shipwrecks, pipelines, wind turbine and oil rig anchors; the space between those points and the turbines, platforms and shipping lanes drawn on a map can be vast. Within that thick space reside the animals caught by fishers and those occupying shipwrecks and energy infrastructure. Three-dimensional or section-based representations of this space are rare, despite significant advances being made in technologies for seafloor mapping. (19)

Time is also missing in traditional plan-based cartography. Lines drawn on paper fail to capture the flows of the ocean—fish, plankton, plastic waste, and water continue to move irrespective of imaginary zones and boundaries—suggesting that bounded-container conceptions of territoriality are fundamentally incompatible with basic properties of the sea. Even boundaries that we now think we can know and draw, like the habitat ranges of fish, are expected to shift with climate change.(20) EPFL laba studio's study of the Barents Sea made evident the extent to which its conditions are cyclical and contingent, with the yearly melting and freezing of sea ice a determining ecological factor.(21) A more dynamic form of time-based representation is used by Forensic Architecture; in their work on the Left-to-Die Boat case, in which sixty-three migrants died while drifting within the NATO marine surveillance area, they created a video report that combines multiple data types—including a voice-over narrative, a timeline, dynamic mapping, and interviews—into a comprehensive reconstruction of events over fifteen days.(22) The emphasis is on establishing relationships over time, in order to establish culpability for lives lost at sea.

Collaborations between academic institutions and local governments have shown the potential for web-based tools that facilitate planning processes in "fluid" spaces. For example, "Flux.land" is a collaboration between researchers from the University of Toronto, the MIT Urban Risk Lab, and Broward County, Florida.(23) Although designed for an urban rather than oceanic context, it navigates a "dynamic hydrological condition" amplified by climate change.(24) As an interactive web-based platform with live updates, the tool helps plan for a condition of flux by "incorporating the indeterminacy of broader environmental systems with the pervasiveness and exactitude of the planning code."(25) The project recognises that even on land, the default to fixity limits the capacity of planning to deal with flux.

The value of such a dynamic interface (whether plan, section, or volume-based) is made evident when considering the uneasiness some fishers have felt at the prospect of being mapped, because they fear that they will be "mapped into a box." Fishing is a dynamic activity, and a classic map made on any given day cannot communicate seasonal, ecological or economic cycles. However, refusing to be mapped produces a sort of "cartographic silence" that means the fishing industry is inadequately represented in the creation of marine spatial planning documents, with representatives of spatially fixed interests assuming that they can always "fish somewhere else." As described by a fishing industry representative: (26)

> On land there is ownership, so there is basis for negotiation. But in the sea we are dealing just with the state. This falls against the fishers because they can just go somewhere else, and there is no basis for compensation. The other industries—oil, cables, and pipelines—have rights attached to a particular place. So we should say now the rest belongs to the fishing industry, then there would be a basis for negotiation.

The fishers note, rightly, that a process of planning which departs from the principle of *land ownership*—a fundamentally terrestrial concept—is not suited to the space of the sea and the activity of fishing. Here, a dynamic, interactive mapping system could alleviate some of these concerns by enabling fishers to more clearly represent their "soft" territoriality, which is based on the complex interplay of high-level regulations and the movement of fish [Fig. 4, p. 86]. Systems such as this might further represent the interests of non-human biota (whales, fish, plankton, seabirds) who similarly exist outside fixed planning norms.

RELATIONAL NAVIGATION IN THE PACIFIC

Oceanic navigators have long relied on relational tools to navigate the sea's fluid spaces. In the Pacific, skilled navigators sailed the world's vastest ocean, travelling from Papua to Hawaii to Aotearoa (New Zealand) to the west coast of South America. The ocean was a space of interconnection, dialogue, and dynamic relationships between humans, islands, sea, and biota. Even the relatively fixed points of islands are viscous, their geographies constantly changing as sandbars shift and volcanoes erupt.

Pacific navigators drew on stars, currents and winds to navigate the vast ocean; two systems-in-motion used to understand a third.(27) "Star compasses" such as those of the Caroline Islands use the rising and setting points of stars around the horizon to visualise directions.(28) Devices such as the Cook Islands' "star peeker," a water-filled coconut to navigate using reflections of the stars, were created for linking the systems of sky and ocean serving as a kind of relational

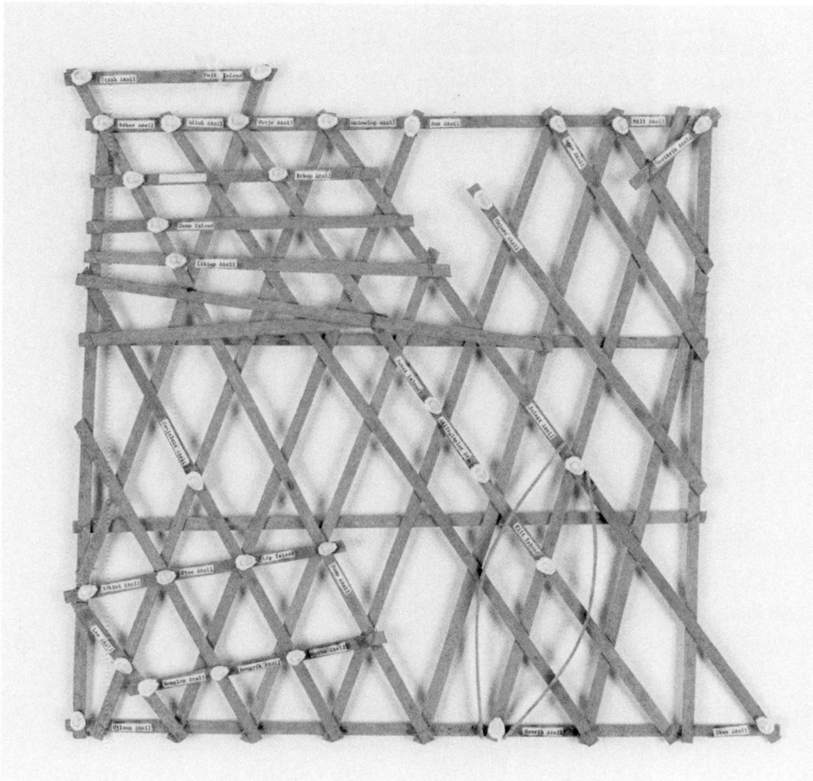

Fig. 5
Stick chart,
Marshall Islands.

map designed for a particular inter-island journey.

Notably, while these atmospheric compasses tell you where you are going, they do not tell you where you are. Their use requires constant attention to where you have come from; because of their atmospheric nature, they may not be available at all times, when clouds cloak the sun and stars or when winds die off. In those cases, one form of knowledge must be supplemented by another: Micronesian navigator Pius "Mau" Piailug, would lie down in the belly of the canoe, reading wave patterns and trajectory by the way the boat rocked.(29)

Micronesian stick charts combine kinesthetic knowledge of ocean patterns with a representational tool woven from panadanus roots and sometimes marked with shells indicating the location of islands. Rather than depending on winds and stars, Marshallese "wave piloting" relies predominantly on an understanding and reading of ocean swells. Stick charts serve as non-cartesian "maps," such as the *wapepe* which models "four interconnected schemas of the ocean: "the wave field, a continuum of wave patterns between atolls (*dilep*), a succession of zones of currents (*jukae*, *rubukae*, and *jeljeltae*) useful in gauging distance, and a series of wave patterns radiating outward from each atoll (kōkļaļ)."(30) [Fig. 5]. Using the chart requires the ability to read, through bodily movement, one's position within the chart. The map is assembled from these multiple navigation systems in the minds and bodies of the navigators.

Oceanic navigation systems require constant negotiation between multiple ways of understanding the environment. As anthropologist Joseph Genz notes, in Marshallese navigation, "A successful sea journey involves a combination of egocentric sensing of environmental phenomena and abstract, allocentrically framed representations." Assemblage models of oceanic navigation suggest that in order to understand any of the ocean's constantly moving and transforming components, no single episteme is sufficient. While many of these ways of knowing the sea were lost with the imposition of dry-ground ontologies, a resurgence of traditional outrigger canoes and navigational projects reclaim oceanic ways of knowing, pushing back against conceptions of space which attempted to convert the mobile and contingent into the fixed and mappable.

REPRESENTING SUBJECTIVITIES AND NARRATIVES

The body of the navigator is but one element in a vast assemblage of human and non-human actors. The very subjectivity of the navigator—the way they relate to other elements in order to build up an inner map—is critical to understanding their physical position, which in turn affects their relationships with other elements in the network. Here it is useful to refer to the tools of actor-network theory (ANT), in particular the actor-network diagram, which maps dynamically interrelated actors in a network and the effects they have on each other.

"The Black Sea Files," Ursula Biemann's video exploration of the geography of the oil pipeline connecting Azerbaijan to the world market, could be seen in terms of this representational approach. Interrelated subjectivities captured in film reveal the lived, highly personal experience of something typically discussed in abstract terms: the international oil market. She highlights the actors and connections that are invisible (displaced Kurds, farmers, the pipeline itself) in order to disrupt sanitised official versions of reality. Biemann uses image-making to construct narratives that form part of an interconnected ensemble of "files". It is through these files that "a subjective, but interrelated, series of scenes and plots" is revealed, combatting a centralising practice of image-making in order to include the many sidelines and secondary landscapes in the geography of Caspian oil.(31)

Image-making that communicates multiple lived realities traces connections within an actor-network diagram, so that newly visible elements fold into larger and more abstract understandings of the whole. A 2012 study attempted to concretise a relational approach to (marine) planning by engaging representatives of the commercial shipping industry in a conversation about their needs and views.(32)

Industry representatives largely felt their safety concerns were being dismissed in MSP processes, in particular their need for buffer zones between shipping lanes and wind farms. As summarised by study author Stephen Jay, the study makes visible the lived experience of a container ship captain on the North Sea—specifically the complex contingent choreography of navigation in shipping lanes:

> the sense of space is far from an even projection of axes, but is a continuously mutating assemblage of perceptions in which relative positions, directions and movements are paramount, calculated using selective information in relation to, and variable signals from, other entities; all this is channelled into hazard-sensitive decisions about progression across intermingling planes.(33)

Like a navigator moving between islands in the Pacific, a ship captain travelling in the North Sea deals with a "continuously mutating assemblage of perceptions" which cannot easily be captured in static form.(34) Following Biemann, the choreography of ships might comprise a "file" that reveals the relevant underlying three-dimensional, time-based factors that feed into a final spatial output (the position of the ship). This "file" could inform and perhaps form part of a what Bruno Latour would term a larger "matter of concern", such as a marine spatial plan.(35) Other dynamic representation techniques could also be deployed that elucidate the time-based, three-dimensional, and contingent relationships between actors in a network.

Sometimes something is so large, complex, and/or incomprehensible that it is effectively impossible to grasp it as a whole. A navigator, whale, or fishing boat finding a path across the ocean represents an actor writing a narrative within an extended, heterogenous, and highly networked space: the sea. Rather than simplifying components of this system so that the whole can be grasped, the tracing of elements through all of their connections and movements—whether a navigator or a single fish—provides a *narrative window* that brings to light components of the network-in-flux. This means working at a tangible scale: rather than starting with ecologies, networks, or policies, what is made visible begins with whales, container ships, underwater vibrations, fish, pieces of plastic, plankton, fishers, or oil rigs. To comprehend the vast, shifting, wet, deep, and multifaceted space of the ocean, thickened ways of seeing, knowing and inhabiting marine space must be brought together. This thickly descriptive narrative window resists the simplification —or legibility—of the whole even as it readily admits its own subjectivity.(36)

(EN)VISIONING MARINE SPACE

Representation establishes a particular image of what exists. The approaches outlined above represent the sea in ways that transcend the static, plan-based, boundary-oriented cartography typical of terrestrial planning. We might see them as a series of "plans"—plans that allow the space of the ocean to be understood as deeper, wetter, softer, more viscous and more potent; they could become a starting point for new planning tools founded on thicker representations. As calls expand for marine spatial planning to become "softer", its representation might also become "thicker": engaging time, volume, narrative, subjectivities, and relationality can help planners engage with these fundamental qualities of the urbanised ocean on a deeply interconnected planet.

Representation is the tool with which we understand the status quo and create visions of the future. As Andreas Faludi observes, spatial planning is "about inserting imaginative visions into the ongoing reconstruction of the spatial fabric of life, including the plurality of territories which this implies."(37) "Thick" representations are the shifting foundations for more aspirational visions of the future.They seek to comprehend the seas' physical and geopolitical viscosity (see chapter 3). Today's oceans are threatened from multiple angles: overfishing, plastic waste, warming waters, ocean acidification, resource extraction, and crowded human activities. Tools that allow us to better conceptualise multiple and competing human and non-human actors can help planners negotiate complex and contested oceanic space. These tools can also change who is included in the planning process. As we strive to better represent, preserve, organise, and repair the oceans, it is essential that we bring to the forefront this complexity of action and habitation while also being projective about what oceanic futures might contain.

(1) On "thick representations," a concept developed from anthropologist Clifford Geertz's use of "thick description" as a way of conceptualizing ethnography, see, e.g., Jens E. Kjeldsen, "The Rhetoric of Thick Representation: How Pictures Render the Importance and Strength of an Argument Salient," *Argumentation* 29, no. 2 (2015): 197–215; Zoe Bray, "Anthropology with a Paintbrush: Naturalist–Realist Painting as "'Thick Description,'" *Visual Anthropology Review* 31, no. 2 (2015): 119–33; Clifford Geertz,. *The Interpretation of Cultures* (New York: Basic Books, 1973).
(2) *Odontodactylus Scyllarus*, commonly known as the "mantis shrimp" has the most complex eyes known in the animal kingdom, containing 12 to 16 types of photoreceptors. Mantis shrimp can detect ultraviolet to far-red wavelengths of light as well as circularly or linearly polarized light.
(3) Philip Steinberg, *The Social Construction of the Ocean* (Cambridge University Press, 2001), 137.
(4) James C. Scott, *Seeing like a State: How Certain Schemes to Improve the Human Condition have Failed* (Yale University Press), 1998.
(5) Willian Cronon, *Nature's Metropolis: Chicago and the Great West (*WW Norton & Company, 2009)
(6) Neil Brenner, ed., *Implosions/Explosions: Towards a Study of Planetary Urbanization*, Jovis Verlag: Berlin, 2014
(7) Andreas Faludi, "Territorial Cohesion, Territorialism, Territoriality, and Soft Planning: A Critical Review," *Environment and Planning A*, 45, no. 6 (June 2013): 1305.
(8) Stephen Jay, "The Shifting Sea: From Soft Space to Lively Space" *Journal of Environmental Policy & Planning* (Feb. 2018): 7.
(9) Epeli Hau'Ofa, "Our Sea of Islands," in *A New Oceania: Rediscovering our Sea of Islands*, eds. Eric Waddell, Vijay Naidu, and Epeli Hau'ofa (University of the South Pacific: Beake House, 1993), 2–16.
(10) Philip Steinberg and Kimberley Peters "Wet Ontologies, Fluid Spaces: Giving Depth to Volume through Oceanic Thinking," *Environment and Planning D: Society and Space* 33, no. 2 (2015): 250.
(11) Stephen Jay, "Marine Space: Manoeuvring Towards a Relational Understanding," *Journal of Environmental Policy & Planning* 14, no. 1, (2012): 84.
(12) Nancy Raewyn Couling, "The Role of Ocean Space in Contemporary Urbanization," (Lausanne, EPFL, 2015), http://infoscience.epfl.ch/record/212706; Larry Crowder and Elliott Norse, "Essential Ecological Insights for Marine Ecosystem-Based Management and Marine Spatial Planning," *Marine Policy* 32, no. 5 (2008): 772–78.
(13) European moves towards macro-regional marine and terrestrial planning are reflected in the EU's "Territorial Agenda of the European Union 2020." "Territorial Cohesion," European Commission, "What is Regional Policy?" http://ec.europa.eu/regional_policy/en/policy/what/territorial-cohesion/, Accessed 13 May 2018.
(14) Jay, "Marine Space," 85.
(15) Jay, "Shifting Sea," 9.
(16) Stuart Elden, "Land, Terrain, Territory," *Progress in Human Geography* 34, no. 6 (2010): 809.
(17) Stuart Elden, "Secure the Volume: Vertical Geopolitics and the Depth of Power," *Political Geography* 34 (2013): 35.
(18) For a discussion of how territory becomes verticalised when we begin to value not only the ownership of the surface, but the capital potential of the geological strata that lie beneath it, see Bruce Braun, "Producing Vertical Territory: Geology and Governmentality in Late Victorian Canada," *Ecumene* 7, no. 1 (2000): 7–46.
(19) Adrienne Bernhard, "The Quest to Map the Mysteries of the Ocean Floor," *BBC Future* (5 April 2018), http://www.bbc.com/future/story/20180404-the-quest-to-map-the-mysteries-of-the-ocean-floor
(20) Nations like Tuvalu are expecting an increase of tuna in their waters as schools migrate towards cooler climes; New England is experiencing a decline of cod and other fish, linked to climate change. Government of Tuvalu, "National Adaptation Programme of Action II"; Emily S.Klein, Sarah L. Smith, and Jacob P. Kritzer, "Effects of Climate Change on Four New England Groundfish Species," *Reviews in Fish Biology and Fisheries* 27, no. 2 (2017): 317–38.
(21) Harry Gugger, Nancy Couling, and Aurélie Blanchard, eds., *Barents Lessons. Teaching and Research in Architecture* (Zürich: Park Books, 2012).
(22) Charles Heller, Lorenzo Pezzani, and Situ Studio, "Report on the Left-to-Die Boat," *Forensic Architecture* (2012), http://www.forensic-architecture.org/case/left-die-boat/
(23) Research team Toronto: Fadi Masoud, Isaac Seah, Jia Lu, Fabio Dias; MIT Urban risk lab: Miho Mazereeuw, Mayank Ojha, Aditya Barve, Kelly Leilani Main, Abraham Qunintero, Chetan Krishna.
(24) MIT Urban Risk Lab,"Flux.land," http://urbanrisklab.org/FluxLand-Sea-Level-Rise-Toolkit
(25) David Vega-Barachowitz, Fadi Masoud, and Roi Salgueiro, "Coding the Third

Condition," *UrbanNext*, https://urbannext.net/coding-the-third-condition/
(26) Ditte Degnbol and Douglas Clyde Wilson, "Spatial Planning on the North Sea: A Case of Cross-Scale Linkages," *Marine Policy* 32, no. 2 (2008): 197.
(27) Lesley Iaukea, "Integrating Geospatial Technology Analysis to Connect Indigenous Knowledge with Modern Science." AGUFM 2019 (2019): U32A–02.
(28) The name Caroline Islands dates to the era of Spanish colonization. The archipelago is comprised of indigenous communities who speak languages including Chuukese, Yapese, Palauan, Chamorro, Kosrean, and Carolinean.
C. Conboy Pyrek and R. Feinberg, "The Vaeakau-Taumoko Wind Compass as Part of a 'Navigational Toolkit,'" *Structure & Dynamics: eJournal of Anthropological & Related Sciences* 9, no. 1 (2016): 32; N. Thompson, "The Star Compass," *Polynesian Voyaging Society*, http://www.hokulea.com/education-at-sea/polynesian-navigation/the-star-compass/.
(29) Thompson, "Star Compass."
(30) J. Genz, "Complementarity of Cognitive and Experiential Ways of Knowing the Ocean in Marshallese Navigation," *Ethos* 42, no. 3 (2014): 337–8.
(31) Ursula Biemann, "Black Sea Files," *World of Matter*, http://www.worldofmatter.net/black-sea-files-0#path=black-sea-files-0.
(32) Jay, "Marine Space."
(33) Ibid., 93.
(34) Ibid., 93.
(35) Bruno Latour, "Why Has Critique Run Out of Steam? From Matters of Fact to Matters of Concern," *Critical Inquiry* 30, no. 2 (2004): 225-48.
(36) In addition to Geertz, see, for a discussion of how thick description combined with "weak theory" can create more wholistic understandings of society, economy, and planet, Julie K. Gibson-Graham, "Rethinking the Economy with Thick Description and Weak Theory" *Current Anthropology* 55, no. 59 (2014): S147-S153.
(37) Faludi, "Territorial Cohesion," 1312.
[Fig. 1] Printed with permission, Bundesamt für Seeschifffahrtund Hydrographie, Hamburg/Rostock
[Fig. 2] Cartography MUST urbanism, June 2014
[Fig. 3] with permission, based on figure in Iain Deas and A. Lord, "From a New Regionalism to an Unusual Regionalism? The Emergence of Non-standard Regional Spaces and Lessons for the Territorial Reorganisation of the State," Urban Studies, 43, no. 10 (2006): 1847–77.
[Fig. 5] Printed with permission from Auckland War Memorial Museum Tāmaki Paenga Hira. 1998.13.17, 55497.

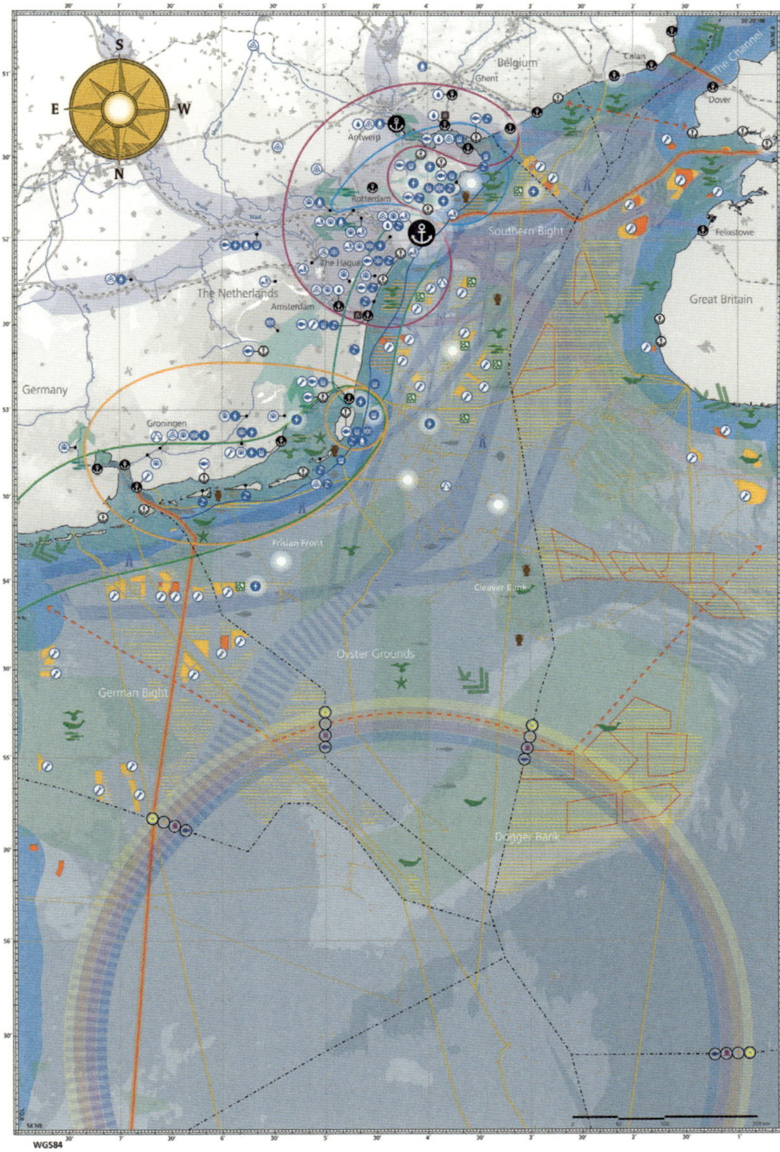

Fig. 2
Dutch North Sea "upside-down" maps, an attempt to reorient and refresh a nation's understanding of its offshore space by seeing it from the "perspective of the sea." (Dutch Ministry of Infrastructure and the Environment with the Dutch Ministry of Economic Affairs).

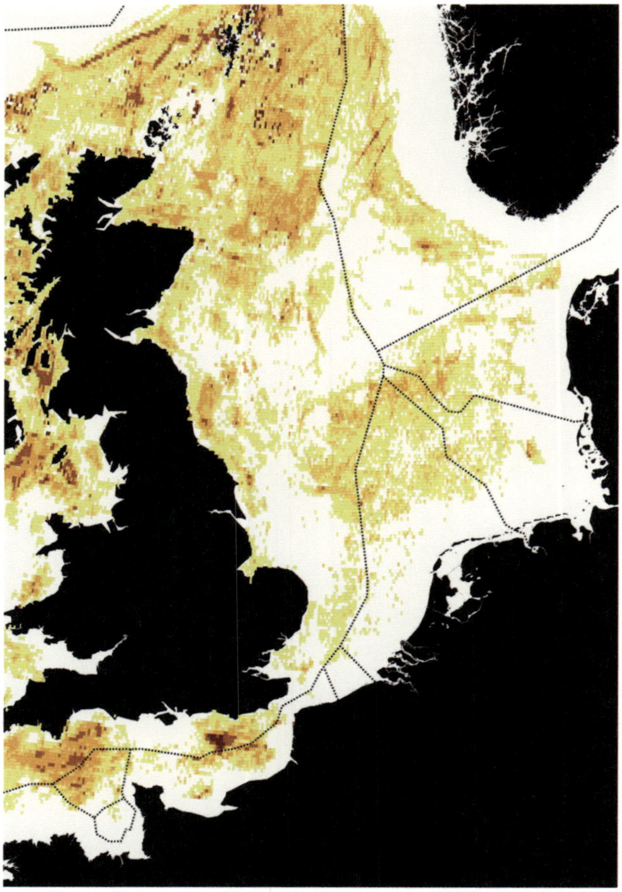

Fig. 4
UK fishing catch crossing EEZs. The map illustrates how UK fishers cross international maritime borders to catch fish in the EEZs, but not the 12-mile-wide territorial waters of neighbouring countries. (Bode)

Fig. 1
Typology of urban Switzerland: alpine fallow lands (brown), alpine resorts (blue), quiet zones (green), networks of cities (orange), metropolitan regions (red).

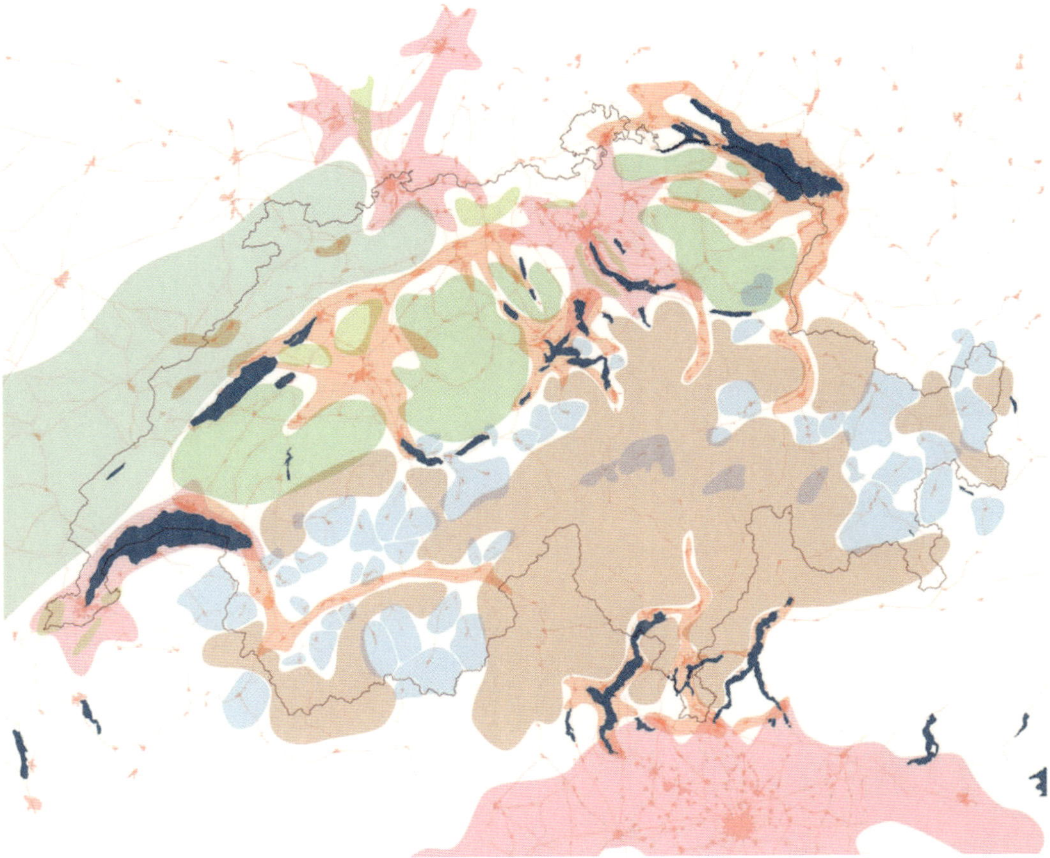

Fig. 1
Carta Marina 1949, full colour facsimile of the original 1539 edition (Olaus Magnus Courtesy of the James Ford Bell Library, University of Minnesota)

Fig. 5
Reuse of Ekofisk oil tank, North Sea, as a centre for sharing holistic data and research, in a marine protected area, 22 km in radius, for artificial reefs. (David Aadland, Mats Edal & Alvar Larsen, BAS 2019)

Fig. 1
The nearby spiral galaxy M106 seen in an optical image, with LOFAR radio emission overlaid. (LOFAR)

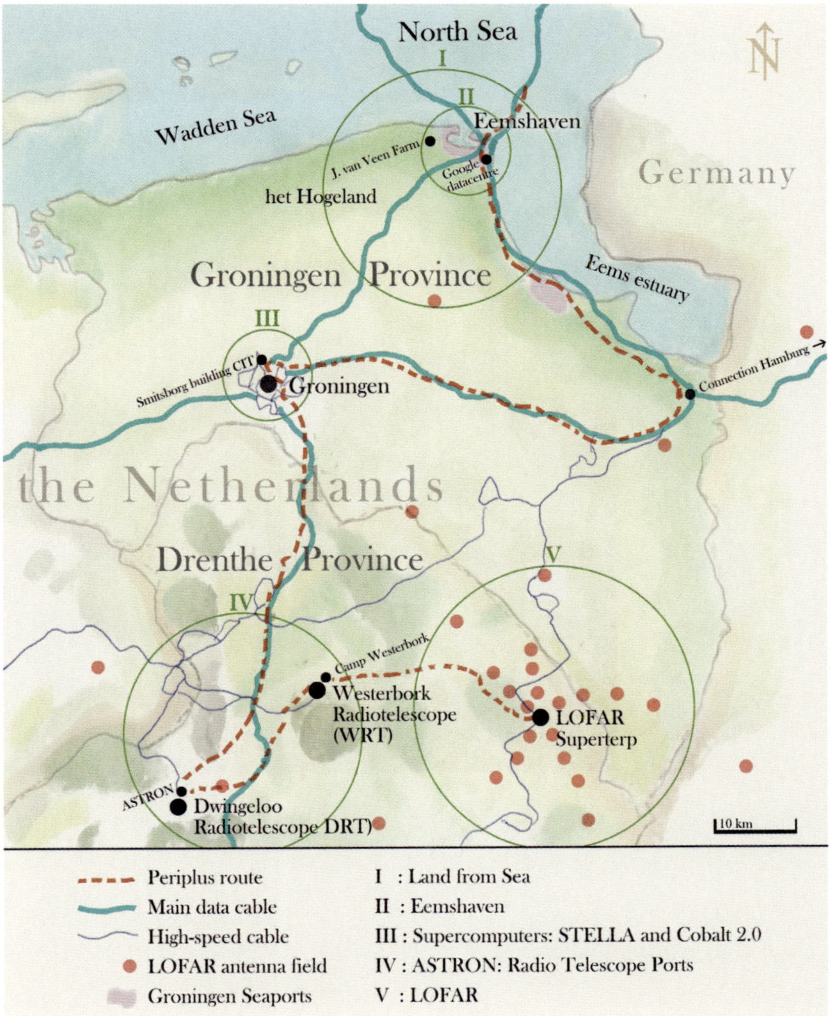

Fig. 3
North Sea Periploi.
(Jan Derk Diekema)

Fig. 4
LOFAR Super Terp. (Aerophoto Eelde/ ASTRON)

Fig. 5
LOFAR Low-Band Antennae (Hans Hordijk/ASTRON)

Chapter 6 ANALYSING EXTENDED URBANISATION: A TERRITORIAL APPROACH*

Christian Schmid

Today's planetary conditions demand a radical rethinking of conceptions of the urban. Christian Schmid explains ongoing territorial transformations through current urban theory, using case studies to propose analytical methodologies and to place this theory into context.

Christian Schmid is Professor of Sociology at the Department of Architecture at ETH Zurich. He has authored, co-authored, and co-edited numerous publications on theories of the urban and of space, on Henri Lefebvre, on the territorial approach of urban analysis, and on the comparative research of urbanisation processes. Together with architects Roger Diener, Jacques Herzog, Marcel Meili, and Pierre de Meuron he co-authored the book *Switzerland: an Urban Portrait*, a pioneering analysis of extended urbanisation. He currently works together with Neil Brenner on the theorisation, and investigation of emergent formations of planetary urbanisation, and together with Milica Topalović he leads a research project on Territories of Extended Urbanization, which is based at the ETH Future Cities Laboratory Singapore.

*An earlier version of this chapter was published as "The Urbanization of the Territory: On the Research Approach of ETH Studio Basel," in *Territory: On the Development of Landscape and City*, ed. ETH Studio Basel (Park Books, Zürich, 2016), 22–48. A shorter version was published as "Analysing Extended Urbanisation," in *Future Cities Laboratory: Indicia 02*, eds. Stephen Cairns and Devisari Tunas (Zürich: Lars Müller Publishers 2019), 157–180. An earlier version also appeared in an Italian translation: Christian Schmid, "Analizzando l'urbanizzazione estesa: un approccio territoriale," in *Confini, Movimenti, Luoghi. Politiche e progetti per città e territori in transizione*, Camilla Perrone and Giancarlo Paba, eds. (Roma: Donzelli editore, 2019), 11-26.

Urban research is increasingly confronted with urbanisation processes that are unfolding far beyond the realm of agglomerations, urban regions, and even mega city-regions. Novel patterns of urbanisation are crystallising in various environments, including in agricultural areas, in the space of seeming wilderness and in the oceans, challenging inherited conceptions of the urban as a bounded zone and a dense settlement type. Today, the entire planet potentially serves as a resource for urban areas. These observations suggest a radical rethinking of conceptions and cartographies of the urban, at all spatial scales, encompassing both built and unbuilt spaces. They have led to the development of the conception of "planetary urbanisation" as a new proposal for the understanding of the urban.(1) This chapter discusses these processes and illustrates them through the work of ETH Studio Basel, which has developed a territorial approach to urbanisation over the past two decades, allowing a differentiated analysis of extended urbanised territories. This approach is also useful for thinking about the urbanisation of the sea, as discussed in this book, and it has particularly inspired the chapters by Nancy Couling and the work of Milica Topalović.

CONCENTRATED, EXTENDED, AND DIFFERENTIAL URBANISATION

To understand the widespread occupation of the earth's surface through various forms of urbanisation, it is necessary to address the meaning of *urbanisation*. Ever since Catalan architect Ildefonso Cerdá coined the term "urbanización" in 1867,(2) many theories and approaches have been developed to grasp and define urbanisation processes. Urbanisation is often equated with the population growth of cities. But this is a highly limited view that relies on only one criterion—population numbers—and focuses exclusively on the growth of urban agglomerations. This conception has been criticised as simplifying and reifying.(3) In contrast, many approaches in critical urban studies understand urbanisation as a polymorphic and multi-dimensional process of transformation. This transformation includes the material structures and practices of the production of urban space, the various regulations of the use and transformation of the territory, and the modalities of everyday interactions.(4)

Henri Lefebvre, in his theory of the production of space, understands urbanisation as the production of *second nature*: natural conditions are transformed through social labour, resulting in material artefacts, infrastructures, and a built environment that makes permanent occupation of the territory possible. Thus, territories are claimed, ploughed, and reorganised in new ways until complex and interdependent urban landscapes emerge. As a result, the city, as a delimited and clearly identifiable unit, fragments and dissipates, and the urbanised territory replaces the once readily discernible form of the city. The historical point of departure is thus given by natural conditions, which have established very diverse preconditions for urbanisation. In a society's interaction and confrontation with natural forces, a second nature emerges which today presents itself as a given, quasi-natural condition; nonetheless it has emerged over centuries, layer by layer. Each layer is determined by very concrete social circumstances that have, to a certain extent, materialised through this transformation process and have thereby also been incorporated into urban space.(5)

As Lefebvre postulated, the results of urbanisation can be represented as an *urban fabric* that is embedded into the territory.(6) This fabric has a material structure: settlements, transport routes, sites where raw materials are extracted, pipelines, high-voltage lines, logistics facilities, and many other elements. An entire urban system, ranging from energy supply and transport systems to diverse information and production networks, is established on the basis of this fabric. An urban practice of networking and linkage also develops, out of which emerge an urban lifestyle and a value system founded on industrial rationality. The urban fabric also involves diverse signs, markings, and symbols, from architectural landmarks to traffic signs and even inconspicuous markings on the wayside.

The urban fabric is more or less tightly woven, with smaller and larger interstices between the strands of its mesh. It has an orientation, which is determined by the *dialectic of centres and peripheries*: the centres never exist without diverse peripheries that supply food and raw materials, water, and energy, and which function as dumping grounds for all sorts of waste or provide recreational areas and serve as ideological and mental compensation planes. As a result, even the putatively "non-urban" areas are drawn into the process of urbanisation: they are linked to urban networks, which are increasingly dominated by an urban logic of production and are concomitantly fundamentally transformed. Urbanisation is thus a reciprocal process, in which both the urban centres and the hinterlands change in concert with each other. Every urban centre inevitably has a hinterland. With industrialisation, this hinterland expands further outward, drawing ever-more remote areas into the urban process.

As Neil Brenner and I have argued, urbanisation can therefore be understood as the simultaneity of processes of concentration and extension: any form of urbanisation generates not only the concentration of people, means of production, goods, and information that leads to *concentrated urbanisation*, but also inevitably and simultaneously causes a proliferation and expansion of the urban fabric, thus resulting in *extended urbanisation*.(7) Food, water, energy, and raw materials must be brought to urban centres, requiring an entire logistical system that ranges from transport to information networks. Conversely, areas that are characterised by extended urbanisation can also evolve into new centralities and urban concentrations. Thus, concentrated and extended forms of urbanisation exist in a dialectical relationship to each other and can, at times, seamlessly merge. This dialectic is complemented and transformed by the relentless churning and transformation of the extant urban fabric leading to *differential urbanisation*.

THE CONCEPT OF TERRITORY

Recognising the phenomena of concentrated, extended, and differential urbanisation demands a new approach to analysing urbanisation processes. The challenge is to capture diverse manifestations of urbanisation and to identify them in specific urbanising territories. This requires a fundamental shift of perspective, as the research has to grasp the urbanisation of the entire territory, and not just analytically isolated settlements or urban regions.

Analysis of the urbanisation of territory is still at an early stage. This is partly due to the nature of the term territory itself: there exists a broad range of definitions, and they are found in diverse disciplines—from philosophy, biology, the political sciences, and geography, to architecture and spatial planning. To date, however, there have been only a few studies that examine the term conceptually or historically.(8) In the diverse genealogies of the term "territory," one can identify two fundamental understandings that still retain great importance. A first understanding, prevalent in the English-speaking world in the fields of political science and political geography, focuses on sovereignty and state power. In a general sense, this position considers a territory to be an area over which a political body—for example, a state—exercises power and control. The territory is understood here as an abstract space that denotes sovereignty, and hence the extent of dominance. Most of the contributions belonging to this line of thinking assign no particular significance to concrete, material qualities—the territory is, as it were, "dematerialised."

A very different conception can be found in the fields of architecture and geography, primarily in the French-, Italian-, and Spanish-speaking worlds, focusing precisely on the materiality of a territory. It is led by the conviction that the territory is produced by human activity, through labour, but also by symbolic means. In one of the classic works on architecture, Italian architect Saviero Muratori comprehends territory as a product created by civilisation, which can be analysed in relation to political economy, ethics, and aesthetics.(9) In geography, Genevan geographer Claude Raffestin has presented one of the most interesting theoretical contributions on territory to date.(10) He links Lefebvre's theory of the production of space with Foucault's reflections on power and proposes an understanding of territory as socially appropriated space. The territory is the result of material actions and mental activities; it comes into being through human labour, through the application of energy and information. The dominant social relations and conditions, and the existing power constellations, are thereby incorporated into the territory. The basic structure of Raffestin's analysis consequently rests essentially on two dimensions: first, on the complex grid of borders that evolve over the course of history; and second, on a system of centralities and networks that crystallise in the territory. The entirety of the borders marking a territory forms a kind of netting that Raffestin designates as "*maillage*." The superimposition and interpenetration of all sorts of borders can give rise to complex political structures that shape the territory and thus also define a specific power structure. Raffestin uses the term "grid of power" that is incorporated into the territory.(11) In a similar sense, it is possible to examine centralities and their concomitant networks of communication and circulation by a multilayered reading of the territory. The emerging systems of centres and related networks may vary considerably, and be either more polycentric or more monocentric, which in turn has great influence on the significance and arrangement of the peripheries, and thus on the entire socioeconomic structure of the territory.(12) In every urban area, however, centres and peripheries generate a specific pattern that exists at all scales: while centres of decision-making and control of the world economy develop at the global scale, sub-centres and urban corridors emerge at the regional scale. This gives rise to an entire system of networks and nodes that stretches out to establish a logistical space.(13) Largely inspired by Raffestin, in the 1990s, Alberto Magnaghi, Giancarlo Paba and their colleagues developed a "territorial approach" to urban analysis, whereby the territory is seen as a neo-ecosystem that draws together the milieus of nature, the built environment, and human beings.(14) They applied this approach in various empirical analyses of the Florence region and put forward the urbanistic project of a locally controlled urbanisation of the territory.(15)

A similar understanding of territory can be found in the writings of Genevan urbanist and architectural historian André Corboz. Like Raffestin, he also defines territory as the product of processes of appropriation, comparing it with a palimpsest: the land is repeatedly worked and reworked, continually being overwritten with a new texture until it resembles an old, perforated and worn parchment. (16) Corboz used this concept to analyse urbanisation in Switzerland, thereby discovering the emergence of a new urban form that he identifies as *ville-territoire* ("city-territory"): this city no longer forms a delimitable unit, but rather a sprawling, polycentric urban region where the old city centres lose their historical functions and the peripheries take on new meaning. What evolves in this process is an encompassing form of the city, a place of the discontinuous, the heterogeneous, and the fragmentary, subject to constant transformation.(17)

These thoughts are consistent with many other, similarly defined concepts, like the "in-between-city,"(18) the "extended metropolis,"(19) the "100 mile city,"(20) and the "postmetropolis."(21) However, all of these concepts still presume that urbanisation is a spatially confined phenomenon, and that a vast field of "non-urban" areas extends beyond urban territories—a field that usually is not further illuminated by the urban analysis. Therefore, it is crucial to go a step further, not only examining how compact forms of the city dissipate through manifold processes and interrelationships within a regional configuration, but also to gain a comprehensive understanding of the urban transformation of the entire territory, with its gradual or sudden changes. This approach, however, requires redirecting the view toward supposedly "non-urban" areas, and examining to what extent they have also been involved in the process of urbanisation. In other words: the investigations should not proceed from an urban centre and then slowly move "outwards," but rather should begin by selecting a large segment of a territory, examining the urban transformations of that entire segment, and in so doing also include, from the very beginning, those areas usually designated as non-urban.

A TERRITORIAL APPROACH TO URBANISATION

Within traditional forms of urban analysis, extended urbanisation is not visible. Analysing extended urbanisation first requires a fundamental shift in perspective: urbanisation can no longer be understood as a spatially bounded phenomenon; it must instead be examined as a comprehensive process that increasingly moulds more regions and repeatedly overwrites them. This new perspective ushers in a whole range of considerations: the focus shifts away from the typical questions that have long been central to urban studies, such as how to define the borders of urban regions or how to distinguish urban from non-urban areas. Instead, it is necessary to examine the diversity of urban manifestations that are inscribing themselves onto the territories and turning them into urban landscapes. This means decentering the focus of analysis, looking from an ex-centric position, one that looks from the periphery and asks where to find traces of urbanisation.(22) This planetary perspective enables a researcher to detect a wide variety of expressions of the urban that have traditionally been excluded from analytical consideration because they are located outside large agglomerations and metropolitan regions and their immediate hinterlands.

In order to examine these extensive urban constellations, new procedures of inquiry are needed, along with modes of analysis and mapping that are capable of portraying the multi-dimensional nature and plural determination of urban territories. Over the last two decades, ETH Studio Basel has developed a specific research approach to address these problems. The project "Switzerland:

An Urban Portrait" played a pioneering role in the development of an appropriate methodology, based on the concept of "drill holes": small sections of the earth's surface that are expected to provide information about typical urban situations are selected and analysed in depth.(23) For this purpose, a specific set of field research methods has been tailored to include literature and analysis of documents, interviews with local experts, specialists, inhabitants, field observations, photographic documentation as well as the use of maps and graphics, which also integrate statistical data. The field research results in a synthetic, qualitative analysis that, through triangulation, superimposes different kinds of knowledge. In this way, individual sections of the territory are exposed, allowing insights into their underlying deep structure. These punctual insights are then expanded to become encompassing analyses of the entire territory, and the sections exposed by the drill holes are consolidated in an overall picture. Cartography plays a central role in this task, as it makes it possible to expand individual results to the entire surface area of the territory being examined. The goal is to take the investigation to such a depth that a dense image of the territory emerges. Different urban configurations can be identified using this procedure [Fig. 1, p. 87].

Working with these methods, the urban portrait did not analyse individual cities or urban regions, but the entire Swiss territory, including seemingly rural areas that it deciphered as specific urbanised landscapes. Even peripheral, agricultural, or tourism-oriented areas located far away from the catchment areas of urban regions are nevertheless shaped by urbanisation processes, as they are embedded in diverse urban networks and settings, linked in many ways to urban centres and, of course, are connected to electronic networks. Everyday life in these areas is characterised by a high degree of mobility, while consumption patterns, lifestyles, and architecture differ only slightly from those in urban centres, rather than fundamentally, as was once the case.(24)

Following this work on urban Switzerland, ETH Studio Basel analysed a selection of contrasting urban areas in different parts of the world presented in "The Inevitable Specificity of Cities."(25) The book not only examines densely populated urban areas, but also forms of extended urbanisation, such as the subtle changes occurring in the still largely agrarian Nile Valley, the massive urban transformations generated by tourism on the Canary Islands, and the urbanisation of the area surrounding Mount Vesuvius [Fig. 2]. Here, the aim was to understand which urban processes are in operation and to discern the specific, but often covert urban structures, territorial regulations, and patterns of socio-spatial differentiation that govern these processes.(26)

Fig. 2
Cultivation and settlement patterns in Assiut, Nile Valley. Subdvision of the fields into different crops.

This analysis paved the way for the development of a territorial approach to analysing urbanisation, based on a transdisciplinary and transductive research procedure. The term "territory" assumes a specific meaning in this context: it can be understood as a socially produced material support for activities and interactions. This definition prepares the ground for a new type of examination, leading to an analysis that tries to capture the entire spatial context of urbanisation. In the project "Territory," ETH Studio Basel selected segments of the earth's surface stretching across several hundred kilometres and containing a great variety of urban situations: urban centres, peripheral and sparsely populated areas, as well as areas dominated by agriculture.(27) The analysis singles out a selection of some essential elements: water, agriculture, extraction of mineral resources, industrial production, and human settlement. The quality of this analysis lies in particular in the systematic layout of the investigation, which allows for comparability of the case studies. The six selected territories show that the urban fabric is considerably more densely woven and the urban imprint is much more widespread and more advanced than might have been assumed. In the analysed segment of Florida, even the areas beyond the settlements have been radically transformed, as a result of, among other things, widespread mining of phosphate for use as fertiliser [Fig. 3]. The landscape in the desert area around Muscat has seen massive earth movements that moulded the landscape in such a way that the original topography is no longer identifiable in some places. In other cases, transformations remain more discrete, as in the extended environs of Hanoi, where, in the densely populated and small-scale areas of rice cultivation, narrow corridors of settlement are developing along local access roads, with urban forms of land use and new building typologies replacing the traditional rural structure. In a similar and related project, Milica Topalović and her team examined the urbanisation of Singapore's hinterland, and also analysed with the same method the urbanisation of the sea in the Singapore Strait (see Topalović, this volume).

ANALYSING EXTENDED URBANISATION (28)

Grasping extended urbanisation means reversing the dominant perspective: the main goal is no longer to examine various forms of settlement space, the spheres of influence, or the catchment areas of large urban centres, but to take a comprehensive look at the urban transformation of the entire territory. By taking this perspective, urban areas are no longer treated as bounded entities, but as open zones: the entire area must be systematically scrutinised and all sorts of traces of urbanisation must be carefully sought in the terrain.

Slightly modifiying Lefebvre's theory of the production of space, three dimensions of urbanisation can be distinguished.(29) The first dimension involves a material transformation of the territory. This begins with the appropriation of the territory through human activities that initially are ephemeral, but over time they increasingly condense and solidify. In this way, a society gradually inscribes itself into a territory and produces an *urban fabric* that spreads out across the landscape. Thus, the entire territory has to be systematically scrutinised and the manifold traces of urbanisation carefully analysed. As discussed above, the urban fabric defines centres and peripheries in a reciprocal relationship. The periphery is therefore not just "natural space," "countryside," or "non-city," but a relational space that can be defined through its relationship with the various centres that dominate it. The extraction of raw materials and the production of agricultural goods in planetary hinterlands is

Fig. 3
The amplified scale of the transformed landscape through phosphate mining, Florida. A clay settling pond, a 10 m high dam can reach dimensions of 2 km by 2 km, creating almost arena-like sceneries.

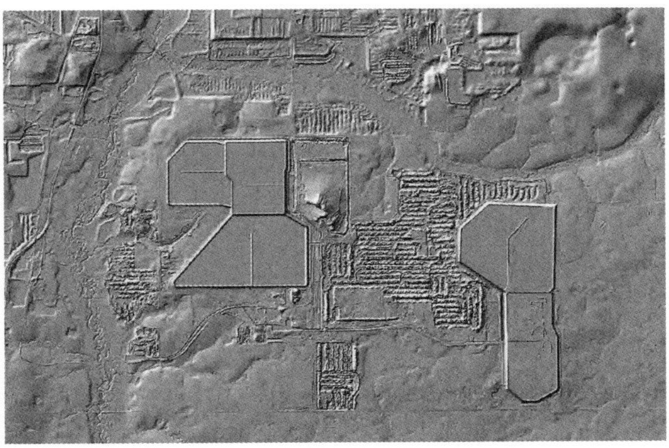

not only a crucial precondition for urbanisation, but also involve a fundamental transformation of the peripheries that are producing them. As a result of extended urbanisation, the urban fabric spreads to cover increasingly remote places, whether sea spaces (which this volume elaborates in detail), deserts, or rainforests.(30)

The production of the urban fabric supports and enables urban practices that connect people and places. This necessitates the analysis of all kinds of *movements of people* that crisscross the territory and at the same time bind it together and define it. In contrast to urban agglomerations and thus concentrated urbanisation, territories of extended urbanisation are usually characterised by longer, more sporadic, and varied forms of mobility. Various forms of circular or temporary migration, where people only migrate for a certain time or follow a recurrent pattern returning regularly to their places of departure, are part of this type of mobility. Concomitantly, there are also movements by people searching for opportunities, operating small businesses, crossing borders to take advantage of fluctuations in prices and exchange rates of currencies, connecting widely ramified social networks, and maintaining extended family ties. With these movements and related activities people create a multi-scalar social reality and produce large and extended urban territories that transgress all kinds of borders.(31)

In a second dimension to be analysed is the question of borders and territorial regulation. Borders mark and identify a territory, they symbolise the demarcation of power, constitute the framework for controlling the territory and form the foundation for *territorial regulation*, which defines specific orders and rules, from traffic ordinances to complex planning systems.(32) An understanding of the social and political character of borders is therefore key: borders are instruments of action, they exert considerable influence on the process of urbanisation and they constitute invisible guidelines for urban development. At the same time, however, they are continually challenged by the process of urbanisation itself, which reveals the inherent tendency to transcend borders and to undermine boundaries, thus disbanding existing territorial entities and redefining them. In this process, borders are overwritten but still may remain effective and thus be able to gain new meaning. An urban territory is therefore an area in which borders are transformed, become permeable, and enter new power constellations.

Often, territories of extended urbanisation are shaped and enforced by a wide range of specific *state strategies* that prepare the ground for urbanisation in many different ways: they homogenise the legal framework for urbanisation, open up a territory for capital accumulation, and create the conditions of further urban expansion.(33) Of special importance are strategic infrastructural projects, such as large-scale high speed railways and highway systems and complex infrastructural initiatives that impose an overarching logic on the territory, such as the "Plan Puebla Panama," a cross-border infrastructure project for southern Mexico and Central America that was ultimately abandoned (34) or, more recently, China's huge "one belt, one road" project.(35)

A third dimension is the differentiation of the territory. A crucial question of extended urbanisation is related to its effect on everyday life: what is the urban under conditions of extended urbanisation? Following Lefebvre's theory, urban space can be understood as a *differential space*, in which differences come to light and interact with each other.(36) Separations and space-time distances are replaced by oppositions, contrasts, superimpositions, and the juxtaposition of disparate realities. Urban space can be defined as a place where differences know, recognise, and explore each other, affirm or negate each other. Differences can be defined in a twofold manner: on the one hand, they characterise the totality of actions, material elements, and relationships that come together in a specific space, and as different people with varying social wealth, history, knowledge, abilities, and needs.

On the other hand, differences can also be generated by networks: the linking up of different areas can create new differences. Urbanisation is characterised in particular by the fact that it overcomes all kinds of borders and brings together previously distant and separate areas. Urbanisation in this sense means the connection and articulation of different (near and far) places and situations. (37) The crucial question however is precisely how such urban experiences unfold and develop, and how people adapt to or resist processes of extended urbanisation. This question has been studied by analysing the effects (or non-effects) of urbanisation in the outskirts of Kolkata, (38) in indigenous and allied resistance against the construction of pipelines across Canada in the province of Alberta connecting a tar sand extraction site to global markets, (39) the urbanisation of Amazonia in Brazil, (40) and the struggle of a small agricultural village at the edge of the Atacama Desert in northern Chile against massive new infrastructure investments that support the nearby mining industry.(41)

Processes of extended urbanisation are transforming the planet in unprecedented and unpredictable ways, often positioning dynamic and depleting areas side by side. Territories of extended urbanisation are therefore more variegated and complex than might be expected. It is urgent to gain a more comprehensive picture and a more systematic understanding of these processes that are increasingly determining the destiny of the planet.

(1) Neil Brenner and Christian Schmid, "Towards a New Epistemology of the Urban?," *City* 19, no. 2/3 (2015): 151–82; Andy Merrifield, *The Politics of the Encounter: Urban Theory and Protest Under Planetary Urbanization* (Athens, GA: University of Georgia Press, 2013).
(2) Ildefons Cerdà, *General Theory of Urbanization 1867* (Barcelona: Actar, 2018); see also Adams E. Ross, *Circulation and Urbanization* (London: Sage, 2018).
(3) Neil Brenner and Christian Schmid, "The 'Urban Age' in Question," *International Journal of Urban and Regional Research* 38, no. 3 (2014): 731–55. Hillary Angelo and David Wachsmuth, "Urbanizing Urban Political Ecology: A Critique of Methodological Cityism," *International Journal of Urban and Regional Research* 39, no. 1 (2015):16–27; Stephen Cairns, "Debilitating City-Centricity: Urbanisation and Urban-Rural Hybridity in Southeast Asia," in *Routledge Handbook of Urbanization in Southeast Asia*, Rita Padawangi, ed. (New York: Routledge, 2019), 115–30.
(4) Henri Lefebvre, *The Production of Space* (Oxford: Blackwell, 1991); David Harvey,*The Limits to Capital* (Oxford: Blackwell, 1982); Christian Schmid,"Specificity and Urbanization: A Theoretical Outlook," in *The Inevitable Specificity of Cities*, ed. ETH Studio Basel, 287–307 (Zurich: Lars Müller, 2015).
(5) Lefebvre, *Production of Space*; Christian Schmid, *Stadt, Raum und Gesellschaft: Henri Lefebvre und die Theorie der Produktion des Raumes* (Stuttgart: Steiner, 2005).
(6) Henri Lefebvre,*The Urban Revolution* (Minneapolis: University of Minnesota Press, 2003); see also Merrifield, *Politics of the Encounter*; Neil Brenner, *New Urban Spaces: Urban Theory and the Scale Question* (New York: Oxford University Press, 2019).
(7) Brenner and Schmid, "Towards a New Epistemology."
(8) See, e.g., Stuart Elden, *The Birth of Territory* (Chicago: University of Chicago Press, 2013).
(9) Saverio Muratori, *Civiltà e territorio* (Rome: Centro Studi di Storia Urbanistica, 1967).
(10) Claude Raffestin, Pour une géographie du pouvoir (Paris: Librairies Techniques, 1980) ; "Space, Territory, and Territoriality," *Environment and Planning D: Society and Space* 30 (2012), 121–41.
(11) Raffestin, *Pour une geographie*, 139.
(12) Ibid., 185ff.
(13) Pierre Veltz, *Mondialisation, villes et territoires: L'économie d'archipel* (Paris: Presses Universitaires de France, 1996).
(14) Alberto Magnaghi, *Le projet local* (Sprimont: Mardaga, 2003).
(15) Giancarlo Paba, Camilla Perrone, and Fabio Lucchesi Andiacopo Zetti, "Territory Matters: A Regional Portrait of Florence and Tuscany," in *Post-Metropolitan Territories*, eds., Valeria Fideli, and Francesco Curci(London: Routledge, 2017).
(16) André Corboz, "The Land as Palimpsest," *Diogenes* 31, no. 121 (1983), 12–34.
17)André Corboz, *Vers la ville-territoire* (Bern: Paul Haupt, 2001).
(18)Tom Sieverts, *Cities Without Cities: An Interpretation of the Zwischenstadt* (London: Spon Press, 2003).
(19)Norton Ginsburg, Bruce Koppel, and T. G. McGee, eds., *The Extended Metropolis: Settlement Transition in Asia* (Honolulu: University of Hawaii Press, 1991).
(20) Deyan Sudjic, *The 100 Mile City (*San Diego, CA: Harcourt Brace, 1992).
(21) Edward W. Soja, *Postmetropolis: Critical Studies of Cities and Regions* (Malden: Blackwell, 2000).
(22) Christian Schmid, "Journeys through Planetary Urbanization: Decentering Perspectives on the Urban," *Environment and Planning D: Society and Space* 36, no. 3 (2018): 591–610.
(23) Roger Diener, Jacques Herzog, Marcel Meili, Pierre de Meuron, and Christian Schmid (ETH Studio Basel), *Switzerland: An Urban Portrait* (Basel: Birkhäuser, 2006).
(24) Marcel Meili, "Is the Matterhorn City?," in *Implosions / Explosions: Towards a Study of Planetary Urbanization*, ed. Neil Brenner, 398-428 (Berlin: Jovis, 2014); Christian Schmid, "Networks, Borders, Differences: Towards a Theory of the Urban" in *Implosions / Explosions: Towards a Study of Planetary Urbanization*, Neil Brenner, ed. (Jovis, Berlin, 2014), 67–81.
(25) Diener, Roger, Manuel Herz, Jacques Herzog, Marcel Meili, Pierre de Meuron, Christian Schmid, and Milica Topalović, eds., *The Inevitable Specificity of Cities* (Zürich: Lars Müller,)
(26) Schmid, "Specificity."
(27) Roger Diener, Liisa Gunnarsson, Mathias Gunz, Vesna Jovanović, Marcel Meili, Inderbitzin Müller, Christian Schmid, eds., *Territory: On the Development of Landscape and City* (Park Books, Zürich 2016).
(28) This section is related to the research project "Territories of extended urbanisation" of the ETH Future Cities Laboratory Singapore, previously published as part of Christian Schmid, "Analysing Extended Urbanisation," *Future Cities Laboratory: Indicia 02*, eds. Stephen Cairns and Devisari Tunas (Zürich: Lars Müller Publishers 2019), 157–80.

(29) Schmid, "Specificity."
(30) See, also, Nancy Couling, "The Urbanization of the Ocean," in *Infrastructure Space*, I. Ruby and A. Ruby, eds. (Berlin: Ruby Press, 2017); Miguel Kanai, "On the Peripheries of Planetary Urbanization: Globalizing Manaus and its Expanding Impact," *Environment and Planning D: Society and Space*, 32, no. 6 (2014): 1071–87; Nikos Katsikis, "From Hinterland to Hinterglobe: Urbanization as Geographical Organization," PhD dissertation, Harvard University, 2016; Urban Theory Lab, "Extreme territories of urbanization," research report (Cambridge, MA: Graduate School of Design, Harvard University, 2015).
(31) Elisa Bertuzzo, *Archipelagos. From Urbanisation to Translocalisation* (Berlin: Kadmos, 2018); Alice Hertzog, "The Lagos-Abidjan Corridor: Migration Driven Urbanisation in West Africa," PhD dissertation, ETH Zürich, 2020.
(32) Schmid, "Specificity."
(33) Brenner, *New Urban Spaces.*
(34) Japhy Wilson, "Plan Puebla Panama: The Violence of Abstract Space," in *Urban Revolution Now: Henri Lefebvre in Social Research and Architecture*, eds. Łukasz Stanek, Christian Schmid, and Ákos Moravánszky (Farnham: Ashgate, 2014).
(35) See e.g. James Sidaway and Chih Yuan Woon, "Chinese Narratives on "One Belt, One Road" in geopolitical and imperial contexts," *Professional Geographer* 69, no. 4 (2017): 591–603.
(36) Lefebvre, *Production of Space.*
(37) Schmid, "Specificity"; Merrifield, *Politics of the Encounter.*
(38) Ananya Roy, "What is Urban about Critical Urban Theory?," *Urban Geography* 37, no. 6 (2015): 810–23.
(39) Stefan Kipfer, "Pushing the Limits of Urban Research: Urbanization, Pipelines and Counter-colonial Projects," *Environment and Planning D: Society and Space* 36, no.3, (2018): 474–93.
(40) Roberto Luís Monte-Mór, "Modernities in the jungle: Extended urbanization in the Brazilian Amazonia," PhD dissertation, University of California, Los Angeles, 2004; Rodrigo Castriota and João Tonucci, "Extended Urbanization in and from Brazil," *Environment and Planning D: Society and Space* 36 no. 3 (2018): 512–28.
(41) Martin Arboleda, "In the Nature of the Non-city: Extended Infrastructural Networks and the Political Economy of Planetary Urbanisation," *Antipode* 48, no. 2 (2016): 233–51.
[Fig. 1] Roger Diener, Jacques Herzog, Marcel Meili, Pierre de Meuron, and Christian Schmid (ETH Studio Basel), *Switzerland: An Urban Portrait* (Basel: Birkhäuser, 2006).
[Fig. 2] Eidgenössische Technische Hochschule Zürich. Studio Basel, Nile Valley: Urbanization of Limited Resources : ETH Studio Basel, Contemporary City Institute, Spring Semester 2009 Student Work (Basel: ETH Studio Basel, 2010).
[Fig. 3] Eidgenössische Technische Hochschule Zürich. Studio Basel, Florida- Private Management of an Urban System. A Territorial Research ETH Studio Basel, Contemporary City Institute, Spring Semester 2011 Student Work (Basel: ETH Studio Basel, 2015).

Chapter 7 BLANKNESS: THE ARCHITECTURAL VOID OF NORTH SEA ENERGY LOGISTICS*

Nancy Couling & Carola Hein

Energy logistics have contributed to the gradual transformation of the North Sea into an industrial void. Referring to the concept of blankness articulated by Roberto Mangabiera Unger and Jeffrey Kipnis, Nancy Couling and Carola Hein call for imaginative architectural interventions that respond to the potential of logistic spaces lodged within the volume of the sea.

Nancy Couling is Assoc. Prof. at Bergen School of Architecture, Norway and an independant researcher in Switzerland. She investigated the urbanised sea as a Marie Skłodowska Curie Fellow at the Chair of History of Architecture and Urban Planning, TU Delft 2017–19 and in her PhD at the EPFL (2015). She taught at the TU Berlin and co-founded the interdisciplinary practice cet-0/cet-01 in Berlin 1995–2010.

Carola Hein is Professor of History of Architecture and Urban Planning (Delft University of Technology). Her books include *Adaptive Strategies for Water Heritage* (2019), *The Routledge Planning History Handbook* (2017), *Port Cities* (2011), *The Capital of Europe* (2004), *Rebuilding Urban Japan after 1945* (2003), and *Cities, Autonomy and Decentralisation in Japan* (2006).

*A version of this chapter appeared as Nancy Couling and Carola Hein, "Blankness: The Architectural Void of North Sea Energy Logistics," *Footprint* 12, no. 23 (2018).

The North Sea is commonly viewed by the public as a void, but in fact it is a saturated space of logistics, the management of intangible flows for example of petroleum, gas, electricity, and of their physical counterparts, such as cables, pipelines and drilling platforms. This paradoxical spatial condition has been gradually constructed by corporations and governments over several centuries, but the process has accelerated due to industrialisation, low fuel prices, and increased availability after the Second World War. The diverse temporalities and fluctuating fortunes of energy logistics can be seen clearly in the development of refineries in ports around the North Sea and the emergence of offshore extraction.(1)

In his comprehensive study of ocean space across historical phases and societies, Phil Steinberg discusses the evolution of a modern Western idealisation of the ocean surface as a "great void."(2) Compared to the view evident in narrative features incorporated in sixteenth-century maritime cartography by the seventeenth century, with the emerging dominance of scientific thought, the sea had become largely empty [Fig. 1, p. 88]. Then, in the eighteenth century, early industrial capitalism, rooted in landed *place*, conceptualised the ocean as non-developable void.(3) This transformation reflects the growth of European sea-powers and their view of the sea as a place to exert and consolidate their political and economic strength, but did not mean territorial domination of the seas; rather, the mercantilist states, in particular the Netherlands and the United Kingdom, aimed to defend the unhindered sea-borne trade on which their economies were based.

The ocean void served nations and growing corporations at the time of industrialisation and changing energy consumption patterns. It was also a time when land masses were becoming more densely populated and scrutinised. The use of petroleum, first as lighting oil and then as engine fuel, at the end of the nineteenth and in the early twentieth century, encouraged investors to scale up industrial petroleum drilling and processing, creating a need to connect areas of production and consumption around the globe. Shipping was the cheapest solution for transportation from sites of production to sites of consumption. The perceived emptiness of the ocean disguised the rapid growth of petroleum shipping, first from the United States and later from around the world to the ports of the North Sea.

Scholars have recognised a correspondence between a nation's energy consumption and its material prosperity: since the use of coal to transform production methods in the industrial revolution in eighteenth-century Great Britain, energy consumption has continuously increased.(4) This tendency has led to the transformation of ocean space, coastlines, ports, and cities through increased shipping of oil, logistical development, and offshore energy production.

Meanwhile, the ocean itself is not only home to a temporary layer of petroleum shipping, it has also long hosted the long-term physical structures of extraction. In 1949, after Soviet engineers discovered offshore oil in commercial quantities, they built the Neft Dashlari settlement, an extensive network of drilling platforms, housing, and leisure structures, around 100 km from Baku and 50 km offshore. This "town" heralded a new era of ocean urbanisation through oil. Twenty years later, the discovery of the Norwegian North Sea field of Ekofisk (1969) by the American oil company Phillips, brought the topographic and geological properties of the northern European continental shelf sharply into focus for national and corporate petroleum companies, inciting them to drill in deeper and rougher waters. The last fifty years have seen vast spatial transformations related to energy logistics both on- and offshore, and a new unfamiliar logistical architecture in the offshore energy sector has begun to emerge.

Oil has a ubiquitous, pervasive presence within our society. The oil industry has inserted physical artefacts in ocean space that are small in comparison to the vast scale of the sea itself, but their presence is underpinned by rigid ordering systems of territorial dimensions.(5) These systems have been set up through legal devices, engineering, and world market logistics rather than integrated political/democratic planning processes. A variety of shields guard the border between the public and logistics spaces. Individuals require specialist knowledge, skills, and security clearances to enter these realms. For the public at large, who do not have passkeys, the ocean takes on an abstract, remote status that is home to select, highly specialised technical interventions.(6) If a commodity is kept at a distance and its materiality negated, its cultural dimension becomes more challenging to excavate. The public imagination is steered by national and corporate advertisement campaigns. Carola Hein's research, among others, unravels the representative imagery that cloaks the black and viscous oil and names the parties who dominate the production of oil narratives. Governments have issued celebratory visuals of oil infrastructure on official documents such as stamps and banknotes, whereas corporations glorify the positive impact of petroleum through advertising, information booklets, and even art. (7) This is a dangerous fiction and at the same time a sleight of hand, since corporations and nations control the spaces of oil and gas in secrecy and concealment, making it extremely difficult to *site* as well as *sight*.(8)

The oil and gas industry is a multinational giant without a face, both ostensibly liberated from and inextricably implicated in state operations. Energy companies with identifiable leaders, such as John D. Rockefeller (the founder of Standard Oil) or Pakhuismeesteren (the local company that first stored oil in the port of Rotterdam), have evolved into a set of corporations with anonymous leadership, which

Fig. 2
The North Sea petroleum grid (Couling)

is reflected in the industry's logistical spaces. Constantly "swapping assets" and reconfiguring ownership constellations, the industry is also made up of numerous operators delivering specific services and has therefore mostly been able to avoid public liability. The largest oil spill in the history of the offshore industry, the 2010 Deepwater Horizon disaster in the Gulf of Mexico, is a tragic illustration of this point.(9) Given the previously mentioned relationship between energy consumption and material prosperity, it comes as no surprise that the objectives of this industry resonate with neoliberal practices in business and politics more generally, even though the UN led countries into the Paris Agreement concerning CO_2 emissions.

Journalists report a particularly contradictory relationship between the UK government's commitment to renewables and the important revenues gained from the oil and gas industry.(10) US president Donald Trump has acted more directly in support of the country's oil industry and has withdrawn from the Paris Agreement.

The dominant presence of multinational energy corporations in ocean space has resulted in the erasure of a common non-industrial (non-oil-based) concept of the sea. The force and spatial reach of the industrial conception is demonstrated by the petroleum grid—an expansive, rigid, invisible ordering system within which offshore operations are embedded. Following significant onshore gas finds in Groningen (NL) in 1959, the petroleum industry, eager to explore the hydrocarbon potential of the continental shelf, pressured the UK and Norwegian governments to proceed with national legislation on sovereignty over the sea bed and natural resources. In March 1965, the Norwegian and UK governments jointly agreed to divide the North Sea into quadrants according to the median line principle of one degree latitude by one degree longitude. On the Norwegian continental shelf, quadrants were then subdivided into twelve blocks of 15' latitude × 20' longitude, corresponding to ca. 10 × 25 km, whereas the UK subdivision contained thirty smaller blocks. This continuous extraction grid formalised the offshore petroleumscape. It has become the state's framework for issuing licences to exploration companies anywhere on the continental shelf [Fig. 2].

The homogeneous, infinitely extendable extraction grid of the North Sea, created by nations under pressure from corporations, exemplifies Henri Lefebvre's notion of abstract space.(11) Lefebvre argues that the political principle of unification (of legislation, culture, knowledge, and education) is imperative to the state project of accumulation, without which it cannot be realised. National interventions work hand in hand with the demands of global corporations in the field of energy logistics. This principle of unification explains the simultaneously abstract and concrete character of the state's institutional space. Passing for *absence*, abstract space in fact conceals the *presence* of operational procedures and their results, and it is intrinsically violent.(12) The half-century of hydrocarbon extraction hinders any attempts to question petroleum narratives and practices.

NORTH SEA ENERGY LOGISTICS

Energy logistics dominates the space of the North Sea at the territorial scale, yet the material traces of this sector have been hard to decipher and pin down. The North Sea has historically formed the central logistical space of a highly active trading realm, which extended east to the Baltic Sea and the central European river system, west across the Atlantic and south to the Mediterranean. Traditionally a trading ground for the exchange of furs, grain, timber, and luxury goods, today the North Sea is characterised by the generation and exchange of energy—an indispensable, shapeshifting, and often invisible commodity.

Since the mid-twentieth century, North Sea oil and gas production has made a vital contribution to global energy supplies, occupying second place in combined offshore oil/gas quantities in 2006 after the Persian Gulf.(13) It is still the location of the most offshore rigs worldwide with a count of 184 in 2018.(14) Yet despite North Sea oil and gas production, the EU as a whole is marked by a significant energy gap between supply and demand and is still 80 percent dependent on oil imports.(15) Energy logistics therefore not only lace through and around the North Sea extraction sites, but also carry out the functions of transport, storage, and relocation of oil and gas from external sources. The sea surface and floor comprise the double "motherboard" of northern European energy transactions.

Energy logistics appears on the surface of the sea as a fleeting, yet continuous stream of shipping, which is becoming increasingly consolidated through electronic systems and dedicated deep-water routes. In Europe's top port of Rotterdam, crude oil, mineral oil products, and LNG accounted for 40 percent of port throughput by weight in 2017 (16), therefore more tonnes of liquid bulk goods travel through North Sea ports than container goods.

The steady, periodic sea surface of shipping is mirrored on the sea-floor by an invisible template of cables and pipelines. As a liquid medium for systems of flow and exchange, the ocean itself is an environment of minimal friction, ease of transfer, and minimal boundaries. Here, legal structures are less solid than on land, where ownership principles have long legacies. Outside the twelve nautical mile territorial boundary, which in economic terms directly translates into tax advantages, the sea is an ambiguous space.(17) The political neutrality of this space, its extra-territorial status endorsed by international law, and the relative technical ease of offshore operations make subsea pipelines more attractive than overland options: "Offshore lines minimize issues of land ownership and concerns of political instability."(18) All states are entitled to lay or maintain cables and pipelines on the continental shelf and coastal states cannot impede such activities.(19) Oil and gas pipelines of differing sizes connect satellite platforms to each other as well as to the main facility on land, while fluids and "umbilicals"—a combined string of steel pipes—deliver additional fluids, controls, power, and communication from the landside. This ubiquitous, invisible underwater infrastructure will remain in place even when it is no longer used—unlike installations. According to decommissioning law, pipelines are not subject to a legal requirement of disposal after use.(20) Unseen from above, they remain as a logistic nervous system threaded through the sea-floor's composite matter.

Not only a petroleum-based energy landscape, the North Sea is also coveted by the post-oil energy industry. Under current international objectives to reduce CO_2 emissions, the North Sea has been earmarked by the EU as a favourable site for the rapid expansion of offshore wind-energy production.(21) Augmenting existing energy logistics, this sector's activities create additional logistical networks of component production (turbines, blades, transformers, monopoles, cables, foundations), assembly, servicing, and delivery routes. These uses compete for space with food production, transportation, military activities, sand and gravel extraction, fish and bird sanctuaries and other protected natural areas. Intensification of all activities has resulted in spatial competition, which all littoral nations must resolve through Maritime Spatial Plans by 31 March 2021.(22) The North Sea has become a crowded and contested realm.

THE POSSIBILITIES OF BLANKNESS

The space of energy logistics across seas and coastlines is continually reorganised by nations and corporations in what David Harvey and Neil Brenner discuss as a process of "creative destruction." (23) This process produces differential, uneven spatial development in ongoing sequences that can destabilise established urban formats. Therefore, energy logistics play a vital role in the shaping of the built environment both on land and at sea—a role in urgent need of recognition by professionals. Architects, engineers, logistic planners and lawyers must take on expanded and intersecting roles in order to find new forms and expressions for this century's spatial challenges, in particular across the land- sea interface. We support architectural interventions that critically reflect on questions of access and visibility, develop new typologies and programmatic overlays, and find architectural expression for the intersection of natural and cultural ecosystems generated by energy logistics.

Infrastructural systems utilised by energy logistics have an important public dimension. Rather than being part of an extended public design brief, urban infrastructure has mostly been hidden underground, functionally restricted to strategic delivery tasks and taken entirely for granted. The question of its larger role in our relationship, for example with nature, has rarely been addressed. The architectural practice Lateral Office proposes that infrastructure could potentially catalyse new economies that are adaptive and responsive to environment and use.(24) Maria Kaika and Erik Swyngedouw draw attention to the things we have previously buried and forgotten, which are returning with urgent environmental questions that we are ill equipped to answer.(25) Understanding the apparent spatial and conceptual blankness of energy logistics is the first step towards a conscious, meaningful, and inclusive design for their extended terrain: tracts of land, sea, and the connecting thresholds. The cases discussed here illustrate the ways in which energy logistics has refused architecture. However, interventions in this field should be fundamental to the field of architecture, and architecture should not refuse energy logistics.

In 1993, Jeffrey Kipnis and Alexander Maymind discussed *blankness* as one of five criteria for a new architecture alongside *vastness*, *pointing*, *incongruity*, and *incoherence/intensive coherence*.(26) At the time, he named this quality partly in relation to postmodern architecture, and blankness was a potential release from collage as the "prevailing paradigm of architectural heterogeneity."(27) The five criteria had first been formulated and introduced by the neo-modern social theorist Roberto Mangabiera Unger in "The Better Futures of Architecture."(28) Unger called for architects to insist on new expressions of collective life in physical form, and for proposals describing possible futures for a more democratic society and a more empowered individual. He urged them to create a greater range of narratives, resist societal norms, and foster conflict between alternatives.(29) According to Unger, architecture must embrace the ambivalence of both pragmatic, established systems and inspirational, transcendent spatial ideas. In his concept of radical-democratic politics, an architectural vision is needed.(30) But such a concept and such a vision are critically lacking in the field of energy logistics.

The political dimension of Unger's argument resonates with the politics of energy logistics in the neoliberal market system. To differing degrees, this logistical space has, over the continuing course of industrialisation, devoured its counterparts of social and technical labour and of historical spaces of trade interaction. Smooth, efficient logistics that developed in the service of the global economy cut off social interactions: security zones at ports and around offshore wind parks and rigs prevent intrusion, compressed shipping turnaround times in ports hinder crews from making real social contact on shore. Energy logistics, particularly offshore, are still blank in architectural terms—that is, is we have not yet ascribed to them democratic, socially relevant meanings; heterogeneous human activities, cultural references, or detailed forms of ownership. In the absence of such common meaning, nations and corporations have prescribed spatial patterns and constructed banal enclosures on land and at sea. The conversation between Kipnis and Unger on the notion of blankness calls the general public to acknowledge energy logistics as a key player in the shaping of our built environment and for architects to consciously move into this domain of design, including its offshore spaces.

For Kipnis, Unger's *blankness* was architecturally optimistic and full of potential. It was neutral, non-ascribed, without formal reference, and combined with other criteria including *vastness*, could enable incongruous entities to enter into dialogue with each other while also avoiding "traditional hierarchical spatial patterns."(31)

Fig. 3
Video still "The Swarm." Little archaeolcgical and data-controller robots operate in intelligent seasonal swarms, working together to monitor the health and cultural value of the North Sea. (Justine Sleurs, Bergen School of Architecture BAS 2019)

Kipnis's new architecture proposed large mute volumes formed by incongruous, unfamiliar geometries that set up unexpected relations to their surroundings and therefore enhanced the heterogeneity of the resulting spaces. We argue that considering oceanic water masses as vast, deep volumes rather than flattened planes can stimulate architectural thinking along the lines Kipnis intends. In addition to volume, they possess cores and density, properties normally associated with solids. While still unfamiliar to architects, these organic geometries are precisely determined according to the oceanographic parameters of depth, currents, bathymetry, temperature, and salinity.

In response to radical transformations generated by a neoliberal mode of operations, energy logistics has developed and expanded unchecked across ocean space. Throughout this process, planners prioritised economic and logistic concerns, but erased the public in

Fig. 4
Reuse of wind-turbine foundations close to the Dogger Bank as a knowledge bank for marine archaeology and species protection. (Li-Cheng Chen, & Justine Sleurs, BAS 2019).

the process. How can the tools of an architect expand and dismantle this sectorial approach to design and communicate an integrated public vision? Rather than the largest periphery, the high seas are the largest public space on earth and require innovative approaches that can both capture the public imagination and develop scenarios in tune with the dynamics of the sea itself. Conceptions of heterogeneous diversified futures for energy logistics, particularly in offshore space, are lacking. We need visions that can create awareness and inspire design research, extending the field of architecture beyond the shoreline and embracing the spatial challenges of the ocean. The sea is not a void or a tabula rasa, but a moving volume housing differentiated habitats and internal spaces, including inherited logistical systems. The role of architecture has long been to translate such functionalities into meaningful habitats. The blankness of sea-borne energy logistics—as a corporate strategy designed to make us look away—must do the opposite: attract attention and inspire architectural intervention. Kipnis's alternative understanding of blankness offers a way of responding to ocean volumes and celebrating architectural manoeuvring in space.

The North Sea has developed historically as a vital logistical space, first filled then emptied of large-scale human interaction, narratives, and imagery. The sea space is now planned, monitored, excavated, mobilised for transport, and operationalised for energy production. As environmental considerations become urgent and fish stocks collapse, as the climate changes and new generations of offshore infrastructure are both installed and dismantled, new architectural interventions are required which re-programme this logistical space with heterogeneous human activities and reinvigorate the public dimension of energy logistics and of our common ocean imagination [Fig. 5, p. 89].

(1) Carola Hein, "Temporalities of the Port, the Waterfront and the Port City" PORTUS: RETE Online Magazine 29 (June 2015), http://portusonline.org/temporalities-of-the-port-the-waterfront-and-the-port-city/.
(2) Philip E. Steinberg, *The Social Construction of the Ocean* (Cambridge: Cambridge University Press, 2001).
(3) Ibid., 118.
(4) Keith Chapman, *North Sea Oil and Gas: A Geographical Perspective* (Newton Abbot: David & Charles, 1976).
(5) Nancy Couling, "Urbanization of the Ocean; Extractive Geometries in the Barents Sea," in *Infrastructure Space*, LaFargeHolcim Forum for Sustainable Construction (Berlin: Ruby Press, 2016).
(6) Nancy Couling, "Formats of Extended Urbanisation in Ocean Space," *Emerging Urban Spaces- a Planetary Perspective* (Berlin: Springer, 2018)
(7) Carola Hein, "Oil Spaces: The Global Petroleumscape in the Rotterdam/the Hague Area," *Journal of Urban History* 44, no. 5 (2018): 887–929. doi:10.1177/0096144217752460.
(8) Sheena Wilson and Andrew Pendakis, eds., "Sight, Site, Cite: Oil in the Field of Vision," *Imaginations: Journal of Cross-Cultural Image Studies* 3, no. 2 (9 June 2012), http://www3.csj.ualberta.ca/imaginations/?page_id=4020.
(9) Lance Duerfahrd, "A Scale That Exceeds Us: The BP Gulf Spill Footage and Photographs of Edward Burtynsky," *Imaginations: Journal of Cross-Cultural Image Studies* 3, no. 2 (6 September 2012): 115–29.
(10) Felicity Lawrence and Harry Davies, "Revealed: BP's Close Ties with the UK Government," *The Guardian*, 21 May 2015, https://www.theguardian.com/environment/2015/may/20/revealed-bps-close-ties-with-the-uk-government.
(11) Henri Lefebvre, *The Production of Space*, trans. Donald Nicholson-Smith (Oxford: Blackwell, 1991).
(12) Ibid., 289.
(13) Lucien Chabason, "Toward International Regulation of Offshore Oil Drilling?," in *Oceans: The New Frontier*, vol. 2011, *A Planet For Life* (Delhi: TERI Press, 2011), 216–19.
(14) Statistica, "Number of Offshore Rigs Worldwide as of January 2018 by Region," Statistics (London ; New York: Statistica Ltd., 2018), https://www.statista.com/statistics/279100/number-of-offshore-rigs-worldwide-by-region/.
(15) North Sea Commission, "CPMR North Sea Commission—Integration Approach to Sustainable Development in the North Sea Region" (Brussels & Gothenburg: North Sea Commission, 27 November 2017), http://cpmr-northsea.org/download/cpmr-north-sea-commission-integration-approach-to-sustainable-development-in-the-north-sea-region/.
(16) Port of Rotterdam, "Throughput Port of Rotterdam 2017," Statistics (Rotterdam: Port of Rotterdam, 2018), https://www.portofrotterdam.com/en/news-and-press-releases/container-throughput-drives-growth-in-rotterdam.
(17) This gave the undersea-routing option for the Nord Stream double gas pipeline in the Baltic Sea significant advantages over alternative routes on land. Interview with Nord Stream Deputy Communications Director, 10/07/12.
(18) Willem Timmermans J, "The Future of Offshore Pipelining," *Offshore Magazine* 62, no. 6 (6 January 2002).
(19) UN, "UNCLOS 1982," 1982, http://www.un.org/Depts/los/convention_agreements/convention_overview_convention.htm.
(20) D. G. Gorman and J. Neilson, eds., *Decommissioning Offshore Structures*, Environmental Engineering (London ; Springer, 1998).
(21) https://treaties.un.org/pages/ViewDetails.aspx?src=TREATY&mtdsg_no=XXVII-7-d&chapter=27&clang=_en
(22) The European Parliament and the Council of the European Union, "Directive 2014/89/EU" (2014), http://eur-lex.europa.eu/legal-content/EN/TXT/?uri=uriserv:OJ.L_.2014.257.01.0135.01.ENG%20.
(23) David Harvey, *The Urban Experience* (Oxford: Blackwell, 1989), Neil Brenner, "Theses on Urbanization," *Public Culture* 25, no. 1 (2013): 85–114, doi.org/10.1215/08992363-1890477
(24) Mason White and Lola Shepherd, "New New Deal: Infrastructures on Life Support," in *Infrastructure as Architecture : Designing Composite Networks*, eds. Katrina Stoll and Scott Lloyd (Berlin: Jovis, 2010).
(25) Maria Kaika and Erik Swyngedouw, "Fetishizing the Modern City: The Phantasmagoria of Urban Technological Networks," *International Journal of Urban and Regional Research* 24, no. 1 (2000): 120–138
(26) Jeffrey Kipnis and Alexander Maymind, *A Question of Qualities : Essays in Architecture* (Cambridge, MA: MIT Press, 2013), 294.
(27) ibid., 292.
(28) Roberto Mangabiera Unger, "The Better Futures of Architecture," in *Anyone*, ed. Cynthia C. Davidson (New York, New York: Rizzoli, 1991).
(29) Ibid., 30.
(30) Ibid., 35.
(31) Kipnis and Maymind, *Question of Qualities*, 294.

Chapter 8 NORTH SEA COSMOS: *A PERIPLUS*

Stephen J. Ramos & Jan Derk Diekema

Traditional navigation frequently used a combination of scientific and subjective methods. In employing Strabos' *periplus*, Stephen Ramos and Jan Derk Diekema take us on a voyage of discovery, below and beyond the North Sea, into the backwaters then out to space. Through this last leap, the authors reassert a subjective sense of wonder apt to be lost amid the intermediate technological landscape of transnational communication cables.

Stephen J. Ramos, D.Des is Associate Professor of Urban Planning and Design at the University of Georgia. He is Editor for the Americas for *Planning Perspectives* and serves on the International Advisory Board of the Leiden-Delft-Erasmus Port City Futures initiative. He was Visiting Professor at TU Delft in 2018. Publications include *Dubai Amplified: The Engineering of a Port Geography* (Ashgate 2010; Routledge 2016), *Infrastructure Sustainability and Design* (Routledge 2012), and *New Geographies* (GSD/ Harvard University Press).

Artist Jan Derk Diekema works in research, media-art, and writing, focusing on urbanisation and human behaviour. He works on temporary urban development for CareX. Diekema organises creative/artist communities and cultural spots throughout the Netherlands and was founder and organizer of artist-exchanges between Groningen and international art-institutes. He is a member of the Port Journey Network.

> *The ocean, as a material space, is particularly difficult to grasp… the representation of a point in ocean-space is a false staticization of geophysical processes. The ocean is constituted by vectors of movement—tides, currents, and waves—but these vectors do not simply occur in the ocean subsequently; they are the ocean… Baudrillard's observation about the map preceding the territory is as true at sea as it is on land. But in the ocean there is a further iteration because the territory washes away the map. Thus we can never truly "locate" ourselves within the ocean. Or, if we must locate ourselves, we require a different kind of "map."*(1) —Philip Steinberg

A DIFFERENT KIND OF MAP

In 1947, in his article titled "Terrae Incognitae," US geographer John K. Wright posed an open question regarding the place of the imagination in geography.(2) Wright described two kinds of geographic knowledge: factual and inferred. His principal interest was in the latter, which he believed could take many forms. Although science had advanced to where virtually no point on earth remained unexplored, from an inferred, subjective perspective, mystery remained: "If there is no *terra incognita* today in an absolute sense, so also no *terra* is absolutely *cognita*"(3) [Fig. 1, p. 90].

Wright invited geographers to include an "aesthetic subjectivity" in their spatial explorations.(4) He recalled discovery travels from the past to reunite the two kinds of geographic knowledge and include the geographic imagination with more traditional mapping methodologies. He termed this holistic research field "geosophy,": "the study of geographical knowledge from any or all points of view."(5) A polylogue.(6)

Over fifty years later, *The Urbanisation of the Sea* is a kindred project. The binary conceptual understanding of sea and land as discrete spaces has proven misguided in the ways it informs spatio-environmental practice and stewardship.(7) We believe Wright's call for an inter- and trans-disciplinary exploratory methodology can help to conceptually move beyond the exhausted binary to better locate ourselves with a different kind of map.

CLASSICAL SEA-LAND-COSMOS TRIANGULATION

Like Wright, we take inspiration from the classical world. Classical geographers (and geographers from many other cultures and time periods) triangulated sea and land exploration with alternating visions of the heavens, cosmos, and the stars. The cosmos helped to orient sea travel and also guided land survey. Triangulation wedded poetic mystery and wonder to the more scientific pursuits of astronomy, navigation, and cartography in a more complete, geosophic frame. 'From any or all points of view,' indeed.

The two most significant sources of Ancient Greco-Roman geography are Strabo and Ptolemy. Their studies of the then

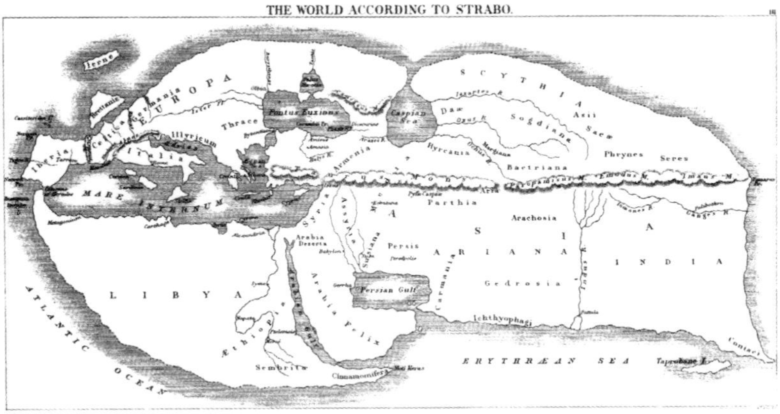

Fig. 2
A modern reconstruction of the world known to Strabo.

inhabited *oikoumene*, (8) particularly when translated into Latin during the Renaissance, informed the subsequent European "Age of Discovery."(9) Each produced a *Geography* (Strabo's predating Ptolemy's by 150 years), but their approaches were starkly different. In Wright's classification of geographic knowledges, Ptolemy's would be the factual and Strabo's the inferred.

In the Ptolemaic version, geography is cartographic, based on precise locational data similar to that obtained by contemporary quantitative Geographic Information Systems (GIS) research.(10) Ptolemy's second-century work, *Almagest*, was a series of mathematical texts, which focused on astronomy and the ecliptic coordinate system of the stars within a geocentric frame. *Almagest* would later be applied to land surveying and seafaring navigation. Ptolemy explored land, sea, and stars in concert to locate and construe the relational, mutually constitutive spaces of each.

Strabo's writings are travel logs of lands and peoples, which account for "differences in social forms and cultural practices... with a marked penchant for the curious, the marvellous, and the exceptional."(11) The Strabonic, more akin to contemporary cultural geography, (12) draws more from poets and playwrights; principally from the blind bard Homer (13) [Fig. 2]. In his ode to Homer's description of Achilles's shield, Strabo sees the foundation of the "science of geography." Similar to Ptolemic cosmography, at the outer edge of the circular shield is Oceanus, a water body that surrounds the land, and out of which rise the sun and constellations after they have bathed in its water during their respective times of the day.(14) Homeric voyages traverse sea and land, with intermittent visitation from gods and constellations, and for Strabo, these triangulated geographies are elemental components of the heroic song.

In her work on Strabo's *Geography*, classicist Daniela Dueck reminds us that although Strabo based his ideas on ancient travel logs and techniques, "*human* change within the rigid framework of the *oikoumene* is in fact what the whole *Geography* is about."(15) Namely, those socio-political agents that are co-joined, networked, and deeply embedded into chorographic narratives and coastal-hinterland spatial configurations.

The sea-land continuum is a thread woven throughout this volume, to which we add the relationship between sea-land and today's heavenly bodies, namely, deep space. The ocean depths and deep space merge as the contemporary "Sirens' songs," which Wright references as the calls draw society toward new mysteries. A *cosmos incognita* to pursue.(16) We conjure the work of Roman Hellenic geographies—instrumental for that particular Mediterranean identity—to triangulate and relocate sea and land with the cosmos in a new age of geospatial information discovery along X and Y axes, and the Z-*axis mundi*.

PERIPLOI

The methodology we adopt is the *periplus* (sing.), which Strabo famously incorporated to map Mediterranean territories for Roman expansion. Literally translated from Greek as "circumnavigation," *periploi* (pl.) were seafaring coastal descriptions of land from the sailors' perspective from the sea.(17) They combined the survey of the biophysical with cultural-historic narratives to produce broader, more complete geographic interpretation. The periplus recorded towns, ports, topography, and waterways. Because maritime routes often stayed close to land for purposes of navigational orientation, the descriptions surveyed land from the sea to chart each. On the eve of Rome's move from Republic to Empire, Strabo employed periploi to make topographic and ethnographic observations, and from these he derived political analyses to inform what was to become empire maintenance. They were situational in each sense of the word. The periplus gazes inward from the sea; an anthropomorphic conceit that imagines how the sea sees land, and into the river tributaries that nourish it.

Trading companies later came to rely on periploi for ocean depth charting and port infrastructure information, combining quantitative measurement and descriptive text in early "mixed-method" cartography.(18) Periploi also presaged contemporary concern with the pretence of objective cartographic representation. The method favours what British geographer Derek Gregory describes as constructive and not mimetic—something fashioned, but not false—to transcend the division of material and metaphorical spaces.(19) Periploi can be viewed as antecedents to this volume's viscous connections and unfoldings where sea and land engage.(20)

Our deployment of the periplus technique in the northern region of the Netherlands is a chorographic infrastructural journal, which travels from the North Sea foreland through the Eemshaven energy/data port at the mouth of the Eems river estuary, and into the hinterland of the Groningen and Drenthe provinces. But rather than take a traditional riverway to enter the land, as Strabo's periplus entered Egypt through the Nile delta, our narrative travels along transnational communication cables. Data travels through amphibian data cables that connect the undersea to the subterranean in distributed infrastructural space, in ways often colloquially referenced in comparable language of channelled water: "flows," "storage," and "treatment." Yet distinct from water, cables distinctly separate material and data substance.

The hinterland journey takes us through the radio telescope sites of the Netherlands Institute for Radio Astronomy (ASTRON) in the Groningen and Drenthe regions, which communicate with the outermost reaches of deep space. We encounter supercomputers in the city of Groningen, travel to the Dwingeloo Radiotelescoop (DRT) —one of the oldest working radio telescopes in the world—and continue via Westerbork Synthesis Radio Telescope to LOFAR, the world's largest radio telescope. Here, ASTRON coordinates an international space research consortium network, which explores information from deep space in pursuit of cosmic discovery. Geographer Fraser Macdonald observes, "Space is a modality for hypermobile information which, in combination with advanced technologies of 'software-sorting,' has enabled a wider 'automatic production of space.'"(21) The *periplus* activates and engages spaces of sea depths, remote, rural Dutch land-seascapes, and outer space in a fully modern, technological sense.(22)

In the periplus, the infrastructure itself is imbued with narrative qualities and capabilities [Fig. 3, p. 91]. The data and energy cables traverse the sea-land continuum, connecting the biophysical to the cultural and historic features of the Dutch landscape. These same cables enable networked communication among international space research stations to strengthen earth's capacity for deep space study. Periploi, once particular to surveys of land from sea, can now include surveys of space from earth. Data ports like Eemshaven function as intermediary nodes at the vertices of the sea-air-cosmos triangulation, so that ports' traditional function at sea-land is also part of ASTRON's space communication "ports." The radio telescope is a new kind of port, embedded in (and enabled by) trade infrastructure from the past, which also joins sea and land to multiverse.

The serial systems of ports are infrastructures that maintain, at once, their traditional functions, while also helping to mediate, translate, and transgress those perceived boundaries of sea, land, and cosmos. The sea-land line looks upward and becomes a triangle. The social realm is also overlaid, networked. Regions once remote and languishing in economic decline, are reimagined and revived in new centralities. These ports communicate energy generation and data processing. They are cosmic ports for discovery of new worlds. We locate ourselves in a different kind of map, a geosophic journey from sea to land to the cosmos.

A NORTH SEA PERIPLUS

Deep below the surface of the North Sea lurk a series of transnational networks of submarine cables and pipelines distributed all over the world by companies and public authorities. These pipelines and cables enable the transfer and trade of natural gas, oil, electricity, and energy, among other material and information.(23) Among networks, submarine communication cables transport 99 percent of international data transfer and are many thousands of miles long.(24) Cable networks are used to transfer enormous amounts of data—via hubs—to "supercomputers" inland. Within broader claims for sea urbanisation, submarine transnational cables clearly comprise the infrastructural sea substrata, in forms similar to infrastructural underground networks in cities and regions for over two hundred years.(25)

Once ashore, these "main" high-speed communication cables each have appropriate anthropomorphic nicknames, such as "the backbone" and "the aorta."(26) Supercomputers onshore are designed to do high-level calculations, and they function best with a direct connection to the "backbone" cable for increased speed and capacity." The infrastructure enables broad data gathering across multiple sites with near-simultaneous complex calculation and analysis. The range of networks enhances capacity for big data transport between sites and supercomputers around the world.

One of the hubs where onshore high-speed data cables are connected to offshore submarine data cables is situated in the Eemshaven seaport, at the mouth of the Eems river estuary in the north-eastern Netherlands. The historic geography transmogrifies in the wind and tides.

LAND FROM SEA

The Eems river estuary meets the Wadden Sea in the south-east section of the North Sea. The exchange produced land over time. Dutch architectural historian Cor Wagenaar characterises the north-eastern Netherlands as "separated from the sea by a narrow band that developed as an ongoing process of give and take. Sometimes the sea swallowed the land; sometimes the process of sedimentation created new land."(27) Strabo described coastal siltation as the sea breathing in and out "like a living being."(28) In the most definitive sense, the northern regions of Groningen and neighbouring Friesland are emblematic of a particular North Sea urbanisation: uniting land and water, the engineered and the organic, town and country, systems and sites. The land-sea scape is alive.

The coastal landscape is comprised of countless acres of grassland and farmland. It is a fertile and efficiently planned landscape of straight ditches, small roads, and old farms. The planned grid sourced by the land consolidation of the nineteenth century is beautifully interrupted by dozens of medieval villages, small rivers, and old trees. Many of the coastal areas are the result of irrigation/draining processes of "polderisation," which helped to maintain above-sea levels for centuries, enabling it to be farmed and inhabited.(29) The villages were built on raised, artificial hills called "terpen" or "wierden."(30) The wierden date from 600 BCE until the first dykes were constructed in the area in the thirteenth century. Some of the villages have no more than ten houses, but all have a church with a tower built from red bricks baked with subterranean clay. The church towers conveyed the civic pride of the villages. There were competitions among them for the highest and the best-adorned towers, with some proudly plastered and painted in white and blue. The verticality—a leitmotif in this axis mundi narrative—punctuates the strong horizontal geography. The dykes, terps, and wierden were all constructed to protect the residents from the sea.

The periplus moves through the North Sea in submarine cables and lines that carry data and energy from Denmark, Norway, England, and beyond to the Netherlands. Approaching the shore, the Wadden Islands are the first sign of land, and at low tide the sandbanks emerge from the Wadden Sea. Eemshaven is the first port of entry.

EEMSHAVEN

The Eemshaven port is one of two main seaports in the Groningen province, located in the sparsely populated "het Hogeland" region in the northern-most area of the Dutch mainland, eighteen miles from the city of Groningen. Eemshaven's founder was the hydraulic engineer Johan van Veen (1893–1959), "father" of the Dutch Deltaplan, which famously prescribed hardscaped geotechnical systems to address water management and flooding throughout the Netherlands.(31) Eemshaven seaport was designed and built in the 1950s and 1960s, near van Veen's childhood farm in the vast northern polder landscape. Van Veen was inspired by the small medieval harbour that once operated there. Throughout his life he advocated for the construction of a modern seaport for the Eems deep-river estuary to help develop the region, and in 1973 his dream was realised when the Eemshaven port was completed.

Eemshaven was designed for oil refining and storage. Its deep estuary entrance, unusual for the northern Dutch coastline, could accommodate big oil ships. But the 1973 oil crisis abruptly put an end to Eemshaven's oil dreams, and decades of regional decline followed.(32) But Eemshaven was revived in the new millennium.

Today, Eemshaven is both an energy port and a data port. These combined port activities have completely changed the future of the seaport and its hinterland, creating new centralities for data and energy transfer and processing. Eemshaven has three operational power stations and extensive energy transfer facilities. There is a large onshore wind farm, and a main energy cable connection with the Gemini Wind Farm (among Europe's largest), located in Dutch waters

52 miles from the coastline in the North Sea.(33) Electricity from a Norwegian hydroelectric power station is transported to Eemshaven by a two-way undersea high-voltage cable. There is also the undersea COBRA cable, which transports wind energy produced in Denmark to Eemshaven. Finally, there are three solar parks and plants that produce energy from waste and biomass. Combined, Eemshaven produces and imports a total of 8,000 megawatts of electricity. This alternative energy capacity, accompanied with the state-of-the-art energy and data infrastructure, have helped persuade companies like Google to locate big data processing centres in the Eemshaven cluster.

Eemshaven's architectural landscape consists of dozens of rectangular buildings without windows. Hundreds of pipelines, cables, fences, and lighting columns populate the site, along with painted metal and concrete facades, and chimneys and silos that rise from a vast, flat coastal landscape. The sea view is blocked by the straight green line of the twenty-five-foot Deltadijk. This wall—more than one hundred miles long—was designed to protect the Netherlands from flooding. Nearly one hundred large onshore windmills complete the technoscape; they are modern versions of the windmills that were built for centuries throughout the Dutch hinterlands. The machines rotate hypnotically in monotones in the rural coastal atmosphere. It is a post-human energy and data-processing settlement that powers and informs distant places and machines.

SUPERCOMPUTERS: STELLA AND COBALT 2.0

The next set of ports along the periplus are the supercomputers that process information. Underground high-speed data cables burrow paths through the landscape to supercomputers, high-tech installations, and data hubs in the hinterland. The main cable from Eemshaven follows the coastline of the Eems river estuary south to the German border; at a divergent crossing, one cable continues on to Hamburg, Germany, and another to the city of Groningen.

In 2005, a supercomputer named "STELLA" (Supercomputer Technology for Linked LOFAR Applications) was connected to the main Groningen data cable network. STELLA was designed to compute unique calculations using data gathered from outer space. STELLA was housed in what was once the Calculation Room in the Smitsborg building at the University of Groningen, which is now the Centre for Information Technology. STELLA was the fastest supercomputer in Europe and the fourth fastest in the world, but supercomputers need updating approximately every five years. STELLA has since been replaced by the Cobalt 2.0 cluster, which runs on graphics processing units (GPUs) and can network computation to multiple cores for increased capacity to conduct deep space research.

ASTRON: RADIO TELESCOPE PORTS

Following cables southward from Groningen city, forests appear. In the Drenthe province, millions of trees, rough heathlands, and sandy plains take over the landscape. This is not the planned, engineered landscape of the "het Hogeland" region, but rather a softer construct. In this part of Drenthe, there are forests that were once planted for logging, and natural open plains with more than 3,500 miles of cycling paths for day trippers and tourists. Where the Groningen province has straight lines on the empty horizon of sea and sky, Drenthe's land form assumes the more sinuous, traditional green face of nature. The only visible reminders of the North Sea are the numerous broken grey shells that pave the small winding cycling paths.

The Netherlands Institute for Radio Astronomy (ASTRON) is housed in an isolated, unremarkable building on the edge of a forest. The Stichting Radiostraling van Zon en Melkweg/Netherlands Foundation for Radio Astronomy (SRZM), the forerunner of ASTRON, was established in 1949 by Dutch astronomer Prof. Jan Hendrik Oort (1900–1992). Oort is regarded as a pioneer in the field of radio astronomy and a central figure in the quest to understand the Milky Way. Next to the ASTRON building stands the Dwingeloo Radiotelescoop (DRT) radio telescope, which was built in 1954, when Johan van Veen was working on the Eemshaven port plan. At the time, the DRT was the biggest radio telescope in the world. It is now one of the world's oldest working radio telescopes. Its eighty-two-foot-wide dish still operates but is only used by amateur astronomers.(34) The DRT is legendary for its historic contribution to the discovery of the Milky Way and the Big Bang in the late 1950s.(35)

Improved technology allowed ASTRON to network its radio telescopic capacity for improved space research, at the Westerbork site further along the periplus. Fifteen miles northeast of the DRT, following a path also paved with North Sea shells, a forest appears that was the venue for much historic suffering. Here, the forest is best known as the location for the Nazi Westerbork transit camp during World War II. Today, there is a memorial centre to commemorate those who suffered at Westerbork, and to learn from the darkest side of human history.(36) The periplus constructs biophysical landscapes with their historic contexts.

The silence of the forest, and that of the memorial centre, is also a silence necessary for conducting further research into the nature of the universe. In the 1970s, also under the direction of Prof. Jan Hendrik Oort, ASTRON built the Westerbork Synthesis Radio Telescope (WSRT)—a series of fourteen radio telescope dishes working together—next to the memorial site.

The WSRT dishes (each also with eighty-two-foot diameter) can be used in concert with radio telescopes in other parts of the world. (37) Two of the WSRT dishes are part of the European VLBI Network, which contains twenty-two radio telescopes, primarily located in

Europe and Asia, but also in Africa and Puerto Rico. "VLBI" stands for "Very-Long-Baseline Interferometry," which is a type of coordinated astronomical interferometer that networks various installations to function together. They form a unique and powerful instrument for space research. An international network of supercomputers and high-speed data connections also enable VLBI networks to function in unison and perform calculations of the mega-data streams the VLBI produces. The result is the most sensitive VLBI network in the world, and the only one capable of real-time observations. Again, improved technological capacity required new sites along the periplus.

LOFAR

Eighteen miles eastward, one leaves the forests behind and enters an open landscape filled with farmlands and former peat bogs. A newer technoscape appears. Hundreds of strange-looking pyramid shapes and dark boxes are distributed throughout the landscape. Since 2009, on the border of the Drenthe and Groningen provinces, lies the centre point of the world's biggest radio telescope.

LOFAR means "Low Frequency Array," and it is a telescope that consists of thousands of small antennas that are combined in fifty-one stations spread throughout Europe. These stations are connected via a high-speed fibre-optic network and the stations are then connected to STELLA and her successors in Groningen. The supercomputer combines the data from the antennas to a virtual radio telescope with a diameter of approximately 745 miles. To cover a large frequency range, there are two distinct antenna types: the Low Band Antenna (LBA—the pyramids) able to measure the earth's lowest observable frequencies, between 10 and 90 MHz, and the High Band Antenna (HBA—the dark boxes) operating between 110 and 250 MHz. Every station has an LBA antenna field and at least one HBA antenna field. These elements are woven into the landscape as an artificial, intelligent nature, seemingly culled from the co-joined imaginations of a naturalist, a planner, and a scientist. An aerial view reveals a more easily recognisable large circular shape, reminiscent of the old terpen and wierden from the "het Hogeland." The "superterp" assembly forms the centre point of LOFAR in the province of Drenthe [Fig. 4, p. 92 & Fig. 5, p. 92].

LOFAR is used to search for the origin of the first galaxies, black holes, and gas clouds just after the birth of the Universe, the Big Bang. LOFAR has already discovered 100,000 "new" galaxies. With over 20,000 antennas and other sensors, it is also used for other projects, such as for research in the field of "precision agriculture" and geophysics. The sensors make it possible to closely examine the growth of crops under different weather conditions and diseases, or to measure the consequences of subsidence in the area. Primarily, however, LOFAR collects enormous datasets from light-years away and sends it through an innovative computer network infrastructure. The data traffic travels from networked telescopes in remote LOFAR stations throughout Europe, through Hamburg, to the Groningen Smitsborg building where the Cobalt 2.0 supercomputer reduces the enormous amount of data to more manageable data sets that astronomers can process and interpret for scientific discovery [Fig. 6].

ASTRON and their partner-institutes are now developing the Square Kilometre Array (SKA), which will be the new most powerful radio telescope in the world. Its hundreds of antennas will be situated in the deserts of Western Australia and South Africa where there is minimal light pollution. The construction of the sites will begin in 2021. SKA will generate unprecedented data volumes and rely on new supercomputers and the worldwide network of high-speed submarine communication cables for its success.

FUTURE PORT

The North Sea periplus leads us to quiet, remote places. Humming in monotones, hidden in forests, listening to the multiverse. They are contextually monumental and declarative, simultaneously autonomous and hermetic in their materiality. The periplus goes beyond the mere assigning of anthropomorphic names to submarine, subterranean, and telescopic infrastructures. We ask technology to speak. We imagine a narration of discovery through geographic elements of sea, land, air, and outer space, which, combined, constitute a more complete, integral space. We draw inspiration from human geographers of the ocean, with the objective conceptualizing this integral space as they describe the ocean's in our epilogue. "A space that is not so much *known* as *experienced*...less a space that we live *on* than one that we live *in;* less two-dimensional surface than a four-dimensional sphere; a space that we can think *from*."(38) These are the "fluid ontologies" that thicken and blur geographies across land, sea, air, and space.(39) This is our understanding of Wright's call for a geosophic frame, which enables us to better conceptualise continuums, data flows, and technoscapes within landscapes and histories.

Fig. 6
LOFAR Regional Network Map (Jan Derk Diekema from ASTRON)

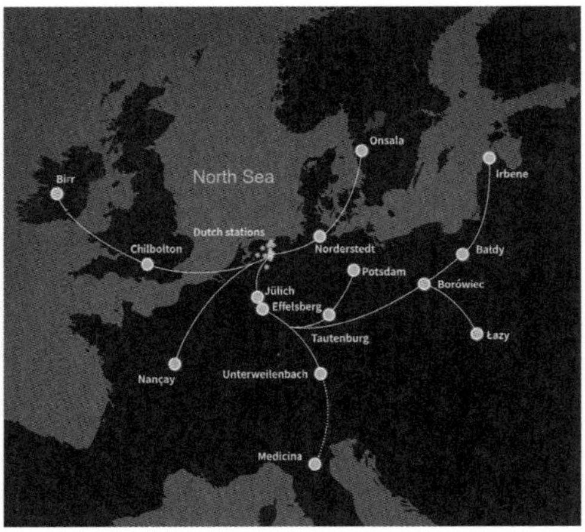

The North Sea can be viewed in section, contemplating maritime depths and outer space distances in verticality, while remaining synchronised with the more traditional, gradient cardinal land orientation. The work of ASTRON and associate institutes is comparable with that of Strabo and Ptolemy. The infrastructural journey conducts and creates new geographies and new ontologies. Travel logs are here made from datasets, and cartographies are high-resolution pictures or 3D-maps of space. STELLA and Cobalt 2.0, in their home in the Smitsborg building, serve as key urban data ports within the broad system. Historic seaports are transformed into data hubs and energy ports, which can communicate radio-telescopic networks across Europe and the entire planet. These new ports become the neuralgic connectors for a contemporary "Age of Discovery," just as maritime ports were for that original age. Cables act as ships, and move seamlessly from sea to land, synthetically merging and forming what anthropologist Tim Ingold calls a "meshwork of natures."(40)

An international network of astronomers produce and share the data generated from these remote infrastructures that we've tried to inhabit in our periplus. How this information will contribute to the formation and reformation of broader political structures here on Earth, as was the case with Strabo's work, remains to be discovered.

(1) Philip E. Steinberg, "Forward On Thalassography", in *Water Worlds: Human Geographies of the Ocean*, eds J. Anderson and K. Peters (Farnham: Ashgate, 2014), xv.
(2) John K. Wright, "*Terrae Incognitae*: The Place of the Imagination in Geography", *Annals of the Association of American Geographers* 37, no. 1 (1947), 1–15.
(3) Wright *Terrae Incognitae*, 4.
(4) Wright *Terrae Incognitae*, 7.
(5) Wright *Terrae Incognitae*, 12.
(6) Julia Kristeva, *Polylogue* (Paris: Seuil, 1977). See also the Center for Postnormal Policy & Futures Studies. Chicago, IL. www.cppfs.org
(7) See Introduction, this volume.
(8) The Greek word "oikoumene" (οἰκουμένη) means the "inhabited earth." See Oxford Classical Dictionary:https://oxfordre.com/classics/view/10.1093/acrefore/9780199381135.001.0001/acrefore-9780199381135-e-8008.
(9) See also Denis Cosgrove, *Geography and Vision: Seeing, Imagining, and Representing the World* (New York: St. Martin's Press, 2008); William A. Koelsch, "Squinting Back at Strabo." *American Geographical Society* 94, no. 4, (2004), 502–18.
(10) Koelsch, "Squinting Back at Strabo."
(11) Cosgrove, *Geography and Vision*, 6.
(12) Katherine Clarke, *Between Geography and History: Hellenistic Constructions of the Roman World*. (Oxford: Clarendon Press, 1999); Koelsch "Squinting Back at Strabo."
(13) Cosgrove, *Geography and Vision*, 7.
(14) Dilip Da Cunha, *The Invention of Rivers: Alexander's Eye and the Ganga's Descent* (Philadelphia: University of Pennsylvania Press, 2019), 46-47; *The Geography of Strabo*, vol. 1, trans. Horace Leonard Jones (Cambridge, MA: Harvard University Press), 13,7.
(15) Daniela Dueck, *Strabo of Amasia: A Greek Man of Letters in Augustan Rome* (London; New York: Routledge, 2000), 45. Emphasis added.
(16) See chapter 4, this volume "Everything has its depth".
(17) Da Cunha, *Invention of Rivers*, 78.
(18) John Hubbart, *The Orientation Navigator; or New Directions for Sailing to and from the East Indies, China, and New Holland* (London: Robert Laurie and James Whistle, 1801); Da Cunha, *Invention of Rivers*, 108.
(19) Derek Gregory, *Geographic Imaginations* (Oxford: Blackwell, 1994), 5; Clifford Geertz, "Blurred Genres: The Reconfiguration of Social Thought" in *Local Knowledge: Further Essays in Interpretive Anthropology* (New York: Basic Books, 1983); Neil Smith, "Afterward: The Beginning of Geography" in *Uneven Development: Nature, Capital, and the Production of Space* (Oxford: Blackwell, 1990).
(20) See chapter 3, this volume.
(21) MacDonald "Anti-Astropolitik", 594. In quote, 'software-sorting' cited from Stephen Graham "Software-Sorted Geographies" in *Progress in Human Geography* 29 no. 5 (2005), 562–680, and 'automatic production of space' cited from Nigel Thrift and Shaun French, "The Automatic Production of Space" in *Transactions of the Institute of British Geographers* 27 no. 3, (2002), 309–335.
(22) Peter Redfield, *Space in the Tropics: From Convicts to Rockets in French Guiana* (Berkeley: University of California Press, 2000).
(23) TeleGeography Submarine Cable Map. https://www.submarinecablemap.com. Accessed 3 February 2020; Keller Easterling, "Cable," in *New Geographies* 1: *AFTER ZERO*. S. Ramos and N. Turan, eds. (Cambridge, MA: GSD/Harvard University Press, 2009), 62-77.
(24) Victoria Woollaston, "The world's nervous system revealed: Interactive map charts 550,000 mile-long network of underwater cables that carry world's web traffic." *The Daily Mail.com*. January 31, 2014, https://www.dailymail.co.uk/sciencetech/article-2549329/Interactive-map-reveals-550-000-mile-long-network-UNDERWATER-cables-carry-worlds-web-traffic.html. Accessed February 3, 2020.
(25) Neil Brenner and Christian Schmid, "Planetary Urbanization", in *Urban Constellations*, ed. Matthew Gandy (Berlin: Jovis, 2011); Nancy Couling, "The Role of Ocean Space in Contemporary Urbanization" (Lausanne, EPFL, 2015). http://infoscience.epfl.ch/record/212706.
(26) "Backbone" is a common terminology for information cabling, and a common metaphor for cable networks as an international information central nervous system. See note 25. AORTA cable comes from a brand name acronym: "Always On Ready Time Architecture." See David W. Conklin. 2006. *Cases in the Environment of Business: International Perspectives* (London; New Delhi: Sage Publications), 479.
(27) Cor Wagenaar, *Town Planning in the Netherlands Since 1880* (Rotterdam: nai10 publishers, 2015), 55.
(28) *Geography of Strabo* 1.3.7-11
(29) Ibid.
(30) Wagenaar, *Town Planning in the Netherlands*, 56.
(31) Han Meyer, *The State of the Delta: Engineering, Urban Development, and Nation Building in the Netherlands* (Nijmegen: Vantilt Publishers, 2016); Johan van Veen, *Dredge, Drain, Reclaim: The Art of a Nation* (The Hague: Matinus Nijhoff, 1962).

(32) Eduardo De Mulder, Ben De Pater, Joos Droogleever Fortuijn, Len De Klerk and Jerry Van Dijk. *The Netherlands and the Dutch: A Physical and Human Geography* (Cham: Springer, 2019), 138.
(33) See https://www.power-technology.com/projects/gemini-wind-power-project/
(34) www.camras.nl
(35) Ernst Raimond and Rene Genee, *The Westerbork Observatory, Continuing Adventure in Radio Astronomy*. (London: Kluwer Academic Publishers, 1996).
(36) See https://kampwesterbork.nl/en/
(37) Richard Strom, Arnold van Ardenne and Steve Torchinsky, *50 Years Westerbork Radio Observatory: A Continuing Journey to Discoveries and Innovations* (Raalte: ASTRON/Van Gorcum, 2018).
(38) Steinberg, Thalassography, xiv.
(39) John Anderson and Kimberly Peters, "A Perfect and Absolute Blank", in *Water Worlds: Human Geographies of the Ocean*, eds J. Anderson and K. Peters (Farnham: Ashgate, 2014) 10-12.
(40) Tim Ingold, "Bindings Against Boundaries: Entanglements of Life in an Open World" In *Environment and Planning A*, 40 (2008), 1796-1810;
[Fig. 2] Reproduced from: Lloyd Arnold Brown, The Story of Maps (Boston: Little, Brown, 1949), p. 56. Penn Museum Archive
[Fig. 6] Image reproduced with permission from Astron (Netherlands Institute for Radio Astronomy)

Nationalpark
Zwischenzone

SWACO
SWACO

Part III EXTENSIONS

Part III brings the discussions of sea spaces and physical extensions across the sea-land continuum to the case study of the North Sea. Urban systems have extended out to sea and reconfigured local coastlines in distinct and unfamiliar ways. Contributions demonstrate how intensively the North Sea is used, by which groups and for which ends, and show the resulting impact on the spatial logic of territory both at sea and on land. They give examples of the instruments which currently regulate this space and highlight the challenges that arise throughout this process—these include not only a variety of seemingly irreconcilable conditions and processes, but also a lack of appropriate imaginaries due to the dominance of limited, land-based conceptions, as discussed in Part II.

With the global petroleumscape in chapter 9, Carola Hein presents a powerful example of extended systems that operate across the land-sea threshold around the North Sea. The historical overview of the global petroleum hub Amsterdam-Rotterdam-Antwerp reveals not only how the petroleum industry and its networked connections have expanded into the built environment, but also how it has created persuasive narratives linking petroleum to idealised historic land- and cityscapes.

Serge van Gessel, Lennert Goemans, and Jan Matthijsen use different types of limits to explain the expanding spatial demands on the Dutch continental shelf in chapter 10. In terms of hydrocarbons and other extractions, wind farms, and policy development, limits are geophysical, economical, ecological, and political as well as spatial. Long-term planning combined with the sea's contingent conditions make the development of different scenarios a useful tool for policy makers to address different limits in the Dutch North Sea.

The reality of an urbanised sea is confronted with the dominant narrative of an enduring ocean wilderness, although the North Sea has been both physically and ecologically transformed over centuries. In chapter 11, Anne-Mette Jørgensen argues that this narrative penetrates planning policy. The acknowledgement of human-made structures as an integral part of the North Sea ecosystem is urgent. National and cross-border planning efforts could then consider longer time frames, offering stability to established ecosystems and supporting higher-quality constructions.

Urbanisation processes in the North Sea have produced viscous conditions that are, in part, deliberately deployed by companies and authorities to their advantage. In chapter 12, Nancy Couling explores diverse forms of the strategic North Sea mixture of land- and sea-based materials and practices. But industrial regulations constrain and separate viscous relations, resulting in abrupt disjunctions and inhibiting potential synergies critical to the development of inclusive, transformative design and practice.

Mega ports are a prime example of such juxtapositions. Susan Dunne addresses this critical question in chapter 13, and traces the space of containerised shipping from the global to the generic in the uncanny confrontation of scale, materiality, and culture around the mega port of Rotterdam. De-contextualised, automated, and inaccessible to the general public, the port causes friction and rupture at the local scale.

The North Sea is also the hopeful site for northern Europe's energy transition to renewables, through the accelerated development of offshore wind energy. In chapter 14, Dirk Sijmons and Maarten Hajer illustrate the scenario developed in order to demonstrate how North Sea wind energy could look in 2050. The authors observe a crisis of the imagination and aim to dislodge the myth that wind energy is small and decentralized. A narrative is told of a North Sea vision within which the sea is completely fitted out as an energy landscape.

Through these contributions, "Extensions" also builds a case for an expanded view of the designer's task, to which Part IV "Cultivations" responds.

Chapter 9 THE GLOBAL PETROLEUMSCAPE OF THE ROTTERDAM/THE HAGUE AREA: AS A MODEL FOR FURTHER RESEARCH*

Carola Hein

Flows of petroleum have shaped the built environment of industrial, retail, administrative, and ancillary spaces, of infrastructures and buildings, as well as their representation. Carola Hein analyses the spatial impact of petroleum on the sea-land continuum through the lens of the port city region of Rotterdam/The Hague.

Carola Hein is Professor and Chair, History of Architecture and Urban Planning at Delft University of Technology. Among other major grants, she received a Guggenheim and an Alexander von Humboldt fellowship. Her current research interests include the transmission of architectural and urban ideas, focusing specifically on port cities and the global architecture of oil. Her books include: *Adaptive Strategies for Water_Heritage: Past, Present and Future*, *The Routledge Planning History Handbook* (2017), *Uzo Nishiyama, Reflections on Urban, Regional and National Space* (2017), *Port Cities: Dynamic Landscapes and Global Networks* (2011), *The Capital of Europe. Architecture and Urban Planning for the European Union* (2004), *Rebuilding Urban Japan after 1945* (2003), *and Cities, Autonomy and Decentralisation in Japan* (2006), *Hauptstadt Berlin 1957–58* (1991). She has also published numerous articles in peer-reviewed journals, books, and magazines.

*This text includes excerpts from Carola Hein, "Oil Spaces: The Global Petroleumscape in the Rotterdam/the Hague Area," *Journal of Urban History*, no. 43 (2018).

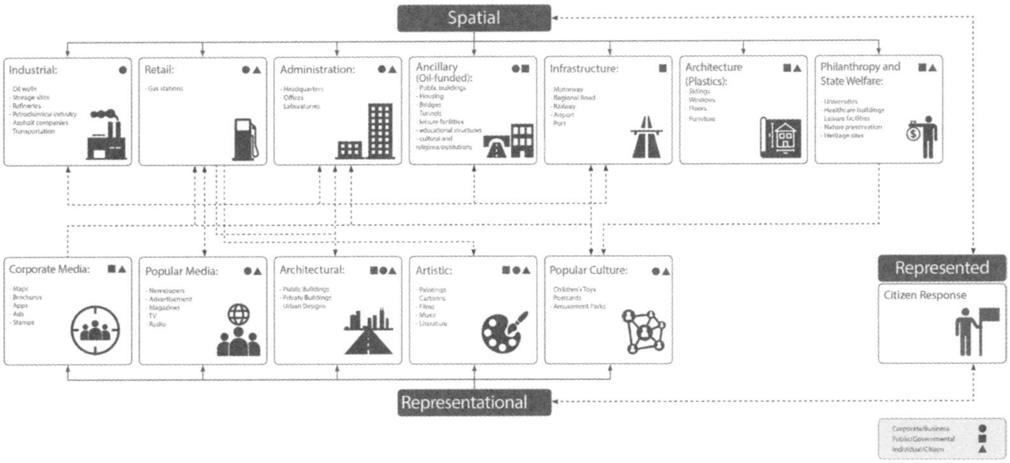

Fig. 1
The hybrid, multiple, shifting, and uneven ways in which many actors collaborate to create the global petroleumscape (Hein)

The emergence of global petroleum networks between producers and consumers around the world has been a key element in the development of shipping, the urbanisation of the sea, and in the construction of new landside structures. The discovery of petroleum in diverse corners of the world has led to the construction of new types of ships and has promoted the use of canals, such as the Suez and Panama canals. The use of petroleum as fuel for the military since the early twentieth century has helped drive the growth of maritime empires, for example, British control over Iranian petroleum. Petroleum has floated on oil for some 150 years, and ports, cities, and regions have thrived on that mixture starting in the mid-nineteenth century.

Petroleum, shipped from many parts of the globe, has shaped port city regions around the world. In the case of petroleum, this dynamic is particularly evident. The landscapes around the North Sea, connected by sea to a flexible maritime foreland, are exemplary of this shipping-based petroleum network. The historic development of ports and cities in the Amsterdam-Rotterdam-Antwerp area offers an example of the opportunities for port cities due to the particularities of the sea, its industrial exploitation, and constructed blankness.(1) Amsterdam, home for refined petroleum products; Rotterdam, the center for crude; and, crossing the Belgian border to the south, Antwerp, the petrochemical hub, the second-largest petrochemical industrial complex in the world (after Houston), have emerged as major entrance gates to the hinterland, notably the German Ruhr area. The land-side development of production spaces of oil is combined with places of administration where decision-makers who control the urbanisation of land and sea, and spaces for consumption of petroleum products.

Once established, these spaces of oil are not only a place of production, but as Henri Lefebvre argues, “also a means of control, and hence of domination, of power.”(2) Spatial practices (the life of inhabitants in a space on sea or land) and representations of space (the approaches of built environment professionals and other actors) intersect with spaces of representation (the images and associations of the users)(3); they are multiple (palimpsestic) layers of physical space and professional and public representation. Together the physical, represented, and everyday practices form what I call the *global palimpsestic petroleumscape*.(4) Each of these layers has similar functions and typologies (style, location, or architectural form) and these layers interconnect to form a single landscape. The concept of the petroleumscape starts with the insight that the diverse spatial emanations of oil—including offshore platforms and pipelines, refineries and storage sites, office buildings and gas stations—are connected through their relation to this single commodity and its group of industrial players. Connecting the actual places where oil is transported, stored, refined or even administered with the representation of these spaces and practices involving petroleum products enables a better understanding of the ways in which oil shapes behaviors and secures continuous demand [Fig. 1].

To highlight how different layers of the petroleumscape have emerged in an exemplary North Sea location, a series of analytical maps shows the various phases in which the industrial, infrastructural, administrative, retail, and ancillary spaces that comprise the spatial layer of the petroleumscape have grown in the Rotterdam/The Hague area in several periods related to the era of the car, comparing 1910, 1940, 1970, and 2000 [Fig. 2 & Fig. 3, p. 177]. The next section follows the maps to explore the emergence of the petroleumscape on the shores of the Dutch North Sea, pointing to the intersection between public/private actors and to the spaces of oil becoming new actors themselves. Progressing in steps of thirty years—examining the end of the lighting oil period, the early years of car development up to the Second World War, the postwar period, and recent decades in which criticism of oil has started to gain ground—this section shows how different layers of the petroleumscape have grown and supported each other in response to maritime flows of oil, while public, private, and citizen actors used

Fig. 2
The Rotterdam/The Hague area in the Amsterdam-Rotterdam-Antwerp (ARA) region

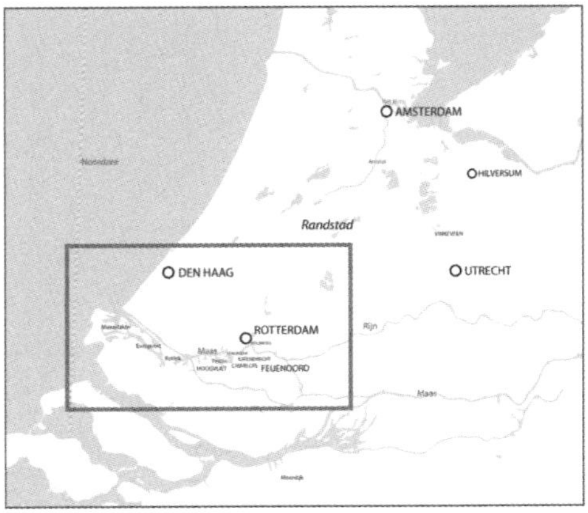

petroleum products and also promoted and depicted their use.

As the series of maps shows, from the earliest locations in the city to the port's extension to the tip of the Maasvlakte in the 1970s, petroleum refining, storage, and transportation have occupied enormous spaces in the port. The growth of the petroleum port did not occur in a vacuum. It was closely linked to petroleum-fueled developments in other parts of the region, notably the construction of administrative and research buildings, retail, and infrastructure. It was also closely linked to representations of these developments.

BLACK GOLD IN THE DUTCH RANDSTAD: ESTABLISHING ROTTERDAM AS A HUB FOR GLOBAL PETROLEUM FLOWS, 1862–1910

The petroleumscape of the Dutch Randstad is anchored in the industrial spaces of the port cities: Amsterdam, Antwerp, and Rotterdam. While Antwerp was initially the biggest importer of petroleum from the United States, Rotterdam has emerged over the last 150 years as the main petroleum hub. It serves as an example of the transformation of a port with multiple local players to a global hub dominated by petroleum interests. The analytical map of the city of Rotterdam illustrates how petroleum storage shifted from its initial location in the city toward the south side of the river and then westward, just as the city constructed new sea spaces, ports, and otherwise expanded, a clear indication of the viscous, shifting territories between sea and land.

In Rotterdam and in other cities around the world, it rapidly became clear that this highly flammable and harmful substance needed special storage—away from structures that could easily be destroyed by fire and away from the city's supply of drinking water. Making sure that it could be transported to and from the port was another challenge, and one that required collaboration among various partners. The construction of water, rail, and road infrastructure at the national scale and the extension of the city borders became key factors in the development of the Rotterdam port, and in turn they facilitated petroleum trade. The opening of the shipping canal, the Nieuwe Waterweg, connected Rotterdam directly to the North Sea in 1872 and facilitated access for the growing number of steamships that transported petroleum. The construction of railway lines to the border, lines that would also come to serve the oil industry, was a second step. The quick growth of the petroleum trade and the need for dedicated facilities flowed from a close collaboration between elite merchants and the municipality and solidified relationships between them.

The construction of new infrastructure and the growth of the city on the sea-land continuum created the foundation for Rotterdam's development as an oil node just as new global players in oil entered the European market. At the end of the nineteenth century, these players were interested in the port of Rotterdam as a turntable and transit point for oil on its way to the rapidly industrializing areas in western Germany. By 1891, several major oil companies had settled in the port, and by 1901, the Koninklijke Olie —one of the predecessors of Royal Dutch Shell—had built there as well. The city on the Maas had emerged as the main entrance gate for global petroleum, outpacing Amsterdam. The advent of major companies that gained control of the entire production and distribution chain—one that was mostly maritime based-had extensively reshaped the port and the oil business. Their interests and commodity flows connected various parts of the world, putting their imprint also on the Randstad.

If demand for lighting oil established Rotterdam as a major oil port, the rapidly growing new demand for benzene as a car fuel triggered its explosive growth. The construction of new refineries related directly to the needs of petroleum produced abroad: in 1907, the company installed a trial distillation facility for petroleum from Borneo, and a trial facility for asphalt followed in 1918.

The multinational setup of companies such as Royal Dutch Shell required close contact between the different headquarters in the Netherlands and the United Kingdom and also had an impact on travel connections across the North Sea. In parallel with the infrastructure created for oil itself, newly emerging aerial connections facilitated the travel of decision-makers among different sites and facilities. The Waalhaven Airport in the Rotterdam port next to the oil facilities opened in 1920 and allowed companies to bring in executives from London as the oil trade expanded.(5)

Pre-war development of oil infrastructures in the port and the capital city had a major impact on post-war rebuilding of bombed-out Rotterdam, illustrating the importance of the path dependencies of oil. In May 1940, on the eve of the Rotterdam Blitz, The Hague was known as petroleum administration headquarters and Rotterdam was the third-largest port in the world after New York and London, and a major entrance gate from the North Sea to the European continent. (6) The port city's leading role in petroleum storage and refining made it a target in the Second World War. Despite extensive destruction, taking advantage of its existing networks, the port rapidly returned to its leading position after the war ended. And the existence of industrial oil structures in the port of Rotterdam was a major factor in establishing a continuity of oil transportation and transformation even as production centres shifted in the postwar era. In the early 1960s, with decolonization in Asia and Africa, most of the oil started coming from the Middle East—the flexible maritime foreland put Rotterdam in contact with global oil producers.

The key role of Rotterdam as a petroleum hub was consolidated through the construction of structures beyond the port and the expansion of the cities of the Randstad; the development of the Dutch highway network in conjunction with the construction of new gas stations alongside them; the rapid growth of traffic; the increasing number of headquarters and research institutions in The Hague, and in neighboring Delft and Zoetermeer; and the construction of the Shell Tower on Weena in Rotterdam, part of the reconstruction effort.

The oil industry's need for access to the port and its hinterland continued to be key to planning and land allocation in the Rotterdam area; several studies document the overlapping interests of Shell and the Rotterdam Port Authority. By the 1950s, the consumer had become an important participant in the petroleumscape. Company publicity promoted the use of their products, highlighting freedom of travel and the beauty of historical landscapes. They produced and handed out many promotional documents—maps, brochures and booklets—that focus on features of the Dutch landscape. Maps can be powerful tools to help users understand space (as shown in the analytical maps made of the Rotterdam port), but they can also create imagined new geographies, and corporations have used them for this purpose for decades.(7) Since the 1930s, oil companies had used free maps to fuel the general public's desire to explore the Dutch landscape (Shell 1931, Texaco 1935). Throughout the twentieth century, oil companies sold or freely distributed road maps that tied the company name to the experience of driving and visiting. The covers of these maps tie company colors and logos to traditional landscapes, to tourist destinations, to historical, scientific, or cultural explorations.(8) They show icons of gas stations in a landscape dotted with oversized windmills and traditional Dutch houses with tulips, enticing the user to explore neighboring cities and regions. Tying the oil companies to traditional landscapes, rather than the industrial ones that petroleum generates, covers like this also promote the car as a vehicle of freedom and discovery.

Company publications geared at the general public continued to construct an imagined landscape different from the one that they were actually building: their focus remains on accessibility of select natural, historical, and cultural spaces. Their focus was primarily on a national and terrestrial scale, one that largely ignored the maritime spaces that served as industrial extensions. While the representational petroleumscape constructs space and identity as well as culture in and for spaces far beyond the ones that they actually occupy, it largely ignored the necessity of shipping for its construction. For the general public, these publications constructed a feedback loop that clearly tied the petroleum actors to the freedom of driving across the land and the joy of leisure.

The oil crises of the 1970s, when major industrial countries faced oil shortages, could have challenged the prominent role of petroleum actors in shaping the built environment. Car-free Sundays in the Netherlands allowed citizens to reclaim highways. The memory of the public was short, and few long-lasting changes occurred. But by that time, Rotterdam was firmly established as a leading oil port, serving consumers notably in the German hinterland. The production sector is huge in scale (with some 5300 ha for industrial sites and 1500 km of pipelines within the port) and its impact on planning decisions is high, but its visibility to the general public in everyday life is low.(9) The pipeline network that links Rotterdam with Antwerp (where the big ships can no longer dock and where the petrochemical industry needs petroleum) and with Germany is largely out of sight.(10) The oil companies share other parts of the infrastructure, such as important rail and highway networks, with general users, who do not easily identify them as part of oil networks either. Recent headquarter buildings such as the one for BP erected in the port area, feature a green roof and advertise a stated turn toward environmental friendliness.

Oil infrastructures have become part of the area's collective imaginary. Heritage debates in the Netherlands document the ways in which spaces of oil have entered the wider public's imagination. Public attitudes about the companies, and about the history of oil in the Netherlands more broadly, affect debates on the selection of monuments for the historic preservation register, which protects some buildings and structures as official parts of the country's history. Historical oil landscapes, including remnants of industrial drilling such as the oil pumpjack Ja-knikker in Schoonebeek, are already included in the register of monuments. As citizens and public decision-makers decide which structures count as heritage, they also decide on a narrative of oil modernity, one that is not usually openly debated. These heritage stories need to be carefully prepared considering both local and global contexts and in line with shared developments around the North Sea.

Changes in the refining business will affect ports, cities, and transportation infrastructure, and those entities will have to formulate planning strategies in response. Places where oil is still physically present will require more extensive clean-up and transformation investment than the headquarters and research buildings or the ancillary buildings that are part of everyday usage. As refineries and storage areas around the North Sea disappear, they will require extensive and specialized cleanup. Even cleaned up, the refineries will be difficult to integrate into their neighboring cities: they will remain valuable to the oil industry due to the extensive specialised networks that they are integrated in and that continue being used, and they are often located in specialized areas of the port that are difficult for ordinary people to access.

This history shows that oil industry, in close collaboration with national governments, has materially not only shaped the port and its links to the sea, but the entire Randstad and its hinterland, through headquarter buildings, retail, infrastructure, and ancillary buildings. Other port cities around the North Sea have experienced similar pressures. They have pursued their own urban, port, and coastal development, ones that still need to be mapped. The petroleumscape, fed by maritime traffic and oil extraction, is an excellent example of the urbanisation of the sea. Using the petroleumscape as an analytical lens allows for a multi-disciplinary investigation of planetary urbanisation as well, allowing us to transcend disciplinary and sectorial borders, to unpack entanglements and relations that cross maritime spaces, and to develop new design approaches that include not only land-based, but also sea-based, spaces and that recognize the viscous nature of the territories at the edge between land and water.

Oil has taken hold of our built environment and corporate and public actors as well as independent artists and citizens who have celebrated it. Citizens and politicians must gain an awareness of the enormous scale of oil's presence and its representation in order to support new energy values in line with a post-oil society, and to create new imaginaries of that post-oil life. We need to recognize the importance of the built environment and its representation—whether established through petroleum or not—in the construction of power systems. A single but world-encompassing industry has created path dependencies in multiple nations and locations; that is, the long lifespan of built things perpetuates oil dependency. This industry continues to shape our value systems, imaginaries, and decision making. All of this makes it particularly difficult for societies to overcome oil dependency and promote new energy practices.

Dominic Boyer and Imre Szeman argued in a 2014 article, "The Rise of Energy Humanities" that "today's energy and environmental dilemmas are fundamentally problems of ethics, habits, values, institutions, belief, and power."(11) They also argue that the failure to imagine new solutions is partly due to a lack of understanding of how oil works in culture and to examine the difficulties we now face in overcoming oil dependency.(12) Studying the spatial and representational layers of the petroleumscape can help us take on the many challenges in replacing them, including cleaning and redeveloping polluted areas, redeveloping and reimagining former oil sites, developing and preserving infrastructure (such as highways) from the oil age, rethinking gas stations and headquarters, and designing new sustainable spaces with as ubiquitous and with as strong an affective character as the spaces of oil.

If the represented layer of the petroleumscape influences how people generate a new physical petroleumscape and its buildings and urban forms, then this inclusive approach to oil is fundamental to any rethinking of energy usage and sustainable architecture and to breaking up the feedback loop.(13) Changing it is perhaps the second step (after understanding history) in creating fossil-free energy landscapes. We also need to generate new imaginaries of fossil-free technologies, images, and practices that allow the general public to embrace these technologies and create new landscapes. Architectural and urban design can help implement such changes, including through studio design at universities. After all, traditional windmills and canals were also originally engineering devices and have now become part of the national imagination and a tourist attraction. Couldn't we achieve the same for new technologies? In the design studio Beyond Oil at the TU Delft, students explore future scenarios and propose transition strategies. In 2018, for example, Ege Cakir proposed large autonomous 'animals' that will roam the site of the former TOTAL refinery in Dunkirk, a port city in Northern France, to clean up the soil and to make the changing remediation landscape a recreational park. Select oil structures—refinery elements and storage tanks—remain as sculptures in the landscape, a strong reminder of the industrial petroleumscape and its negative impact on the environment and health [Fig. 4, p. 178]. History, both its writing and its remnants in the built environment, is a powerful tool in relation to design: we can help shape the future by carefully re-reading and re-presenting the past.

(1) Nancy Couling and Carola Hein, "Blankness: The Architectural Void of North Sea Energy Logistics," *Footprint*, no. 23 (2018).
(2) Henri Lefebvre, *The Production of Space* (Blackwell, 1991). 26–27
(3) Lukasz Stanek, *Henri Lefebvre on Space: Architecture, Urban Research, and the Production of Theory* (University of Minnesota Press); Lefebvre, *The Production of Space*; Henri Lefebvre, *A Critique of Everyday Life* (London: Verso, 1991).
(4) Carola Hein, "Analyzing the Palimpsestic Petroleumscape of Rotterdam," *Global Urban History Blog* (2016); "Port Cities: Nodes in the Global Petroleumscape between Sea and Land," *Technosphere Magazine* (2017); "Between Oil and Water. The Logistical Petroleumscape," in *The Petropolis of Tomorrow*, ed. Neeraj Bhatia and Mary Casper (New York: Actar / Architecture at Rice, 2013); "Global Landscapes of Oil," *New Geographies* 2 (2009).
(5) Ferry de Goey, *Comparative Port History of Rotterdam and Antwerp (1880–2000): Competition, Cargo and Costs* (Amsterdam: Aksant, 2004); Reginald Loyen, Erik Buyst, and Greta Devos, *Struggling for Leadership: Antwerp-Rotterdam Port Competition between 1870–2000* (New York: Springer, 2003).
(6) Ferry de Goey, *Ruimte Voor Industrie. Rotterdam en ee Vestiging Van Industrie in de Haven 1945–1975* (Rotterdam1990). Gerard J. Borghuis, *Veertig Jaar NAM: de geschiedenis van de Nederlandse aardolie maatschapij 1947–1987* (Aardolie Maatschappij B.V., 1987)
(7) Denis Wood, *Power of Maps* (New York City: Guilford Press, 1992).
(8) For map covers and the Rotterdam refinery map by BP from 1970, see "Oil Company Roadmaps from the Netherlands," http://www.petrolmaps.co.uk/country/maps-nl.htm (last visited 15 July 2015).
(9) Port of Rotterdam, Netherlands, "Port of Rotterdam" http://www.ship-technology.com/projects/portofrotterdam/ (accessed 15.7.2015)
(10) There is also an extensive NATO pipeline system; see "Central Europe Pipeline System (CEPS)" (http://www.nato.int/cps/en/natolive/topics_49151.htm?selectedLocale=en) (accessed 15.7.2015)
(11) Dominic Boyer and Imre Szeman, "The Rise of Energy Humanities: Breaking the Impasse," *University Affairs* (2014), http://www.universityaffairs.ca/opinion/in-my-opinion/the-rise-of-energy-humanities/ (accessed July 4 2017).
(12) See, e.g., Jo Clarke, Mel Evans, Hayley Newman, Kevin Smith, Glen Tarman, eds., *Culture Beyond Oil: Not If but When* (London: Platform, 2011), http://platformlondon.org/cbo.pdf (July 10th 2017); Imre Szeman, Sheena Wilson, and Adam Carlson, eds., *Petrocultures: Oil, Energy, and Culture* (Montreal: McGill-Queen's University Press, 2017); Imre Szeman and Dominic Boyer, Energy Humanities-an Anthology, (Baltimore: Johns Hopkins University Press, 2017).
(13) Dominic Boyer, "Special Collection: Energopower and Biopower in Transition," *Anthropological Quarterly* 87, no. 2 (2014).

Chapter 10 NORTH SEA UNLIMITED

Serge F. van Gessel, Lennert J. Goemans, & Jan Matthijsen

The North Sea is a complex composition of spaces, development potentials, resources, and infrastructure. The dynamic interaction of these components together with the changing North Sea ecosystem, is discussed by Serge F. van Gessel, Lennert J. Goemans, and Jan Matthijsen in terms of different limits, in particular how they influence policy-making on the Dutch continental shelf.

Serge F. van Gessel, serge.vangessel@tno.nl: Researcher and adviser at TNO - Energy Transition focusing on the role of sub-surface energy in climate and energy policy.

Lennert J. Goemans, l.goemans@minez.nl: Senior policy officer at the Dutch Ministry of Economic Affairs and Climate Policy, working in the field of integrated area development, water, nature, energy, and mobility.

Jan Matthijsen, jan.matthijsen@pbl.nl: Researcher at the Dutch Environmental Assessment Agency (PBL), working in the field of climate, energy, air quality. and spatial planning.

If you are standing on the beach or sailing on a ship, the North Sea looks wide and empty. For spatial planners and policy makers, however, the opposite is true. The North Sea is one of the most densely used and industrialised seas in the world [Fig. 1, p. 179]. The Dutch continental shelf measures about 58,000 km2 and accommodates 4,000 km of shipping routes with 260,000 vessels passing each year, 160 oil and natural gas platforms connected by 4,500 km of gas transport pipelines, 3,300 km of energy and communication transport cables, six "Natura 2000" areas (total 11,400 km2), fishing grounds, areas for military use, and ten wind farm areas, five of which are to be built before 2023. For the highly urbanised Dutch society, the North Sea is therefore a crucial space, fulfilling vital functions and inextricably linked to the land-side areas of settlement it serves. Policy-making for the sea is becoming equally as complex as it is on land.

The Dutch national administration is the main authority for planning and regulating the Dutch part of the North Sea. The room for manoeuvring is first of all set by fixed physical boundaries in the form of natural resources and capacities at the surface (e.g., aggregates) and sub-surface (oil and gas). The latter are more specifically defined here as geological boundaries and have been the driver for the extensive industrialisation of the North Sea for the past fifty years. The resulting infrastructure opens opportunities for re-use and at the same time sets limits on where future activities can take place. In addition, there are delineations such as nature protection areas (e.g., Natura 2000), licenses, and areas targeted for specific purposes (e.g., shipping lanes, military practice areas). These are regarded as policy (or legal) boundaries, which are negotiable and demarcate the rules for planning the seascape, preserving aspects of the landscape either as a part of nature or culture, and exploiting physical space and commodities.

The ambition to accomodate national and international developments relating to the energy transition, nature conservation, fishery, marine feedstocks, and more will lead to new and increasing pressures on the North Sea. These developments will result in new or redefined physical boundaries (e.g., sites for wind farms, new infrastructure) and adaptation of policy boundaries. These changing boundaries present us with new challenges, but to what extent? Will the number of wind farms in the North Sea be limited by policies intended to encourage a robust North Sea marine life and will there be enough space left for fishing? When will limits be irreversably crossed, and what would be the consequences of unlimited development? Scenario studies help us investigate possible pathways, bottlenecks, and solutions. Not a blueprint for solutions, they are useful as a way to identify and explore the ingredients of future policy strategies. They allow consideration of the complex and dynamic parameters characteristic of sea-space and of multiple perspectives in a fluctuating, uncertain environment. They can offer a "maritime" perspective that contrasts with the "extensions" of land-based logic that have until recently determined the space (with or without planning).

GEOLOGICAL BOUNDARIES

The industrialisation of the North Sea is largely connected to the discovery of oil and gas. This is reflected in the vast network of hydrocarbon production facilities and interconnecting gas transport pipelines that enable the extraction of numerous oil and gas accumulations in the United Kingdom, Dutch, German, Danish and Norwegian Exclusive Economic Zones of the North Sea. The mining of aggregates (mainly sand for coastal suppletion and surface leveling on land) represents another industrial activity related to coastal protection.

Natural gas and oil have their origins in geological processes covering a total period of some 300 million years.(1) During this time, the North Sea area transformed repeatedly between swamp, desert, delta, and shallow sea environments. The presence of oil and gas fields in the North Sea is the end result of sediment deposition in these environments (source rocks, reservoir rocks, and sealing rocks), deep burial in a net-subsiding basin (initiating the generation of oil and gas from organic matter) and rock deformations (creating large-scale structures in which the generated oil and gas became trapped). The spatial outline and characteristics of oil and gas fields are unchangeable on human time-scales and jointly define the geological boundaries. The same holds true for the distribution of aggregate resources in the North Sea and sea floor morphology.

PHYSICAL LIMITS OF EXISTING INFRASTRUCTURE

While geological boundaries are fixed, the purpose and relevance of geological space (i.e., the use of the resource as well as the remaining space after production) may vary over time as the political, economic, and societal context changes. This is clearly illustrated by the historic exploration and development of natural gas resources in the North Sea. In 1959, the onshore giant natural gas field of Groningen was discovered, followed by policy decisions to deploy natural gas as a national resource for residential heating. As a result, gas quickly became the number one energy resource for the Netherlands. The production of natural gas was further stimulated by growing demand in neighbouring countries. Although the first natural gas discoveries in the Dutch sector of the North Sea occurred in 1962, it took another ten years before offshore production came online; the industry postponed the construction of offshore hydrocarbon production and transportation infrastructure until the volume of discovered reserves justified the investments. Then, economic conditions for production improved as new legislation and the policy for small gas fields by 1974 guaranteed sales of offshore natural gas.(2)

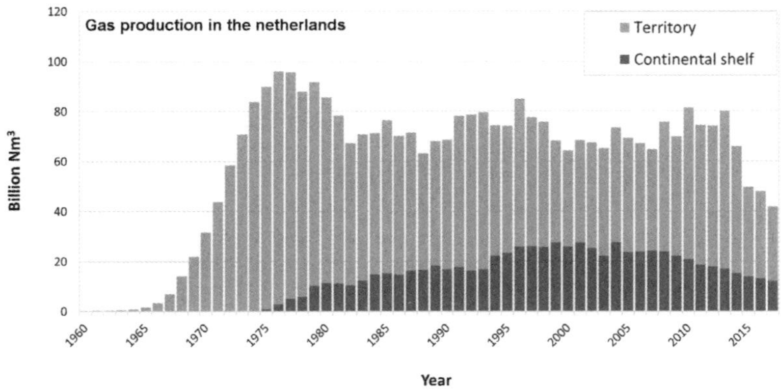

Fig. 2
Hydrocarbon developments in the Netherlands

The development of hydrocarbons was further stimulated by the 1970s oil crisis, which encouraged domestic production to safeguard the Netherlands and other countries against energy supply crises. Production peaked at the start of the twenty-first century [Fig. 2].

Since 2010, the production of hydrocarbons on the Dutch continental shelf has been declining. According to current projections, by 2040 natural gas production in the Netherlands will be less than 5 billion m3 per year.(3) Most gas fields will cease production by 2030. When production stops, the owner of the platform is legally obliged to remove the infrastructure and close off access. However, because of the high costs of abandonment as well as the potential strategic and economic value of offshore infrastructure, it may be worthwhile to investigate whether the heritage of over fifty years of offshore petroleum history can be re-deployed to help fulfill climate goals and renewable energy ambitions.

Several initiatives investigate the added value of re-using depleted natural gas fields and linked infrastructure in order to support the accelerating development of offshore wind energy and the reduction of CO2 emissions.(4) The first option is the electrification—using wind power—of platforms still in use to decrease offshore natural gas consumption and CO2 emissions linked to hydrocarbon production. The second option is deployment of suspended gas production platforms or potential future artificial islands as energy hubs for redirecting, transforming, and converting electricity from wind energy. By using hydrogen as a carrier for wind energy and the existing gas network for transport, congestion problems in the power grid may be solved (specifically at the landing points) when the number of offshore wind farms increases.

The third option relating to the potential use of depleted fields and infrastructure concerns the sub-surface storage of CO2, which is considered to be the only viable solution for a significant emission reduction in the short term. Studies have indicated that depleted natural gas fields in the Dutch continental shelf hold ample storage capacity to sequestrate CO2 from major emitters until 2050 and beyond.(5) A fourth alternative involves energy storage. Offshore natural gas fields and platforms could be used to buffer energy in the form of hydrogen. This way, energy can be stored when there is a surplus of wind power, and at times of low wind, hydrogen can be produced to sustain power output at desired levels.

The above options all depend on the availability of hydrocarbon infrastructure and natural gas fields. This means that both existing geological limits and infrastructure limits will influence the future development of the North Sea. With the presence, relocation, or development of other functions, conflicts of interest may arise where policy boundaries are needed for decisions and regulation.

POLICY BOUNDARIES

To the Netherlands, the North Sea is of great socio-cultural and historical significance. The current Dutch national policy vision for the North Sea has been established in the North Sea 2050 Spatial Agenda and incorporated into the North Sea Policy Document. Both documents take international policy into account, for example, as set forth in the European Marine Strategy Framework Directive.(6) The main goal of the European Marine Strategy Framework Directive is to achieve a Good Environmental Status, meaning that marine resources are used in a sustainable manner, ensuring their continuity for future generations.(7) The Netherlands will benefit from a safe, clean, healthy, and ecologically diverse North Sea that helps satisfy economic and social needs. This goal, however, becomes progressively ambitious, since the uses of the sea are in a state of transition due to several factors, including the depletion of oil and natural gas reserves under the North Sea and climate change and an increasing number of environmental pressures.

Together with civil-society organisations, the new Dutch policy for the North Sea aims for desired use in terms of space, time, ecology, and economy, and to continue to develop the natural potential of the sea and coast. Therefore, the Dutch national government follows a development-based approach to the sea, one that leaves room for new initiatives and flexible management. Based on this vision, the emphasis in the period from now until 2050 will be on five themes: building with nature, the energy transition at sea, multiple/multifunctional uses of the space, connecting land and sea, and accessibility/shipping. International collaboration and export opportunities play a significant role in all five themes. In this respect, the physical boundaries present the possibilities and limitations of options, while policy provides directives for planning and regulation.

The Dutch policy for the North Sea focusing on energy transition has been laid down in consequtive versions of the National Water Plan (NWP) 2009–2015, where the areas "Borssele" and "IJmuiden Ver" are designated and the "Hollandse Kust" and "Ten Noorden van de Waddeneilanden" are "search areas," where in principle, construction of wind farms is allowed.(8) Through an interim revision of the NWP beginning in 2014, "Hollandse Kust" and "Ten Noorden van de Waddeneilanden" were designated for wind energy at sea. This policy is being continued in the NWP 2016–2021.(9)

Within the boundaries of the NWP and in collaboration with several stakeholders, the Dutch national government implemented the policy goals with two road maps for wind energy [Fig. 3, p. 180]. The first road map, aimed at 4.5 GW of generating offshore wind capacity, was published in 2014 in a policy brief provided to the parliament, followed by an update in 2018 with an additional 7.0 GW of offshore wind by 2030, published by the Dutch Ministry of Economic Affairs and Climate Policy, bringing the Netherlands' total offshore wind capacity to 11.5 GW.(10) Once operational, these offshore wind farms would make an important contribution toward reaching the goal of reducing greenhouse gas emissions 49 percent by 2030 compared with the base year 1990, the climate goal set by the Dutch Climate Bill, which is the national implementation of the 2015 Paris Climate Agreement.

Preparations for the first wind farm zone under the 2030 road map "Hollandse Kust (west)" with a total capacity of 1.4 GW, are being developed by the Netherlands Enterprise Agency (RVO.nl) and the Dutch national electricity transmission system operator (TenneT), to be followed by "Ten Noorden van de Waddeneilanden" (0.6 GW) and "IJmuiden Ver" (4 GW). In compiling the road maps, several policy principles have been applied. Free visual horizons are preserved as much as possible. Wind farms in nature preservation areas, sand extraction areas, shipping lanes, and military areas are prohibited. Reducing the national cost is also an important issue, meaning that wind farms must be situated close to the coast, which may produce friction with the policy principle of preserving free horizons. Wind farms have a standard size of about 0.7 GW so the grid connection can be standardised, contributing to a significant cost reduction. Finally, the multiple use of space has been prioritised whenever possible. As a result, wind farms will also be open for recreational use.

CHANGING BOUNDARIES

Pressure on space and the ecology of the North Sea will continue to increase in the coming decades. What are the spatial and ecological consequences of plausible developments in the North Sea and, in particular, on the Dutch continental shelf? What are the policy implications?

We chose to investigate the future of the North Sea in 2030 and 2050 using scenarios.(11) These North Sea scenarios do not represent policy plans or blueprints for the future, but describe possible and desirable future states of the North Sea and the developments and policies required to achieve them. We developed the North Sea scenarios by applying two development pathways to two important scenario dimensions:

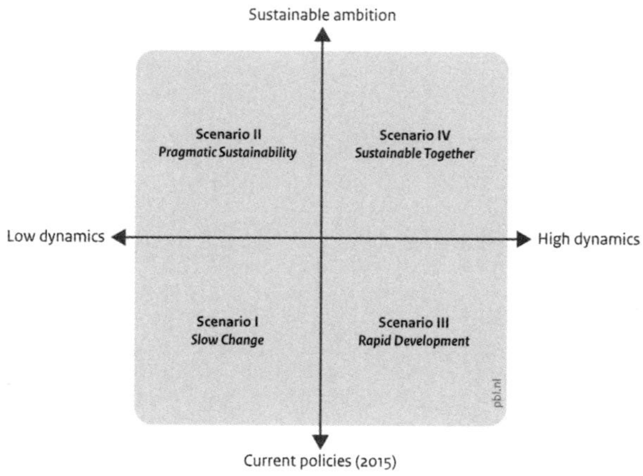

Fig. 4
Positioning of the North Sea Scenarios (PBL)

1. the economy and society—low or high dynamism;
2. policy ambition—current policies or sustainable ambitions.

Combining these two development pathways results in four scenarios [Fig. 4].

The scenario study addresses ongoing policy developments concerning the future of the North Sea. These developments include the Paris Climate Agreement, EU Marine Strategy Framework Directive, the EU directive for Maritime Spatial Planning, and the North Seas Energy Cooperation.(12)

The scenarios focus primarily on the main Dutch policy themes regarding the North Sea: the energy transition, resilient ecosystems and a sustainable food supply. We will also address defence and cultural heritage, although in less detail. We have selected two of the scenarios as representative opposite use cases. [Table 1] gives an overview of the main differences per policy theme between scenarios I and IV. Scenario IV is the only scenario in which the Netherlands attains its national climate goal and scenario I is the opposite scenario in terms of the chosen dimensions.

The maps give a comprehensive overview of the situation on the Dutch continental shelf and in the surrounding North Sea as a whole according to the scenarios for 2050. These maps also show spatial developments in parts of the exclusive economic zones of the other North Sea countries.(13) [Fig. 5, p. 181 & Fig. 6, p. 182].

In the scenarios, it is assumed that all oil and natural gas activities will have stopped on the Dutch continental shelf by 2050. The point at which this takes place depends on developments in CO2 and fossil fuel prices in the scenarios: by 2030 in scenario IV and by 2050 in scenario I. To give some idea of the developments in oil and natural gas in each scenario, the maps show the situation for 2030.

Scenario I, "Slow Change," is a business-as-usual scenario under unfavourable socio-economic and political conditions (e.g., partial implementation of climate agreement, hard Brexit). By 2050, a limited

	Scenario I "Slow Change"	*Scenario IV "Sustainable Together"*
National and international developments	Stagnating globalisation and partial implementation of climate agreements	Continued globalisation and climate agreements implemented
National and international policy	Focus on growth and jobs, hard Brexit, and greenhouse gas reduction target of 45% compared with 1990	Focus on circular economy, trade agreement with UK and greenhouse gas reduction target of 100% compared with 1990
Energy transition	12 GW offshore wind power, oil and natural gas reserves depleted, no Carbon Capture and Storage (CCS)	60 GW offshore wind power, oil and natural gas reserves quickly uneconomic, 50 Mt CCS
Resilient ecosystems	Same nature areas as in 2015, biodiversity also improves outside nature areas, Good Environmental Status achieved in around 2030	International nature network realised, biodiversity improves the most in this scenario, Good Environmental Status (high ambition) achieved around 2030
Sustainable food supply	Some innovation in fisheries sector, sustainable in the long term; limited developments in aquaculture	Strong innovation in fisheries sector, sustainable in the very short term; very strong developments in aquaculture
Shipping	Shipping activities move northwards	Shipping activities move to Scandinavia and the Baltic
Cables and pipelines	Oil and natural gas infrastructure remains in place after 2030; few electricity cables and connection points; twice as many telecommunications cables as in 2015	CCS infrastructure and possibly pipelines for hydrogen from steam; many electricity cables and connection points, 3 "energy hub islands"; 4 times as many telecommunications cables as in 2015
Sand extraction	60 million m^3	40 million m^3
Recreation	Strong decrease	Increase
Defence	More intensive use of exercise areas	Less intensive use; more movements to and from bases

Table 1
General description of the physical, and environment changes in the scenarios

number of wind farms have been installed over an area of less than 5 percent of the Dutch continental shelf [Fig. 5, p. 181]. (yellow area) Fishing is forbidden within this area. The nature reserve area remains the same size it was in 2015 (green area). Current policies will lead to the so-called Good Environmental Status by 2030. The hard Brexit, as assumed in Scenario I, will have a particularly large impact on the seabed (demersal) fishing industry. Demersal fishing will move to the Dutch, German, and Danish part of the North Sea, increasing the pressure on fish stocks in these areas caused by an overcapacity of fishing vessels. This may necessitate further cutbacks in the sector. In 2050, climate policies will have led to a failure to reach the goals of the Paris Agreement with a greenhouse gas reduction of only 45 percent in the Netherlands.(14) As a result, the global temperature increases by 2 °C by 2050 and 4 °C by 2100. The North Pole remains ice-free for longer periods of the year, opening up a northern shipping route between north-western Europe and Northeast Asia. Seawater temperatures increase due to climate change, acidification of the sea continues, and sea level will rise by 35 centimetres by 2050. Consequently, the Netherlands needs more sand from the North Sea for coastal protection.

In Scenario IV, "Sustainable Together," sustainable policy ambitions are put into practice within a setting of high socio-economic developments and geopolitical conditions favouring international cooperation. Globalisation and growing environmental awareness result in ambitious global action to reach the goals set by the Paris Climate Agreement, resulting in a lower climate change impact than in Scenario I [Fig. 6, p. 182]. The contributing elements to the North Sea in Scenario IV are many more wind farms, capture and storage of CO2 in depleted natural gas fields, and the early retirement of offshore oil and natural gas production. By 2050, wind farms cover up to about 25 percent or less of the Dutch continental shelf. The Netherlands becomes a net exporter of electricity, and part of the electricity it generates is used to produce green gas such as hydrogen. A more efficient infrastructure system at sea and on land is developed to accommodate the large growth in wind energy and wind farms located further offshore. Two new infrastructural elements are added in these scenarios: one or more "energy hub islands" and a network of high-capacity interconnection cables for wind farms.(15)

Nature has the greatest amount of protection in this scenario, leading to a considerable improvement of biodiversity in the North Sea. The main contributors to this improvement are the creation of international nature networks and a ban on fishing activities in nature area. A sustainable food supply is achieved in this scenario through a transition from fishing to aquaculture. There is a shift in demand to more plant-based food, which means that sustainable sea vegetable farming also expands considerably. Fish farming takes place in offshore closed-containment systems (sea farms). Some of the wind farms are designed to include aquaculture and fishing activities to mitigate the impact on the fisheries sector.

OPPORTUNITIES, BOTTLENECKS, AND SOLUTIONS

Changing circumstances and pressure factors may radically change the North Sea in the coming decades. The directions of change vary considerably in the different scenarios. In all scenarios, specific problems arise which need special attention and dedicated action.

In Scenario I, "Slow Change," the physical boundaries are subject to more severe impacts of climate change (sea level rise or ecosystem changes). In the short term, a hard Brexit has a strong impact on policy boundaries on the North Sea for the fishing sector. In the longer term, the scenario includes a continuation of severe impacts of climate change. The impacts can be seen as a consequence of international policy inaction and they need solutions in the form of adaptation strategies.

In Scenario IV, "Sustainable Together," many problems are assumed to have been tackled by future national and international policy actions. A rapid increase in wind power is combined with improved biodiversity and/or fishing, meaning that biodiversity and nature protection areas can profit from the presence of wind farms and, within these farms, fishing may be allowed subject to restrictions. Timely steps are taken to facilitate the transport of electricity to land, possibly including the conversion of electricity into hydrogen and the construction of energy hub islands. Future policy actions in this scenario result in a vast increase of multiple uses of space. However, these policies are largely still to be developed and the outcome highly uncertain. For instance, we assume that measures can be taken to sufficiently protect nature given the vast growth of wind farms and other activities on the North Sea in Scenario IV, but it is unclear whether this will be possible. There are signs that birds and also bats may suffer from a vast network of wind farms across the North Sea without interventions like switching off wind turbines during migration. But even with such interventions, it remains uncertain whether the negative effects on birdlife can be sufficiently abated given the unprecedented increase in wind farms. The negative effects of wind farms on underwater nature are believed to be minimal and may even be positive, however the effects have been measured with only a limited number of wind turbines present. Negative effects may also add to other environmental pressures such as climate change. These sorts of problems ask for agile policy actions and the need for continuous monitoring.

DISCUSSION AND CONCLUSION

In this chapter we reflected on the physical/geological and policy boundaries associated with the development of the North Sea. In the future these boundaries will change. The geological evolution of the North Sea has established distinct and unchangeable limits with respect to hydrocarbon resources and storage capacities, yet these restrictions also present multiple options for re-deployment of depleted oil and natural gas fields and infrastructures. We are standing at a cross-roads with regard to the further development of the North Sea sub-surface. Will we exit and abandon the existing oil and natural gas infrastructures all together, or do we enter a new era where we redeploy these for CCS, energy storage, and the support of renewable energy generation? Timing is important when it comes to synergy between oil and natural gas exploitation, offshore wind energy, CCS, and possible conversion into the sub-surface storage of hydrogen. What options are available in terms of achieving the best result, and what are the obstacles? The answer to these questions will largely depend on the continuation of oil and gas exploration (to buy more time) and a timely and successful roll-out of CCS activities. In this respect, the economics of infrastructure maintenance, the investment climate, and the regulatory framework will influence future boundaries.

In 2019, the Dutch national government began consulting with North Sea stakeholders in order to establish broad support for agreements on future developments of the Dutch part of the

North Sea. This bottom-up approach has resulted in the North Sea Agreement of the negiotiating parties on 5 February 2020, which will —when adopted by the grassroots supporters—form the governance basis for the implementation of North Sea policies as set forth in documents such as the Strategic North Sea Agenda 2030.(16) The national North Sea Agreement includes, among other measures, important further development of wind farms, a restructuring of the fishery fleet, and measures to restore the resilience of marine ecosystems.

CHANGING BOUNDARIES

The scenarios presented in this chapter were established by the Dutch Environmental Assessment Agency (PBL) in 2017 and have contributed to the North Sea Agreement by providing a common view on possible future developments and a common basis for further joint fact-finding with broad support of stakeholders. The scenarios involve plausible future developments. Since we published these scenarios, some of the possible developments have already occurred, for example Brexit in Scenario I and an ambitious, legally binding national climate goal for 2030 in Scenario IV. Although real developments are part of different scenarios, the bandwidth of all four can still be viewed as representative. Insights of the study as a whole are therefore still useful and relevant.

Planning and policy-making for the sea is different from that for land. Utilisation of the sea historically has been led by maritime industries, with a limited number of stakeholders and limited concerns for planning. Increasing use means increasing groups and affected parties with a range of different interests and concerns: social, heritage, recreational, ecological, and economical. Legislation of sea space is also increasing at national and international levels at the same time as the energy transition has become more urgent. Sea space plays a crucial role in the transition. These factors can be seen as part of urbanisation processes, where extensions of land-based needs have led to the proliferation of spatial limits to the sea. In addition, the ecological capacity of the sea itself is also limited. At the cross-roads where we, as policy planners, now stand, we cannot draw on previous experience: the sea is a recent realm of policy-making, hence future speculations are full of unknowns and new tools must be sought and developed. The scenarios described are examples to explore ways forward within this complex, urgent, volatile, and challenging situation.

(1) Theo Edward Wong, D. A. J Batjes, and Jan de Jager, *Geology of the Netherlands* (Amsterdam: Royal Netherlands Academy of Arts and Sciences KNAW, 2007).
(2) "Kleine Gasvelden", (small gas fields), archive of the Dutch national website, https://web.archive.org/web/20120331124219/http://www.rijksoverheid.nl/onderwerpen/gas/gasexploratie-en-productie/kleine-gasvelden (31 March 2012, in Dutch)
(3) Dutch Ministry of Economic Affairs and Climate Policy, *Natural resources and Geothermal energy in the Netherlands 2017*, (The Hague: Dutch Ministry of Economic Affairs and Climate Policy, 2018).
(4) Klimaatwinst door systeemintegratie op de Noordzee (North Sea Energy), 2018.
(5) EBN and Gasunie, "Transport en Opslag van CO2 in Nederland", (2018) (A national assessment on CO2 transport and storage in Dutch), https://www.ebn.nl/wp-content/uploads/2018/07/Studie-Transport-en-opslag-van-CO2-in-Nederland-EBN-en-Gasunie.pdf
(6) Dutch Ministry of Infrastructure & the Environment and Dutch Ministry of Economic Affairs,"Policy Document on the North Sea 2016-2021" (The Hague: Dutch Ministry of Infrastructure & the Environment, December 2015), https://www.noordzeeloket.nl/en/policy/noordzeebeleid/@166985/policy-document/; Ministry of Infrastructure and the Environment and Ministry of Economic Affairs, "North Sea 2050 Spatial Agenda" (The Hague: Ministry of Infrastructure and the Environment, 28 July 2014), https://www.noordzeeloket.nl/en/publications/
(7)"Achieve Good Environmental Status", the main goal of the Marine Directive is to achieve Good Environmental Status of EU marine waters by 2020. Last updated 31 December 2019, https://ec.europa.eu/environment/marine/good-environmental-status/index_en.htm
(8) Dutch Ministry of VROM and the Dutch Ministry of LNV, *National Water Plan 2009–2015* (The Hague: Dutch Ministry of VROM and the Dutch Ministry of LNV, 2009). https://www.noordzeeloket.nl/publish/pages/126213/nationaal_waterplan_2009-2015.pdf
(9) Dutch Ministry of Infrastructure and the Environment and the Dutch Ministry of Economic Affairs, 2015. National Water Plan 2016–2021, The Hague. https://www.noordzeeloket.nl/publish/pages/122261/national_water_plan_2016–2021_4948.pdf
(10) Dutch Ministry of Economic Affairs, *Windenergie op zee* (The Hague: Dutch Ministry of Economic Affairs, 2014); https://www.noordzeeloket.nl/publish/pages/122001/kamerbrief_over_windenergie_op_zee_3373.pdf
Dutch Ministry of Economic Affairs, *Routekaart windenergie op zee 2030*, (The Hague: Dutch Ministry of Economic Affairs and Climate, 2018), (https://www.noordzeeloket.nl/publish/pages/142779/kamerbrief-routekaart-windenergie-op-zee-2030.pdf.
(11) Ed Dammers, Susan van 't Klooster, Henk Hilderink, Arthur Petersen, Willemijn Tuinstra and Bert de Wit, "Building scenarios for the environmental, nature and spatial planning policy", PBL publication no 3434, (The Hague: PBL Netherlands Environmental Assessment Agency, 2019).
(12) For details on the scenario study see the full report: Jan Matthijsen, Ed Dammers and Hans Elzenga, The Future of the North Sea. The North Sea in 2030 and 2050: a scenario study (The Hague: PBL Netherlands Environmental Assessment Agency, 2018), https://www.pbl.nl/sites/default/files/downloads/pbl-2018-the-future-of-the-north-sea-3193.pdf
(13) The locations, purpose, and size of the future wind farms, nature reserves and other possible developments are envisaged by the Netherlands Evironmental Assessment Agency purely for this publication.
(14) The Paris Agreement's central aim is to strengthen the global response to the threat of climate change by keeping a global temperature rise this century well below 2 degrees Celsius above pre-industrial levels and to pursue efforts to limit the temperature increase even further to 1.5 degrees Celsius.
(15) Energy hub islands would be like large oil platforms or more permanent structures built by hydraulic filling with sand. Such islands can serve as a location to manage electricity produced from neighboring wind farms.
(16) Noordzeeloket, "Development of the 2030 North Sea Strategy", https://www.noordzeeloket.nl/en/policy/development-2030/

Chapter 11 THE ANTHROPOGENIC SEASCAPE AND THE ENERGY TRANSITION: THE NEED FOR A NEW PERSPECTIVE ON MARINE NATURE AND HUMAN-MADE STRUCTURES

Anne-Mette Jørgensen

The North Sea is witnessing a frenzy of construction and dismantling activity, not only in the field of energy infrastructure, but also in the re-composition of once-natural habitats. Anne-Mette Jørgensen overturns the binary preconceptions about the human-made and natural ecosystems in the North Sea that still dominate planning, and shows what we risk losing in adhering to them.

Anne-Mette Jørgensen is an independent consultant and co-founder of North Sea Futures, an organisation focused on the relationship between offshore energy infrastructure, ecosystem services and other societal values in the North Sea. From 2010 to 2015, she led the Living North Sea Initiative (LiNSI), a North Sea-wide, science-based, multi-stakeholder programme exploring new opportunities for restoring a healthy and rich North Sea ecosystem through alternative approaches to decommissioning.

For humans, the North Sea has primarily been the realm of nomadic activities, namely fishing and various forms of water transportation. It has become a symbol of undisturbed wilderness, open horizons, and untamed nature.(1) However, in reality the current ecosystem of the North Sea is largely anthropogenic, shaped by centuries of human activity. With the ongoing urbanisation of the sea, this process will be further intensified. Since the discovery of oil and gas in the North Sea in the 1960s, the sea has become increasingly occupied by static installations that limit nomadic activities. With the dramatic growth of offshore wind and other energy-related fixtures projected for the years 2020 to 2050, a process of urbanisation is taking shape through cables, pipelines, maintenance activities, and artificial islands. The North Sea is becoming a physical extension of the land surrounding it, rather than a separate entity. To manage this process effectively, we need a new perspective on human-made structures in maritime spatial planning, one that accepts that the North Sea is a seascape of largely human manufacture, and one that is less based on sectoral distinctions and binary oppositions such as land/sea, nature/artificial, temporary/permanent, and open/closed space. A new perspective may allow decision-makers to work from a longer-term, more integrated vision of North Sea space and the interrelations between the growing number of semi-static, land-connected installations and the (human and marine) life around them. A new perspective could also help reduce costs of the energy transition and increase the quality and stability of the provision of ecosystem services.(2)

OFFSHORE INSTALLATIONS AND THE ENERGY TRANSITION

At present, some 1300 oil and gas installations are operational in the North Sea, including subsea installations fully under water and around 4000 wind turbines.(3) These installations are located in water depths ranging from 2 m (Mittelplatte in the German EEZ) to more than 800 m (Ormen Lange, Norwegian EEZ) and they occupy some 1,400–1,900 km2, or less than 0.5 percent of the total area of the North Sea.(4) So far, wind farms are located relatively near the coast in water depths of less than 30 m, but increasingly they are being constructed in deeper waters farther offshore.

With the transition to renewable energy and a shortage of space for onshore energy production, the current situation is expected to change dramatically over the next thirty to forty years. By 2050, it is projected that all oil and gas production in the North Sea will have ended, with related infrastructure either being reused or moved to shore. It is expected that between 10,000 and 25,000 new wind turbines will have been installed, occupying almost 10 percent of the total area of the North Sea (see chapter 14). For the Dutch part of the North Sea, scenarios have been presented in which energy-related activities occupy almost 25 percent of the area.(5) This implies a thirty- to forty-fold increase in the area reserved for energy production in the North Sea, meaning that it will be partially closed to those who might wish to use the sea for other purposes, including traditional nomadic ones. As wind farms are sited farther offshore, maintenance and the transportation of electricity back to shore become more expensive, which has led various stakeholders to propose constructing a maintenance island, on the Doggerbank, for example, possibly in combination with hydrogen production and storage. Such an island would be the first permanent settlement on the North Sea.(6)

Next to the rapidly growing spatial claims for energy production, the Netherlands Environmental Assessment Agency (Planbureau voor de Leefomgeving; PBL) estimates a 40 percent growth in shipping activity in the North Sea by 2050 and a two- to sixfold increase in the area occupied by telecom cables.(7) The North Sea is rapidly becoming an extension of industrial and urban settlements onshore. Meanwhile, the Convention for the Protection of the Marine Environment of the North-East Atlantic, known as the OSPAR Convention (OSPAR), has set a goal of protecting 10 percent of the North Sea as a marine protected area; many scientists and green NGOs would like to see 30 percent of the ocean "kept pristine and wild."(8) The result is that traditional activities like fishing are being limited to ever-smaller areas and fishers, like nomadic people on land, experience their culture and way of life as fundamentally threatened.(9)

OFFSHORE INSTALLATIONS AND THE NORTH SEA ECOSYSTEM

Despite the talk about "pristine and wild" areas, today's North Sea ecosystem is largely human-made or anthropogenic. Large areas that are now described and sometimes protected as "sandy habitats," were previously partially covered by "hard substrate" such as oyster and sabellaria reefs, boulders, moorlog, and cold-water coral reefs [Fig. 1.a, p. 183 & Fig. 1b, p. 184]. In 1883, 32 percent of the bottom of the Dutch North Sea was covered with oyster reefs. Now, as a result of intensive oyster fishing and bottom trawling, 98.5 percent is sand.(10) In the British, Danish, and German parts of the North Sea, similar changes have taken place. Today, North Sea "reefs" are — except for a few coastal locations — to a large extent made up of built structures, which have been placed on the sea bed for other reasons: oil and gas installations, wind turbines, pipelines, cables, and shipwrecks. Most of them are in areas with a soft sea bed of sand, gravel, or mud. [Fig. 1.b, p. 184 & Fig. 2, p. 184].

Although the area occupied by these structures is relatively small, they add significant biodiversity, because soft and hard substrates provide the basis for fundamentally different ecosystems. The presence of these structures has an impact — positive or negative — on almost all of the services provided by marine ecosystems [Fig. 3].

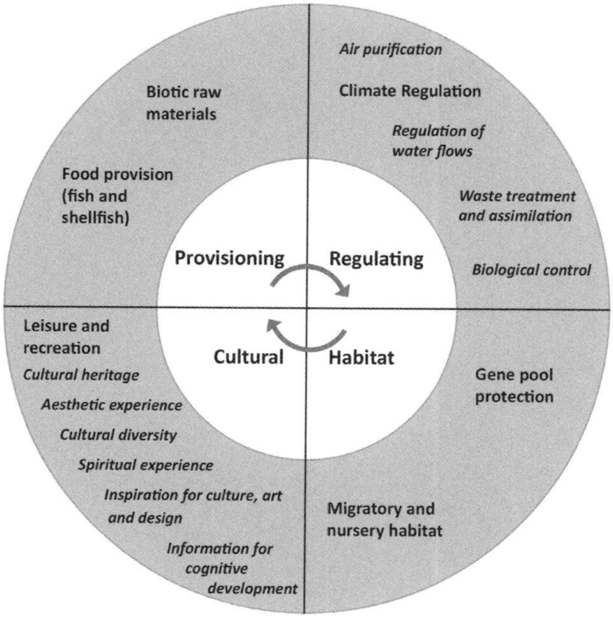

Fig. 3 Ecosystem Services for Marine Areas (Couling)

Offshore installations provide migratory and nursery habitats for reef-dependent species, (thereby protecting the gene pool), sometimes at the cost of other species that prefer a soft sea bed; they influence water flows and the ability of marine ecosystems to absorb nutrients (regulating); they generate additional biomass that provides food and biotic raw materials (provisioning), and they influence cultural services, for example by disturbing the aesthetic and spiritual experience of an open horizon (negative) and by serving as a landmark for orientation for sailors and fishermen (positive).

While the initial construction and placement of offshore installations may have a significant negative impact on the marine ecosystem (e.g., in terms of noise, sea bed disturbance, and vibrations), over the years, many of these structures come to host rich ecosystems that are home to a large variety of species, including some that are threatened, protected, and commercially valuable.(11) The richness of biodiversity on and around offshore structures is not only caused by the presence of hard substrate but also is due to the safety zones around the installations, which function as de facto marine protected areas.(12) Studies have shown that some offshore installations in the North Sea are interconnected with each other and with natural reefs. For *Lophelia pertusa* corals, for example, these installations seem to function as stepping stones connecting natural reefs that are otherwise isolated from each other.(13) [Fig. 4]. Interconnectivity is crucial to long-term species survival, especially in the face of climate change, which will force species to move to new areas with colder water.

With the growth in the quantity and proximity of offshore installations, the cumulative impact of the energy transition is likely to fundamentally change the North Sea ecosystem in ways that are still largely unknown.(14) The process may be compared to the process of terrestrial urbanisation, where the urban environment comes to play an increasingly important role in the survival of species, but with the fundamental difference that under current practice, offshore energy installations, being constructed and removed every twenty–thirty years, are much more transient than terrestrial infrastructure.(15) This transience is being shaped by the spatial planning and regulatory framework governing the offshore installations and a lack of integration of this framework in marine conservation policies. Maybe some "urban thinking" could help improve the coherence of policies governing "natural" and "artificial" ecosystems in the North Sea and hence increase ecological richness and stability.

LEGAL BASIS: TEMPORARY USE AND NATURE VERSUS HUMAN-MADE

In today's world, most people who experience the North Sea do so only from the coast, while enjoying leisurely activities like swimming, (kite-)surfing, sun-bathing, or taking a walk, enjoying the beauty of the sand, the open horizon, and the untamed waves and wind. Or we experience it through nature movies showing the richness of life underneath the waves. Our perception of the North Sea is clearly dominated by the image of an undisturbed wilderness and we do not like that image being disturbed by the sight of offshore installations or other reminders of the industrial work that takes place in harbours and further offshore. (16) Regulatory and maritime spatial-planning frameworks tend to reflect and reinforce the experience of nature, leisure, and industrial activities as separate realms by taking a highly sectoral approach, in which "nature" is attributed a high degree of permanence in time and space, whereas most human activities are seen as transient and generally as disturbing "original nature."(17)

Though maritime spatial planning is intended as "an integrative process to cope with the increasing demand for maritime space... while preserving the proper functioning of the marine ecosystems," the maps resulting from such processes reveal the extent to which it really is a matter of dividing nature and human activities and different sectors.(18) [Fig. 1, chapter 5]. There are remarkably few overlaps between sectoral activities and no reference to types or values of ecosystems in areas that are dedicated to human activities. In the recently presented Dutch North Sea Agreement, multifunctional use of space has been formulated as a guiding principle, which implies that "in the future, an offshore wind farm will never be just a wind farm."(19) This approach could allow for a larger amount of viscosity in spatial planning, recognising that human activities and rich ecosystems need not be mutually exclusive. However, it is in its

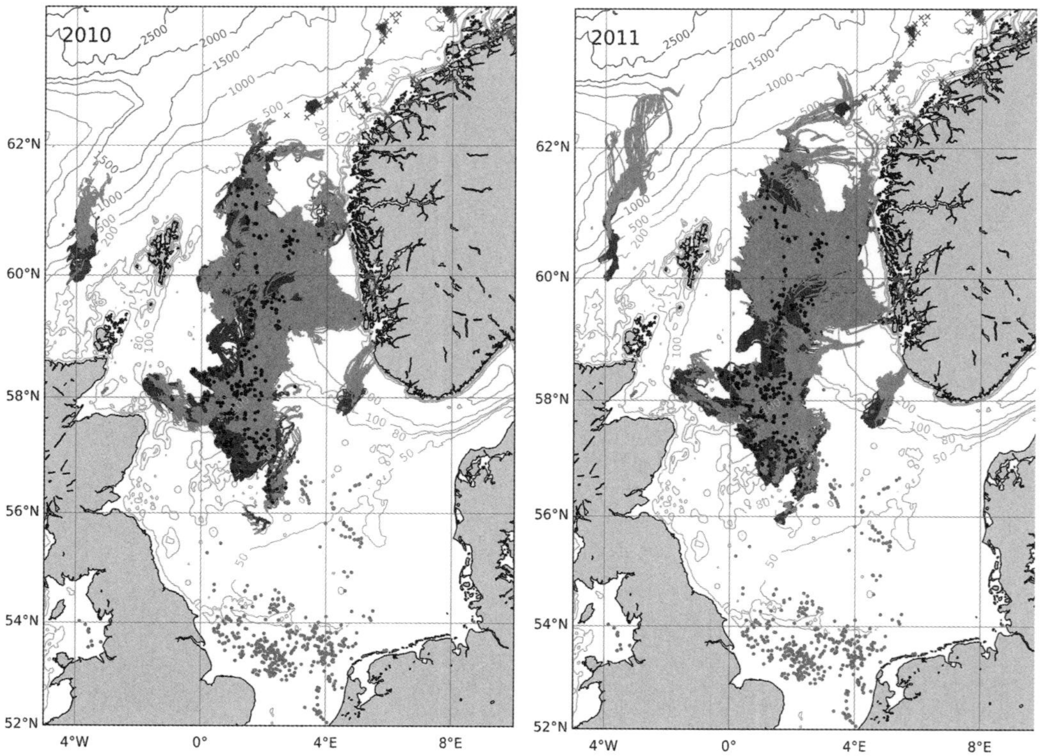

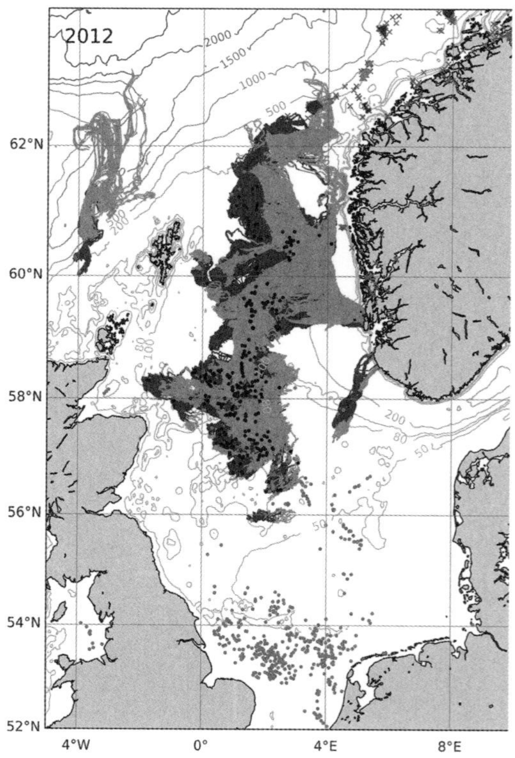

Fig. 4
Inter-annual variability in dispersal pathways of coral larvae released from North Sea oil and gas structures. Pathways of pre-competent (dark grey) and competent (light gey) larvae over deep-sea, shelf and fjordic coral ecosystems. Polygons northwest of Norway indicate coral marine protected areas and zones of high coral density and the crosses indicate occurrences of natural populations off the coast of Norway. Black (grey) dots indicate oil and gas structures included (excluded) from the analyses.

first stages in the Netherlands and still needs to be implemented in formal policies. In practice, so far, wind farm operators—like oil and gas operators, shipping, and aquaculture—remain hesitant about combining functions that may add to costs and risks.

National and international regulations and maritime spatial plans consistently assume that *all* man-made offshore structures are transient. Even formal artificial reefs, which are constructed to restore or compensate natural ecosystems, "should be designed and built in such a way that they could be removed, if required" (emphasis added).(20) In the case of offshore energy installations, permission to make use of an area is time-bound. According to OSPAR Decision 98/3, which has been implemented into national laws, all disused offshore installations should be removed to shore and the sea bed returned to its original state, with some specific exceptions, defined by weight, age, and material. For installations fulfilling exception criteria (listed in Annex 1), operators may apply for a derogation from the rule of full removal to shore, providing an Integrated Assessment (Annex 2).(21) Also, for offshore wind turbines, the general rule is that they should be removed when the operating permit expires and the sea bed has to be returned to its original state (the UK provides an exception, allowing for scouring protection to be left in place).(22) For oil and gas installations, this built-in transience has a clear rationale, as the reservoirs being exploited are limited. For renewable energy installations and artificial reefs, the rationale is less obvious. The essence of renewable energy is that the energy source is unlimited, whereas artificial reefs tend to increase their value over time. In the future, it is expected that many offshore wind farms will be "repowered," that is, they will continue to produce energy under a new permit. Currently, the assumption is that even in such cases, the sea bed has to be returned to its original state, before new wind turbines are constructed in the same location.(23)

In contrast, nature conservation policies are based on an assumption of nature as *permanent and static* in terms of location. Protected areas, for example, Natura 2000 areas, are protected because they have at a certain point been designated as "important habitats" of particular species.(24) Interactions with non-protected species or habitats inside or outside the area are not taken into consideration. Nor does there seem to be a procedure for handling temporal changes in what are "important habitats," for example, as a result of climate change, availability of food, environmental factors, or changes in the possibilities for a species to move from one area to another. Within this framework of conservation, human-made structures are at best perceived as irrelevant (and more often as disturbing), even if they provide a range of benefits for endangered species.(25)

The emphasis on transience of human-made structures and the focus on conserving "original nature" gives rise to some remarkable inconsistencies. Whereas recent years have seen increasing attempts to actively restore or redevelop historical reefs at a significant cost, valuable "accidental reefs" are being removed at even larger costs.(26) An illuminating example is the protection of *Lophelia pertusa* reefs (a cold water coral), which are being mentioned as one of the endangered species and habitats to be protected within the OSPAR region.(27) [Fig. 5]. Whereas some natural *L. pertusa* reefs have become so small and damaged that larvae have to be actively imported from elsewhere to revive them, other *L. pertusa* colonies have been shown to benefit from the supply of larvae from colonies living on oil and gas installations.(28)

However the official and often repeated policy response to questions from oil and gas operators is that "it [*L. pertusa]* would not have occurred without the presence of the platform and therefore would not be considered as constituting an Annex I habitat" (i.e., a habitat that needs to be protected).(29) Hence, the installations are being removed, even though they might play a key role in the survival of natural coral reefs. Similarly, the offshore wind farm at Vindeby in Denmark was removed in 2017, despite being surrounded by ten Natura 2000 areas with reef habitat listed as protected and an Environmental Impact Assessment (EIA) indicating that local cod fisheries could decline as a result of the loss of habitat provided by the wind farm. Meanwhile, Denmark imported rocks from Norway to restore local boulder reefs less than 100 km away, because the original boulders had been removed and used for construction work.(30)

Most recently a special programme, De Rijke Noordzee, has been launched to make nature restoration an integral part of offshore wind farm construction. Without a change of perspective and policies on the transience of human-made structures and on what types of nature or habitats are worth protecting, however, it is highly unlikely that nature or habitats that are developed within a wind farm will survive when the wind farm is being decommissioned.(31)

CONCLUSION

Humans have played a dominant role in shaping the North Sea —a role we must accept. When planning for the energy transition, we need to acknowledge that the cumulative impact of installations being removed and constructed over several decades will have a major impact on marine ecosystems and there is no reason why we should necessarily view renewable energy installations as transient. Acknowledging these facts opens up new possibilities for how we can make use of human-made structures and allow them to support valuable ecosystems and threatened species and at the same time minimise negative impacts.

In order to facilitate ecosystem restoration, we need to consider marine ecosystems as viscous and changing (e.g., as a result of climate change) and human-made structures as a potentially permanent and integral part of the wider ecosystem. Future research should focus on better understanding the cumulative impact of the growing number

Fig. 5
Lophelia pertusa corals on the legs of the decommissioned platform North-West Hutton, North Sea. (BP)

and specific locations of offshore installations and on exploring how we can make use of them to enhance pressured species' possibility of adaptating to changing conditions. How can human-made structures be placed, designed, and used in such a way that they do not impede the movement of birds and bats, but do facilitate interconnectivity and safe movement of underwater species considered valuable, provide attractive habitats and enough food for marine life and humans, help keep the water clean and clear and give us humans a sense of beauty and belonging when we approach or enter the realm of the sea?(32) Accepting a larger degree of permanence of offshore installations and other human-made structures will help increase the stability of this new, human-made infrastructure for marine life and at the same time help reduce the most significant negative environmental impacts, which tend to take place in construction and removal phases. It may also help reduce costs, as (parts of) the infrastructure may be reused or used for more than one purpose—e.g., energy production and protein production—generating higher returns and providing opportunities, for example, for shared use of maintenance facilities.

Considering human-made structures as potentially permanent clearly has major consequences for other human activities, in particular the "nomadic" ones, and hence for the spatial planning process. Combining functions will be a must and maps resulting from maritime spatial planning exercises will no longer look the same: the hard divisions between nature, static human activities, and "nomadic" human activities will become blurred. For the "nomads," it will be necessary to adapt so they can operate safely in conjunction with human-made structures, but also offshore energy operators will have to consider how they can facilitate safe operations of nomadic activities—through adapted design, opening up for combined use of space, developing new, combined business models, and so on. Such an approach requires a process in which science, government, and the various stakeholders closely cooperate and are willing to adapt their perspective and explore innovative solutions to potential conflicts of interest. It also demands an integrated, long-term, cross-border vision and spatial plan and a much stronger integration of policies regulating offshore energy activities, other human activities, and nature conservation policies.

With the dramatic increase in offshore energy installations following the energy transition, human-made structures can no longer be seen as transient, insignificant elements in an undisturbed marine wilderness. Together with existing habitats and marine ecosystems, they need to be seen as the backbone of future seascapes—a backbone that at the same time provides sufficient stability for marine life to thrive and grow and allows for "nomadic" activities to continue to develop and innovate toward safe co-existence and collaborative use of our North Sea commons.

(1) See e.g., the World Wildlife Fund's presentation of the North Sea as the "largest nature area of The Netherlands" (https://www.youtube.com/watch?v=N9TroqJ4TWo) and artists' representations of the North Sea from William Turner and Caspar David Friedrich to modern Peter Rush.
(2) *"Ecosystem services are the benefits people obtain from ecosystems. These include provisioning services such as food, water, timber, and fiber; regulating services that affect climate, floods, disease, wastes, and water quality; cultural services that provide recreational, aesthetic, and spiritual benefits; and supporting services such as soil formation, photosynthesis, and nutrient cycling."* (UNEP, *Millennium Ecosystem Assessment*m 2005. Ecosystems and Human Well-Being: Synthesis" (Washington, DC: Island Press, 2005). Archived copy: https://web.archive.org/web/20131203005715/http://www.unep.org/maweb/documents/document.356.aspx.pdf accessed on July 27th, 2020). See also figure 3, in which supporting services are mentioned as habitat services in line with current TEEB (The Economics of Ecosystems & Biodiversity) terminology (see http://www.teebweb.org/resources/ecosystem-services/).
(3) Joop W. P. Coolen, "North Sea Reefs. Benthic Biodiversity of Artificial and Rocky Reefs in the Southern North Sea," (PhD thesis, Wageningen University and Research, 2017); OSPAR Commission. *OSPAR Inventory of Offshore Installations - 2015*. https://odims.ospar.org/layers/geonode:ospar_offshore_installations_2015_01. Accessed 30 October 2018. These numbers are somewhat outdated, but they are the only official numbers covering the entire North Sea area. WindEurope, *Offshore Wind in Europe - Key Trends and Statistics 2017* (Brussels, 2018).
(4) This calculation is based on the following assumptions: 650 - 1300 O&G installations with each a safety zone of 500m = 510 - 1020km2; 4000 wind turbines with an average safety zone of 0,22km2 = 880km2. In total some 1400–1900 km2 are now reserved for energy production.
(5) Generation.Energy en PosadMaxwan in opdracht van het Ministerie van EZK, *Ruimtelijke Uitwerking Energiescenarios* (Maart 2020).
(6) See, e.g., the North Sea Wind Power Hub (https://northseawindpowerhub.eu/project/) and https://chriswestraconsulting.nl/2019/05/unieke-kans-voor-de-nederlandse-offshore-industrie/
(7) Jan Matthijsen, Ed Dammers, and Hans Elzenga, *The Future of the North Sea. The North Sea in 2030 and 2050: A Scenario Study* (The Hague: PBL Netherlands Environmental Assessment Agency, 2018).
(8) Seas at Risk, *Blue Manifesto*, https://seas-at-risk.org/images/pdf/publications/SAR_BLUE_MANIFESTO_DEPLIANT_A4_plie_BaT.pdf
(9) It is worth noting that development of offshore energy and other static activities is certainly not the only threat to the "nomadic" culture of fishing communities. As described e.g. in Elspeth Probyn, *Eating the Ocean* (Duke University Press, 2016), the largest threat to the traditional culture of fishing communities is the intensification and industrialisation of fishing itself, in combination with regulatory frameworks that largely fail to regulate the exploitation of the "high seas," with severe consequences also for coastal fisheries.
(10) Coolen, *North Sea Reefs*.
(11) Ibid; C. Stenberg, J. G. Støttrup, M. Deurs, C. W. Berg, G. Dinesen, H. Mosegaard, T. Grome, and S. Leonhard, *Long-term Effects of an Offshore Wind Farm in the North Sea on Fish Communities* (Marine Ecology Progress Series, 2015); S.E. Gass, J.M. Roberts. *The Occurrence of the Cold-water Coral Lophelia pertusa (Scleractinia) on Oil and Gas Platforms in the North Sea: Colony Growth, Recruitment and Environmental Controls on Distribution* (Marine Pollution Bulletin, 2006); Victoria L. G.Todd, Edward W. Lavallin, Peter I. Macreadie *Quantitative Analysis of Fish and Invertebrate Assemblage Dynamics in Association with a North Sea Oil and Gas Installation Complex* (Marine Environmental Research, 2018).
(12) Oil and gas installations are surrounded by a 500 m safety zone, which is closed to all human activities unrelated to the installation. Access to wind farms is limited in all countries, especially for fishing.
(13) Lea-Anne Henry, Claudia G. Mayorga-Adame, Alan D. Fox, Jeff A. Polton, Joseph S. Ferris, Faron McLellan, Chris McCabe, Tina Kutti and J. Murray Roberts, "Ocean Sprawl Facilitates Dispersal and Connectivity of Protected Species," Nature Scientific Reports 8 (2018).
(14) R. G. Jak and J. E. Tamis, "Screening Impacts of Offshore Infrastructures on Marine Species Groups: A North Sea Case Study for System Integration," North Sea Energy II (2019).
(15) Menno Schilthuizen, *Darwin Comes to Town: How the Urban Jungle Drives Evolution* (New York: Picador, 2019).
(16) Michael Pye, *The Edge of the World* (London: Penguin Books, 2014).
(17) Elizabeth R. Johnson and Irus Braverman, *Blue Legalities. Governing More-than-human Oceans* (Duke University Press, 2019) discusses the short-comings of regulatory frameworks governing marine space and the tensions between ocean governance and the large amount of gaps in our knowledge of ocean systems;

temporal aspects of ocean systems, in which past and future get mixed up with the present e.g., through consequences of long-past decisions on dumping or CO2-emissions being expressed in the current crisis of our oceans; the tensions between laws seeing the ocean as a global commons versus laws dealing with marine space as a repository of profitable commodities; and the failure to incorporate the perspectives of non-human inhabitants of oceans into laws and regulations. Many of these themes are reflected in the way that regulatory frameworks governing the North Sea deal with human-made structures versus "real nature" and other dichotomies discussed in this chapter.

(18) https://www.msp-platform.eu/msp-eu/introduction-msp

(19) Overlegorgaan Fysieke Leefomgeving, *Het Akkoord voor de Noordzee*. Extra Mijlen voor een Gezonde Noordzee (15 juni 2020). See also chapter 10.

(20) OSPAR Commission, "OSPAR Guidelines on Artificial Reefs in Relation to Living Marine Resources," (Reference number: 2012-3), Art. 4.2.

(21) OSPAR Commission, "OSPAR Decision 98/3 on the Disposal of Disused Offshore Installations" (Sintra, July 1998).

(22) Katie Smyth, Nikki Christie, Daryl Burdon, Jonathan P. Atkins, Richard Barnes, and Michael Elliott, "Renewables-to-Reefs?—Decommissioning Options for the Offshore Wind Power Industry," *Marine Pollution Bulletin* 90 nos.1-2 (2015): 247-58.

(23) Personal communication from wind farm operators.

(24) See, e.g., OSPAR Commission, "OSPAR List of Threatened and/or Declining Species and Habitats"
(Reference Number: 2008-6); https://ec.europa.eu/environment/basics/natural-capital/natura2000/

(25) Ashley M. Fowler, Anne-Mette Jørgensen, Jon C. Svendsen, Peter I. Macreadie, Daniel O. B Jones, Arjen R. Boon, David J. Booth, Robin Brabant, Emily Callahan, Jeremy T. Claisse, Thomas G. Dahlgren, Steven Degraer, Quenton R. Dokken, Andrew B. Gill, David G. Johns, Robert J. Leewis, Han J. Lindeboom, Olof Linden, Roel May, Albertinka J. Murk, Geir Ottersen, Donna M. Schroeder, Sunil M. Shastri, Jonas Teilmann, Victoria Todd, Gert Van Hoey, Jan Vanaverbeke, and Joop W. P. Coolen, "Environmental Benefits of Leaving Offshore Infrastructure in the Ocean," *Frontiers in Ecology and the Environment* 16, no. 10 (2018): 571-78; I. S. Fortune and D. M. Paterson, "Ecological Best Practice in Decommissioning: a Review of Scientific Research," ICES *Journal of Marine Science* 77, no. 3 (2018): 1079–91.

(26) Historical reefs are reefs that are known to have been historically present in a certain location, but are now (almost) gone. This fits with a narrative of restoring original nature and is expected to increase the chance that a restored reef will form a successful ecosystem. See, e.g., Naturstyrelsen, *Blue Reef—Restoration of Stone Reefs in Kattegat/ Restaurering af stenrev i Kattegat*. (Copenhagen, 2013) or WWF. *Aanleg oesterbank en 3-D geprinte riffen primeur voor Noordzee* (Zeist, 2018) https://www.wnf.nl/nieuws/bericht/aanleg-oesterbank-en-3-d-geprinte-riffen-primeur-voor-noordzee.htm, Accessed on 15 January 2019.

(27) OSPAR Commission, "OSPAR List of Threatened and/or Declining Species and Habitats"

(28) Henry, *Ocean Sprawl*.

(29) CNR International, "Environmental Statement for the Decommissioning of the Murchison Facilities," (Aberdeen, 2013). An "Annex I habitat" is a habitat type described in Annex I of the "OSPAR List of Threatened and/or Declining Species and Habitats."

(30) A. M. Fowler, A. -M. Jørgensen, J. W .P. Coolen, D. O. B. Jones, J. C. Svendsen, R. Brabant, B. Rumes, and S. Degraer, "The Ecology of Infrastructure Decommissioning in the North Sea: What We Need to Know and How to Achieve it," *ICES Journal of Marine Science* 77, no. 3 (2019): 1109–26, https://doi.org/10.1093/icesjms/fsz143.

(31*) De Rijke Noordzee*. https://www.derijkenoordzee.nl/

(32) This opportunity was also presented recently in the Friends of Ocean Action paper, "The Business Case for Marine Protection and Conservation." http://www3.weforum.org/docs/WEF_Business_case_for_marine_protection.pdf

[Fig. 1a] O. T. Olsen, *Piscatorial Atlas of the North Sea* (London: Taylor and Francis, 1883).

[Fig. 1b] Printed with permission Joop Coolen, 2018

[Fig. 2] Printed with permission, Ibid.

[Fig. 3] Adapted from the UN Millennium Ecosystem Assessment 2005.

[Fig. 4] Adapted and reprinted with permission from Henry, *Ocean Sprawl*.

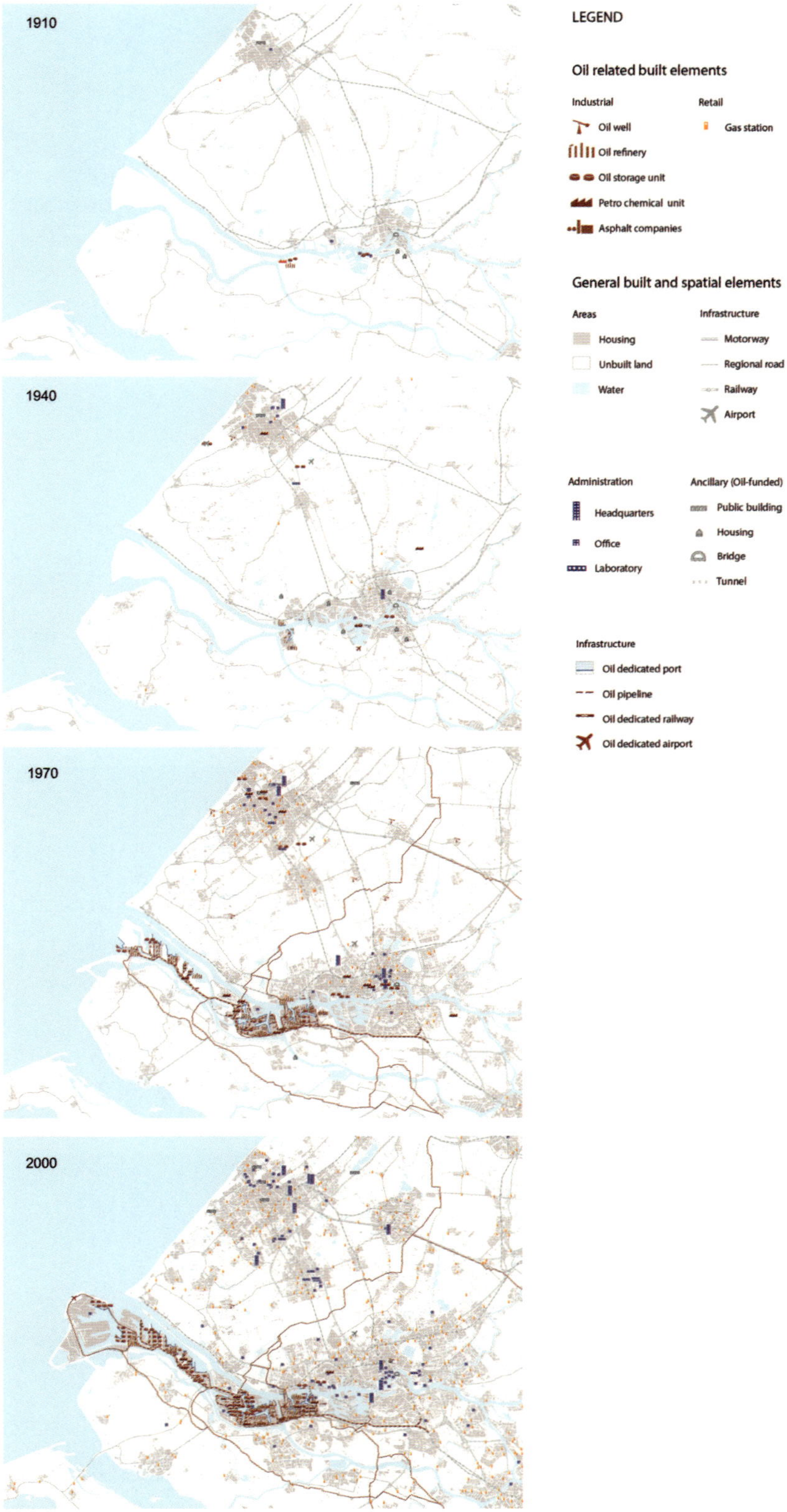

Fig. 3
The ARA area and the growth of the petroleumscape in four periods: 1910, 1940, 1970, and 2000 (Carola Hein and Arnoud de Waijer)

Fig. 4
Post Industrial
Safari (Ege Cakir)

Fig. 1
Current space utilisation North Sea, the Dutch continental shelf. (noordzeeloket)

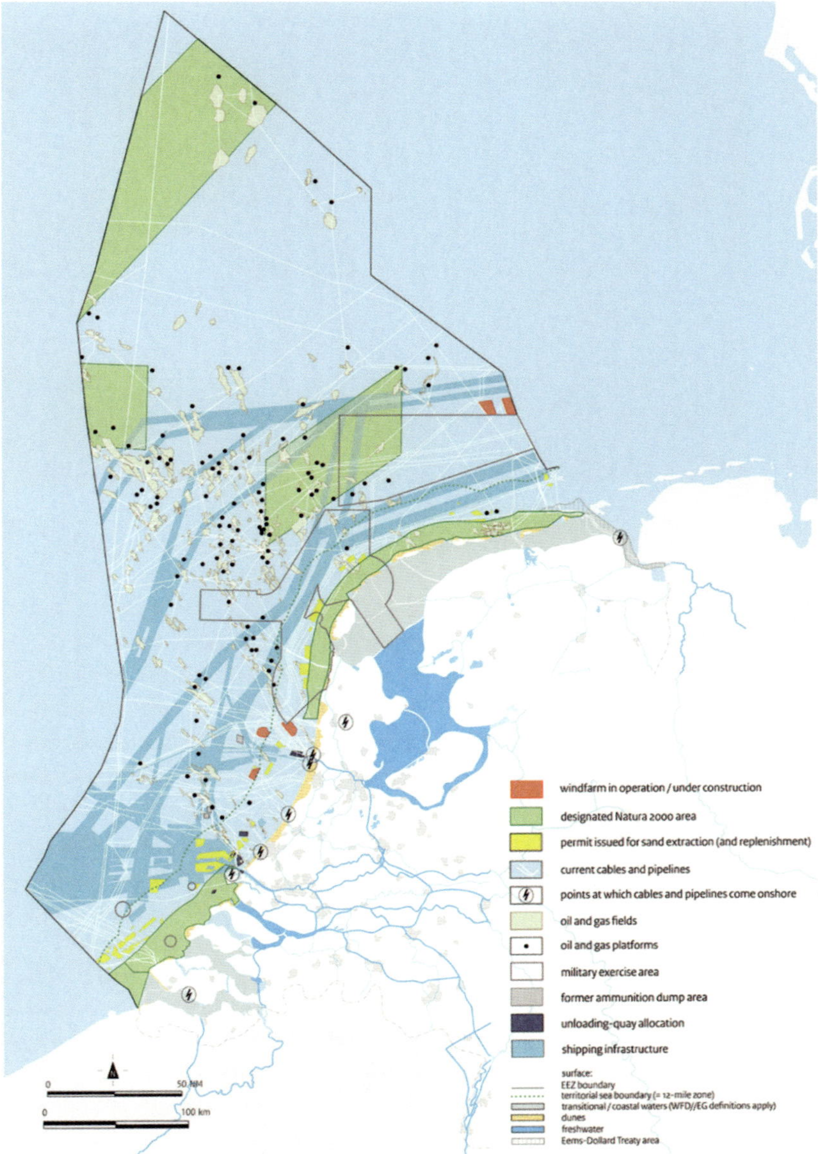

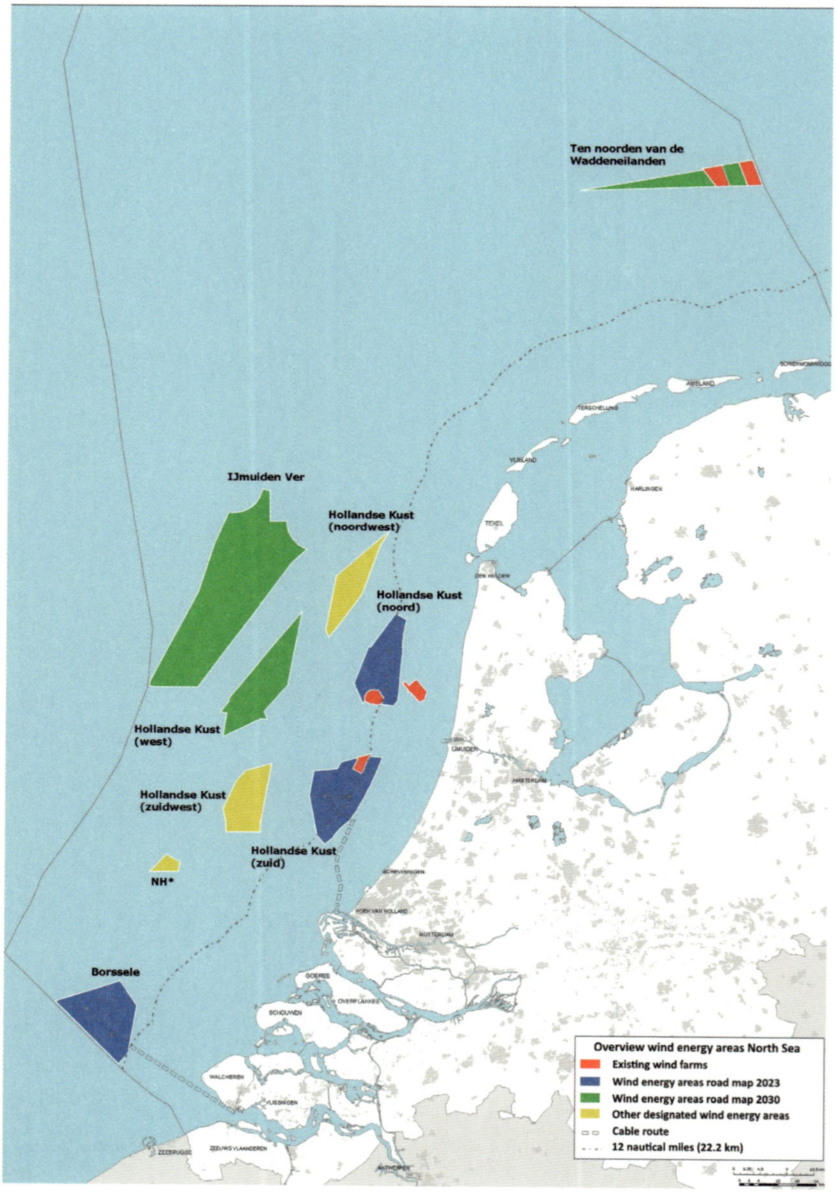

Fig. 3 Existing and planned development of wind farms in the North Sea, Dutch continental shelf (noordseeloket)

Fig. 5
Dutch continental shelf in 2050 under scenario I, "Slow Change."

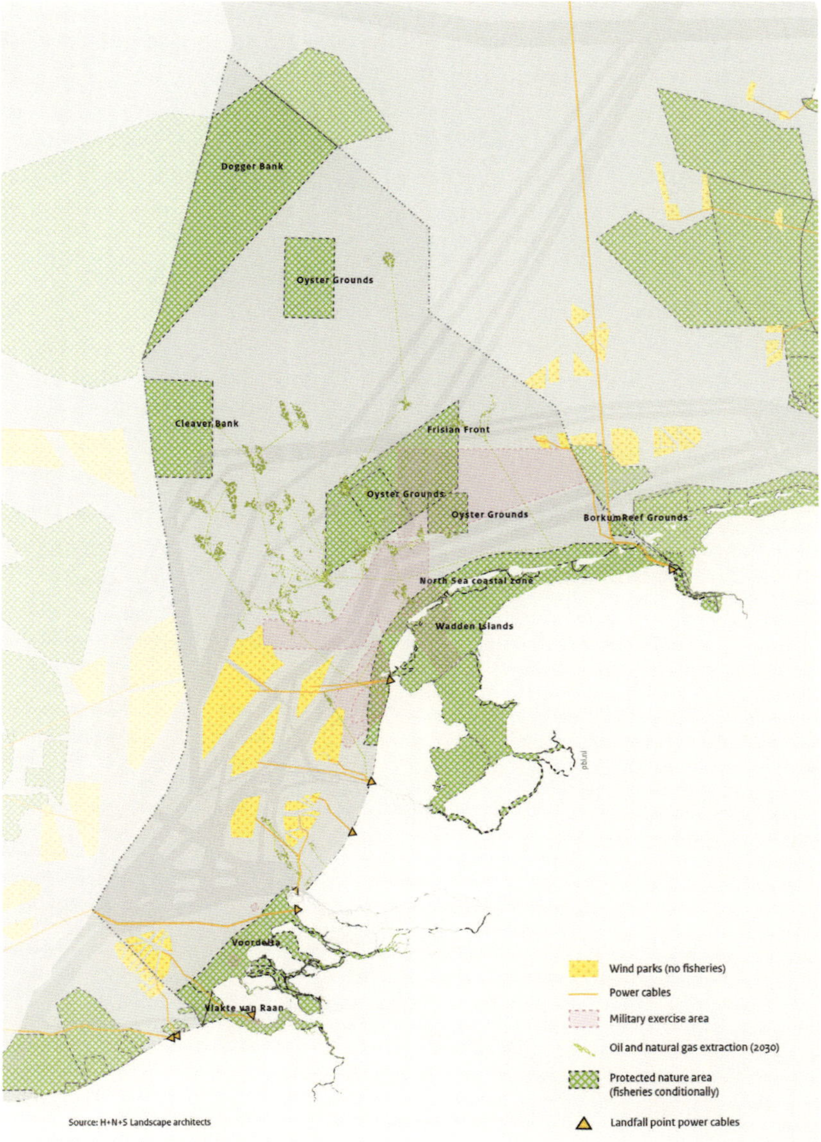

Fig. 6
Dutch continental shelf in 2050 under scenario IV, "Sustainable Together."

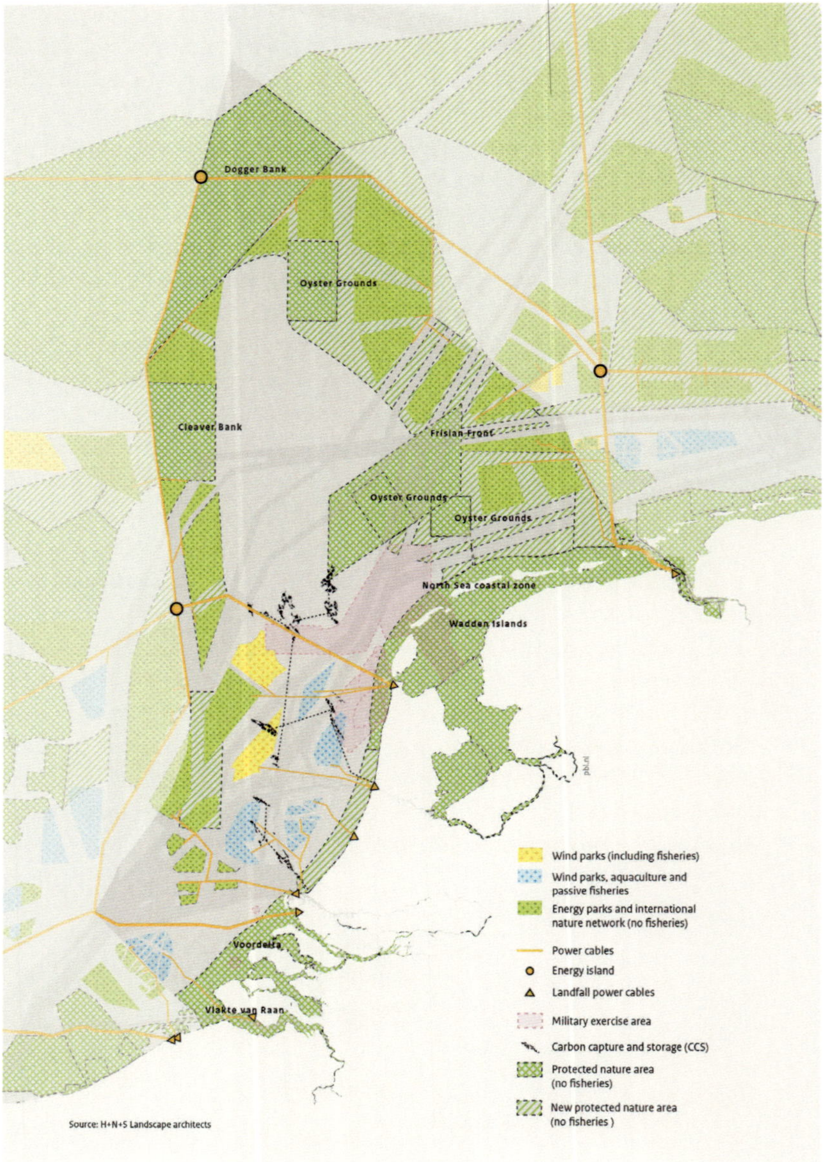

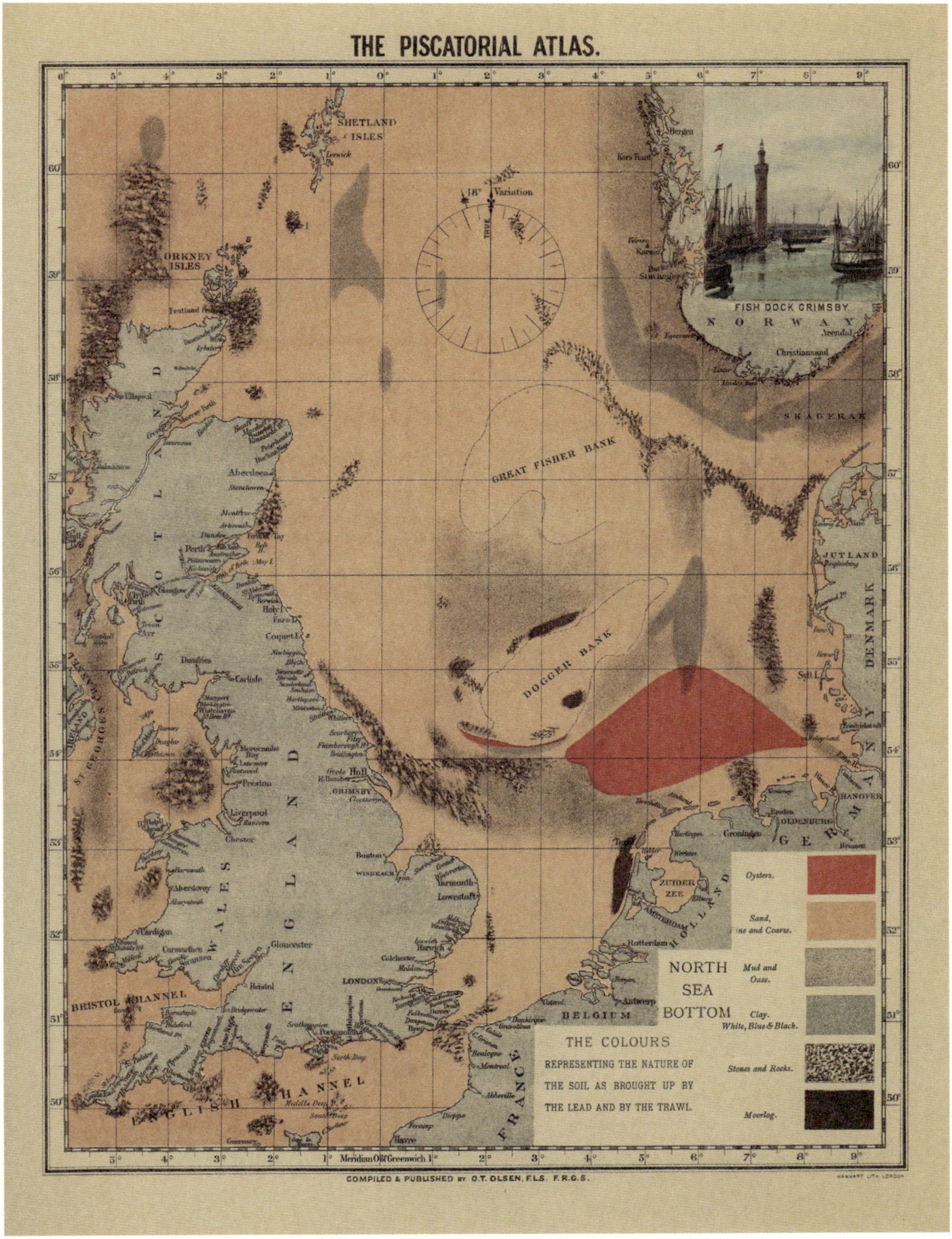

Fig. 1.a
Benthic habitats are oysters (red), sand (soft pink), ... and moorlog (a peatlike material of rotten organic matter from the the period when the North Sea was not yet a sea) (black)

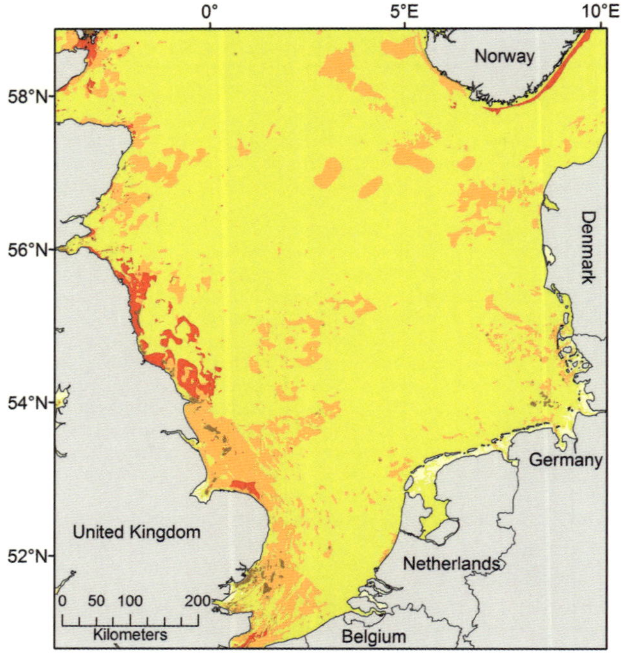

Fig. 1.b
Benthic habitats are sand and mud (yellow), mixed (brown), coarse sediment including gravel (orange), and rocky reef (red).

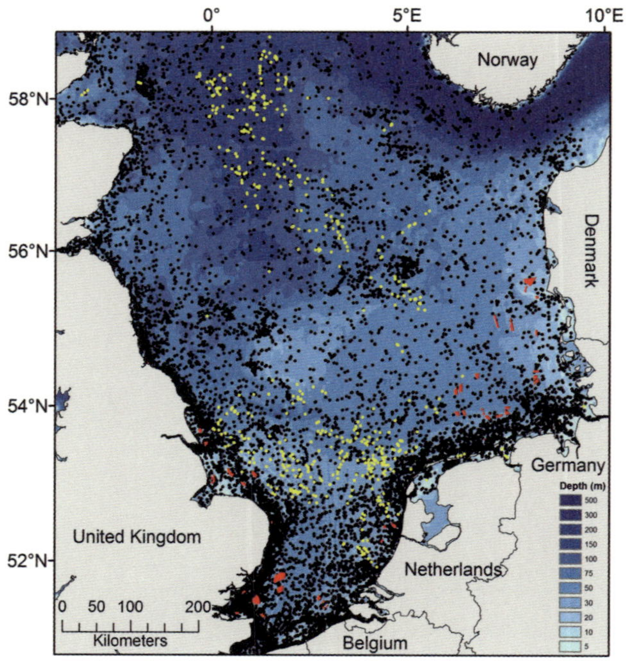

Fig. 2
Locations of O&G platforms (yellow dots), wind turbines (red areas), and shipwrecks (black dots) in the North Sea in 2015.

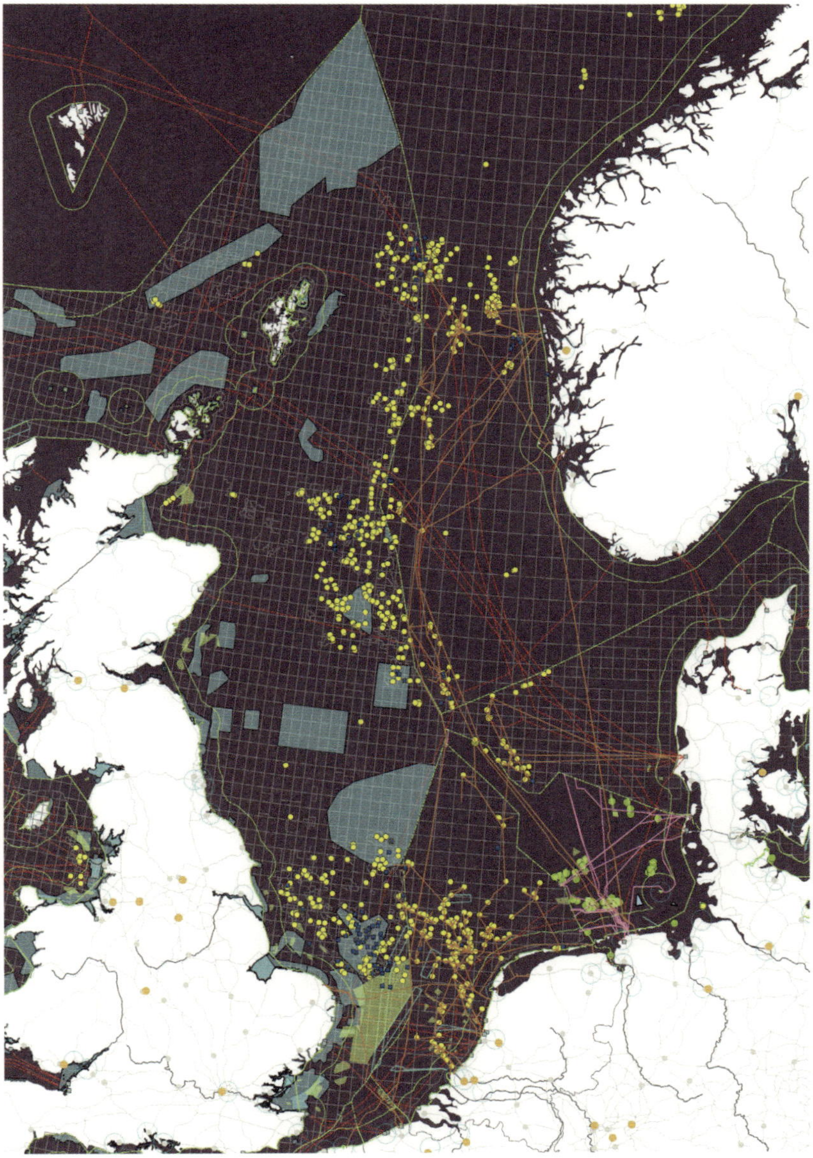

Fig. 3
North Sea
Urbanised (Couling)

Fig. 4
Decommissioned
Frigg field (Total)

Fig. 7
Offshore
dependency
(Shuai Wang, Paris
Malaquais School
of Architecture,
2018)

1.

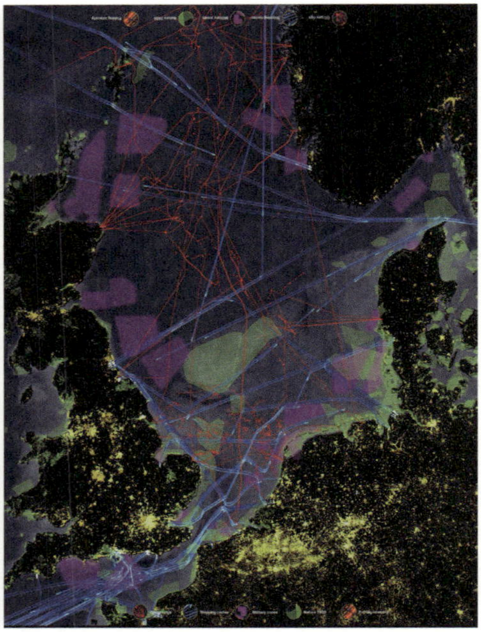

2.

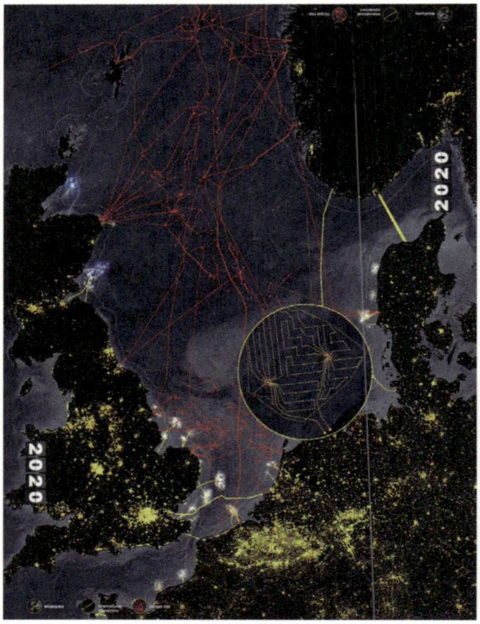

3.

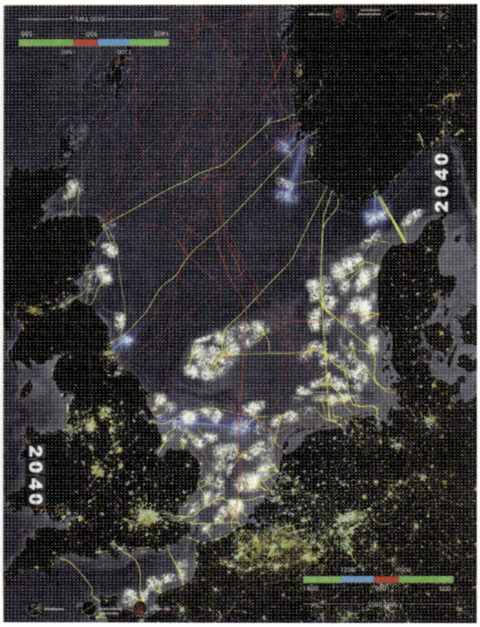

4.

Fig. 1, Fig. 2, Fig. 3, Fig.4
Stills of the Odyssey: Fig. 1 seasonal south-westerly winds, Fig. 2 Oil/gas rigs, shipping routes, military zones, Natura 2000 areas and fishing intensity 2016, Fig. 3 initial stages with an exemplary wind farm 2020, Fig. 4 Spatial view 2040 towards the 2050 target of 25,000 turbines with an average capacity of 10MW

Chapter 12 EXTENSIONS AND VISCOSITIES IN THE NORTH SEA

Nancy Couling

An incongruous and selective mixture of maritime and land-based systems is to be found throughout the North Sea–systems that do not normally belong together. By taking a closer look at three examples, Nancy Couling shows us that the potentials of urbanisation in the North Sea lie in its viscosity, heterogeneity, and resistance to categorisation.

Currently Assoc. Prof. at Bergen School of Architecture, Norway, Nancy was awarded a Marie Skłodowska Curie Individual Fellowship at the Chair of History of Architecture and Urban Planning, TU Delft 2017–19 with the project "Oceanurb: The Unseen Spaces of Extended Urbanisation in the North Sea." Trained as an architect at Auckland University, New Zealand, she completed her PhD at EPFL in 2015 after much international practice experience and cofounding her own interdisciplinary practice in Berlin 1995–2010. Co-editor of the prize-winning "Barents Lessons-Teaching and Research in Architecture" (2012. Zürich: Park Books), she frequently publishes and lectures and is a member of the research group "Territories of Extended Urbanisation," led by the ETH Zurich, & FCL Singapore.

Fig. 1
Scheveningen pier
2019 (Couling)

Surfers at Scheveningen paddle out from the shore, framed by the Port of Rotterdam's industrial silhouette. A line of ships ploughs the horizon. This popular recreational beach has been "nourished" with sand dredged from offshore sites.(1) Interspersed with art projects, seasonal bars modelled on international themes line the beach alongside equipment rental stands, injecting the seafront with an atmosphere of relaxed enjoyment, a contemporary version of the bathing culture that became established here in 1818. Scheveningen is fashioned in fairground style, with activities and people gathered around the recreational sea, an arena facing the infamous pier and the horizon [Fig. 1].

Seawards, two munitions dumping sites organised after the Second World War lie submerged just beyond the territorial waters.(2) Removing munitions is hazardous: explosions spread toxic material through the sea, so for now, testing is being carried out and the munitions are disintegrating naturally, their metallic coatings corroding in seawater like "ticking time-bombs."(3) Recent changes to the Dutch shipping routes approved by the International Maritime Organisation steer vessels around these danger zones, through complex intersections serving one of the world's busiest shipping spaces. The rerouting also aims to provide space for new wind farms.(4) Among those, by 2023, at least one, Hollandse Kust zuid, will be visible from the coast.(5)

The beach is a viscous place where land and sea interact. While at Scheveningen this interaction will soon include new wind farms, less perceptible elements such as corroding metal will also play an active spatial role and be drawn into existing viscous relations. Scheveningen is carefully constructed to promote engagement with the sea, but is also an example of the restriction of viscous space characteristic of Dutch hydraulic engineering: the land is pushed forward into the sea space, and the sea is held back from the land. The Scheveningen dike was strengthened in 2010–2012 with an urban upgrade and coastal protection design by Spanish architect Manuel

De Solà-Morales, which incorporated a layered promenade and a beach extension to lessen the impact of storm surges.(6)

The Dutch strategy of offensive separation of land and sea became established in the early nineteenth century.(7) Before then, people who lived behind the dunes and in other less protected places had to physically negotiate the viscous time and space between land and sea. Since the second half of the twentieth century, the separation has been accompanied by ongoing processes of urbanisation, within which land-based systems and elements have extended far offshore to serve the oil and gas industries, while a second-generation effort to capture wind is taking hold around the sea's liminal edge. At the same time, the view of the horizon—the "open sea" experience—has been preserved from the shore, exemplified by the beach promenade, which in Scheveningen is combined with the dike. This situation represents a conceptual inversion of land/sea relations: in order to connect to the human experience, the familiar visual sea is constructed and preserved as an edge adhering to the land, while the industrial sea unfolds beyond the sightlines. Connecting these two realms, dedicated channels penetrate the coastal condition at selected landings.

Testing concepts introduced in chapter 3, this chapter uses viscosity as a tool to think through the mixture of land and sea-based elements, practices, and modes of operation resulting from urbanisation processes. Territorial regulation, construction of the built environment, and habitation are spatial practices developed on land, manifest largely in the composition of urban agglomerations. The maintenance of open trade-routes, free of territorial claims, the quasi-autonomous, itinerant status of vessels at sea, and the history of alternative forms of social organisation are practices developed in a fluid maritime environment. In the urbanisation taking place in the North Sea, elements of both land and sea exist in parallel, are enmeshed, sometimes fully merged, juxtaposed, and frequently in full contradiction.

Under natural conditions, the viscous mixture of land and sea would occur at the coast or around shallow offshore banks. Using a large-scale lens to observe the North Sea as a whole reveals an unfamiliar space, composed of redrawn relations between inherited understandings of the *open sea* and scattered sites of industrial production exported from *land*. At this scale, the condition of viscosity is no longer purely coastal. Linear connections penetrate deep into the sea space, remaining largely invisible until emerging in unevenly dispersed material clusters and geometrical formations. Do these stretched connections define a contemporary land-sea dividing line, or is such a line today obsolete? I aim for an understanding of the specificities of this urbanised sea, and to represent spatial relations across the land-sea divide that have seldom been considered in urban debates. This interest is driven by the architect's desire to discover the design implications of spatial relations. Such an understanding could challenge the terrestrial limits apparent in the design disciplines and promote holistic, imaginative, responsible planning at sea.

This chapter first uses conceptual and theoretical sources to contextualise the inherent sea space as distinct from land. It then explores the viscosities of the North Sea through three aspects of urbanisation: territorial regulation, the built environment of the oil and wind sectors, and the offshore as a lived space. These explorations tell different stories using different protagonists and do not add up to a single narrative, rather they describe a collection of spaces in transformation. Geographer Andrew Barry argues, "The North Sea is multiply enacted through practices...that are not necessarily interested in being aligned."(8) The design task is therefore not to attempt to align the partially autonomous and discrete materials, flows, and practices of the North Sea, but to recognise and loosely gather them in their common space while paying attention to intersections and interdependencies.

PART I

EXTENSION

Existing land-based systems of urbanisation have been extended into the space of the sea through new offshore industries that were first built up on land and did not exist in the North Sea prior to the Second World War.(9) Maritime transport and fishing have expanded or intensified based on pre-existing practices and patterns of movement rather than involving something altogether new.

Extensions have been executed by governments and companies according to the logic of colonising a new frontier. In particular, at the birth of North Sea oil in December 1969, at the Ekofisk field on the Norwegian continental shelf, the climate encouraged risk-taking, stretching the technological state of the art to new vertical depths and wave heights—and in the North Sea both were a result of overcoming new offshore distances.(10) Due to the geographical location of subsea hydrocarbons, oil and gas production took place far offshore. Two of the major formations—the Central Graben and the Viking Graben—form an irregularly shaped zone spreading down the UK/Norwegian border in the middle of the North Sea, making more pronounced the direct linear nature of extensions from land. Eyon Weizman proposes a clear distinction between frontier and border: while the border is the static, linear result of a "relatively symmetrical" balance of power, the frontier is in flux, not yet clarified, advancing and retreating according to the pull of utopian visions, technological possibilities, or climate change. The overlaid meeting lines of Exclusive Economic Zones (EEZs) constitute the nine North Sea borders. Although these were rationally decided over a relatively short period, as Weizman notes, "The pattern of the

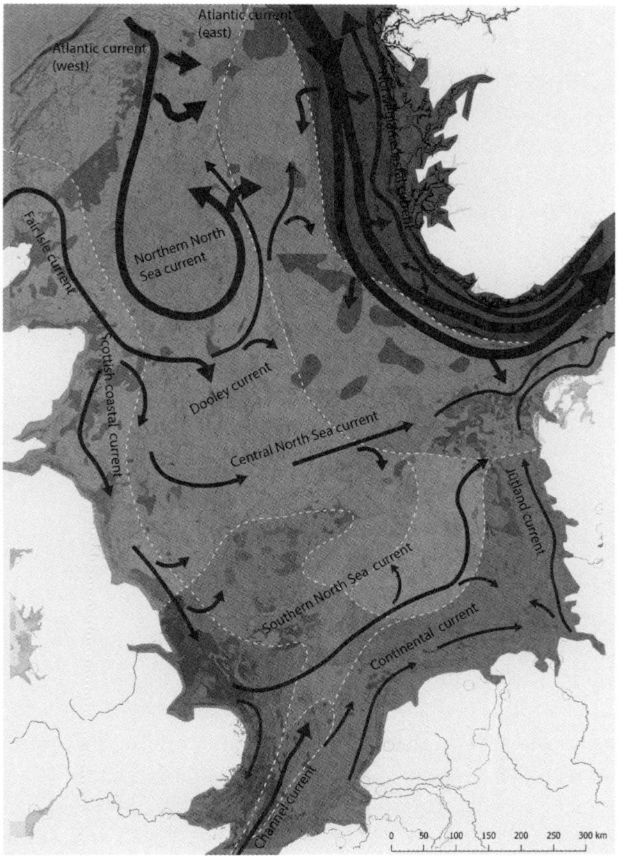

Fig. 2
Hydrographic regions and currents of the North Sea (Couling)

frontier's geographical expansion is highly irregular...occupying geographical 'islands' above isolated fields of energy resources."(11)

THE SEA

Urban systems extending into the North Sea have encountered a distinct material, spatial, and sociocultural realm. The inherent space of the sea volume is made up of a liquid mass. Thick and kinetic, this mass has properties associated with solids, such as density, weight, and cores. Water masses are home to a multitude of travelling species, including inorganic objects such as oil rigs. To physically occupy or interact with this space is to prise it apart, exerting great pressure to resist density, depth, and oceanic movement, striking a balance between capturing its inherent kinetic force and overcoming friction.(12) The opening and displacing of water required to move a vessel forward makes shipping a comparatively slow means of transport: a typical roll-on-roll-off vessel travels at around 17 knots, equivalent to ca. 31.5 km/h. The image of a heavily laden freight vessel carving through the sea aligns with Weizman's "wedges," which he uses to describe infrastructure that opens up new terrain for colonisation.(13)

Salinity and temperature characteristics of the North Sea waters plus currents and bathymetry result in a natural division of water masses into nine hydrographical regions [Fig. 2]. Historically, the natural features of these regions—the currents, predominant winds, and tides—were important for locating the best fishing grounds and for determining navigational routes, hence they were closely related to spatial conceptions and sociocultural practices. The North Sea boasts excellent fishing grounds, and parts of the sea have long been well-charted and understood intimately as places.(14)

Throughout history, human use of the sea and the coastal zones in particular have created what Danish archaeologist Christer Westerdahl calls "maritime cultural landscapes"—opening up a new understanding of mariculture as comparable to agriculture.(15) According to Westerdahl, the relationship between sea and land is binary in maritime societies, involving two distinct cognitive elements where the sociocultural realm of the sea has developed cognitively in opposition to land.(16) The land-sea relationship has been understood as both antagonistic and complimentary.

Traditionally, urbanisation processes of maritime trade displayed systems of order distinct from land. They exploited the ocean's fluidity by prioritising movement, maintaining flows, and resisting territorial claims. Fluid ocean trading systems operated together with place-bound settlement systems in mutual dependency, resonating with the dialectic relationship between concentrated and extended urbanisation theorised by Neil Brenner and Christian Schmid.(17) Until the mid-twentieth century, such fluid conceptions of space were well-aligned with commercial interests and upheld outside of the traditional territorial waters up to three nautical miles from the coastline. Even in the highly industrialised sector of container shipping, the ocean is not a fixed highway: experience negotiating waves and weather remains essential for navigation. As recounted by journalist Horatio Clare, "Our captain practically danced us through the Singapore Strait, navigating by lights, depths, charts, instinct and instruments all at once, as the thick tropical night was stormed with charging ships."(18)

In oceanographic terms, the coastal zone—"the area influenced directly by the presence of both land and open sea"(19)—can be defined by diverse parameters: light reaching the sea bed, freshwater fluxes, nutrients, organic matter from land, the influence of wind-generated waves on the sea bottom, and the frictional influence of the coastline. These parameters result in a loose definition of the area with waters less than 20 m deep, extending an estimated distance of 10–20 km from the shoreline.(20) However, at the Wadden Sea, for example, shallow water can extend more than 50 km from the shoreline. People acquire an understanding of the elasticity of interstitial zones through direct experience of the rising and falling tide, which many associate the natural rhythms of the planet.(21)

Beyond the contact zones and under "natural" conditions, sea space is therefore characterised by temporal, spatial, and conceptual separation from land. It is also separated from inherited land-based spatial understandings of enclosure, ownership, and accumulation through static permanence. Sea and land remain distinct environments, each with fundamental differences that are inscribed in our spatial imaginations and inherited systems of control and governance.

PART II: LAND-SEA VISCOSITIES

TERRITORIAL REGULATION

"Welcome to the UK." Around 2:00 am, the peep of a mobile phone announces the entry of the Rotterdam-Hull ferry into UK waters. This otherwise imperceptible electronic border currently stands to split the North Sea almost directly in two through Brexit negotiations. The "Fishing for Leave" campaign initiated by UK fishermen advocated a closed UK maritime territory and was an important part of the Brexit rationale. As an EU-member, the UK shared their maritime biomass with the entire EU fishing fleet. Brexit therefore initiates a new chapter in North Sea territoriality, the radical formalisation of which began with the 1958 UN Convention on the Continental Shelf, ratified by Denmark in 1963, the UK in 1964, and the Netherlands in 1966, with the mutual acceptance of international offshore boundary lines closely following. The rapidity of these agreements, which divided the North Sea into national segments, was motivated by scientific observations that geological formations in the North Sea could potentially contain hydrocarbons. Gaining access required a new system of offshore spatial organisation and national borders were extended out to sea to create EEZs.(22) What was pushed forward for oil will now have an important impact on the North Sea fishing industry.

From their inception, the EEZs were inscribed with a clear mandate of extraction and production as well as special privileges. Conceived as the limit of a nation's geographical continental shelf, this limit was initially defined by the 1958 Convention as "to where the depth of the superadjacent waters admits of the exploitation of the natural resources of the said areas."(23) Hence the continental shelf itself became a new form of specialised "zone." In her historical overview of the development of special zones, Kellar Easterling argues that zones that emerged in the US in the 1950s with special exemptions for sorting and manipulation, but also for the manufacturing of goods, developed into "a more thoroughly abstracted and formulaic instrument," which was distinct from their forbears—the maritime spaces of free ports.(24) Developed out of a tradition of special maritime trade zones, ironically the maritime space of the EEZ was more attuned to what had been developed on land.

On the map, the EEZ and the petroleum grid bear witness to the vast project of territorial appropriation of the North Sea for production and hence to the urbanisation of the maritime [Fig. 3, p. 185]. But the EEZ is also a "grey" and viscous space, where precisely these mechanisms of urbanisation are selectively subject to a fluid maritime logic. Easterling calls the waters at the extended national boundaries "slushy, violent, conflicted, dangerous, and ... clogged with traffic."(25) The outer EEZ border does not delineate sovereignty —this is limited to the twelve nautical-mile-edge of territorial waters, beyond which the "high seas" still exist in terms of free passage for all commercial vessels and the right of all nations to lay cables and pipelines. Yet nations have sovereign rights to exploit the resources of their continental shelf, which is subtly legally distinct from the EEZ.(26)

THE CONSTRUCTED ENVIRONMENTS OF OIL AND WIND

Vertically aligned with the hydrocarbon-bearing geological formations thousands of metres below the surface, the physical construction of temporary offshore production sites involves the transfer and installation of vast quantities of materials and the delivery of continuous rounds of labour. While most offshore construction in the North Sea took place in the 1970s and 1980s, selected projects are still being developed: Equinor will reopen the Martin Linge field discovered in 1976, operated by the French group Total, then closed in 2016. The development is already over time and budget while oil prices fall. This field and the recent state-of-the-art Johann Sveldrup field utilise a higher degree of offshore automation and are ironically proudly powered by "clean" Norwegian hydro-electricity, making "oil and gas production on Equinor's new giant field 25 times cleaner than the global average."(27)

Currently the sole truly transverse North Sea ferry passes not far from the Martin Linge field on the Denmark–Iceland route, affording rare, if distant, encounters with the industrial giants of oil and their layers of field history. The Troll field hosts the largest object humans have ever moved. In 1995, the last and the tallest (472 m) concrete deep water structure to be built in Norway, the 650,000 tonne Troll A platform was towed out to the field amid a sense of industry triumph. From the ferry, you can see the Heimdal and Alvheim platforms crouching on the horizon and the low silhouette of the Armada Kraken.This is a field of "heavy oil" recently tapped in 2017, but discovered in 1985. It had long remained undeveloped because companies preferred to produce the less viscous Brent grade oil. Further on, the ferry slides past the Frigg field, marking the UK/ Norwegian border and named after the Norse goddess of love and wife of the chief god Odin. Completed in 1977, then shut down in 2004, the decommissioning process of the Frigg field was completed in 2010, with the removal of the topsides, but the field still hosts an ensemble of concrete gravity base structures protruding out of the sea, the largest of which is around 100 m in diameter [Fig. 4, p. 186].

Oil extraction depends on a geographically specific resource and is therefore inherently immobile, using a construction system adapted from land to resist the forces of the sea. However most rigs and platforms are technically "vessels," registered under particular flags and relocated around the sea according to different work "contracts." The heavy, complex material arrangements of offshore oil production are a selective hybrid of static and moving elements —of invisible connecting lines and isolated physical production points, of concentrated human habitation intersecting with pathways of whales, harbour seals, and seabirds. Even the sway of a concrete-based rig can be felt by workers on arrival. The resulting viscous mixture of the urbanised North Sea is uneven and granular, difficult to grasp and to represent. A land-based map will not acknowledge the dispersed industrial metropolis within a 100 km radius of Martin Linge, but maritime maps are thickly studded with information, revealing the geography of a fluid, multi-layered space described through bathymetric lines, sea-floor formations, physical markers, and electronic borders. While the specialised petroleum grid is not represented, field installations are important maritime landmarks [Fig. 5].

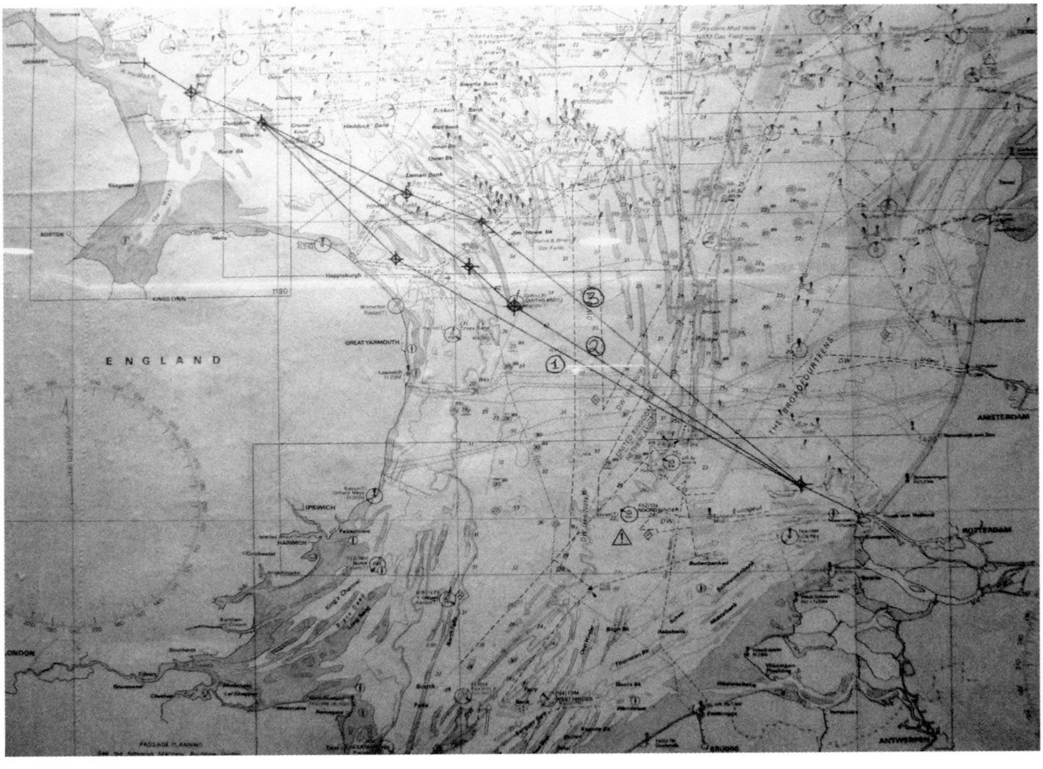

Fig. 5 Navigational maritime map (Couling)

Just as urban extensions reach deep below the sea to extract hydrocarbons and to execute post-oil carbon storage, new generation offshore energy farming extends upwards into the above-sea air space to capture the wind. This is not a blank, empty space; according to Pierre Bélanger, it is a "thick, fuzzy and complex space" inhabited by birds, clouds, sounds, and more.(28) Here the swipe-area of the blades defines the wind turbine's largest dimension, described by manufacturers in terms of football fields. Below, the sea bed affords construction stability and the sea surface provides access and large-scale "smooth" uninterrupted areas where wind speeds are unencumbered by surface friction. In a similar way to oil, offshore wind is invested in minimising friction and maintaining optimal flows.(29) Such vast smoothness hardly exists on roughly textured built land divided by ownership rights. The North Sea is by contrast a "state" space, divided up from the outset according to the rationale of production and now seen by littoral governments as the site destined to host increased renewable energy production to meet the obligations of the 2015 Paris Agreement (see chapter 14).

The Wadden Sea is particularly viscous. The first German offshore wind farm Alpha Ventus was constructed in the North Sea just one year after the Wadden Sea was declared a UNESCO World Heritage Site in 2009. Hence these two unlikely neighbours are destined to remain in what Gugger and Costa call "forced co-existence."(30) Local shrimp fishermen have watched the expanding wind industry with scepticism and observed a lack of knowledge of underlying currents and shifting sandbanks as cables laid for wind farms are washed free by the currents. Offshore wind employees have engineering rather than maritime backgrounds. The accumulated environmental effect on wind patterns is still unknown and its impact on fishing, which is not currently permitted in German wind farm areas due to the risk of damaging cables, has not been considered. The land-based logic of enclosure and exclusion is applied to increasing offshore wind areas, while the maritime logic of fluid mobility is becoming less and less feasible for coastal fishermen, who cannot simply relocate in their 15-18 m vessels that are not adapted to conditions further offshore and where the species for which they have a licence will not be found.(31)

Particularly in Germany, offshore wind has been politically driven and has been allocated large areas in Europe's first legislative Marine Spatial Plan.(32) But it has also been kept at least 32 km from the coast in order to preserve the open seascape, and visible hub heights are limited to 125 m.(33) From the landside, a constructed "ring of nature" is preserved around the valuable Wadden Sea tidal seascape—itself a cultural landscape extended and modified over hundreds of years of human intervention. Beyond lies an energy zone capable of producing 6,436 MW, equal to 8.3 percent of total German power production.(34) Power cables from this zone must be squeezed through dedicated channels tunnelled below the floor of the protected Wadden Sea to emerge behind the dike at transformer stations. The channel itself is near capacity, and the high-tension infrastructure delivering power to the rest of Germany is not yet installed, hampered by NIMBY objections. While legislation has been designed to separate the productive sea from the recreational sea, public environmental action has also been behind these decisions, exerting influence out into the 12 nm territorial sea limit, but not into the state space of the EEZ. Along the littoral zone, social viscosity has limited the Wadden Sea's mineral viscosity.

OFFSHORE LIFE

As North Sea oil runs dry, an estimated 60,000 people are still working on the North Sea continental shelves in the oil and gas industries. Hook-up and completion at the Martin Linge field, for example, is a complex process with a workforce of around 2000 in three shifts of between 600 and 700 people offshore at any one time. In the wind energy industry, the manpower required to maintain wind farms has been grossly underestimated. Consequently, Vattenfall has constructed a stand-alone fifty-berth accommodation platform for the Dan Tysk windfarm, 70 km from the closest North Sea port of Esbjerg.(35) Ørsted maintenance and operations teams in North Germany work in shifts, sleeping on board a service operation vessel based close to the cluster of four parks, from which the crew return in a three-week rotation.

Offshore work has a long tradition in fishing and seafaring, where crews lived in cramped quarters for long periods, but were on the move in the large space of the sea. Life on an oil platform is different. Particularly in coastal Norway, offshore workers felt a strong connection to the sea and responded to the sense of adventure associated with the early days of North Sea oil. But on a rig, at least 35 m above the wave-safety level and pressed under the low North Sea sky, an encounter with the sea must be deliberately sought out, as the daily working life is overwhelmingly internalised and ritualised. Nothing happens by chance: offshore workers describe their days and nights being strictly regimented "like a rest home" from 5:30 am to 22:30 pm.(36)

Despite the advantages of rig life, described as time off, good comradeship, and good wages, since 2016 spatial and temporal constraints have been imposed on the UK continental shelf by financial cuts and a deterioration of living conditions. On Shell platforms the established rhythm of two weeks on and two or four weeks off has changed to three on and three off.(37) Workers describe the increased personal strain and the chronic tension building up the week before flying out. Personnel have been added on board to execute overdue maintenance tasks concurrent to ongoing production. To cope with this increase, cabins are shared by three employees, recreational areas have been sacrificed, and galley meals are strictly rostered in rapid 10-15 minute seatings.

Offshore accommodation places temporary living alongside work, under corporate control, within which there is no individuality, no ownership, and no spatial agency. Even surrounded by sea, viscosity in everyday life is reduced to a minimum. In 2016, workers on seven Shell platforms went on strike against pay cuts and new conditions including the intensified three-week rhythm.(38) Workers had suffered several rounds of redundancies with the downturn in North Sea oil, but saw that management wages were still increasing. Despite difficulties, many welcome the "otherness" of the offshore environment and remain. Like oil, this lifestyle is sticky, but the viscous mixture of land and sea is deceivingly inverted: sea life is more regimented than the two or three weeks of freedom on land.

CONCLUSION

Territorial demarcation, construction of a built environment, and sedentary habitation are spatial practices developed on land. To urbanise the maritime through these practices is to provoke a fundamental disjunction between the two systems. While the threshold of exchange between sea and land is permanently crossed and urban systems advance and retreat in mutating formations, the ways in which this process unfolds are also marked by selective adoption of maritime logic. EEZs at once exert sovereignty and uphold free global passage for vessels and sea-floor infrastructure. The spaces constructed for energy production with heavy and resilient materials are temporarily fixed but are also classified as floating vessels and the regulation of periodic residency offshore follows cycles comparable to traditional maritime industries, but is characterised by extreme measures of control in tight, static spaces. The "otherness" of sea space is selectively upheld at the same time as activities systematically undermine its open border conditions, constant movement, and multi-dimensional spaces. The viscous coastal zone has also become selective in what belongs to the mixture of land and sea: views of industrial monuments are not yet admitted, while the open sea is upheld as a cultural artefact.

Viscosity is a condition that can help us read these contradictions in a new light, to accept the irreconcilable mixtures and avoid inherited forms of categorisation. The North Sea is a cultural product—urbanised, occupied, transforming in unexpected ways. Astride Niemani recommends that "We must learn to be at home in the quivering tension of the inbetween. No other home is available."(39) The challenge to designers in the North Sea is to find ways to cultivate diversity without accepting an overriding techno-capitalist approach and to negotiate the emergent and viscous mixture of the urbanised and the maritime.

Volumes of concrete and steel in the North Sea are still negligible in comparison to the volume of water. The increase in viscosity is therefore predominantly metaphorical. However, these materials interact with marine life and build new interdependencies. Viscosities are that which "sticks, congeals and attaches to other things."(40) Offshore oil installations attract large numbers of fish due to slightly warmer water temperatures and food scraps tossed overboard. Along with wind parks, they act as small marine protected areas. Rigs and platforms are biotopes for seabirds and introduced foundations provide new hard substrates for marine species.(41) It is rumoured that seals have taken over the cleaned-out caverns of the huge Ekofisk oil tank, which is the size of a city block and has been "cold" since 1998.(42) The 1500-person ferry MS Norröna trails thin silk ribbons across the North Sea that collect plankton samples for international oceanographic research. Hence the North Sea as a whole is being transformed in a multitude of more and less discrete ways through additional material and cultural layers composed of memory, decay, secretions, coatings, and adhesions, at different scales and speeds, in both biological and industrial time. Viscosity offers designers a way forward within a space of diverse, non-aligned trajectories that periodically intersect and mutually transform their common realm of interaction.

ACKNOWLEDGEMENTS
Thank you to interviewees Gunleiv Hadland, Norwegian Petroleum Museum; Daniel Høyland and Chriss Thomas Grimstad, CCB (NO); Walter Brown, Gavin Mowat and Alexandros Fotakis, Shell platforms (UK); Johann Looden shrimp fisherman (DE), and Paul Fetcher, Scottish Fisherman's Association (UK), for generously contributing their insights into offshore working life and operations in the North Sea fishing and oil and gas sectors.

(1) ICES, "Greater North Sea Ecoregion - Ecosystem Overview'" (2018), http://www.ices.dk/sites/pub/Publication Reports/Forms/DispForm.aspx?ID=35099.
(2) Dutch Ministry of Infrastructure and the Environment and Dutch Ministry of Economic Affairs, "Policy Document on the North Sea 2016–2021" (December 2015), https://www.noordzeeloket.nl/en/policy/noordzeebeleid/@166985/policy-document/.
(3) OSPAR Commission, "Encounters with Chemical and Conventional Munitions 2013," Assessment sheet munitions (London, 2015), https://www.ospar.org/site/assets/files/7413/assessment_sheet_munitions_2015.pdf. Harald Franzen, "Ticking Time Bombs on the Bottom of the North and Baltic Sea" | DW | 23.08.2017', *DW.COM* (23 August 2017), https://www.dw.com/en/ticking-time-bombs-on-the-bottom-of-the-north-and-baltic-sea/a-40200208.
(4) Dutch Ministry of Infrastructure and the Environment and Dutch Ministry of Economic Affairs, "Policy Document on the North Sea 2016–2021."
(5) See chapter 10, this volume.
(6) Leo Oorschot, "Regeneration of the Urban Coastal Area of Scheveningen: Pearl by the Sea," *TRIA Territorio Della Ricerca Su Insediamenti e Ambiente* 11, no. 2 (2013): 171–84.
(7) Nikki Brand, "Urban Flood Control in The Netherlands: A History," *Revista M* 11, no. 1 (1 January 2014): 38–51, https://doi.org/10.15332/rev.m.v11i1.951.
(8) Andrew Barry, "Petrochemical Zones," (Viscous Space- the offshore physicality of the North Sea between solid and liquid, TU Delft: TU Delft, 2018), http://viscousspace.com/.
(9) See chapter 6, this volume.
(10) Stig Kvendseth K, *Giant Discovery. A History of Ekofisk through the First 20 Years.* (Norway: Phillips Petroleum Company, 1988).
(11) Eyal Weizman, "The Geometry of Occupation," (Borders, Centre of Contemporary Culture, Barcelona, 2004), http://www.cccb.org/rcs_gene/geometry_occupation.pdf.
(12) See chapter 4, this volume.
(13) Weizman, "Geometry of Occupation."
(14) Philip E. Steinberg, *The Social Construction of the Ocean* (Cambridge: Cambridge University Press, 2001).
(15) Christer Westerdahl, "The Maritime Cultural Landscape," *International Journal of Nautical Archaeology* 21, no. 1 (1992): 5–14, https://doi.org/10.1111/j.1095-9270.1992.tb00336.x.
(16) Christer Westerdahl, "The Binary Relationship of Sea and Land," in *The Archaeology of Maritime Landscapes*, ed. Ben Ford, When the Land Meets the Sea (New York, NY: Springer, 2011), 291–310, https://doi.org/10.1007/978-1-4419-8210-0_16.
(17) Neil Brenner and Christian Schmid, "Towards a New Epistemology of the Urban?," *City* 19, no. 2–3 (4 May 2015): 151–82, https://doi.org/10.1080/13604813.2015.1014712.
(18) Horatio Clare, "A Freight Adventure: Sailing the Oceans on a Container Ship," *Financial Times* (December 2013), https://www.ft.com/content/4e62c3c8-666d-11e3-aa10-00144feabdc0.
(19) Matti Leppäranta and Kai Myrberg, *Physical Oceanography of the Baltic Sea* (Berlin: Springer, 2009), 262.
(20) Leppäranta and Myrberg, *Physical Oceanography*.
(21) Nancy Couling, Paola Alfaro d'Alençon, and Medine Altiok, "Narrative Cartography: Capturing a Holistic Perspective on Waterscapes," *European Journal of Creative Practices in Cities and Landscapes* 2, no. 1 (20 December 2019): 11–36, https://doi.org/10.6092/issn.2612-0496/8808.no. 1 (20 December 2019
(22) See chapter 7, this volume.
(23) United Nations, "Convention on the Continental Shelf," (29 April 1958), https://treaties.un.org/doc/Publication/UNTS/Volume%20499/volume-499-I-7302-English.pdf.
(24) Keller Easterling, *Extrastatecraft: The Power of Infrastructure Space* (London: Verso, 2014).
(25) Keller Easterling, *Enduring Innocence : Global Architecture and Its Political Masquerades* (Cambridge, MA: MIT, 2005),70).
(26) David Langlet, "Nord Stream, the Environment and the Law: Disentangling a Multijurisdictional Energy Project," *Scandinavian Studies in Law* 59, (March 2014): 80–108.
(27) https://www.equinor.com/en/magazine/electrification-of-oil-and-gas-platforms.html
(28) Pierre Bélanger, "Altitudes of Urbanization," *Tunnelling and Underground Space Technology*, Urban Underground Space: A Growing Imperative Perspectives and

Current Research in Planning and Design for Underground Space Use, 55 (1 May 2016): 5–7, https://doi.org/10.1016/j.tust.2015.09.011.
(29) See chapter 3, this volume.
(30) Harry Gugger and Barbara Costa, 'Urban-Nature: The Ecology of Planetary Artifice', *San Rocco* 10, no. Ecology (2014).
(31) Interview conducted with local shrimp fisherman, December 2017, Grietsiel, (DE).
(32) See fig. 1, chapter 5, this volume.
(33) BSH:Federal Maritime and Hydrographic Agency, "Marine Spatial Plan for the Exclusive Economic Zone of the Baltic Sea," December 2009, http://www.bsh.de/en/Marine_uses/Spatial_Planning_in_the_German_EEZ/documents2/Spatial_Plan_Baltic_Sea.pdf.
(34) Vera Eckert, "German North Sea Wind Capacity Rose Almost to 2020 Target Last Year - TenneT," *Reuters* (13 January 2020), https://www.reuters.com/article/us-windpower-north-sea-tennet-idUSKBN1ZC144.
(35) "Die Nordstory - Das Offshore-Hotel Wohnen Und Arbeiten Auf Der Plattform" (NDR Norddeutsche Rundfunk, 19 July 2018), https://www.ndr.de/fernsehen/sendungen/die_nordstory/Das-Offshore-Hotel,sendung635630.html.
(36) Interviews conducted with offshore workers by author; see doi 10.4121/uuid:6c360a50-062d-4451-965b-2ec14e38b33c
(37) The Norwegian rule is still currently two weeks on/four weeks off.
(38) Andrew Ward, "North Sea Oil Workers Strike over Jobs and Pay," *Financial Times* (4 August 2016), https://www.ft.com/content/e655db44-5999-11e6-9f70-badea1b336d4.
(39) Astrida Niemanis, "Hydrofeminism: Or, On Becoming a Body of Water," in *Undutiful Daughters: New Directions in Feminist Thought and Practice*, ed. H. Gunkel et al., (New York: Palgrave Macmillan, 2012), 108https://www.palgrave.com/gp/book/9780230118317.
(40) Karen Lutsky, Ozayr Saloojee, and Scott Emily Eliza, eds., *Viscosity—Mobilizing Materialities*, Uminn Papers on Architecture 4 (Minneapolis-Saint Paul: University of Minnesota School of Architecture, 2017), https://issuu.com/umndesign/docs/viscosity--mobilizing_materialities.
(41) See chapter 11, this volume.
(42) H. D. Trotter, "The Ekofisk Tank--A Concrete Gravity Structure In The Norwegian North Sea" (Annual Meeting Papers, Division of Production, American Petroleum Institute, 1974), https://www.onepetro.org/conference-paper/API-74-B001. See image 5, chapter 7.

Chapter 13 MEGA PORTS AND GLOBALISM, ON LAND AND OFFSHORE: CONCEPTUALISING COMPLEXITY

Susan Dunne

Approaching the mega port of Rotterdam at the human scale is a daunting task. With students and colleagues, Susan Dunne infiltrates the port and surrounding area to reveal a series of uncanny disjunctions at the edge condition of global infrastructure.

Susan Dunne is an associate professor in ENSA Paris Malaquais School of Architecture, a researcher in the LAA lab (www.laa.archi.fr/ ENSA Paris La Villette), and a practicing architect, with an MSc in Architecture from Trinity College, Dublin. Her area of expertise is transport infrastructure, which she has been working on for over three decades. Her research is currently concerned with the question of maritime infrastructure, and the different stakes at play on land and offshore. She leads an interdisciplinary master studio "Changing Cities" which focuses on mutating urban environments and un undergraduate studio centred around "What's Becoming of Water?" She has taught in France, Ireland, Northern Ireland, Holland, Austria, Italy, Turkey, and Hong Kong.

This chapter seeks primarily to highlight how deconstructing maritime infrastructure—in the framework of architectural education—can inform and question the stakes at play, at both territorial and local scales. To illustrate this point, we will review investigations carried out in the architectural master studio “Changing Cities: Mega Ports and Globalism, on Land and Offshore.”(1) Grounded in the use of architecture as an analytic device, observation platform, and participative forum, the Changing Cities studio, as the name suggests, questions evolutionary forms of urbanity. The studio embraces a multi-scalar, multi-disciplinary (anthropology, urbanism, geography), and experiential research/project approach.

In the first part of this chapter we will look at how new forms of production and distribution have transformed port cities into logistics hubs with immeasurable ramifications, and how common representations of the ocean and containerisation have contributed to blurring our understanding of the extent of these infrastructural extensions.(2)

In the second part we will discuss how the predominance of global industrial interests over local concerns has created many uncanny disjunctions. The juxtaposition of incongruous situations; such as the siting of an oil refinery next to a residential area, an automatic container terminal next to a medieval town, or a chemical treatment plant next to a bathing area, are to be found all around the port of Rotterdam. These binaries (industry/nature, automation/cultivation,) or antagonistic proximities are rarely discussed, or assessed in conjunction, and it is precisely these edge conditions that we chose to look at in detail. The multimedia representations illustrated were created by the students in connection with their particular paths of enquiry and chosen sites in the port of Rotterdam.

In the final part of this chapter we will focus on how transport systems are intrinsically related to digital networks (or system design). We will consider how spatial networks have become more and more de-contextualized, and why, as a result, we need new tools to analyse the spatial and environmental consequences of global networks.

FROM THE GLOBAL TO THE GENERIC: DECONSTRUCTING INFRASTRUCTURE AND ITS RAMIFICATIONS

The exponential growth of delocalised manufacturing, mass production, and twenty-four-hour online shopping has set in motion extensive supply chains, which in turn, have fuelled the construction of global terrestrial and maritime infrastructures.(3) As cargo traffic grows and operational requirements evolve, roads are widened, canals are deepened, and bridges are raised. Forests, agricultural lands, and villages are cut in two, lakes are filled in, seas are dredged, and earthworks are extensively built. New bigger ships, barges, and trucks are manufactured and freight lines are extended to facilitate the passage of container-conveyer belt infrastructure across the globe. The inter-nodal points of ports, airports, freight stations, and truck parks, are also continuously being re-dimensioned and upgraded to meet the latest requirements, technological "advances" and growing fleets.

If we apply logistics logic, maritime infrastructure is an extension of land infrastructure, and vice versa: both networks are part of the same global trade route.(4) Of all goods, 90 percent travel by sea. "The sea in the age of containerisation has become the conveyer belt of global trade, a site of 24/7/365 operations," to cite writer Ying Sze Peck's apt assessment.(5)

Despite the growth in maritime traffic and in containerisation in particular, there has been little interest shown in the consequences for the ocean. Geographer Philip Steinberg points out that a possible contributing factor may be "the era's emphasis on movement and speed" and the perpetuation of the "great void ideal." He explains that "The aim is to annihilate any unique characteristics of the environments across which the containers move" and states that "trade is reduced to movement."(6) By focusing primarily on the speed and movement, we lose sight of the contents and their cumulative effect and by perpetuating the "great void ideal of ocean space," the ocean loses its substance and is rendered placeless.

In Allan Sekula's documentary film "The Forgotten Space," which he shoots in part from the deck of a container ship, the sea is still, almost abstract, and the journey is primarily flat and monotonous.(7) The enormous ship piled high with containers dominates the seascape and pushes indifferently across the ocean. We are numbed or haunted by the anonymity of the environment. Sekula points out again and again in his writings how "anonymous" the containers and their contents are, and "how the concrete movement of goods can be explained in its totality only through recourse to abstraction."(8)

To compound the matter, there are very few comprehensive maps available representing the activities taking place at sea that are akin to land-use maps. High-resolution satellite views exist for most of the earth's land surface, but not for the sea. Maritime passage charts and land maps are two very separate constructs—the two milieus are rarely represented together.

Global trade and offshore economies flourish beyond land boundaries and many countries yield large profits from their offshore activities. Looking at regions from a sea and land perspective together gives us a much broader understanding of today's geopolitical stakes. In an attempt to create a somewhat comprehensive picture of both milieus and of maritime infrastructure and its ramifications, we began by mapping the North Sea and the South China Sea and surrounding lands as continuous geographies and by representing the maritime infrastructure in conjunction with

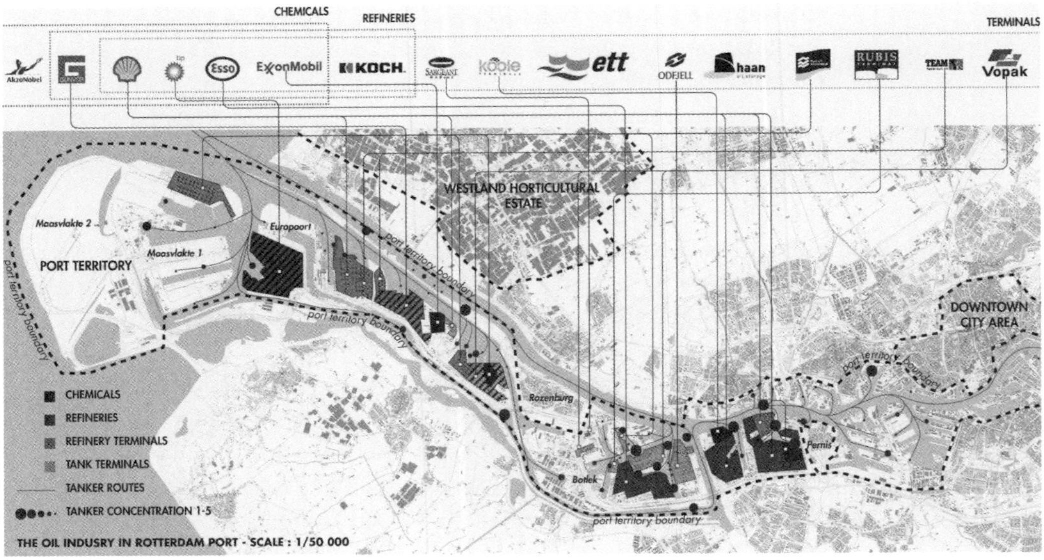

Fig. 1
Location map of petro chemical plants and study areas, port of Rotterdam. (Djuna Patin, Paris Malaquais School of Architecture, 2018)

the land infrastructure. In this way, a complex yet impressive picture emerges beyond the landmasses and helps reveal the interconnected complexity of the geography and infrastructure on land and at sea.

GLOBAL PORTS

Terminal design (ports, airports, exchange platforms), just like transport network design, is a spatial translation of supply chains and flow processes. The port, like the sea, is a "site of 24/7/365 operations," a machine for processing goods from land to sea, river, rail, and road. Unnecessary stoppages are avoided; less than 5 percent of the containers are opened for inspection.(9)

The arrival of giant container ships, lift on-lift off and roll on-roll off technologies, and digital port networks have revolutionised global ports and container shipping. They have brought about a total change in the way ports operate and are spatially organised. The modern container port is automated; the chain supplies are seamless, odourless, and soulless. Global ports and particularly container terminals are generic in nature. Global transport logistics dictate their territorial layout.

We carried out comparative research on three global ports: Rotterdam, Singapore, and Hong Kong.(10) Although located in different parts of the globe, they offer similar port facilities, and are connected to global web port systems. Each port houses a similar number of container terminals, petrochemical industries, dry bulk (sand, ore, coal, agribulk), and break bulk facilities (individually loaded goods); each accommodates comparable maritime traffic and is built primarily on reclaimed land, securitised, and distanced from the city centre.

Where they differ though, is in how they have adapted the infrastructure to their particular geographies, and their geographies to the infrastructure. The port of Hong Kong, for example, which is exposed to recurrent cyclones and tropical climatic conditions and sits alongside steep mountainous terrain, is made up of several independent sheltered terminals and floating docks, sited throughout the bay. The port of Rotterdam, on the other hand, which is situated below sea level, is equipped with heavily engineered dams, dikes, and gigantic locks to facilitate sealing off the port in the case of a storm surge [Fig. 1].

The layouts and engineering of the three ports are different, but they all cover extensive territories. The port of Rotterdam, for example, measures approximately 12,713 hectares including the waterways, and the land area measures approximately 7,903 ha while the downtown city area (intramural) measures only 326 ha.(11) Rotterdam port is the eleventh-largest port in the world, the biggest in Europe, and in 2019 it saw a freight throughput of 469.4 million tonnes.(12)

Global ports depend on vast logistics platforms, commonly situated outside the port boundaries. In the port of Rotterdam, there are several logistic platforms. The Westland Horticultural Estate, situated to the north-west of the port, is an impressive example of a very large-scale industrial horticultural zone covering an area of roughly 2,000 hectares and dedicated to planting, growing, packing, storing, selling, and distributing fruit and flowers. The "smart" sterile glasshouses, fitted with the latest automation technologies and disinfection techniques, function on a pre-programmed 24-hour clock, 357 days a year.

The glasshouses, adjacent to the farmers' houses, back onto immense truck garages. The house is no longer *just* a home, it is also an office/commercial/industrial outlet. The boundaries between residential, agricultural, and industrial are no longer distinguishable [Fig. 2].

Adding up the spatial and environmental footprints of the global port(s), logistic platforms, transport corridors, and the offshore installations and activities would be an impossible endeavour and not to a small degree because of the scale, but also because of the inaccessibility of relevant information, blurring of boundaries, abstraction of processes, and the perpetuation of the "great void" myth about the ocean.

FROM THE GENERIC TO THE UNCANNY: CONCEPTUALISING SITUATED DISJUNCTIONS

The recent industrial expansion and digitalisation of the port of Rotterdam has not only transformed the port and surrounding territories into a vast logistics and industrial hub, but has created many points of friction (ruptures of scale, land use, temporalities) at the local scale.

Fig. 2
Westland Industrial Horticultural Estate. (Dusica Eric, Paris Malaquais School of Architecture, 2019)

Discussing "Practice of Place," contemporary artist Emma Smith states that:

> It raises questions of how we measure an experienced space and of how tactical modes of habitation—walking, cycling, collaborating, encountering, playing, mapping, drawing, and acting—influence our understanding and are about engaging with space and how it is inhabited rather than just representing it.(13)

During field trips with the students, we set out to inhabit the port as wholeheartedly as possible and in the spirit of Smith's "Practice of Place," visited most of the port by bike, boat, bus, and on foot. We mapped, sketched, constructed installations, and enacted performances, questioning the essence of the sites and stakes at play, and we met with the port authorities, port operators, marine crew, local actors, and inhabitants. These actions and encounters became catalysts for the conceptual pieces developed afterwards. These were no ordinary site visits. Travelling for days around a port that measures roughly 40 km long by 12 km wide, facing the wind and the rain, breathing in the fumes and the pungent smells, watching remote-controlled port systems and measureless industrial landscapes where there is hardly a person in sight, left us with an unsettling sense of having experienced something that was impossible to add up, or fully comprehend. The students selected emblematic sites or situated disjunctions in the port of Rotterdam for greater scrutiny. The sites are not static circumscribed areas; they represent loosely a number of symptomatic situations particular to the port of Rotterdam, and together they help create a picture of the complexity of the territory. We put the emphasis at this stage on capturing "the spirit of place," rather than trying to get a complete picture, which would have been impossible, in any case. The combination of affective and analytical methods in the production of research-led architectural investigations is, in our opinion, of greater epistemological value than the assessing of only readily visible and quantifiable aspects.

CONCEPTUALISING SITUATED DISJUNCTIONS

1.PERNIS: LIVING NEXT DOOR TO SHELL

Pernis, our first study area, situated at the east end of the port, is a sub-municipality of the city of Rotterdam, with 4,845 inhabitants [Fig. 1]. It was once an isolated farming village. Today, it is better known as Shell Village. The Pernis Shell refinery, built in the 1960s, revamped in the 1990s, right next to Pernis Shell Village, is Europe's largest refinery, processing 404,000 barrels per day of crude oil.(14) Most of the employed inhabitants of Pernis work in, or in connection with, the Shell refinery or adjacent tank terminal. Shell works hand in hand with the local council, investing considerable sums of money in leisure, social services, and residual heating (from the refinery), and on landscaping projects for the town. Small ponies, and a few sheep, reminiscent of the farming village, graze in the enhanced landscaped borders surrounding the town.

From within, the village appears at first to be an isolated residential area completely separated from the refinery, by the adjacent motorway and metro line. In fact, a private road connects the two sites on its northern edge, and a barge dock with storage facilities, dedicated to transporting refined oil products, can be found on the "residential side" of the site. The physical, social, and economic interconnections are deeply embedded in the two territories.(15)

In a small dwelling, in the middle of the town, there is a Shell museum run by local inhabitants, which welcomes visitors to view the collection of Shell merchandising (from decorative plates to old photographs, old maps, tableware, books, and other Shell paraphernalia). The museum glorifies and celebrates Shell's past and present activities.

The Pernis model invites us to focus on the two areas in conjunction and to question the incredible proximity, intricate relations, and the difference in morphology and scale between the industrial plant and residential town, and to note the *thinness* of the enhanced landscaped borders surrounding the town [Fig. 3].

2.EUROPOORT: INHABITING INDUSTRIAL LANDSCAPES

Europoort, our second study area, is a heavily industrialised area, in the western centre of the port, covering roughly 2,000 hectares, comprised of six extensive petrochemical installations (two refineries, two refinery terminals and two tank terminals), a dry bulk (coal, ore, and sand) terminal, a liquid bulk container terminal, and ferry terminal [Fig. 1]. At a distance of about 500 metres, on the opposite bank of the canal, behind trees and a fence, can be found a small mobile restaurant, De Albatros, and a popular campsite, Kruiningegors. Both are dots in the middle of the industrial expanse.

We spent several days in De Albatros café, talking with André, the café owner, the campers, and other visitors who went there for hot snacks, and to shelter from the rain. We noted how the decor, made up of matching check tablecloths, lamps, and (permanently closed) curtains, personal mementos, and holiday pictures, created a cosy and personal oasis. The campers we met spoke of how they returned there, year after year, to fish, relax, and contemplate the (industrial) landscape. Rather than assessing the industrial area in purely industrial terms, we chose to look at the area through the eyes of the campers and the restaurant owner (André), to question their view of the habitability of domestic areas next to such a large industrial environment.

The conceptual pieces developed afterwards took on a somewhat dystopian quality. Inside a black steel space frame, the interior of André's café was created in miniature, down to the curtains, tablecloths, pictures, flower arrangements, and souvenirs with which he had adorned his café. The model invites us to look closely at the two environments, to recognise the uncanny confrontation of scale, materiality, and culture. It reveals the stark contrast and tension inherent in the insertion of intimate domestic spaces in immense industrial landscapes.

Europoort is conveniently hidden and inaccessible. There are buffers or landscaped borders all around it: fences, walls, trees, rivers, canals, roads and motorways (as there are around all the terminals and large industrial plants in the port), cutting it off physically and visually from the neighbouring towns of Pernis, Brielle, Oostevoorne, and Rozenburg. The towns function like little autonomous islands.

Fig. 3
Pernis Shell refinery on the left and residential town on the right. (Romane Bennatar, Sevdalina Valkova, and Lara Swiecickiy, Paris Malaquais School of Architecture, 2019)

Dedicated to making the most of their towns, residents compete in tidy town competitions, flower shows, and sporting events. Like André in his café, they too—on another scale—are proudly making their spaces homely, attractive, and welcoming, despite the industrial sites that loom large next door.

3.BOTLEK: UPSIDE-DOWN OIL LANDSCAPES

Botlek, our third study area, in the eastern centre of the port, is a heavily industrialised area comprised of five tank terminals and an extensive oil refinery, covering an area of roughly 270 hectares.(16) [Fig. 1]. The site is highly securitised and sealed off from neighbouring areas. Being able to only visualise the gleaming oil fortress from the outside, we spent most of the time mapping and drawing, behind the security fences, and sourcing information at a distance. The secrecy and security issues raised many debates about what is visible and what is invisible—what is withheld and what is told and how much access to, or knowledge of, such installations do we really have for assessment.

Saskia Sassen draws attention, in her book *Expulsions: Brutality and Complexity in the Global Economy*, to the vast quantities of dead land, dead water, and the expulsions of habitats across the globe that are caused by large-scale industrialisation and how, “In sufficient concentrations, industrial waste, including heavy metals and greenhouse gases, can render an environment so toxic that plants cease to grow and even people become sterile.”(17) After meticulously drawing and building models, and investigating the refinery processes, the Botlek student group created allegorical figurations inspired by Sassen’s writings, questioning the “invisible” effects on the subsoil of refining industrial quantities of oil.

Fig. 4
Botlek: Upside-Down Oil Landscapes. (Djuna Patin, Paris Malaquais School of Architecture 2018)

Birds fly below the upturned trees,
remnants of a past forever buried deep below layers of viscous oily soil, and the smoking industrial chimneys of the refinery.
Susan Dunne

The gleaming image we have of oil refineries is intentionally disturbed by the layers of toxic waste and damaged earth suggested in the upside-down subterranean world hidden below the refinery, represented in an additional conceptual model. At first sight, the work is deceptive. It is tempting to keenly admire its aesthetic value, until we realise that there is an underworld, another dimension, where the natural elements have been replaced, reversed, destroyed [Fig. 4].

4.MAASVLAKTE 1: NATURE VERSUS INDUSTRY

Maasvlakte 1, our fourth study area, on the south-western seafront of the port, built in the 1970s on a large reclaimed land extension, covers roughly 2,000 hectares, and is comprised of an oil terminal, a dry bulk terminal, three container terminals, and a toxic waste plant [Fig. 1]. During the last decade, a nature and sport theme park (Natuurstrand), composed of a fishing area, sea-sports area, and nudist beach, was constructed just behind the toxic waste lake (slufter) and landfill site.(18) The siting of such amenities and natural areas next to what is known to be one of the most toxic areas in the port provoked many debates. One can only speculate that the (toxic) liquid vapour clouds that form above the lake must at some stage return to the ground and penetrate other water bodies and have significant effects on neighbouring ecosystems. While exploring the area, we spotted a deer grazing in front of the vast industrial landscape. This key moment, captured on video, led to a journey questioning the place of nature next to industry and raised issues about what parts of the territory are really "natural," and about how nature-like sport is used as a device.

The bust of a deer, imaging the opening scene in the video, was sculpted in plastic straws, evoking subtly the question of oil extraction and transformation, and the orchestration of nature next to industry [Fig. 5]. From zoos to theme parks, artificial environments are created, hewn from the raw materials of the natural world, which are then reshaped and altered to depict a passive image of nature. These buffer zones of pacified nature serve to create an idealised image in the foreground and keep other less than ideal realities at a safe distance in the background.

5.MAASVLAKTE 2: ABSTRACT LANDS AND CONCRETE FUTURES

Maasvlakte 2, our fifth study area, on the western seafront, is the last extension to the port of Rotterdam. Phase 1 was (partly) inaugurated in 2012. It houses the latest completely automated container terminal and container exchange route known as the Rotterdam World Gateway and covers an area of roughly 2,000 hectares.

The conceptual pieces developed in this case by the students questioned how decisions made in boardrooms in the city, far removed from the territories where they are enacted, lead to the fabrication of a de-contextualised port, removed from its culture and geography, an abstract place, yet so concrete and frighteningly real. The question of sand extraction and land reclamation became the motor for an eerie

Fig. 5
Straw model of a deer (Pierre Johan Gicquiaud, Paris Malaquais School of Architecture 2018)

conceptual model of a boardroom design meeting, figuring bodies buried in the bodies of earth that were used for the land reclamation (of Maasvlackte 2). The tone of the piece was undoubtedly dark, outlining clearly that lives (and livelihoods) are at stake, and not only human ones, when geographies are destroyed and new extensive lands are manufactured and automated.

Given the immensity and technicity of such automated territories it is next to impossible to imagine what forms of cultivation or habitation could be permitted, or deemed sustainable in such places today, without a reasoned deceleration, downscaling, and redistribution of the infrastructural installations [Fig. 6].

6.OFFSHORE INSIDIOUS DEPENDENCE: VITAL ARTERIES

This last piece inquires into the insidious dependency we nurture with the offshore and how hooked up to the consumer network we are: it feeds us and we feed it [Fig. 7, p. 187]. Maritime routes are vital arteries of contemporary society. Offshore oil, gas, and mineral extraction are fast-growing sectors and economies.(19)

The image "puts a light on" the hidden intricate connections that exist between offshore rigs, port infrastructure (namely in this case the port of Rotterdam), underwater networks, and the few remaining fish in the sea, inviting us to review the extended maritime infrastructure and the damage our consumer dependency is causing marine ecosystems.

The question of the intensity and the immensity of the multiple networks that link the land to the ocean has yet to be seriously identified and evaluated. What is clear though is that land and sea infrastructure are intrinsically enmeshed and increasingly de-contextualised. In the case of the global port, the downtown city centre is a circumscribed quarter, physically removed from the port infrastructure. The port functions in a controlled space and sphere, regulated by extra-territorial dimensions (generic systems, global shipping scale, and nonstop connectivity). It is these extra-territorial conditions that are superseding regional geographies and climates, and creating rude awakenings and disjunctions for local cultures and habitats.

In each of the case studies or situated disjunctions discussed above, it was difficult to precisely assess the industrial footprint, not least because of the size and technicity of the installations, but also because of the intricate relations fostered between the inhabitants (consumers) and the industrialists, and the security measures and devices that were implemented to protect or hide the sites. However, the ruptures of geographies, scale, land use, life styles, technologies, and temporalities were clearly visible between the extensive global infrastructure, the downtown city, and the shrinking, isolated towns and habitats.

SYSTEM INFRASTRUCTURE: VIRTUALLY NO LIMITS

The systems that characterise spatial system design (infrastructure) are similar in nature to virtual system design in that they embrace similar philosophies and comparable goals: the productivity of the system is paramount and the physical embodiment is about packaging the system. Location is secondary.

Fig. 6 Maasvlakte 2- Boardroom decisions and De-contextualized lands (Adrien Renborn, Ana Varanda sa Leite Guimaraes, and Fengyi Zhang)

Terminal network or system design is generic in nature, be it a computer, an airport terminal, or a port. Such systems can be applied in almost any location, as the main criteria for quantifying and qualifying them have to do with their efficiency, economy, and generic attractiveness—not their cultural rootedness or specificity. For example, ports have been built on purpose-made islands, on rocky mountainous terrain, and on marshy lands. Dry ports are springing up in rural as well as in urban areas. Global ports look alike throughout the globe.

Virtual and spatial systems (transport infrastructure), are also intricately interrelated: the growth of one influences the growth of the other. Trafficking and connecting in the virtual world impacts the real world, but distances you from the consequences. Who asks themselves or knows how far goods travel or what type of infrastructure is built as a result of one-click online buying and massive consumerism?

The question we may ask is, as Vandana Shiva puts it, infrastructure for which structure? Shiva explains,

> An infrastructure holds together a structure. However, increasingly, the word infrastructure is being used without specification of the structure of society that it supports. In World Bank jargon, the assumption is that infrastructure should support a fossil fuel-based society for the elite, with the needs and rights of the poor not taken into account.(20)

What is happening in Rotterdam is taking place in many other global port cities; they too are being restructured around flows of capital, transport, and energy rather than around neighbourhood or community. Paul Virilio states that "the architecture of systems has definitively replaced architectural and urban systems." He notes that transport inter-modal hubs are replacing the "rooted urban experience" as speed and connections are becoming the predominant considerations in the increasingly mobile society we live in.(21)

Globalisation has changed the way we operate. In architectural education, we also need to change our ways of thinking and our methods to take into account the consequences of global infrastructure, and how it imposes its scale and systems on different milieus and vast territories.

Conceptualising complex infrastructural networks is one of the ways we can demystify systems and their complexity and arouse concern and emotion about their growing impact. It also gives us the freedom to question different sides of the situation, not only the network as a system, but also the living elements affected by the system. Infrastructure or network technology is too often designed and managed by "experts" who are concerned with their own particular discipline and not trained or expected to act outside their disciplinary borders.

The spatial view that urban design and architecture can offer is urgently needed in analysing the consequences of territorial infrastructural development. Our engagement is about enlightening communities and motivating industrialists to question the relevance, scale, and impact of the system overload, and to work toward a more reasoned and participatory deceleration, rather than blindly feeding the conveyer belt of global trade.

(1) The investigations discussed here were carried out by the teachers, Susan Dunne and François Bruneau, and the master's degree students, during the Changing Cities studios (2018 and 2019) at the Paris Malaquais School of Architecture.
(2) The immeasurable ramifications referred to here are the multiform infrastructural extensions that service global trade routes on land and offshore, including, but not exclusively, the roadways, freight-rail lines, canals, logistic areas, parking lots, pipelines, cables, data centers and other sea bed infrastructures and networks. The intention here is to stress that these entities are part of the same global supply chain system and are interdependent - when the industrial components or vehicles are re-dimensioned the infrastructure follows suit.
(3) When considering maritime cargo (growth) figures there are 2 principal measures to be taken into consideration, capacity expansion and traffic growth "The world container ship fleet has experienced profound development since the 1990s. Carrying capacity has increased by a factor of 6, from 1990 to 2014. Ship size has increased continuously. The biggest ship was less than 2000 TEUs at the beginning of the 1970s, less than 5000 TEUs at the beginning of the 1990s, today it is 18,000 TEUs. Empty traffic (empty containers) has grown even faster than the world traffic, 234% vs. 223% in the 2000s." Nguyen Khoi Tran, Hans-Dietrich Haasis, *An empirical study of fleet expansion and growth of ship size in container liner shipping*, International Journal of Production Economics, January 2014
(4) The China's Belt and Road Initiative (BRI) is a typical example of an integrated large-scale land-sea infrastructure project.
(5) Ying Sze Peck, "The Dialectic of Calm Waters: The Forgotten Space's Documentary Pictures," *Art Papers* 42.02 (2018).
(6) Philip E. Steinberg, *The Social Construction of the Ocean* (Cambridge: Cambridge University Press, 2001). pp 164-165
(7) Allan Sekula, *The Forgotten Space* (Wildart Film, 2010).
(8) Allan Sekula, *Fish Story* (Rotterdam: Witte de With, 2014[1995]).
(9) The containers have a barcode tracking label on the outside which is scanned and checked for conformity with the port-net system during port custom operations. In the case of non conformity or spot checks a limited number of containers are opened for scrutiny. The figure (less than 5 percent) was stated by the port operator guide in the port of Rotterdam (during field trips in 2018 and 2019). It is not surprising considering the emphasis put on streamlining and optimizing the flow system.
(10) The comparative research on the three ports included a functional, spatial, geographical, and historical analysis. This was done by using corporate, state, open and academic sources and by using use the same mapping and representation techniques for the different ports in order to compare effectively.
(11) The port of Rotterdam (Rotterdam: Marinke Steenhuis ed.nai010 publishers, 2015) pp 26-38 and https://www.portofrotterdam.com/en/our-port/facts-figures-about-the-port
(12) Ibid.
(13) Emma Smith, *Practice of Place* (London: Bedford Press, UK, 2015).
(14) https://www.portofrotterdam.com/en/our-port/facts-figures-about-the-port
(15) The nearest house in the town of Pernis is 450 meters away from the Shell refinery's gas storage tanks. The Shell refinery is a Seveso site and as such is classified as a high risk industrial plant.
16) https://www.portofrotterdam.com/en/our-port/facts-figures-about-the-port
((17) Saskia Sassens, *Expulsions: Brutality and Complexity in the Global Economy* (Cambridge, MA: Harvard University Press, 2014). p 155
(18) The *slufter* is a 250-hectare open-air liquid depot for extremely contaminated dredged material and synthetic chemical substances. Surrounded by a 24-metre-high landfill boundary, the lake bottom is 28 metres below sea level.
(19) Analyse- Les abysses: une promesse pour l'avenir, Focus- Pétrole et gaz *offshore*, le défi des grands fonds *Diplomatie, les grands dossiers* - N° 33, *Géopolitique des mers et des océans*, juin-juillet 2016. p 8-12
(20) Vandana Shiva, *Soil not Oil: Environmental Justice in an Age of Climate Crisis* (London: Zed Books, 2016). p 63
(21) Paul Virilio, *L'espace critique* (Christian Bourgois Editeur, 1984)

Chapter 14 2050: AN ENERGETIC ODYSSEY —PERSUASION BY COLLECTIVE IMMERSION*

Maarten Hajer & Dirk Sijmons

The grand scale of North Sea wind-enery potential is laid out in an installation for the International Architecture Biennale Rotterdam in 2016. With this project, Dirk Sijmons and Maarten Hajer demonstrate the power of design in unleashing the imagination.

Maarten Hajer is a Dutch political scientist and urban and regional planner, Professor of Public Policy at the University of Amsterdam, and was chief curator of International Architecture Biennale Rotterdam (IABR) 2016. Educated at the universities of Amsterdam and Oxford he has published widely on city politics, public space, political discourse, environment and democracy.

Dirk Sijmons is a landscape architect, one of the three founders of H + N + S Landscape Architects and was also a Professor of Landscape Architecture at TU Delft. He was chief curator of IABR–2014–"Urban by Nature" and received the "Landscape & Energy- Designing Transition" prize (2014), the IFLA–Sir Geoffrey Jellicoe Award, & the Landezine International Landscape Award (LILA) in 2017.

*This essay was previously published in Scenario 07:*Power, Fall 2019 https://scenario-journal.com/article/2050-an-energetic-odyssey/*

WHAT IS AN ENERGETIC ODYSSEY?

"2050: An Energetic Odyssey" was designed as a large floor projection of 5.5 × 8 metres for the International Architecture Biennale Rotterdam 2016, with a theme of "The Next Economy"(1). Using an animated narration, we created an immersive experience to show how the deployment of 25,000 wind turbines on the North Sea could provide some 90 percent of the electricity demand of the countries bordering the North Sea by 2050.(2)

MOTIVE: A DOUBLE CRISIS OF THE IMAGINATION

We observed a crisis of the imagination. In discussions of the energy transition, there is a common assumption that fossil fuels require big installations and centralised state power, while renewables are small and decentralised. This is coupled with disbelief and scepticism that "soft renewable" sources will ever be able to fuel an industrial society like the one that exists. Rather than reiterating "small is beautiful," we wanted to show that a future of renewables can involve a massive investment: Big is Beautiful.

We presented an imaginary in which the North Sea would be the powerhouse of renewables. We explained how, given the right political ambition and "Chinese building speeds," an energy landscape of thousands of wind turbines might fit in one of the world's most intensively used coastal waters. This grand operation could even result in a positive boost for the marine ecosystem [Fig. 1, Fig. 2, Fig. 3 & Fig. 4, p. 188].

THE ANIMATED NARRATIVE

The story is told in twelve minutes. At times the narrative closely follows what you see in the projection, and for large parts it roams more freely using the animation as a backdrop to the steadily unrolling story of the deployment of 25,000 wind turbines. Other dynamic elements are a year-counter to gauge whether we are on track to meet the 2050 deadline, and pop-up infographics showing the energy used, the jobs lost and won by replacing fossil fuel with a renewable offshore industry, the construction island needed to convert AC to DC. Probably the most impressive is the illustration of how a turbine park can be shut down when flocks of migrating birds are approaching. At these times the voice-over and the animation are meticulously synchronised. Approaching the end, we let the sun come up in the animation while inserted aerial films show the rather moderate visual impact of the wind turbine parks from the shore. The floor projection is supported first of all by a 12 metre concertina fold containing the scenarios, calculations, and the construction details of the renewable future [Fig. 5]. Secondly, large flat screens showing contrasting images of the human engineering and the rich underwater life of the North Sea. A third screen summarises the most important key figures of the narrative.

BEHIND THE SCREEN: THE MAKING OF...

The interactive production of the installation, in the "free cultural domain" of the IABR, forged a coalition of key actors. These actors not only contributed financially but also gave "in kind" contributions lending their specialists to inform the narrative and to discuss "landing rights" for the intervention. It made the animation an intense collaboration between designers and scientists, and a snowball effect of an expanding consortium with expert input from builders, offshore specialists, ministries, energy firms, a transmission system operator, port authorities, and environmental and nature NGOs. Stakeholders used preliminary versions of the installation and the maps we produced for their deliberations. Environmental NGOs organised a conference of marine ecologists from the North Sea countries, with the animation used as a backdrop to discuss the pros and cons of such an operation, as well as the ecological development possibilities that they could identify.

IMPACT

Showing the early concepts of the presentation started a buzz, word got around, and ultimately we were invited to give a "sneak preview" of this giant floor projection to the energy ministers of the twenty-eight European countries during the Dutch presidency of the EU. Moreover, on the 6th of June 2016, an agreement was signed between the UK, Ireland, Norway, Sweden, France, Denmark, Germany, Belgium, and the Netherlands to boost cooperation on turning the North Sea into our central energy landscape. Of course, this agreement was not "design driven." But interviews reveal that sharing the animation and the narrative played a role in this process.(3)

Based on the animation, a business-led coalition formed at the IABR exhibition to urge the Dutch government to speed up its policies regarding the energy transition. The Odyssey (again) demonstrated the power of research by design.(4) It shows that with this kind of research it is possible to address problems that will never have a paying client. In our day-to-day practice, our ability to contribute to the big environmental questions of the day may be limited, but research by design in free cultural or academic realms considerably broadens the scope of design.

Fig. 5
A part of the twelve-metre concertina fold with the scenarios and calculations

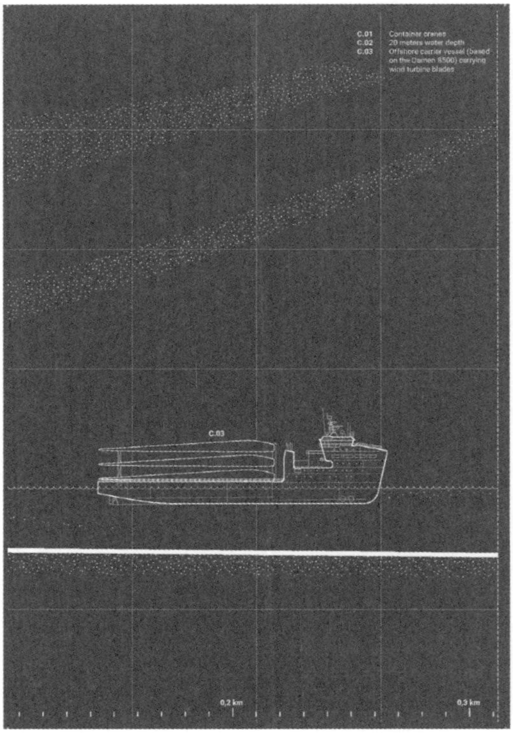

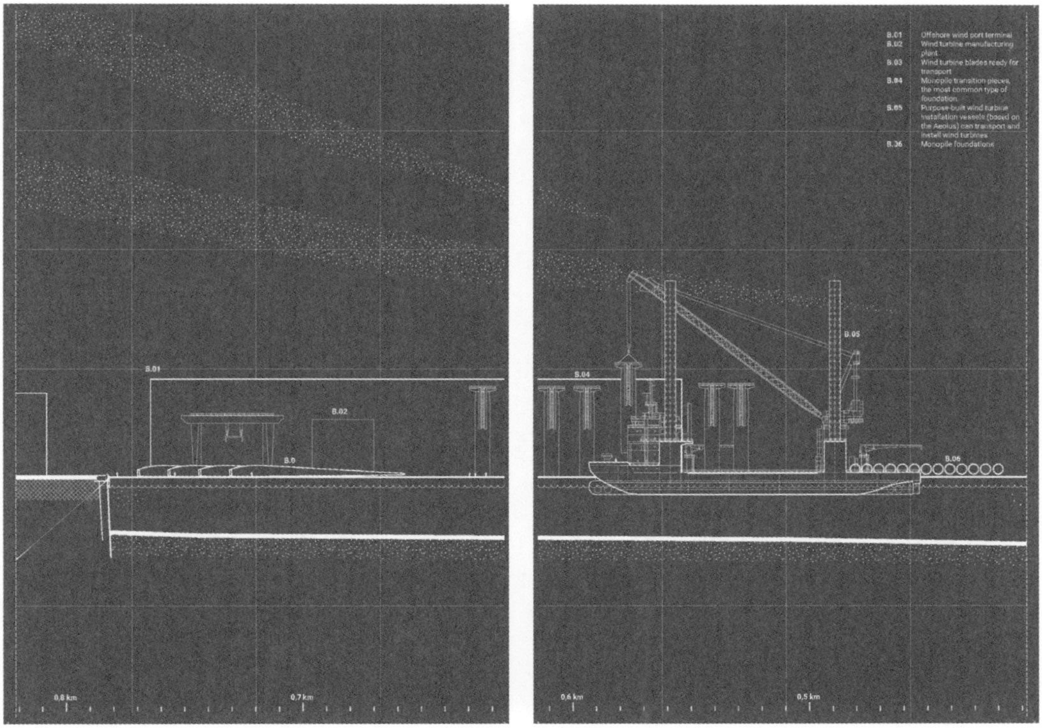
B.01 Offshore wind port terminal
B.02 Wind turbine manufacturing plant
B.03 Wind turbine blades ready for transport
B.04 Monopile transition pieces, the most common type of foundation
B.05 Purpose-built wind turbine installation vessels (based on the Aeolus) can transport and install wind turbines
B.36 Monopile foundations
B.01
B.02
B.0
B.04
B.05
B.06
0,8 km
0,7 km
0,6 km
0,5 km

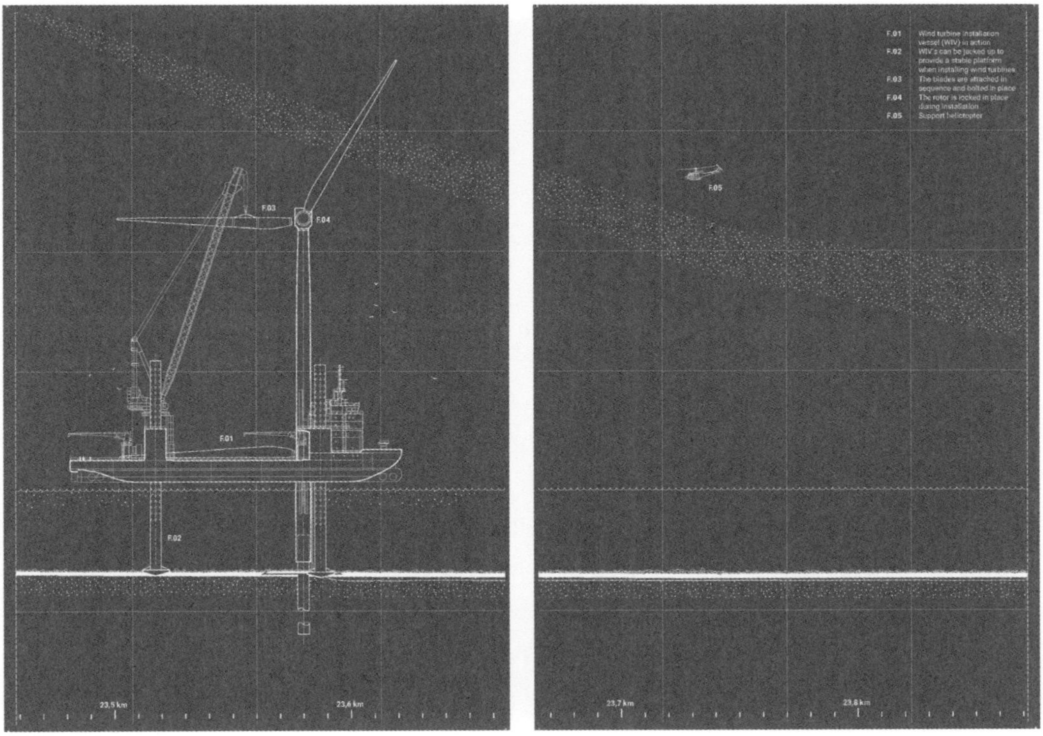
F.01 Wind turbine installation vessel (WIV) in action
F.02 WIV's can be jacked up to provide a stable platform when installing wind turbines
F.03 The blades are attached in sequence and bolted in place
F.04 The rotor is locked in place during installation
F.05 Support helicopter
F.03
F.04
F.01
F.02
F.05
23,5 km
23,6 km
23,7 km
23,8 km

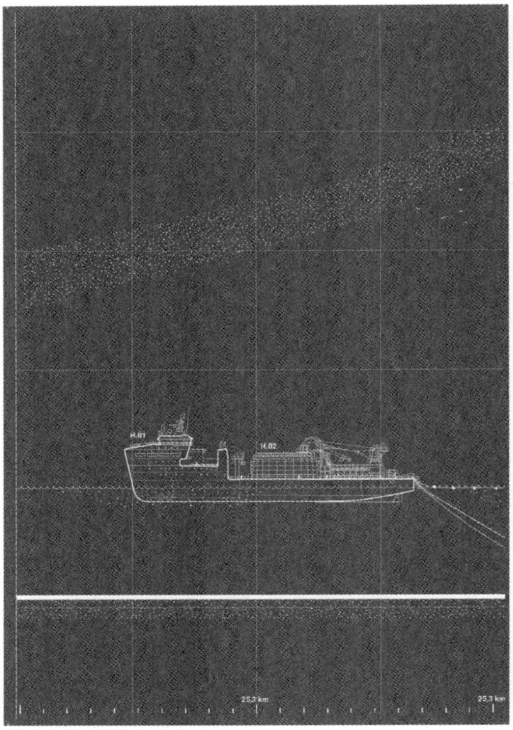
H.01
H.02
25,2 km
25,3 km

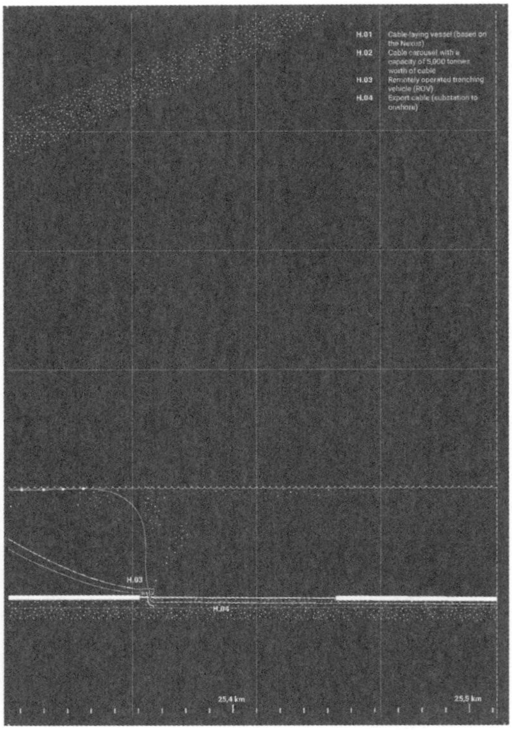
H.01 Cable-laying vessel (based on the Nexus)
H.02 Cable carousel with a capacity of 5,000 tonnes worth of cable
H.03 Remotely operated trenching vehicle (ROV)
H.04 Export cable (substation to onshore)
H.03
H.04
25,4 km
25,5 km

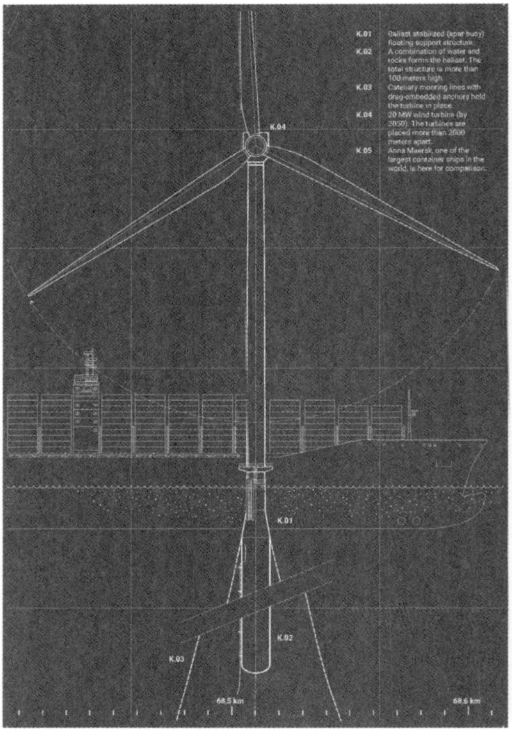
K.01 Ballast stabilized (spar buoy) floating support structure.
K.02 A combination of water and rocks forms the ballast. The total structure is more than 100 meters high.
K.03 Catenary mooring lines with drag-embedded anchors hold the turbine in place.
K.04 20 MW wind turbine (by 2050). The turbines are placed more than 2000 meters apart.
K.05 Anna Maersk, one of the largest container ships in the world, is here for comparison.
K.04
K.01
K.02
K.03
68,5 km
68,6 km

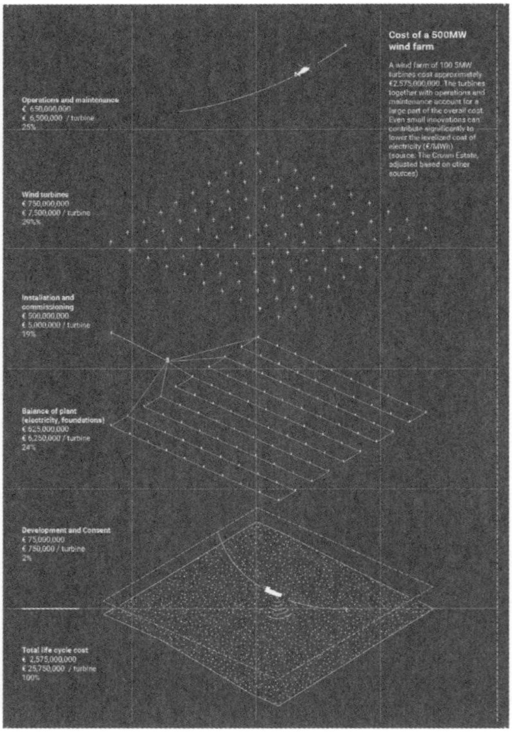
Cost of a 500MW wind farm
A wind farm of 100 5MW turbines cost approximately €2,575,000,000. The turbines together with operations and maintenance account for a large part of the overall cost. Even small innovations can contribute significantly to lower the levelized cost of electricity (€/MWh). (source: The Crown Estate, adjusted based on other sources)
Operations and maintenance
€ 650,000,000
€ 6,500,000 / turbine
25%
Wind turbines
€ 750,000,000
€ 7,500,000 / turbine
29%%
Installation and commissioning
€ 500,000,000
€ 5,000,000 / turbine
19%
Balance of plant (electricity, foundations)
€ 625,000,000
€ 6,250,000 / turbine
24%
Development and Consent
€ 75,000,000
€ 750,000 / turbine
2%
Total life cycle cost
€ 2,575,000,000
€ 25,750,000 / turbine
100%

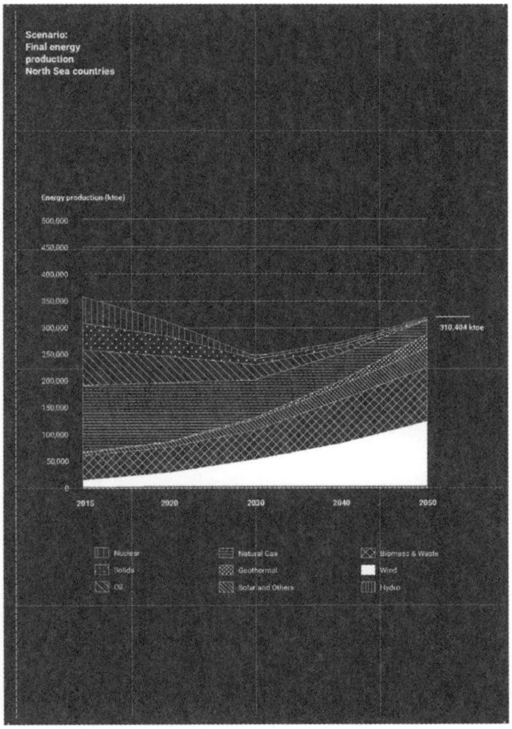
Scenario:
Final energy
production
North Sea countries
Energy production (ktoe)
500,000
450,000
400,000
350,000
300,000
250,000
200,000
150,000
100,000
50,000
0
2015
2020
2030
2040
2050
310,404 ktoe
Nuclear
Solids
Oil
Natural Gas
Geothermal
Solar and Others
Biomass & Waste
Wind
Hydro

2050—AN ENERGETIC ODYSSEY, Commissioned by the International Architecture Biennale Rotterdam in the context of IABR—2016—THE NEXT ECONOMY. Concept and narrative: Maarten Hajer & Dirk Sijmons
Realised by H+N+S Landscape Architects, Tungsten Pro, ECOFys
In Partnership with:
Ministry of Economic Affairs of the Netherlands, Royal Dutch Shell, Port of Rotterdam, Van Oord Offshore, RWE, European Climate Foundation, Port of Amsterdam, Zeeland Seaports, TenneT, Natuur&Milieu Foundation,
With expert advice from:
PBL: Environmental Assessment Agency of the Netherlands, The Crown Estate, TU-Delft, Eneco, EBN, ROM3D

(1) IABR—2016 *The Next Economy*, Catalogue, Rotterdam, 2016.
(2) Watch the animation at: https://www.iabr.nl/en/film/2050_webvideo
(3) Maarten A. Hajer and Peter Pelzer. "2050—An Energetic Odyssey: Understanding 'Techniques of Futuring' in the transition towards renewable energy. *Energy Research & Social Science 44* (2018) 222–231.
(4) Dirk Sijmons. *When Research by Design takes Politics on a Sabbatical Detour*. In *The Next Economy*, Catalog of The Next Economy, Catalog of the IABR—2016, George Brugmans and Jolanda van Dinteren, eds.

"K"LINE
CAUTION
9'-6"
HIGH
MGW=34,000kg for UIC railway transport
KKFU 676219 3
45R1
MAX. GROSS
TARE
NET
CU.CAP.
35.000 KGS
77.160 LBS
4.560 KGS
10.050 LBS
30.440 KGS
67.110 LBS
67.6 CU.M.
2.388 CU.FT.
CIMC
905333 5
35000 kg 77160 lb
4590 kg 10120 lb
30410 kg 67040 lb
67.5 m³ 2384 ft
TTNU 833847
45R1
TTNU 846912
45R1
TRITON
www.tritoncontainer.com
TTNU 828431 8
45R1
MAX GROSS
TARE
NET
CU.CAP.
35,000 KG
77,160 LB
4,490 KG
9,900 LB
30,510 KG
67,260 LB
67.5 CU.M.
2,384 CU.FT.
CAUTION

E1

DOCKWISE
BLACK MARLIN

Part IV CULTIVATIONS

Part IV embraces the complex, paradoxical conditions that frequently accompany exchanges between sea and land. It questions the essential relations between humans and nature, which have been overturned through the processes of industrialisation. We propose a rethinking of concepts that might seem familiar and use the term cultivation to describe tending to the second nature of a space such as the North Sea.

The six contributions included in Part IV demonstrate the application of innovative research and design methods that tackle the spatial challenges of the sea. They reveal and represent previously unseen relations through cartography and propose new means of access, forms of spatial organisation, and interaction. Projects presented here illustrate the concept introduced in Part II, of planning *from the sea to the land*. Several contributions seek to reassert connectivity and consider how this could influence interactions, dialogue, public involvement, and planning at the territorial scale. In addition to critically appraising the different cases in question, these chapters have been selected for the visionary nature of their design and representation. They cover a broad geographic range, from the Zandmotor in the Netherlands to the Mediterranean, the Pacific and the Singapore Strait. Cultivation evokes the persuasive power of new visions, perspectives, and experiments capable of reasserting and recalibrating our cultural relationship to the sea. "Cultivation is the opposite of extraction."(1) Cultivation takes time.

The intensity of interactions around selected North Sea coastal sites and the associated problems of ecological degradation and sea level rise provide fertile ground for new forms of adaptation and co-existence. In chapter 15, Taneha Bacchin proposes adjusting human rhythms to new water management strategies and to give viscosity space to perform tasks of ecological exchange and coastal protection.

A further example of planning for exchange between sea and land is illustrated in chapter 16 by Niccolò Bassan, Elisabetta Manea, Alberto Innocenti, and Francesco Musco. The authors demonstrate how the design process can be used to transcend legislative and conceptual barriers, to identify shared challenges, and to integrate a diverse group of stakeholders.

In particular in the case of the Netherlands, the border between land and sea is unclear and has been constructed and redesigned over centuries. In chapter 17, Satellietgroep show how their artistic projects pose essential questions that challenge preconceptions about the relations between humans, climate, and nature and offer poignant, palpable forms of reconnection and reflection.

Exemplary historical maps provide inspiration for the Mediterranean projects discussed by Medine Altiok in chapter 18. They convey the richness and importance of maritime space during specific periods and communicate that territorial responsibility was shared between many entities—something that could be reimagined through port city exchanges in this liquid territory.

The Singapore Strait is an archetypal urbanised maritime space. Milica Topalović summarises this condition in chapter 19, pointing out its salient features in this context, how the maritime industries dictate the sea-land interface and the urgency of addressing this urbanisation through design.

The separation between extreme maritime industries and the general public, achieved through technological supremacy, preferential treatment by authorities, and the sheer, unimaginable depth and distance of offshore locations, is a problem that can be tackled through architectural representation of imaginative scenarios. This point is made by Design Earth in chapter 20, where the object of the architectural device, "the aquarium," is to bring the public into close emotional contact with the exploitation of the Pacific Ocean, thereby aiming to "reclaim and cultivate response-ability."

(1) Interrobang-curators, Oslo Architecture Triennale 2019, "The Architecture of Degrowth: An Open Call" (OAT, 2018), http://oslotriennale.no/uploads/images/Open-Call-OAT-2019.pdf.

Chapter 15 NORTH SEA LANDSCAPES OF COEXISTENCE

Taneha Kuzniecow Bacchin

The South-West Delta in the Netherlands and the Thames Estuary in England both face extreme sea level rise and ecological degradation. Taneha Bacchin and her students take these conditions as an opportunity to launch a gradual revolution that redefines the land-sea edge as a productive and protective ecosystem.

Taneha Kuzniecow Bacchin is an architect, researcher and educator. Her research and projects focus on the relationship between landscape architecture, infrastructure and urban form. Her current work deals with the changing nature of the territorial project, addressing spatial, ecological, and political aspects of water-related risks, with ongoing projects in the North Sea, the Arctic, and India. Her work has been funded internationally and exhibited at the Venice Architecture Biennale 2002 and 2018, and São Paulo Architecture Biennale 2013. She is Assistant Professor of Urban Design Theory and Methods, and Research Leader of the Delta Urbanism Interdisciplinary Research Program at the Faculty of Architecture and the Built Environment, Delft University of Technology, where she also leads the Transitional Territories Graduation Studio.

This essay presents five graduation theses from the interdisciplinary studio "Transitional Territories" offered by TU Delft's Faculty of Architecture and the Built Environment.(1) From 2017 to 2020, the studio focused on the North Sea as common ground for the mediation of multiple agents acting at the sea-land continuum. This pedagogical project employed research-by-design to map some of the controversial aspects of the North Sea as territory (e.g., the large variety of coastline habitats, management, and ownership practices) and, later, to envision different forms of co-habitation. The five selected projects illustrate a line of inquiry studied in the studio: the effects of the altered nature of the North Sea habitat and the projection of a possible/desirable synergistic approach between land-use occupation and environmental risk management. The selected projects respond to envisioned scenarios developed within the context of the studio, taking singular but related positions on the present and future state of urbanity, ecology, and climate in the North Sea geographic space.

PREMISES

As a territory, the North Sea is the product of dynamic relations between natural processes and human activities. A dense urbanised ground, it has been shaped by the — mostly divisive — relation between flows of goods, capital, data, and people, the oil, gas, and fishery industries and, most recently, climate adaptation and clean energy infrastructure.(2) The nature and materiality of its habitats, edge conditions, and the succession of its multiple layers define the North Sea as an artefactual body of water. As a relatively small geographic space, it has, throughout history, been a point of departure for global infrastructural and industrial, environmental, and geopolitical interventions. The five projects briefly presented in this essay employed chorologic and topographic analysis to examine, transform, and finally unfold the possibility of new spatial constructs and forms of habitation in a viscous mixture of land and sea.(3) All the projects consider the recalibration of edge spaces at sites exposed to extreme sea level rise and eutrophication in two specific landscapes: the South-West Delta in the Netherlands and the Thames Estuary in England. The recalibration is designed as intention and concept, using material and ecological practices to modify the relation between different forms of land use, sociocultural practices, and environmental performance. This method gave form to new infrastructures, concrete or abstract, that set some of the agents and forces present in the sea-river-land continuum in a synergistic fashion.

The examples described in this essay investigate the altered nature of the North Sea territory, taking the current pressures of extreme urbanisation, pollution, and environmental decay, coupled with future scenarios of clean energy production and accelerated sea level rise, as a design opportunity. These present-day conditions form the base for a spatial strategy that enables a gradual revolution: the transformation of hectares of coastal and riverine borders into living ecological infrastructures. Dissolving the static edge between land and water is central to this approach, enabling spatial interventions to act as a coastal and riverine flood risk management strategy as well as enabling new forms of economy. The projects employ multiple scales and temporal programming—connecting interventions at the macro (regional) scale to nano (process) levels, and from meso (urban) to micro (architectonic) levels. As a result, the compilation of the five projects introduces the possibility of a new sea-land relation, composed by the propagation of patterns of cultivation for new industries while providing space for carbon sequestration and ecological and hydrological rehabilitation from inland areas to the sea.

STUDIO PROPOSITION: NORTH SEA ALTERED NATURE AND THE ARCHITECTURE OF EXTREMES

When projecting the long-term geography of the North Sea, some important limitations were identified in the nature of its resource space. Whether considering reduced coastal edges, depleting nutrient levels, demand for infrastructure expansion, or ecological management, each theme included a call for cooperation and synthesis between different forms of human and non-human living systems and the oceanic space. Working within critical axes ranging from moderate to extreme climate change and from local to globally influenced socioeconomic development, the studio delineated scenarios that depicted what could be defined as radical outcomes, extreme climate settings, or uncertain images of the future. Yet, somehow, as we looked closer, we began to recognise pervasive interrelations between politics, economy, ecology, and space.

To place this in context and establish the basis for a common narrative within the studio, the produced scenarios assumed that the effects of climate change are negative and vary depending in part on the cooperation of political actors and their ecological and spatial awareness. Economically, the scenarios showed that the speed of our divestment from fossil fuels, toward, for example, renewable energy systems, will depend on both shared investment and political motivation as well as the key limit or availability of extractable oil. In turn, the ecological scenarios considered driving economic factors such as fishing industry production capacities in relation to changing sea temperatures and levels—involving, for example, fish migration toward northern parts of the sea due to warming southern waters.

Direct anthropogenic impacts encompass the disturbance of nutrient balance, marine pollution, and resource depletion. At the same time, indirect anthropogenic impacts—predominantly through climate change (sea level and temperature rise)—account for shifts within the North Sea's biotopes and habitats, as previously explained. With these impacts intensifying at an unprecedented pace and the outcomes being largely unknown, any projections remain speculative. However, it is evident that negative feedback loops are beginning to dominate the ecosystems of the North Sea and adjacent bodies of water.

Finally, the studio explored the spatial implications of an extreme sea level rise on coastal areas. The extreme scenario of a global mean sea level rise 15 mm yr–1 (10–20 mm yr–1, likely range) and global temperature rise of 1.5 degrees Celsius acts as a warning for North Sea coastal countries.(4) The North Sea and its adjoining bodies of water constitute one of the major forces of climate issues in the region. The maps identified the Dutch coastline and the Thames Estuary as the most vulnerable areas, showing the spatial delineation of the projected flooding extent and the socioeconomic defence types currently in place. Taking other factors into consideration such as sea level rise and the North Sea currents, the projected changes point to coastal erosion and adhesion, affecting not only the coastline, but also patterns in urbanised cities. The southern coastline between England, France, Belgium, and the Netherlands is in a constant state of change, while the northern area of Scotland and Norway are the most stable areas, experiencing minimal impact, even with the projected sea level rise.

The extremity of change demands that actors take a collaborative approach, responding to earth forces and the microenvironments of each region; differentiating between the British Isles and the coastal regions of Belgium, the Netherlands, Germany, Denmark, and Norway. The shift toward cross-national collaboration and microclimate responsiveness maintains the possibility of addressing a number of different issues within the territory.

Overall, regardless of the chosen projection, the studio argued that the rapid increase and instability of earth forces, such as sea level rise, must inform a change of perception, intention, and practice—one that works with, rather than against the new state (of extremes). The following five projects illustrate ways in which this change can potentially be implemented.

RESTORING SYSTEMIC PROXIMITIES: TOWARD THE RE-TERRITORIALISATION OF THE DUTCH RIVIERENLAND, South-West Delta, the Netherlands (Isabel Recubenis Sanchis)(5)

Uncertain and extreme climate events challenge a particular territoriality that is reliant on the control of groundwater and river dynamics within urbanised Deltas.(6) In the Netherlands and particularly in the Dutch river area (Rivierenland in Dutch), new adaptive approaches to spatial planning and hydraulic engineering have already resulted in “Room for the River”, a national planning

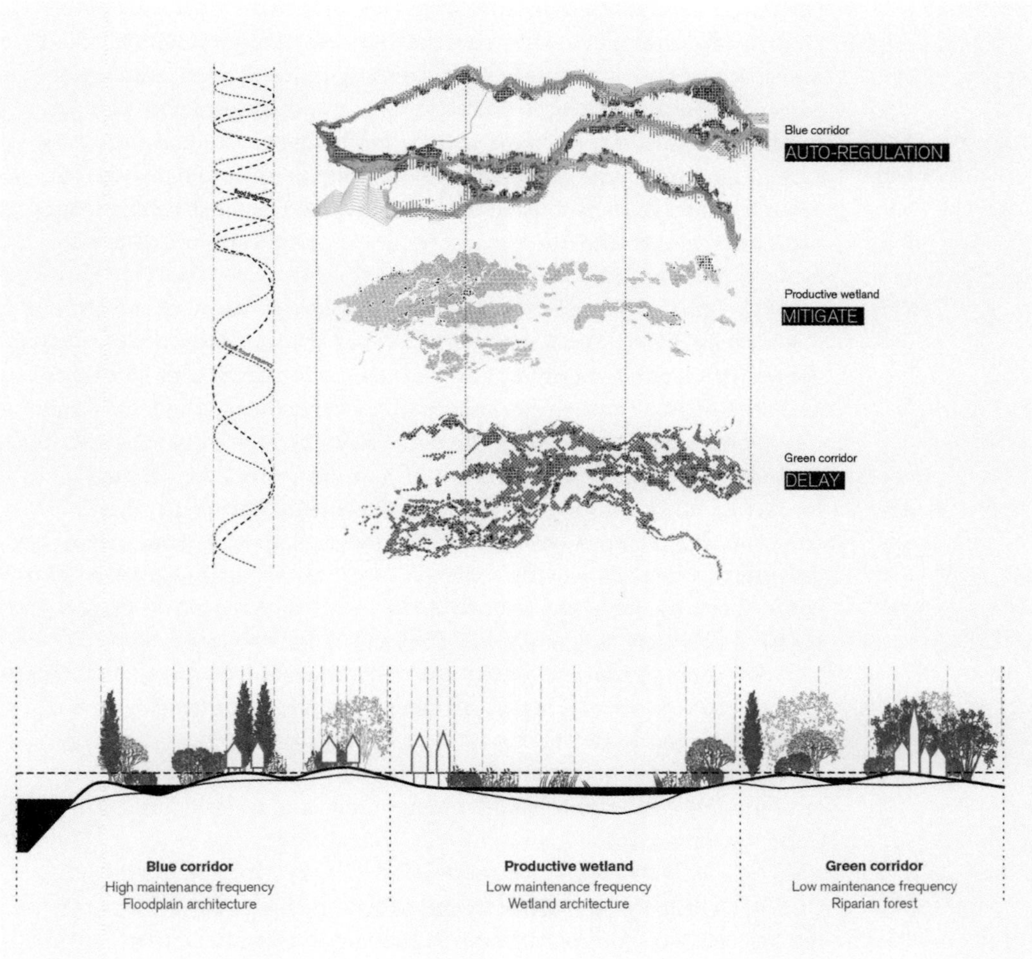

Fig. 1 Macro-Framework: Extreme-discharge function. Three geomorphological conditions with a type and frequency of flood disturbance and specific extreme discharge function: auto-regulation (blue/ river corridor), mitigation (wetlands), delay (green/ coarse-grained soil corridors). (Isabel Recubenis Sanchis, TU Delft 2020)

policy project that gives more space for the river while improving the spatial qualities of affected areas.(7) However, there is still a need to go beyond the physical, cultural, and programmatic separation in flood management between active areas—assigned to embanked rivers—and passive areas—assigned to the urbanised territory. The definition of these dualities in the Dutch territory not only feeds a model based on flood vulnerability—working under certain levels of river discharge—but it also leaves a fragmented landscape.

Aiming to embrace climatic uncertainty and river discharge extremes within highly urbanised floodplains, this project proposes a process-based approach to planning and a design based on radical connectivity throughout the Dutch Rivierenland watershed, where every part of the urbanised territory plays a role in the active management of floods and ecosystem restoration [Fig. 1]. The approach guides a specific spatial transformation consisting of a new topography of repurposed flood channels and depressed areas strategically distributed throughout the urbanised catchment and the cultivation of a green infrastructure of agroforestry patches as riparian corridors. The decentralisation and dispersion of the flood and green network throughout the entire regional matrix upscales the space for groundwater and river dynamics by downscaling flood-related spatial interventions.(8) This model opens the possibility for a local management of flood events and regenerates the forested land cover of the watershed, all of which delays and reduces the hydrograph peak during extreme discharges, reducing the likelihood of flood-related disasters.(9)

The main outcome of the thesis is a process-based planning and design framework for the hybridisation of the territory by increasing ecological densities and buffer capacities, which upscales the green and blue infrastructure per land management unit—the plot—and functional layer as a result. The framework guides a transformational pathway where the synergetic coupling of functions is activated locally by landowners, triggering the cultural appropriation of the proposal. The project is positioned within an emerging urban paradigm, one that redefines the act of urbanisation as an act of reterritorialisation, where occupation is aligned with the ecology and shifting climatic frequencies of the particular territory.(10)

Extreme climatic events require that land be managed differently in order to restore and maintain the soil capacity to delay, store, and discharge water. The thesis explores the idea of performative land units by restoring the proximity to the river and the subsequent —economic, flood management and land regeneration—opportunities.(11)

CULTIVATED ECOLOGIES: OPERATIONAL LANDSCAPES OF MATERIAL PRODUCTION AS FLOOD-RELATED RISK INFRASTRUCTURE, Greater Thames Estuary, South-East England, UK (Sarantis Georgiou)(12)

This thesis elaborates on a theoretical, epistemological, and design research framework for the possibility of an operative synthesis of, on the one hand, climate-related risk management (flood exposure from sea level rise and coastal/tidal flooding, fluvial flooding, and/or pluvial flooding) and, on the other, the planning and design of operational landscapes of material production, as a means for sustainable ecological development.

Contemporary practices of managing ecological, environmental and climatic risk rely heavily on a "mitigation" approach, where the imperative is the restoration of a prior "natural" order or the spatial planning of the next waves of development and urbanisation according to the evaluation of the internal logic of natural processes. However, this line of thinking severely hinders the possibility of a creative and proactive reorganization of human processes of material production precisely because it presupposes a "nature-society rift."(13) Similarly, the negative externalities associated with the extensive and intensive operationalisation of vast terrestrial terrains are viewed as singular phenomena to be addressed in situ and not as opportunities to fundamentally reconceptualise contemporary planetary urbanisation.(14)

This work is built on the premise that to properly address climate-related risk, one has to also address unsustainable patterns of material production and the physical and functional organisation of urbanisation. In contrast to the predominant approach of placing the emphasis on the "city", and following the development of the concepts of "concentrated" and "extended urbanisation" through the construction of gradients of "agglomeration" and "operational landscapes,"(15)(16)(17) this thesis attempts the opposite: by shifting the analytical centrality from agglomerations to the operational landscapes that sustain them, we are able to formulate an urbanisation hypothesis that addresses the requirements of the latter not as externalities of the former (thus hindering the capacity of the framework to be adequately socio-ecologically sustainable) but as the fundamental elements of the planning and design of the urban fabric. The thesis suggests that integrating within the urbanised landscape biophysical processes and ecosystem functions, which are central to the performance of operational landscapes, would offer climate-related benefits.

Assuming that this integration is an act of construction of the urban landscape which also partakes in its economic activities, this work reformulates Henri Lefebvre's opening statement in "*The Urban Revolution*": "society has been completely urbanised", as follows: "the urban has been completely operationalised," and attempts to elaborate on the coming-into-being of this reality: the project of the cultivation of the urban.(18) The proposal discusses the possibility that "agglomeration landscapes" become hybridised with "operational landscapes," meaning that contemporary cities and urban regions renounce their sole correspondence with the secondary and tertiary sectors of the economy and, in turn, take on the role of encompassing primary (i.e., material) production as well. The design and planning framework establishes the ways in which different compositions of forest plots, croplands and / or pastures could be adapted within existing urban areas and result in a landscape structure that performs for water-sensitivity. The geomorphology, geology, surface hydrography, and hydrology of the landscape influence water-regulation and flood-risk management, as well as the structure of the open space and the land-use/land-cover types.(19) Part of the ecological region of the Greater Thames Estuary that is most exposed to different forms of flooding is used as a case study, here referred to as the "border interface zone." The analysis considers the current landscape composition, the land-use/land-cover class types that exhibit the greatest potential for transformation and their relation to water-regulation and flood-risk management. The design proposes suitable crop species and organises the crops in such a way as to provide water-sensitive performance as flood- risk infrastructure [Fig. 2, p. 265]. Existing spaces are reconfigured internally as well as receiving patches of forestry, cropland and/or pasture. These spaces become "cultivated landscape ecologies," contributing to a new landscape image.(20)

RE-NATURED ECONOMY: FROM POLLUTANTS TO PRODUCTIVE LANDSCAPES, South-West Delta, the Netherlands (Aikaterina Myserli)(21)

In light of climate change, it is clear that as a result of ecosystem derangement and the debasement of local economies in the name of globalisation and free trade, capitalism has almost exhausted its source of nourishment: nature. Cities seem to be more connected to the planetary system of production and trade than to their surrounding context.

To place humanity within natural processes and to define humans as custodians of nature's ecological heritage, are interventions well-discussed in the fields of urban, landscape, and environmental theory, however there are still challenges regarding their implementation. The question is: which new ecologies of the Anthropocene could transform negative outputs of our current economic model (pollutants, waste flows) into inputs of new productive landscapes?

The Dutch-Flemish Delta is used as the test bed for a new projective ecology. Pollutants causing eutrophication (nitrogen, phosphorus, CO2, algae) are captured in order to facilitate processes that generate value (food production, energy) and trigger a shift in economy that will both reshape the deltaic landscape as well as set the foundations for a bio-based future economy. At the core of this proposal lies the transformation of underperforming crops (mainly produced via arable farming, grasslands, and flower production) into algae crops in enclosed tubular systems that do not require fresh water but contribute to wastewater treatment and convert discharged nutrients into valuable [bio]products [Fig. 3, p. 266]. Traditional agriculture uses vast quantities of fresh potable water and releases phosphorus and nitrogen into the water through the extensive use of fertilisers. In addition to enclosed algal systems, the proposal investigates the creation of new wetlands by re-flooding polders with high saline soil and non-profitable crops; establishing macroalgae ponds in their place. These ponds may function as a model of filtration "layers" for agricultural and industrial discharges that would reduce the level of pollutants in the water and could bring back benthic and pelagic species that are currently forced to migrate.

A system where pollutants are subverted into resources requires, on the one hand, the transformation of local industrial systems from linear to circular (closed loops of flows, semi-open systems) and a new material economy (circular systems that generate value out of pollutants and a market for renewable resources) on the other. It is noteworthy that in order to project a vision and develop an efficient strategic framework for such a shift in economy, it is crucial to understand and work with the relationships between large-scale regional strategies and more detailed, local design solutions. In this case, the temporal dimension is of utmost importance; fossil fuel depletion is a reality and a shift in economy toward renewable sources will take place in the years to come, therefore pollution reduction means pollutants may not provide sufficient input for a bio-based economy in the future. The proposed hypothesis is therefore a transition in time, an intermediate stage toward sustainable economic development. In the end, as pollution becomes historical, nature becomes a landscape of flows and fluids that co-exist and co-evolve.

REVERSED RISK: PROTECTIVE PRODUCTIVE CYCLE BASED ON TIDAL FORCES IN ESTUARINE TERRITORIES, Thames Estuary, England (Alexandra Farmazon)(22)

With more than 80 percent of Thames River banks transformed into concrete storm walls and the Thames Barrier in place since the 1970s, the dynamic tidal force is persistently causing storm surge flooding and flash floods throughout London's dense urban areas.(23) This makes the UK coastline a priority North Sea area—both in terms of event frequency and of prospective impact. Despite this urgency, the UK Environment Agency's funding for maintaining flood assets has fallen by 14 percent nationally. Recent investigations undertaken by the *Financial Times* quote John Pettigrew: “It is important that the UK is seen as a place that is attractive to inward investment. In terms of the energy sector, a lot of infrastructure needs to be built in the UK over the next few years. Post-Brexit, it is important that it is coming in.”(24) While funding for the energy sector is increasing, the UK's flood defense plans are inadequate and lagging behind in investment.(25) As a consequence and if inundated, the Greater Thames Estuary region, currently containing 1 million properties, would suffer direct damage of at least £ 97.8 billion at 2003 prices.(26) Surely, the increased investment on the energy sector is justified as the North Sea is facing an era of fossil fuel depletion and overpriced electrical energy urgently demands a transition to clean, renewable sources. The UK is a leading power with the most extensive Exclusive Economic Zone coverage in the North Sea, including several fossil fuel extraction platforms that are currently being transformed into energy farms. This opens the opportunity to research and design productive landscapes triggered by coastal dynamics as a possible paradigm for energy futures. Therefore, this thesis proposes a spatial strategy that integrates coastal risk management and energy production with new ecosystems and land-use typologies.

Already, in shifting the focus of energy production to the maritime territories that engage in exchanges with the land, we are implicitly discussing coastal flood strategies. From a theoretical and practice point of view, there would be a clear interdependence between the hydrodynamics of the territorial sea and the adaptive coastal response to risk. However, the UK planning system regards these issues as separate entities, under separate departments, directly subordinated to Her Majesty The Queen. From the central government level, to the regional, county, and village level, flood risk and energy efficiency are managed separately under the Department for Business, Energy and Industrial Strategy (BEIS) and the Department for Environment, Food and Rural Affairs (DEFRA), while spatial planning is addressed through the Department for Communities and Local Government (DCLG), thus making any communication difficult if not impossible.

In response to these conditions, this project aims to bring these separated fields together through a new coherent, integrated approach linking flood risk and energy transition pressure. It proposes a strategy for production in estuarine waters, requiring a control body that involves all implicated departments and ensures the coordination of vision, policy, and investment. The project looks beyond the 2030 effective lifespan of the Thames Barrier and explores an alternative system of hybrid infrastructure that can reverse the flood risk factor toward a profitable tidal energy source, creating a protection/production cycle, simultaneously defending and "fuelling" the city, as well as retrieving its original investment [Fig. 4, p. 267]. Practically, understanding the value of natural forces, paired with adaptive capacity patterns builds a gradient of spatial and performance suitability. This creates a system of critical intervention areas directly supporting and conserving their anthropic activity within the urban system. A coherent spatial assessment framework is proposed, which results in identification of critical locations and a paired governance implementation model. The following design approach then zooms to a system where a restrictive, regeneration urban area is transformed into natural protected landscapes.
As a result, the protective infrastructure boosts the regional economy by promoting an agricultural transition to aquaculture and an energy self-sufficient urban district.

A NON-STRAIGHTFORWARD ARCHIPELAGO,
South-West Delta, the Netherlands (Neil Moncrieff)

As Erle C. Ellis has suggested, "In the Anthropocene, there is no possibility of removing human influence from ecosystems: anthropogenic transformation of the terrestrial biosphere is essentially complete and permanent."(27) Ellis also claims that few remaining natural systems demonstrate no human impact and it is at the junctions between natural and urban systems where the impact

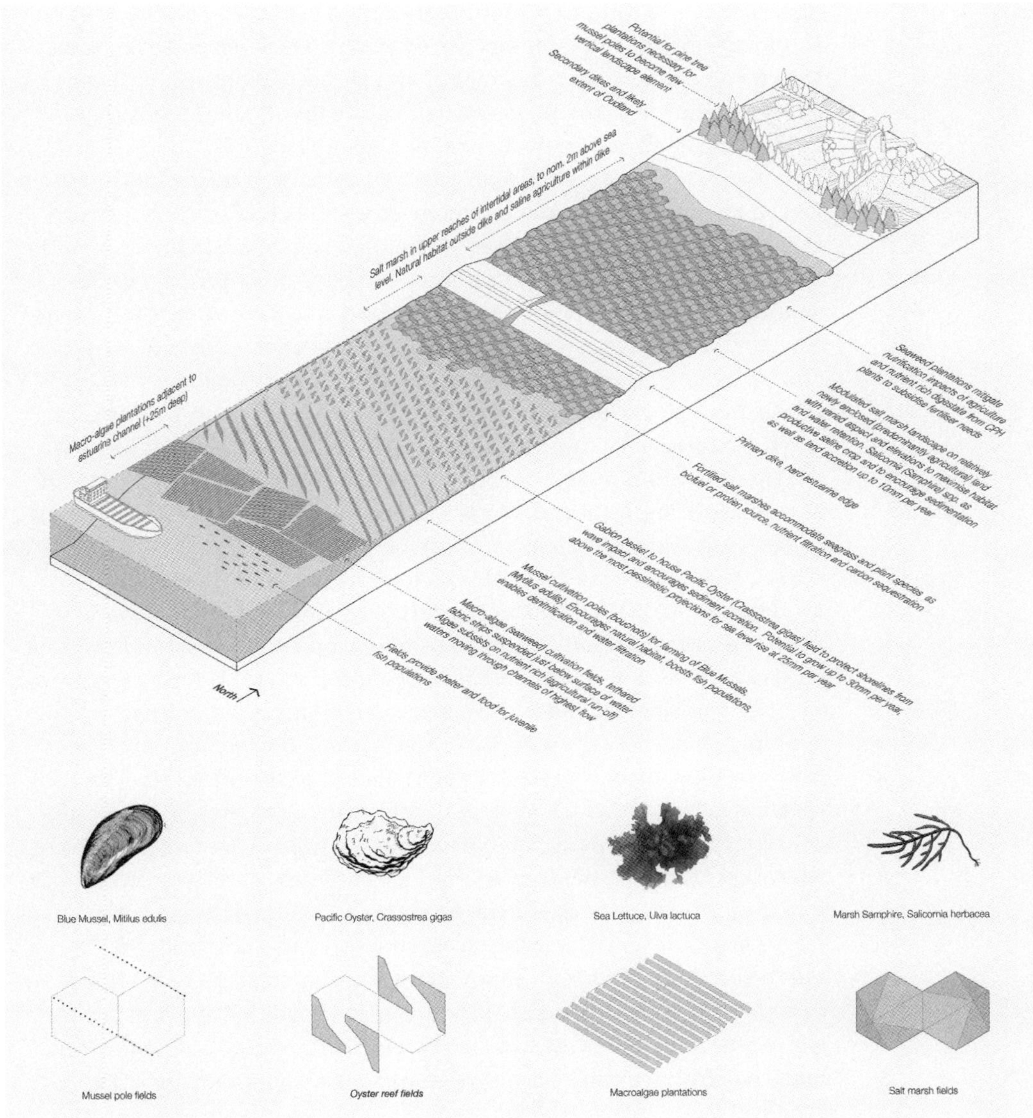

Fig. 5
New spatial typologies at Oosterschelde (Neil Moncrieff, TU Delft 2020)

of, for example, habitat degradation, pollution, or resource over-exploitation, as well as the complex series of interactions between culture and landscape are most apparent.(28) As neither system holds sway, this is also where local interventions might have the broadest impact: both in terms of the cultural changes exerted on the environment and the psychological and behavioural impacts that these environments exert over the occupying communities.

The Dutch relationship to landscape is particular and the physical construction and ordering of the landscape in response to the ever-present threat of inundation has had as much impact on the cultural psyche as it has on the deltaic groundplane. The question is whether the elements that come together to compose the unique visual and cultural character of the Dutch landscape might be replicable, or at least employed again in different ways, to address today's environmental and existential threats. What might be a contemporary estuarine equivalent of the traditional patterned, agricultural, and infrastructural polder landscapes?

A possible consequence of the contemporary re-evaluation of Dutch flood and water management strategies could be a return to more naturalistic estuarine conditions within the South-West Delta. This has the potential to re-animate natural systems and habitats as well as bolster cultural connections to, and across, this landscape. But how could this re-naturalisation benefit the urban landscapes and economies that negotiate the transition between one of Europe's densest urban, industrial, and logistics corridors from Brussels and Antwerp to Rotterdam, and the equally congested territory of the southern portion of the North Sea? Could a new spatial typology of designed ecologies (nature-based solutions) prompt a re-orientation of both natural and urban ecosystems within the delta toward greater social, economic, and ecological efficiency and resilience? Can alternative spatial organisation driven by an alternative notion of flood protection, productive landscape infrastructure and a new land-use transitional delta logic respond to different tidal forces over time?

This project suggests four new ecosystems and land-use typologies, namely mussel pole cultivation fields, oyster reef installations, macroalgae (seaweed) plantations and salt marsh meadows. The design and spatial arrangement of these ecosystems is driven by their Oosterschelde context, conforming to a new, shared spatial grid, in turn defined by the individual productive and/or locational requirements of the ecosystems themselves [Fig. 5].

These new typologies should improve environmental, biodiversity, and habitat values as well as reorient the delta flood defence and water management systems, moving away from hard, engineered measures (as typified by the Deltaworks) toward softer, more naturalistic infrastructures that are able to keep up with sea level rise. This designed deployment of ecosystem engineering measures also aims to be of economic, cultural, and social benefit, with strong spatial characteristics that could foster community, visual, and economic connections to the new landscape. The system could expand and close functional and systemic loops (e.g., carbon, nutrient, and productive cycles) as well as facilitate the broader intellectual, logistics, and cooperative networks required to distribute biomass, local power or heat, and new seafood products.

ACKNOWLEDGEMENTS
"North Sea: Landscape of Coexistence" was a studio brief developed for Transitional Territories Studio together with Hamed Khosravi, starting in the academic year 2017–2018. Design and research mentors from both TU Delft's Urbanism and Architecture Departments of the Faculty of Architecture and the Built Environment between 2017 and 2020 contributed to the project. The five selected Urbanism Master Theses presented in this essay were supervised by Taneha Kuzniecow Bacchin (studio leader, Section of Urban Design, Delta Urbanism Research Group), Diego Sepulveda Carmona (Section of Spatial Planning & Strategy, Delta Urbanism Research Group), and Evert Meijers (Section of Urban Studies). The author would like to acknowledge the contributions of Isabel Recubenis Sanches, Sarantis Georgiou, Aikaterina Myserli, Alexandra Farmazon, supervised together with Diego Sepulveda Carmona and Neil Moncrieff, supervised together with Evert Meijers. The author thanks the contributions and reflections of Emily Aquilina, Filippo La Fleur and Geert van der Meulen (Delta Urbanism Research Group researchers) and Transitional Territories Studio students regarding the studio sub-theme "North Sea Altered Nature and the Architecture of Extremes."

(1) "Transitional Territories Studio," Delft University of Technology, accessed September 18, 2020 https://www.tudelft.nl/en/education/programmes/masters/architecture-urbanism-and-building-sciences/msc-architecture-urbanism-and-building-sciences/master-tracks/urbanism/programme/graduation/transitional-territories/
(2) Nancy Couling, "Formats of Extended Urbanisation in Ocean Space," in *Emerging Urban Spaces- a Planetary Perspective*, eds., Philipp Horn, Paola Alfaro d'Alençon, and Ana Claudia Duarte Carduso, (Springer International Publishing, 2018), XII, 219.
(3) The study of the causal relations between geographical phenomena occurring within a particular region. GEMET General Multilingual Environmental Thesaurus, s.v. "Chrology," https://www.eionet.europa.eu/gemet/en/concept/10644
(4) 'Global Warming of 1.5°C. An IPCC Special Report on the Impacts of Global Warming of 1.5°C above Pre-Industrial Levels and Related Global Greenhouse Gas Emission Pathways, in the Context of Strengthening the Global Response to the Threat of Climate Change, Sustainable Development, and Efforts to Eradicate Poverty' (Intergovernmental Panel on Climate Change, 2018), https://www.ipcc.ch/site/assets/uploads/sites/2/2019/06/SR15_Full_Report_High_Res.pdf.
The rate of global mean sea level rise is projected to reach 15 mm yr–1 (10–20 mm yr–1, likely range) under RCP8.5 in 2100, and to exceed several centimetres per year in the 22nd century. Projected RCP8.5 is a high greenhouse emission scenario in the absence of policies to combat climate change. O. Pörtner, D.C. Roberts, V. Masson-Delmotte, P. Zhai, M. Tignor, E. Poloczanska, K. Mintenbeck, M. Nicolai, A. Okem, J. Petzold, B. Rama, N. Weyer (eds.)]."IPCC, 2019: Summary for Policymakers," in *IPCC Special Report on the Ocean and Cryosphere in a Changing Climate*. 2019, https://report.ipcc.ch/srocc/pdf/SROCC_FinalDraft_FullReport.pdf
(5) Isabel Recubenis Sanchis, "Restoring Systemic Proximities: Towards the Re-territorialization of the Dutch Rivierenland," Master's thesis, Delft University of Technology, 2020.
(6) Claude Raffestin, "Space, territory, and territoriality," *Environment and planning D: society and space* 30, no. 1 (2012): 121-141, defines territoriality as the ensemble of relations that a society maintains with exteriority and alterity for the satisfaction of its needs.
(7) Jeroen Rijke et al., "Room for the River: Delivering Integrated River Basin Management in the Netherlands," *International Journal of River Basin Management* 10, no. 4 (1 December 2012): 369–82, https://doi.org/10.1080/15715124.2012.739173.
(8) Richard Forman T, "Land Mosaics: The Ecology of Landscapes and Regions," in *The Ecological Design and Planning Reader*, ed. Forster Ndubisi, Land Use Planning (Washington, DC: Island Press, 2014), defined regional matrix as the mosaic patterns in landscapes and regions according to the patch-corridor-matrix model.
(9) J. A. Jones, "Hydrologic Processes and Peak Discharge Response to Forest Removal, Regrowth, and Roads in 10 Small Experimental Basins, Western Cascades, Oregon," *Water Resources Research* 36, no. 9 (2000): 2621–42, https://doi.org/10.1029/2000WR900105.
(10) Gilles Deleuze and Félix Guattari, *A Thousand Plateaus: Capitalism and Schizophrenia*, 11th print. (Minneapolis: University of Minnesota Press, 2005), define deterritorialization as a process of detachment between forms of occupation and the landscape dynamics of a place, reterritorialization refers to processes of reattachment.
(11) Filippo La Fleur, Taneha Kuzniecow Bacchin and Isabel Recubenis, "Next-Constructed Natures: Next Generation Infrastructure Design Under Conditions of Extremes" research report, Delft University of Technology, 2020; Taneha Kuzniecow Bacchin, "Performative Nature. Urban landscape infrastructure design in water

sensitive cities." PhD diss., Delft University of Technology and UNESCO-IHE Delft, 2015.
(12) Sarantis Georgiou, "Cultivated Ecologies: Operational landscapes of material production as flood-related risk infrastructure". Master's thesis, Delft University of Technology, 2019.
(13) Jason W. Moore, "Toward a Singular Metabolism: Epistemic Rifts and Environment-Making in the Capitalist World-Ecology," in *Grounding Metabolism*, ed. Nikos Katsikis and Daniel Ibanez, vol. 6, New Geographies (Cambridge, MA: Harvard Graduate School of Design, 2014).
(14) Neil Brenner, "Introduction: Urban Theory without an Outside," in *Implosions / Explosions : Towards a Study of Planetary Urbanization* (Berlin: Jovis, 2014), 14–30.
(15) Brenner, "Urban Theory."
(16) Nikos Katsikis, "On the Geographical Organization of World Urbanization," *MONU Geographical Urbanism*, 20 (2014).
(17) Nikos Katsikis, 'The "Other" Horizontal Metropolis: Landscapes of Urban Interdependence', in *The Horizontal Metropolis between Urbanism and Urbanization*, ed. Paola Viganò, Chiara Cavalieri, and Martina Barcelloni Corte, (Cham: Springer, 2018), 23–45,
(18) Henri Lefebvre, *The Urban Revolution* (Minneapolis: University of Minnesota Press, 2003),1
(19) Taneha Kuzniecow Bacchin, "Performative Nature; Urban Landscape Infrastructure Design in Water Sensitive Cities" (Doctoral Dissertation, Delft, TU Delft and UNESCO-IHE, 2015), http://resolver.tudelft.nl/uuid:10f06b60-0f67-45b4-9390-785445a0dc7b.
(20) The design of a hybrid green-blue-grey landscape mosaic based on soil regeneration, primary production and flood risk management parameters. Filippo La Fleur, Taneha Kuzniecow Bacchin and Isabel Recubenis, "Next-Constructed Natures: Next generation infrastructure design under conditions of extremes" research report, Delft University of Technology, 2020.
(21) Aikaterina Myserli, "Re-Natured Economy: From pollutants to productive landscapes." Master's thesis, Delft University of Technology, 2018.
(22) Alexandra Farmazon, "Reversed Risk: Protective productive cycle based on tidal forces in estuaries territories" Master's thesis, Delft University of Technology, 2018.
(23) With a span of 520 metres across the River Thames near Woolwich, protecting 125 square kilometres of central London from flooding caused by tidal surges, the Thames Barrier is one of the largest movable flood barriers in the world. It's steel gates are raised under storm surge conditions to protect London from flooding from the North Sea, remaining closed until the water level downstream has reduced to the same level as upstream. "Thames Barrier," GOV.UK, accessed October 1, 2020, https://www.gov.uk/guidance/the-thames-barrier.
(24) Sylvia Pfeifer and Andrew Ward "UK energy grid warns that political risks threaten investment" *Financial Times*, March 4, 2018, https://www.ft.com/content/d3490bc8-1e16-11e8-956a-43db76e69936
(25) Robin McKie "UK flood defence plans are inadequate, warn scientists" *The Guardian*, February 23, 2020, https://www.theguardian.com/environment/2020/feb/23/uk-flood-defence-plans-inadequate-warn-scientists
(26) Richard Jonathan Dawson, J. W. Hall, P. D. Bates, and R. J. Nicholls, "Quantified analysis of the probability of flooding in the Thames Estuary under imaginable worst-case sea level rise scenarios." *Water Resources Development* 21, no. 4 (2005): 577–91.
(27) Erle C. Ellis, "A Taxonomy of the Human Biosphere," in *Projective ecologies*, eds. Chris Reed and Nina-Marie E. Lister (Cambridge, MA: Harvard University Graduate School of Design, 2014), 168-183.
(28) Erle C. Ellis, "Anthropogenic Transformation of the Terrestrial Biosphere." *Proceedings of the Royal Society A: Mathematical, Physical and Engineering Science*, 2011. 369(1938): p. 1010–1035.
[Fig. 2] Based on ""Ordnance Survey: OS Open Data." 2019. Accessed 08.04.20 https://www.ordnancesurvey.co.uk/opendatadownload/products.html. Rural Payments Agency. 2018. Crop Map of England: Product Specification - v.2018.2; Ordnance Survey: OS Open Data." 2019. Crop Map of England (CROME) 2018.

Chapter 16 LAND-SEA INTERACTIONS IN MARINE SPATIAL PLANNING: A CASE STUDY IN TUSCANY

Niccolò Bassan, Elisabetta Manea, Alberto Innocenti, & Francesco Musco

Through their work on the Tuscan Archipelago, Niccolò Bassan, Elisabetta Manea, Alberto Innocenti and Francesco Musco take us through the challenges of considering land-sea Interactions within the Marine Spatial Planning process and demonstrate the potential of research by design in overcoming them.

The authors constitute the research team of the Planning Climate Change Lab of the Iuav University of Venice:

Niccolò Bassan, architect and planner, MSc in Maritime Spatial Planning from the Universidad de Sevilla, Universidade dos Açores, and Iuav University of Venice.

Elisabetta Manea, post-doctoral researcher, PhD in Marine Biology and Ecology from the Polytechnic University of Marche.

Alberto Innocenti, architect and urban planner, double degree PhD student at the University Iuav of Venice and University of Copenhagen.

Francesco Musco, associate professor, urban and regional planner, PhD in Analysis and Governance of Sustainable Development," director of the master degree programme in Planning and Policies for Cities, Territory and Environment and dean of the Erasmus Mundus Master Course on Maritime Spatial Planning.

The sustainable management of coastal and maritime spaces is gaining increased attention among research institutions, universities and governments around the world.(1) Maritime activities and the exploitation of marine and coastal resources to boost the so-called "blue economy" have rapidly increased, reaching unsustainable levels worldwide.(2) The constantly increasing exploitation and unplanned use of marine resources have compromised the health of marine and coastal ecosystems, undermining their ability to provide services on which socioeconomic well-being relies.(3) Many activities compete for the same spaces and resources, leading to increasing conflicts. Moreover, in many cases difficulties in identifying jurisdictional boundaries of maritime areas have led to transnational disputes.(4) Some of the equity and sustainability imbalances will become more acute in the medium- and long-term as a result of climate change, potentially leading to overlapping negative effects, especially in coastal areas due to sea level rise.(5)

Maritime Spatial Planning (MSP) is a tool used to anticipate conflicts in maritime space while reducing anthropogenic pressures on coastal and marine ecosystems in a way that favours a sustainable blue economy.(6) The planning of maritime space needs to be coordinated with land planning, since land- and sea-based activities are interlinked. In addition, dynamic, viscous marine and coastal environments contrast with land-sea planning binaries, considerably complicating planning and management. MSP may support the integration of land-sea planning regimes by properly assessing interactions among human activities and natural flows crossing the terrestrial-marine interface.

Land-sea interaction (LSI) can be defined as a "complex phenomenon that involves both natural processes across the land-sea interface, as well as the impact of socioeconomic activities taking place in the coastal zone."(7) However, the absence of a recognised approach for LSI analysis and limited and uncertain data complicate the overall task. In response to these shortcomings, we chose a research-by-design approach that offered maximum flexibility. This helped us overcome land and sea conceptual barriers, shifting from a land-based spatial logic, with fixed spatial and legal delineation, to a more fluid, integrated, land-sea approach. LSI was also a way to engage local stakeholders, involve them in the planning process, and collect meaningful information. We then "translated" input from local stakeholders into a graphical language, stimulating the production of shared cartographies and new perspectives. The aim was to better comprehend the porous space of analysis, reasserting connectivity between land and sea realms. We tested this approach in a case study of the Tuscan Archipelago under the framework of the EU-funded SIMWESTMED (Supporting Implementation of Maritime Spatial Planning in the Western Mediterranean Region).(8)

MARITIME SPATIAL PLANNING: DEFINITION AND PURPOSE

Maritime Spatial Planning (MSP) is used to manage maritime areas by allocating different uses in space and time. It can be defined as a public process developed to find solutions to problems concerning the use of marine space and to allocate space for human activities while supporting their sustainability. At an international level, MSP was first promoted by IOC/UNESCO, which in 2006 organised the first international workshop on the use of MSP as a tool to implement ecosystem-based management (EBM), leading to the publication of the first international MSP guide.(9) At the European level, international attention then led to the establishment of the MSP Directive (2014/89/EU), in which EU coastal member states agreed to develop national maritime spatial plans by 31 March, 2021, with a minimum review period of ten years.(10)

Concerns have been raised about MSP implementation processes.(11) In fact, there has been little assessment of the potential negative and distributive effects of MSP, which is unfortunate considering the risks of lobbying and the appropriation of common maritime space. Consequently, the current MSP implementation panorama requires a radical turn, focusing on more equity-based, democratic decision-making and a fairer distribution of ocean wealth. Some of the negative impacts of MSP can be overcome by ensuring broader stakeholder and rights holder consultation and adopting more flexible planning processes.

MSP should also involve an adaptive approach in which the management cycle is conceived as a continuous learning process and measures adopted are reassessed.(12) The role of design is essential to impart flexibility to the process and ensure representation of the different commons, ecologies, and cultural ties. Design becomes a means of engagement, giving visibility to local needs and boosting transparency.

MSP has been implemented in many locations worldwide. However few pilot projects existed in the Mediterranean region, until the EU recently co-financed several projects on MSP in the European basins, including the Adriatic.(13)

LAND-SEA INTERACTIONS WITHIN AN MSP FRAMEWORK

Although a standard definition of LSI does not exist, three main typologies can be identified.(14) First, there are natural land-sea processes, particularly related to the flow of water and nutrients and organisms between terrestrial, freshwater, and marine ecosystems. They ensure functioning of coastal and marine ecosystems and can be altered by human effects. A second typology concerns cross-system threats, including economic activities originating on land and affecting the marine environment or vice versa. These can be categorised according to their source, the affected realms (terrestrial, freshwater, marine), the direction of influence (seaward or landward), the main effect (e.g., altered flow of water, pollutant transfer), and the sector to target for intervention (e.g., urban areas, industry). Finally, there are socioeconomic interactions, because people are part of the ecosystem, interrelated with both land and sea.

Planning at sea should not disregard the terrestrial domain, although planners need to be mindful of the differences in management authorities and responsibilities. Terrestrial and marine environments are connected by ecological, biogeochemical, and oceanographic processes. Although a significant amount of non-systematic research exists around LSI discourse, there is no standard methodology for integrating LSI in a MSP process. Exploring LSI by using design and mapping can provide new insights, shifting from a rigid "planning" logic, with fixed spatial and legal delineation, to a more fluid approach.

RESEARCH BY DESIGN

Research by design promotes discussion and spatial analysis, especially in multi-scale contexts where there is a need to acquire knowledge from the field. Design is used as "a way of inquiring, a way of producing knowledge."(15) Research by design is a way to plan for the future in projects that concern complex environmental challenges.(16) Planners face continuously changing conditions and shifting political and economic programmes, therefore the process of planning should involve feedback sessions, in which critical assessment, comparability, and evaluation take place through sketching.(17) Design is especially useful for adapting the overall MSP planning process since external factors of climate change, migration, economics, and social processes need to be managed even in the absence of a "master plan." Design methods can explore several scenarios at once, imagining multiple futures. This process promotes innovation, exceeding the limits of pure scientific knowledge both in a methodological and theoretical way.(18) Design methods are particularly adapted to the analysis of LSI due to the numerous variables and uncertainties involved. We tested this approach in the Tuscan Archipelago case study of the SIMWESTMED project (2016-2018)(19), specifically during feedback sessions with local stakeholders. In this project, research by design primarily involved mapping and sketching, which facilitated direct visual communication of the acquired knowledge.

CASE STUDY AND RESULTS

The Mediterranean Sea has a wide variety of marine habitats and a high degree of biodiversity, but recent rapid economic and demographic development has increased anthropogenic pressures on the marine environment. Overexploitation of natural resources has led to the urgent need to find the right balance between economic needs and the conservation of the marine environment; overfishing, for example, has widely affecting the whole basin.(20) Past management initiatives concerning sustainable use of marine resources in the Mediterranean have been criticised for failing to reflect real conservation priorities.(21) Because the socioeconomic development of Mediterranean countries depends on marine resources and space, it is especially important to manage such resources sustainably and preserve their integrity.

The Tuscan Archipelago represents the specificities of the Mediterranean basin: it is a recognised hot spot of biodiversity, presenting diverse marine habitats of great ecological value, and numerous maritime activities take place there. We used a research-by-design approach in the Tuscan case study to better address and analyse LSI within an MSP context [Fig. 1]. We explored the socioeconomic potential of the coastline in this region and identified major hot spots of anthropogenic pressures affecting the environment. The LSI analysis was structured in three main phases: design, feedback, and redesign. In the first phase, we collected meaningful information regarding the case study and established criteria for compiling maps. We decided to develop single thematic maps and to summarise them in diagram maps that highlighted essential features. This supported feedback sessions with local stakeholders and rights holders, previously identified with the help of local authorities and engaged through specific events meant to explain the benefits (and risks) of actively participating in the MSP process. Preliminary outputs were shared to gather stakeholders' feedback. After we collected and mapped all the stakeholders' information, it was possible to redesign and update the previous mapping. This generated more complete knowledge and we were able to condense the information in a final diagram map, which shows the main areas and interaction hot spots. The results were incorporated in the case study's overall MSP planning proposal.

Fig. 1
The case study boundaries and satellite image (ESA 2014)

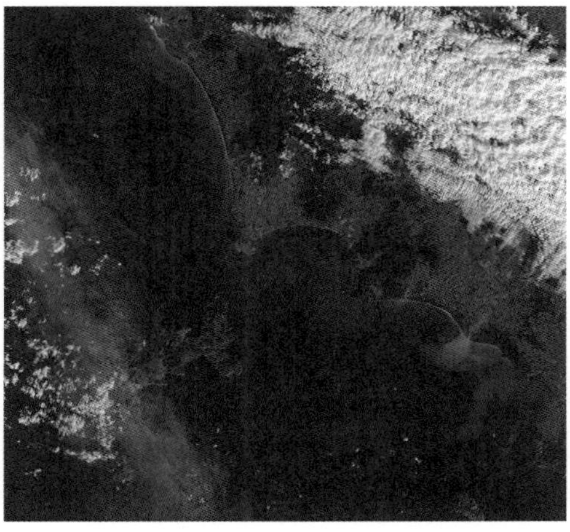

Following the main internally recognised methodological "steps," an initial assessment was carried out through desk-based research, including current environmental, socioeconomic, and governance information.(22) The existing multi-level strategic documents (international, national, and regional) were analysed to identify preferred future development trajectories, as well as high-level environmental and economic objectives established for the planning area. The initial assessment showed that the case study's coastal area presents high ecological and socioeconomic value due to the important environmental components found in shallow waters (less than 30 metres deep) that deliver many ecosystem services [Fig. 2] Seagrass meadows cover part of the coastline, supporting the area's high degree of biodiversity, increasing its resilience to erosion and providing food sources, shelter, and breeding grounds for numerous marine species, including some of commercial value, such as hake (*Merluccius merluccius*) and rose shrimp (*Parapenaeus longirostris*).

Conservation activities are encouraged in the area through the presence of several protected sites, including the Tuscan Archipelago National Park [Fig. 2] Often protected sites and regimes spatially overlap, creating complexity in analysing the governance schemes (i.e., determining who is the responsible authority, which protection measures are mandatory, and which areas have prohibitions on particular activities). Although marine and land systems present important differences from an environmental point of view, these two realms are strongly connected through shared ecological processes. (23) Nonetheless, in the Tuscan Archipelago there is a lack of coordination between land and marine conservation tools that do not address the many anthropogenic effects on the natural environment at the land-sea interface.

Fig. 2
Environmental and infrastructural frameworks in the area (Bassan, Manea, Innocenti, Musco)

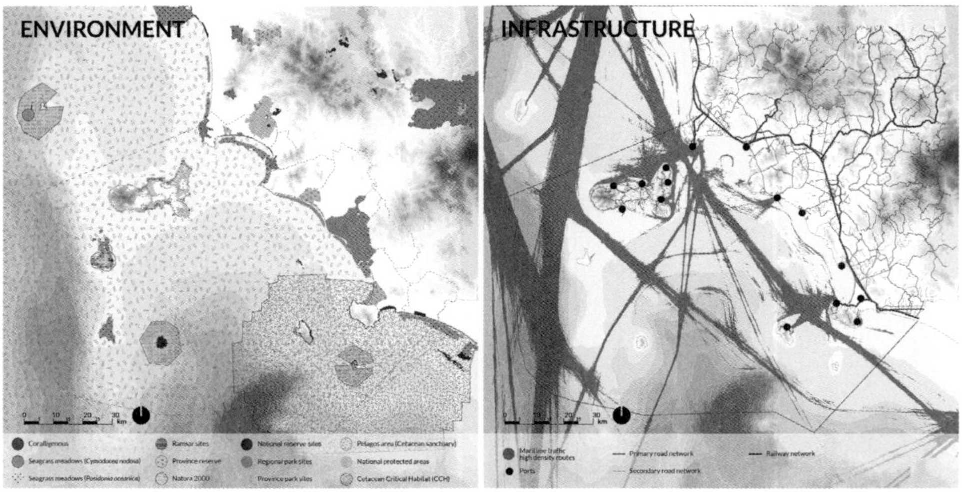

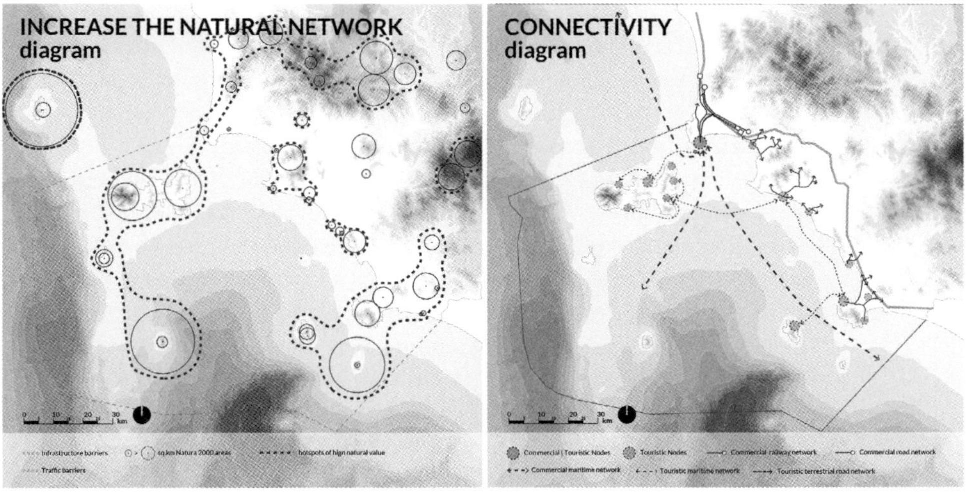

Fig. 3 Diagrams of possible increased natural networks and transport connectivity in the area. (Bassan, Manea, Innocenti, Musco)

LSIs are also influenced by transport infrastructures and fluxes [Fig. 2]. Accounting for these “infrastructural barriers” helped us understand how to mitigate impacts and conflicts. Maritime activities such as shipping, fishing, sailing, and movement of passengers require dedicated port infrastructures, which usually negatively affect coastal habitats. From the perspective of commercial shipping, LSIs not only involve connections with the different ports, but also with the road transport system. For these reasons, the transportation sector determines a high percentage of LSI in the area, supporting the overall connectivity, which assists socioeconomic development, but involves considerable environmental impact (e.g., habitat fragmentation, noise, pollution).

The dual nature of transport systems, as vectors of connectivity and as barriers, was assessed in the study. The flexible approach to design facilitated engagement with local administrators and stakeholders and we were able to define the main issues through collaborative mapping and immediate feedback. Results suggested that traffic decongestion measures should be applied and activities be monitored to reduce environmental pressures. In addition, with a communicative approach and the use of iterative mapping, the identification of transport connectivity gave input that can be used to optimise these networks [Fig. 3].

On the other hand, in order to promote natural connectivity, we developed diagram maps showing possible ecological corridors in a wider natural network. This network covers both land and sea territories in a comprehensive way, with the aim to facilitate preservation of land, coastal, and marine environments [Fig. 3]. We used these results to demonstrate the need to proceed cautiously when planning with uncertainties and with poor data quality/quantity, and to understand where to apply localised measures and monitoring activities.

The case study area includes landscapes of great value, while also hosting important productive activities. There is clearly great potential for developing sustainable tourism throughout, especially in light of farmhouse activities and "slow" agriculture practices (olives and wine). Local tourism depends on environmental quality and yet is recognised as one of the main sources of direct and indirect environmental pressures, often exacerbating the fragile equilibrium between activities on the coastline and the capacity of natural resources to recover.(24) An example is the depletion of water resources due to excessive exploitation of aquifers resulting in saline intrusion. The degree to which such activities affect the coastal and marine environment at the land-sea interface needs to be assessed in the absence of a defined terrestrial boundary that might help determine the real source of touristic pressures. Especially in this context, land and sea planning frameworks must "talk" in order to avoid inconsistencies.

To overcome the lack of definition to the limits of analysis, we assumed a buffer zone around the coastal beach areas, diving sites, and main infrastructures in the area. This helped define primary areas of interaction between tourism and the environment [Fig. 4, p. 268]. The buffer zone made it possible to see possible impacts of touristic activities on the environment (e.g., habitat degradation, marine litter, and pollution), and to stimulate further research and monitoring that might reduce such impacts.

Land-based activities such as agriculture and industry indirectly affect maritime sectors, contributing to environmental degradation through the discharge of contaminants that reach the sea by rivers. This can lead to habitat loss and hypoxia/anoxia events (depletion of oxygen) as a result of eutrophication (dense vegetative growth) due to excessive nutrient loads entering the sea. Through a cascading effect, this environmental degradation can negatively affect maritime activities such as fish farming.(25) In the case study area, these interactions were mapped to delineate places where in-depth research is necessary to better understand environmental quality. Additional research could also support planning processes in addressing sustainability objectives more effectively. Some intensive fish farming facilities are already present in the area, but the establishment of further fish farms could have a detrimental impact on other activities in addition to impacting the overall environment. Through design we were able to show the interrelations between productive land-based and maritime activities, underlining interconnections between environmental components and demonstrating why these relations should be carefully assessed.

In this context, where interactions between land-based activities and the environment involve trade-offs, we were able to detect multiple connections in a dense potential network of interactions through mapping and design. This analysis helped us identify and design the main overlaps of interactions and fluxes [Fig. 5, p. 268]. The work involved a communicative, explorative approach, with the aim of structuring a series of measures to be included in the MSP pilot. (26) This phase was essential in approaching such a complex topic by unfolding new knowledge and connecting with local stakeholders. LSI was one of the significant components that reflected conflicts and synergies among uses and between uses and the environment.

CONCLUSION

Land and sea are connected via complex interactions. These interactions often influence people's livelihoods. Any strict division between land and sea domains, planning frameworks, and binaries is essentially an "artificial" construct that follows political-administrative demarcations and priorities. LSI research can help transcend land and sea binaries. It recognises the sea as a cultural space in which local needs, perceptions, and values should be taken into account.

In the case study, research by design allowed us to explore the value of the natural and anthropic environment and to consider benefits provided to local communities. It also allowed us to discern hot spots where activities overlap, possibly conflicting or complementing each other. Thematic maps based on the acquired spatial information helped overcome data limitations and underpin visual perceptions. In fact, they were highly effective in both communicating and analysing knowledge acquired of the area, as well as in suggesting potential solutions, especially in such a multi-sectorial context. Design allowed us to acquire a general understanding at the scale of our analysis, orienting future downscaling to deepen site-specific contexts with the support of more detailed data. Furthermore, this approach facilitated engagement with local stakeholders, enabling the co-production of knowledge throughout the overall planning process. We aimed to extend the analysis landwards, while being aware of the absence of definite terrestrial boundaries. We included some land activities and infrastructures in the analysis, looking for positive and negative interactions between them, as well as with the coastal environment and sea space. Within the poorly-defined LSI framework, our approach aimed at exploring the land-sea interface continuum, building a basis for the implementation of a LSI methodological framework in the context of MSP.

Land and maritime planning differ. They involve different priorities, institutional and legal frameworks, and conceptual approaches- aspects which are fundamental when considering the "urbanisation of the sea", in relation to both land and sea regimes. The need for new tools is evident. Land planning is focused on private rights while maritime planning focuses on controlling activities in the common space of the sea. This creates a complex socioeconomic picture with various communities, stakeholders, and actors interested in the same geographic space, while also creating difficulties in adapting traditional frameworks used in land planning to the maritime domain. Maritime and terrestrial planning systems require good coordination to produce aligned outputs and meet the goals of ecosystem-based management and sustainable development. Terrestrial planners need sufficient understanding of marine and maritime matters, while marine/maritime planners need to understand land-based implications of marine planning.

This exercise tried to overcome many of these differences, highlighting LSI effects and perceiving the main LSI hotspots through "unconventional" tools such as design. Research by design can help "translate" between disciplines. It can be adopted in data scarce conditions as well as on a large scale to address anthropogenic and natural processes and dynamics that cross land-sea boundaries (to improve reliability, this approach should be accompanied by science-based analytical approaches). The research-by-design approach applied to the LSI analysis turned out to be a highly communicative tool, able to incorporate not only spatial data but also socio-ecological perspectives in a way that was supportive of the MSP process. It was a reflective practice in which critical assessment took place through sketching, continuously going back and forth between inquiry and proposal. Testing such an approach in such complex planning contexts as the Tuscan Archipelago, can pave the way to better understanding and implementation of an LSI methodological framework, and to better coordination between land and sea planning regimes.

(1) United Nations Development Program, "2030 Agenda for Sustainable Development" (2017) https://sustainabledevelopment.un.org/sdg14
(2) European Commission. "Communication from the Commission to the European Parliament, the Council, the European economic and social Committee and the committee of the regions: Blue Growth opportunities for marine and maritime sustainable growth". COM (2012) 494 final.
(3) Benjamin S. Halpern, Kimberly A. Selkoe, Fiorenza Micheli, and Carrie V. Kappel, "Evaluating and Ranking the Vulnerability of Global Marine Ecosystems to Anthropogenic Threats," *Conservation Biology* 21, no. 5 (2007): 1301-15.
(4) Stephen Jay, Fatima L. Alves, Cathal O'Mahony, Maria B. Gomez, Aiobheann Rooney, Margarida Almodovar, Kira Gee, Juan Vivero, Jorge Gonçalves, Maria da Luz Fernandes, Sarah Twomey, Inmaculada Prado, Catarina Fonseca, Luis Bentes, Guida Henriques, Aldino Campos and Olvido Tello, "Transboundary Dimensions of Marine Spatial Planning: Fostering Inter-Jurisdictional Relations and Governance" *Marine Policy* 65 (2016): 85-96.
(5) Robert J. Nicholls and Anny Cazenave. "Sea-level rise and its impact on coastal zones," *Science* 328.5985 (2010): 1517–20.
(6) European Union. "Directive 2014/89/EU of the European Parliament and of the Council of 23 July 2014 establishing a framework for Maritime Spatial Planning", *Official Journal of the European Union*, Brussels (2014)
(7) European Commission (2017) https://webgate.ec.europa.eu/maritimeforum/en/node/4090
(8) Supporting Implementation of Maritime Spatial Planning in the Western Mediterranean Region (SIMWESTMED) - EASME/EMFF/2015/1.2.1.3/02/SI2.742101
(9) Charles N. Ehler and Fanny Douvere, "Marine Spatial Planning: a step-by-step approach toward ecosystem-based management." *Intergovernmental Oceanographic Commission and Man and the Biosphere Programme* (2009)
(10) European Union. "Directive 2014/89/EU of the European Parliament and of the Council of 23 July 2014 establishing a framework for Maritime Spatial Planning" *Official Journal of the European Union*, Brussels (2014)
(11) Wesley Flannery, Geraint Ellis, Melissa Nursey-Bray, Jan PM van Tatenhove, Christina Kelly, Scott Coffen-Smout, Rhona Fairgrieve, Maaike Knol and others, "Exploring the winners and losers of marine environmental governance/Marine spatial planning: Cui bono?/More than fishy business: epistemology, integration and conflict in marine spatial planning/Marine spatial planning: power and scaping/Surely not all planning is evil?/Marine spatial planning: a Canadian perspective/Maritime spatial planning–ad utilitatem omnium/Marine spatial planning: it is better to be on the train than being hit by it/Reflections from the perspective of recreational anglers ...", *Planning Theory & Practice* 17(1), (2016): 121-151.
(12) Tundi Agardy, John Davis, Kristin Sherwood and Ole Vestergaard, "Taking steps toward marine and coastal ecosystem-based management: An introductory guide", *MarXiv* (2011)
(13) Andrea Barbanti, Pierpaolo Campostrini, Francesco Musco, Alessandro Sarretta and Elena Gissi, "ADRIPLAN Conclusions and Recommendations: A short manual for MSP implementation in the Adriatic-Ionian Region", *CNR-ISMAR, Venice, Italy* (2015) Kemal Pınarbaşı, Ibon Galparsoro, Angel Borja, Vanessa Stelzenmüller, Charles N. Ehler and Antje Gimpel, "Decision support tools in marine spatial planning: present applications, gaps and future perspectives", *Marine Policy*, 83, (2017): 83-91.
(14) Jorge G. Alvarez-Romero, Robert L. Pressey, Natalie C. Ban, Ken Vance-Borland, Chuck Willer, Carissa Joy Klein and Steven D. Gaines, "Integrated land-sea conservation planning: the missing links," *Annual Review of Ecology, Evolution, and Systematics*, 42, (2011): 381-409.
(15) Brent Allpress, Robyn Barnacle, Lesley Duxbury and Elisabeth Grierson, "Supervising practice-led research by project in art, creative writing, architecture and design," *Brill Sense*, (2012): 1-14.
(16) Rob Roggema, "Research by Design: Proposition for a Methodological Approach," *Urban Science*, 1.1, (2017)
(17) J.M. De Jonge, "Landscape architecture between politics and science: an integrative perspective on landscape planning and design in the network society," (2009) Mette Ramsgaard Thomsen and Martin Tamke, "Narratives of making: thinking practice led research in architecture," *In Communicating (by) Design*, (2009): 1-8.
(18) Jurgen Rosemann, "The conditions of research by design in practice." *Research by Design, Proceedings of the International Conference Proceedings A. Faculty of Architecture Delft University of Technology in Co-Operation with the EAAE/AEEA, Delft, The Netherlands*, (2000): 1-3.
(19) Elisabetta Manea, Niccolò Bassan, Federico Fabbri, Daniela Addis, Alberto Innocenti, Marina Markovic, Francesco Musco, Elena Gissi, "Tyrrhenian case study. General description of the Tyrrhenian Case Study," *EU Project Grant No.: EASME/EMFF/2015/1.2.1.3/02/SI2.742101. Supporting Implementation of Maritime Spatial Planning*

in the Western Mediterranean region (SIMWESTMED), CORILA (2018)
(20) Athanassios C. Tsikliras, Anny Dinouli, Vasileios-Zikos Tsiros and Eleni Tsalkou, "The Mediterranean and Black Sea fisheries at risk from overexploitation," *PloS one*, 10(3), (2015)
(21) Jose Antonio García-Charton, Angel Pérez-Ruzafa, Conception Marcos, Joachim Claudet, Fabio Badalamenti, Lisandro Benedetti-Cecchi, Jesus Manuel Falcon, Marco Milazzo, Patrick Joseph Schembri, Ben Stobart and others, "Effectiveness of European Atlanto-Mediterranean MPAs: do they accomplish the expected effects on populations, communities and ecosystems?," *Journal for Nature Conservation*, 16(4), (2008): 193-221.
(22) Ehler and Douvere. "Marine Spatial Planning: a step-by-step"
(23) Maria Beger, Hedley S. Grantham, Robert L. Pressey, Kerrie A. Wilson, Eric L. Peterson, Daniel Dorfman, Peter J. Mumby, Reinaldo Lourival, Daniel R. Brumbaugh and Hugh P. Possingham, "Conservation planning for connectivity across marine, freshwater, and terrestrial realms," *Biological Conservation*, 143(3), (2010): 565-575.
(24) Marilena Papageorgiou, "Coastal and marine tourism: A challenging factor in Marine Spatial Planning," *Ocean & coastal management*, 129, (2016): 44–48.
(25) Alice Newton, John Icely, Sonia Cristina, Ana Brito, Ana Cristina Cardoso, Franciscus Colijn, Simona Dalla Riva, Flemming Gertz, Jens Wurgler Hansen, Marianne Holmer and others, "An overview of ecological status, vulnerability and future perspectives of European large shallow, semi-enclosed coastal systems, lagoons and transitional waters," *Estuarine, Coastal and Shelf Science*, 140, (2014): 95–122.
(26) Elisabetta Manea, Federico Fabbri, Niccolò Bassan, Alberto Innocenti, Alessandro Sarretta, Giulio Farella, Davide Di Blasi, Fabio Garaventa, Andrea Barbanti, Pierpaolo Campostrini, Marianna Morelli, Francesco Musco, and Elena Gissi, "Tyrrhenian case study. Management focus: the Tuscan Archipelago," *EU Project Grant No.: EASME/EMFF/2015/1.2.1.3/02/SI2.742101. Supporting Implementation of Maritime Spatial Planning in the Western Mediterranean region (SIMWESTMED), CORILA*, (2018)
[Fig. 3] Open Source: https://de.wikipedia.org/wiki/Abraham_Cresques#/media/File:Europe_Mediterranean_Catalan_Atlas.jpg;

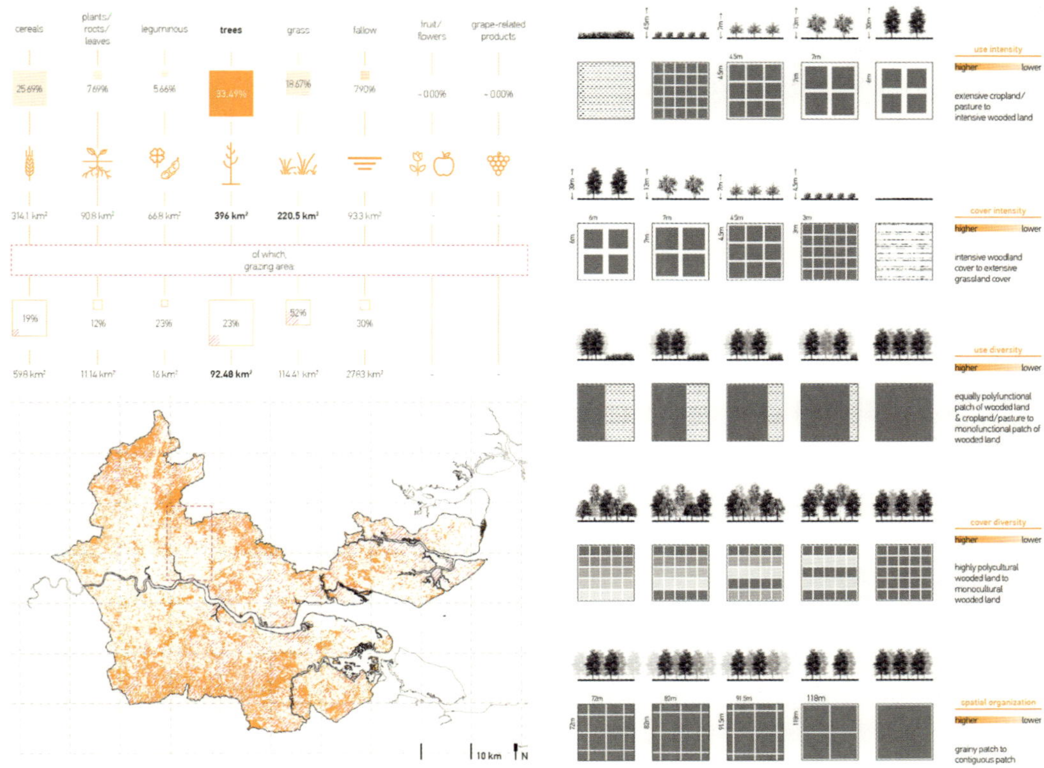

Fig. 2
Relative cover of different crops for the border interface zone of the ecological region of the Greater Thames Estuary (left) and designed (proposed) organisation of ecological density (right). (Sarantis Georgiou, TU Delft 2020)

Fig. 3
Nano-scale floating hubs-Algae exhibition area (Aikaterina Myserli, TU Delft 2020)

Fig. 4
Reconstructed functional typology—Oyster farm development inside the inner tidal barrage (Alezandra Farmazon, TU Delft 2020)

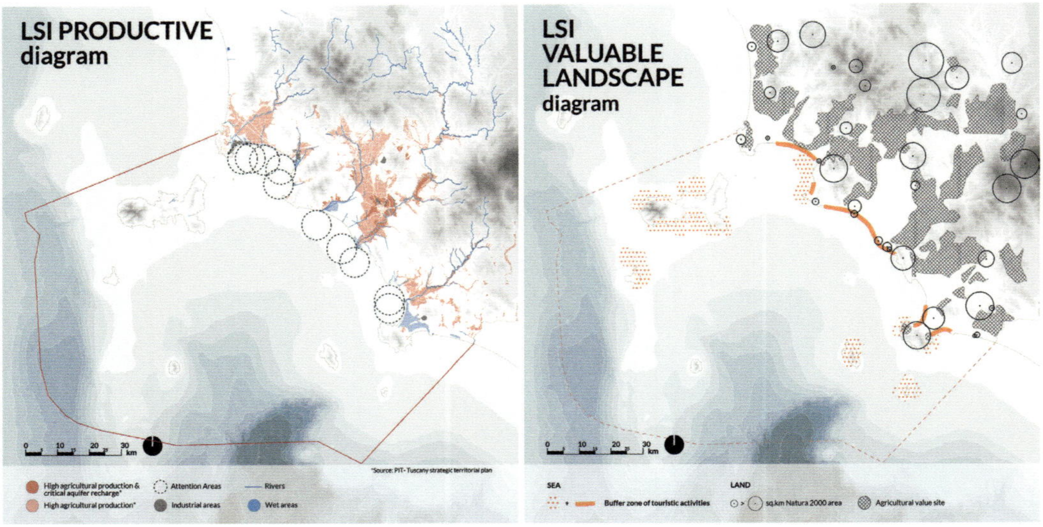

Fig. 4
Productive and valuable landscape diagrams of the area. (Bassan, Manea, Innocenti, Musco)

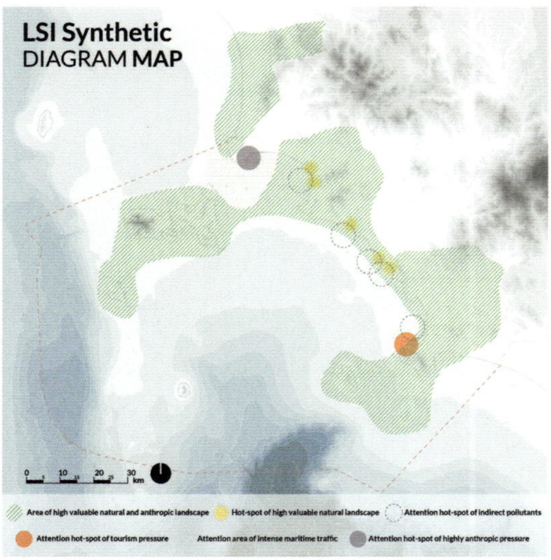

Fig. 5
Land-sea interactions synthetic diagram of the Tuscan Archipelago. (Bassan, Manea, Innocenti, Musco)

Fig. 1
Sarah Cameron Sunde, 36.5 / a durational performance with the sea; Satellietgroep 2015 (Florian Braakman)

Fig. 3
Theun Karelse, Fossils Soup; Satellietgroep 2015 (Florian Braakman)

Fig. 4
Berndnaut Smilde,
Breaking Light;
Satellietgroep
2015 (Annnegret
Kellner)

Fig. 3
Map of Europe and the Mediterranean from the 1959 copy of the Catalan Atlas of 1375. (Abraham Cresques)

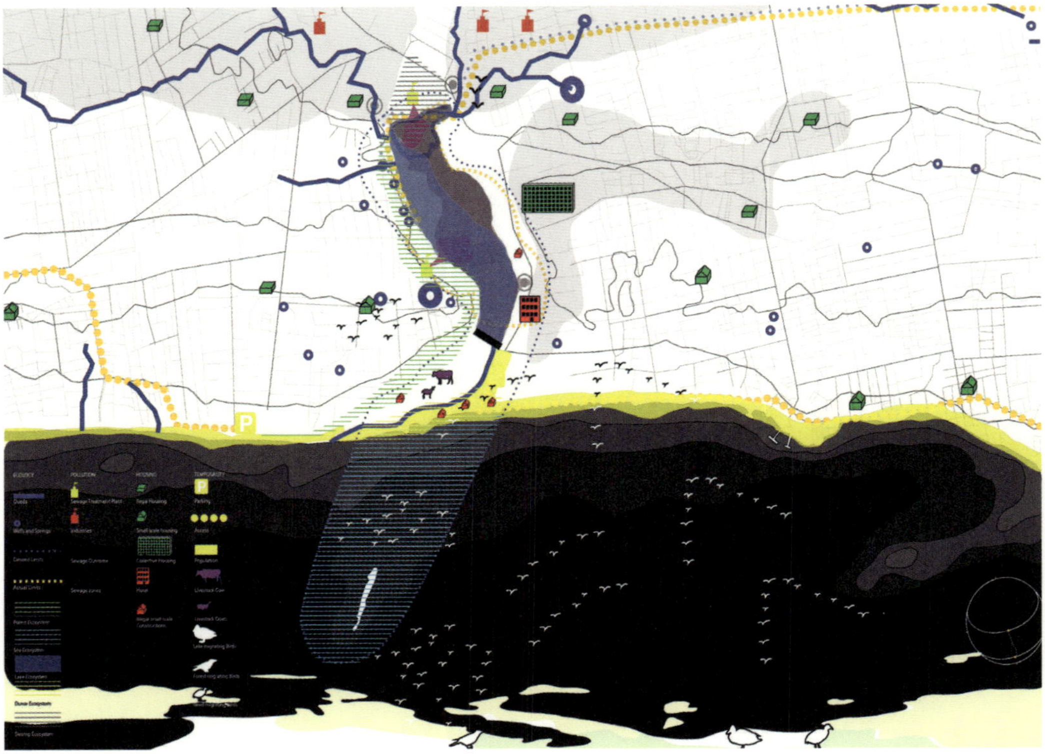

Fig. 6
The protection of Lake Reghaia is in conflict with the pollution caused by nearby industries. Algiers (Mittelmeerland 2012)

Fig. 1
Borderzone archipelago, southwest Singapore (Bas Princen, 2016)

Fig. 4
Below the Water Towers (Design Earth, Pacific Aquarium 2016)

Fig. 5
Iron Towers (Design Earth, Pacific Aquarium 2016)

Chapter 17 WHO IS NATURE?

Artists' Collective Satellietgroep

Artists ask different questions. Satelleitgroep gathers artists around the Zandmotor in the Netherlands to carry out investigations that open up important discussions about relations between people, water, nature, time, and climate.

Lotte Milene Bosman (NL, 1987) is a visual artist, focusing on the shifting understanding of nature and landscape over time. The human role in nature is an important as- pect of her work, but she also takes a playful approach toward the landscape. Bosman received her MFA in painting at Minerva Art Academy in 2012. Since 2015, Bosman has been part of the artists' collective Satellietgroep.

Jacqueline Heerema (NL, 1958) is a Dutch conceptual artist, mediator and independent (sub)urban curator, studied Monumental Art and Environment at the Royal Academy of Art The Hague and Theoretical Museology at Leiden University. Heerema is fascinated by the construction of 'time' and changing perceptions of value systems, which we often take for granted. Her focus is on the in-between-ness of the natural and the artifactual to create space for reciprocity and polyphony in a changing world. As part of her artistic practice, Heerema co-founded artists collective Satellietgroep in 2006 and is artist-curator since then.

Satellietgroep is an artists collective that explores the reciprocal relations of humanity and nature from an artistic perspective, with a focus on the sea, (coastal) landscape transitions, climate and the impact of humanity on the environment in the Netherlands and abroad. In 2018, Satellietgroep posed the question *Who is nature?* With the exhibition program *Climate as Artifact—Klimaat als mensenwerk* Satellietgroep positioned dialogue about climate and the impact of humanity as a geological force in the cultural domain. Materializing ideas through art and redefining climate as an artifact, as something we make, helps to increase our sensitivity and to see connections within the natural world and between our actions and our environment. www.satellietgroep.nl

HOW VISUAL NARRATIVES IN ART AND DESIGN CAN OVERTURN PREVAILING UNDERSTANDINGS OF ENVIRONMENT.

On a summer's day at 8:15 am, a woman in a red suit walked into the North Sea. As soon as the water was up to her ankles she stopped and stood still, looking out over the water and staring at the horizon. The tide came in and the water started to rise, but she did not move. She hardly blinked. The sun climbed higher in the sky until it reached its highest point, then started to sink again, along with the sea. Children were playing in the water, birds flew over, and people were passing by. Apart from the buildings and pathways around the bay, the only static thing was that particular lady in her bright red suit.

It was August 15, 2015, at Katwijk aan Zee, in The Netherlands. The woman is Sarah Cameron Sunde, a New York-based theatre-maker and performance artist, who came to the Netherlands as part of an ongoing public performance with the sea and stood in the water for almost thirteen hours—a full tidal cycle [Fig. 1, p. 269]. The project began in 2013, after New York City was hit by Hurricane Sandy and the artist was startled by how ill-prepared the city was for climate change and sea level rise. Sunde's durational performance with the sea brought new awareness to a huge and extremely diverse audience. Moreover, she created a sense of community as people were invited to stand in the water with her. Passers-by in the morning or early afternoon commented that it was a little ridiculous to stand in the sea for so long. But when they returned in the evening they had brought family and friends and while the sun was setting and Sunde walked out of the sea, a whole crowd had gathered around the bay and everyone was clapping and telling each other that they just had witnessed something wonderful and even magical. People realized that they were in this together. That the sea is as threatening as it is beautiful.

There are several elements in this work that demonstrate how art can function as a visual narrative that strengthens cultural perspectives of sea and land. The artist takes this aspect of the work very seriously by performing the piece on each continent, thus pointing out that different cultures, different seas, and different landscapes are all connected and all subject to change due to global warming. People all around the world are slowly starting to rethink how they and the planet are interrelated and new questions arise around the understanding of time and the perception of place. The challenge we are facing is not merely technical or political, it is first and foremost a cultural challenge. This chapter aims to demonstrate how redefining climate as a cultural artifact through artistic practice helps us to break free from conventional attitudes in order to develop essential new perspectives.

Our case study investigates the experience of nature on the Zandmotor, a temporary and artificial extension of the beach on the west coast of the Netherlands. [Fig. 2] The Zandmotor is a human intervention in nature. It can be regarded as the largest cultural

Fig. 2
The Zandmotor, 2012 (Joop van Houdt)

statement of its time, at least in the Netherlands and perhaps even in Europe, in terms of the shifting relationship between people and water. Here, a piece of land has been added that is designed to change under the influence of sea currents and sand drifts. The Zandmotor is built to generate knowledge about future relationships between people and water, through the deposit of 21.5 million cubic meters of sand on the foreshore. On the Zandmotor, all issues related to climate change around people and water come together: it is situated in a rising salty sea with an urbanised hinterland (the metropolis Rotterdam-The Hague), bordered by dunes from which drinking water is extracted, while new dune formations enlarge the freshwater bubble beneath the Zandmotor.

We will be drawing from our own experiences and projects that were developed on the Zandmotor to illustrate our statement and to explain how we came to the question "who is nature?"

A DIALOGICAL SPACE OFFERED BY ART

In an essay on environmental aesthetics and the land art of Robert Smithson, Anja Novak refers to the American philosopher Arnold Berleant, who pointed out that "our environment is not simply the physical world that surrounds us (...) but actually occurs in our perceptual and active involvement with the world" (1). By taking people outside and offering them new experiences on a somewhat familiar site, it becomes possible to have a lasting impact and to trigger new philosophies. Earlier, Friedrich Nietzsche maintained that one should not start with thinking, but with being outside and experiencing. That is what changes you.(2) And a third philosopher, Helmut Plessner, claimed that "man not only lives and experiences his life. He also experiences his experience of life."

—which means that people live in three worlds at the same time: the outer world, the inner world, and the shared world of culture (which Plessner calls "Mitwelt"). All three statements urge us to leave our comfortable couches and climate-controlled offices and go outside and interact with people and with our environment—the first step toward revaluing, and reconnecting to, the space we inhabit in order to develop new narratives. It is not the way the world is changing that makes us rethink how we live our lives, rather it is the stories we tell each other. Can the conversation itself then, when it is staged or initiated by an artist in a specific atmosphere, be a work of art? When we posed the question "who is nature?" most people first raised an eyebrow, but soon realized that it wasn't necessarily a question that needed to be answered with factual explanations. What is important is to start the conversation.

SAND STORIES

Designers Nadine Sterk and Lonny Ryswyck from Atelier NL produced glass from the "wild sand" that was deposited at the Zandmotor in 2011.(3) The glass industry normally uses only pure white sands, which can only be found in a small number of sand quarries worldwide. In order to challenge the conventions of the conservative contemporary glass industry, Atelier NL has been collecting wild sands from dunes, beaches, and sandpits in various places all over Europe since 2010—constantly experimenting with this natural material, including studying geological time, particle size, chemical composition, and microscopic imaging. Their project "SandBank" reveals the potential of local, wild sands. For this project, the designers followed the path of ancient Roman glass traders, took samples of eighty sands, mapped and classified them, created special sand-boxes and carried out multiple tests to produce different types of glass. Sands from different locations provide varied results because of their wide mix of minerals and other components that adhere to the grains, yielding different colors and textures. The research and development are time-consuming, but essential for the designers to demonstrate the value and potential of raw materials and to reveal the full richness of sand's distinctive elements.

There are two important aspects to this work: the celebration of the beauty of diversity and the questioning of our use of natural resources for industrial objectives. Displaying the glass or drinking from it opens up conversation and brings new stories to the table; stories about the Zandmotor, where the sand was collected; stories about the North Sea, from where the sand had been dredged, and stories about land formation through sediments brought in from rivers and the sea into the Dutch Delta, then further shaped by people.

Other stories within the work reach far beyond the local. An example is the designers' contact with Denis Delastrac, the award-winning director of the documentary *Sand Wars*.(4) His film documents the disappearance of many of the world's beaches due to the large industries and building companies' insatiable need for concrete, which requires sand. The so-called sand mafia exists on a global scale and people are being killed over sand. Sand is illegally dredged from particular countries, already causing the disappearance of some Indonesian islands and resulting not only in the loss of the environment, but also livelihoods and whole ecosystems. These are stories that need to be shared. Atelier NL's sand glass addresses our sensitivity and imagination and speaks of global challenges from a local perspective, thus bringing them closer to us. Through the materialisation of concepts and data, art offers a sensory experience that can help us exchange facts about the natural world and people's relationships with it, but more importantly, it can effectuate different ways of being and perceiving.

THE SIMULTANEITY OF TIME

The sand of the Zandmotor is classified as Pleistocene sand, as it was dredged from the bottom of the North Sea in an area that 11,000 years ago was part of the mainland (Doggerland) connecting Britain and continental Europe. For this reason, the sand contains an unusually high concentration of fossils. Artist Theun Karelse found a mammoth tusk when he was on the Zandmotor one evening. Holding the piece in his hand brought him back to a time when the Netherlands, as we know it, did not yet exist. When a geologist drills a hole in the ground, the drill goes through different layers of time. The deeper it goes, the older the soil horizon it touches. On the Zandmotor, it is the reverse, since the top layer of the seabed was excavated first and the deepest part dredged was placed five meters above sea level. The artist wanted to share the incredible sensation that came with his realization and new understanding of time through fossils such as a mammoth rib and the tooth of a woolly rhino that he found—objects that date back to the Last Glacial Maximum and are between 20,000 and 40,000 years old. Karelse wondered whether people today could still experience something of that old time through those fossils.(5) The result was a fossil soup and the group that ate it were the first people in millennia to taste mammoth again [Fig. 3, p. 269]. In the artist's own words, the project and the writing that came with it "contemplates the parallels and differences between the last climate change event and the current one, in terms of ecology and culture and it explores what a positive agenda for the future could mean".(6) Looking back and experiencing the deep memory that is stored in the ground underneath our feet can help us to develop scenarios for the future—a deeper understanding of place naturally leads to a deeper understanding of time and of the way in which we experience time. When thinking about the future, we should eliminate the linear way of thinking that is so deeply rooted in western thought and recreate a more symbiotic way of thinking of relations between people and nature. This is not a plea to return to a simplified way of life, but to look at people who have passed on their skills and knowledge of the natural world over thousands of years, and take them as an example; they probably have much to teach us.

The Columbian-Canadian anthropologist Wade Davis has travelled to the most remote parts of the planet and worked with indigenous people from all over the world. His research shows that many of these people have the ability to "sense the world beyond their body," meaning they have an ability to see from the perspective of other creatures or objects, for example rocks, water, or clouds (7). This type of understanding requires much sensitivity and imagination —yet we all possess these bodily and mental powers, therefore we can relate to Davis's position. Keeping the concept of bodily sensation, or understanding through sensory experience brings to mind a project by visual artist Esther Kokmeijer. In December 2015, she tested how climate-proof we are in the Netherlands. On a cold winter night, a group of people stayed with her in a sweat lodge on the Zandmotor, then dived into the ice-cold water. Stories and experiences were shared while the artist directed the activities and documented the group's body temperatures. The project showed how people can adapt to different and extreme circumstances in the process.

The biological success and resulting expansion of the human species means that the entire planet has become subject to cultural influences. However, through the work of Wade Davis, we learn that despite the fact that indigenous people probably witness and suffer the most from the rapidly changing conditions due to global warming, they maintain a positive, holistic perspective on systems change and immediately look for solutions. Rather than counting species or developing mathematical models, they see cause and effect in an exact material manner—in every insect, mammal, or flower, and in the way their own lives are changing. One could argue that many indigenous communities display an incredible resilience through their ability to adapt and their enormous respect for the natural and spiritual world, which means that, the people of the future on this planet will probably be much closer to nature than most people are today.

BEYOND THE NATURAL OR ARTIFICIAL: CLIMATE AS ARTIFACT

Opposing pairs such as culture and nature, male and female or past and future no longer offer valid categories of contemporary reality. At the same time this dualism is deeply rooted in our thinking and our language. We lack the vocabulary for the coexistence of land and water and for the constant and omnipresent interaction between people and nature. The Zandmotor is an artificial peninsula, branded as "nature." The Wadden Sea is UNESCO World Heritage and is described as a unique natural site, as if there were no islands or dikes in that area, as if there haven't been any people that have been just as dependent on that sea as the fish, as the birds, as the worms, or the weeds. Moreover, people create new conditions where certain rare species can survive, only due to human intervention.

Nature is frequently discussed as needing to be protected, restored, or maintained, since the influence of mankind is omnipresent and taking on immense proportions, causing irreversible damage. We argue that the latter statement is a cultural position. Humanity is changing ecosystems, causing mass extinction, but also creating new conditions. This makes humankind a geological force and thus equal to nature. But do people see themselves as nature? People's understanding of what nature is changes throughout time and new insights greatly influence human perception. After centuries of humankind attempting to dominate nature, we recently started talking about nature as a force that is starting to "strike back." Despite the fact that nature has always been beyond the control of humans, a flood is no longer seen as a result of bad policy or poor engineering, but is more or less regaining its divine status; humanity is being punished. We do not know what the effects will be in the long term of our actions over the past 500 years. Looking at geological time, including ice ages and interglacial periods, it seems quite impossible for humanity to actually destroy the planet. But the world as we know it today will never return. So what type of nature are we currently trying to protect? Does this consist of all the organic nature, all flora and fauna that are known to us? Are we also aiming to protect all inorganic nature, every mountain and every rock, iceberg, sandy beach; the oceans that we desire and fear? Are we aiming at conservation of the current state? The general public appears to have an idealistic idea of what nature is and what the world should look like, and slowly our environment is adjusted to fit that image, becoming a representation of nature. If we continue in this direction, going out to the North Sea might become like going out to the zoo or to an aquarium. But we are also nature and since the beginning of humankind, the planet has been cultivated, making nature part of our cultures, and slowly turning the world into an artifact.

Our expanding cities have been named people's largest artifact.(8) But it was the Dutch landscape architect, emeritus professor and co-inventor of the Zandmotor, Dirk Sijmons (see chapter 14), who recently wondered whether by now the climate might be our biggest artifact. Defining people as nature and the climate as an artifact could just be a philosophical or linguistic exercise, in order to discuss the question "who is nature?" However redefining these concepts through art is an essential task, since this requires an intensive and constructive use of human sensitivity and imagination. Visual narratives and artistic actions that invite the public to go outside and perceive the world with a critical but open mind can make a lasting impression. It helps us to bring abstract concepts or things that are seemingly beyond our control closer to ourselves. Climate is a hyper-object: according to the British philosopher Timothy Morton, we know that it exists, but we can't comprehend it.(9) Materializing ideas through art and redefining climate as an artifact, as something we make, helps to increase our sensitivity and to see connections within the natural world and between our actions and our environment.

This approach is particularly relevant to the Zandmotor, since it is a pilot project to generate knowledge for future coastal protection. Despite common belief, the Zandmotor is not built to protect the Dutch coastline, but is primarily a research site. Meanwhile, nature organisations and the provincial administration promote it as a place where people can experience and enjoy "rough nature." Thus, by not telling the real story, people are excluded from what is actually happening in public space. As Stephen Mintern wrote, the Zandmotor is "the first of its kind," which "means that the public have no preexisting idea of how to occupy the space, it is a space void of any memory, therefore allowing for new more singular interactions with the space."(10) This means that we have to find new ways of interacting with our environment, thus creating new stories.

During his Zandmotor residency with Satellietgroep, artist Berndnaut Smilde looked into ways of imposing a natural phenomenon onto the surroundings. He was interested in the artificial aspect of the Zandmotor, in interfering with the location, and investigated the values people project onto weather phenomena. He wrote:

> Size and proportions are unreal on the Zandmotor because I no longer appear to be accustomed to (unused) emptiness. That's why I sometimes felt alienated and strangely enough I lacked a sense of overview. How do you relate to 21.5 million cubic meters of sand?

Smilde then wondered what was "underneath" the Zandmotor. What was on the exact opposite side of it? The antipode turned out to be a "meaningless" coordinate in the ocean (somewhere near New Zealand). There wasn't even a satellite image available of the exact spot. Then the artist realized that the location of the Zandmotor used to be, and soon probably will be, just as undefined. The artificial peninsula is designed to exist for no more than twenty years, making its existence even on a human timescale almost negligible.

Artists pose different questions and transform these into visual experiences or objects, through which we can understand what our environment means to us, or what it could mean. Smilde works with natural phenomena, which makes his work appealing but also extra confusing. Do we appreciate the natural phenomenon, or the fact that he was able to produce it himself? During his residency, Smilde refracted the light of a lighthouse in order to project a rainbow onto the landscape. He turned a natural phenomenon into an artificial one that he could control, and project this onto a human-made landscape [Fig. 4, p. 270]. Ironically, the public still has the sense that they are witnessing one of these small wonders of nature.

BUILDING WITH NATURE, OR, EPHEMERAL CONSTRUCTIONS

The Zandmotor exemplifies a shift in attitudes toward nature and toward the sea. Where dikes were meant to build "against nature," the Zandmotor is an example of "building with nature." This a cultural shift within which people acknowledge that we live in one world and we have to work with nature rather than destroy it. Nevertheless, it is still building, yet the human-made aspect was more or less conveniently forgotten as soon as the Zandmotor was constructed. The Dutch artist Maurice Meewisse aimed to acknowledge the societal aspect of the Zandmotor with his Coffee Break performances in the summer of 2017. Meewisse wanted to stress the human-made aspect and the heavy labour that comes with land reclamation. Every workday he went to the Zandmotor, dug up some stools that he had made from driftwood or drift palettes and had his fifteen-minute coffee break, during which people were invited to join him for small talk and coffee, after which he buried everything again. It took him over three hours to have this short coffee break and Meewisse kept the work up for one month [Fig. 5]. At first sight, this might seem as ridiculous as standing in the sea for thirteen hours, but just as with Sarah Cameron Sunde's work discussed previously, it is much more than a humorous metaphor. The routine becomes something of a ritual and the fact that all the work is done in order to have some time to rest and reflect reinforces the importance of contemplation and conversation. Meewisse becomes a little like a contemporary Nietzsche, who went for five-hour walks, five days a week, for ten years. The production of new ideas or perspectives on the world that we inhabit does not start with thinking, but with being outside and experiencing.

Fig. 5
Maurice Meewisse, Coffee Break; Satellietgroep 2017 (Jacqueline Heerema)

But what if all there is left to experience on a specific site is a memory? The Zandmotor can be regarded as a suicidal landscape (11). It was built to dissolve. Taking into account that people had just witnessed the rise of a new type of landscape where there was "no preexisting idea of how to occupy the space," a new landscape that offered new insights and produced new knowledge concerning coastal protection and climate change, where people were confronted with times long gone, with the power of wind and sea, where people once again displayed their technical proficiency, and where we developed a new understanding of environment, a new understanding of who we are and where we stand, makes it difficult to accept that this too, is only temporary. How can we deal with an ephemeral phenomenon when it feels so solid and well researched? What does it mean to construct new narratives that do not correspond with prevailing concepts, knowing that these ideas in the near future will not be backed up by the physical entity of the place where these ideas originated? In order to understand and deal with the cultural shifts and dilemmas that come with the construction of new landscapes, it is essential that the humanities and social studies are involved. People and cultures are part of changing climates and changing environments. Technical inventions or solutions can bring about cultural change, but most solutions aim at preserving the current state. We argue that in order to develop new, inclusive narratives that can contribute to the establishment of significant cultural changes, we need to acknowledge that people are nature and that nature has become culture.

WHO IS NATURE?

The human desire to understand abstractions leads to new inventions, critical research, and a poetic contemplation of our environment. One of the most challenging aspects of the arts is the ability to pose different kinds of questions—those that people don't usually ask. In January 2006, the artists' collective Satellietgroep kicked off with the question *To whom belongs the sea?* To celebrate over twelve years of pioneering and to prepare for an unforeseen and challenging future, in January 2018, we started to rethink our perceptions of culture and nature with the question "Who is nature?" Satellietgroep invited seventeen artists and designers to jointly create a public program based on shared fascinations. This developed into an exceptional project, namely the exhibition program *Climate as Artifact – Klimaat als mensenwerk*. For the first time, climate is positioned in the *cultural domain*. Without judgement, without a preconceived position, we are curious to see the opportunities that climate (change) can offer us.

In the run-up to the exhibition, monthly informal meetings took place with the participating artists and special guests from different domains. In addition, there evolved a supporting program, where artists in smaller group presentations tested their artistic research with the public and entered into dialogue with scientists, philosophers, and each other. Following the practice of Satellietgroep as alternative academy and appreciating the sea and shores as vital learning environment of time and space, our visitors had the opportunity to engage with the artists who worked on-site, contribute to the ongoing process of artistic research, share their insights, and discover through the arts a multitude of fields of knowledge. Experts in the fields of nature, climate, geology, archeology, oceanography, philosophy, zoology, botany and spatial planning—as well as a canoe builder from the Marshall Islands—actively contributed to the making of new art works and public dialogues. This method also leads to an exhibition program that differs from the more traditional exhibitions. It is closer to a knowledge lab; a space for experiment, discussion and wonder; a workshop, learning center and meeting place, where all your senses are claimed.

With special thanks to the participating artist and designers Berndnaut Smilde, Sachi Miyachi, Nishiko, Esther Kokmeijer, Maurice Bogaert, Aliki van der Kruijs, Jos Klarenbeek, Maurice Meewisse, Lotte Geeven, Theun Karelse, Thijs Ebbe Fokkens, Giuseppe Licari, Onkruidenier, Josje Hattink, Masha Ru and all engaged experts, visitors and partners. More information: www.satellietgroep.nl

(1) Novak's essay "Engaging Environments. The practice of Robert Smithson and Olafur Eliasson as an Instance of Environmental Aesthetics" can be found in "Robert Smithson: Art in Continual Movement a contemporary reading," eds. by Ingrid Commandeur and Trudy van Riemsdijk-Zandzee. P. 21 (Alauda publications, 2015).
(2) Quote from Henk Manschot's lecture "Nietzsche als gids bij ecologische problemen. De verbeelding aan de macht!" De Nacht van de Filosofie, April 14, Nest, The Hague.
(3) Atelier NL is a Dutch design and research collective that develops products focusing on the richness of the earth and the value of local raw materials.
(4) *Sand Wars* is produced by Rappi Productions, La Compagnie des Taxi-Brousse, InfomAction, Arte France, with the support of the Santa Aguila Foundation. It premiered in 2013 in France and is distributed worldwide by PBS International.
(5) Theun Karelse reflections on the project: https://fo.am/blog/2015/03/30/mammoth/
(6) http://theunkarelse.net/writing.html
(7) Quote extracted from an article by Jim Robbins, "Native Knowledge: What Ecologists Are Learning from Indigenous People,"April 26, 2018. https://e360.yale.edu/features/native-knowledge-what-ecologists-are-learning-from-indigenous-people
(8) J. Portugali, *Complexity, Cognition and the City*. P. 211 Springer Heidelberg Dordrecht Londen New York, 2011.
(9) Roos van Tongerloo en Isabelle Veltman. 'Als we het klimaat willen redden is dit onze enige reddingsboei'. February 6, 2018. https://brandpuntplus.kro-ncrv.nl/brandpuntplus/deborah-coen-klimaat/
see also: *Hyperobjects: Philosophy and Ecology after the End of the World* by Timothy Morton, 2013.
(10) Mintern. S. The Sand Engine as a Productive Void. Discussing the Spatial Value and Public Appropriation of the Sand Engine.
(11) Quote Jan de Graaf

Chapter 18 MITTELMEERLAND: THE MEDITERRANEAN AS A LIQUID TERRITORY

Medine Altiok

Mediterranean port cities are diverse entities that share a common fluid space that supports exchange between them. Medine Altiok's Mittelmeerland design workshops test the potentials of seven port cities in relation to the sea, rather than anchored to land.

Medine Altiok is a German architect, graduated from the AA London. She is founder of Mittelmeerland.org, an initiative dealing with the urban transformation in the Mediterranean territory. She has been teaching Architectural Design at ETH Zurich from 2005-10, as programme director of the *Mittelmeerland*-Visiting Schools at the AA London since 2011 and as Visiting Professor at Bilgi Uni Istanbul in 2016/17. She is currently researching for her PhD with RWTH Aachen and runs her own practice in Zurich.

Once deemed the centre of civilisation, in the last century, and especially since the Second World War, the Mediterranean Sea has been divided by politics, religion, and the boundaries of nation-states into a contested and complex border zone. The Mediterranean region continues to share a common climate and ecology and growing shipping networks and ports still connect its various shores. But the Mediterranean is being transformed by urbanisation.

An important transformative force involves not only what is happening on land, but also how people are using the sea, deforming the sea floor, and changing laws that regulate such activities. The sea is increasingly busy with traffic related to the increase in trade and container shipping and new infrastructure projects that cross the Mediterranean. The construction of new shipping highways and the expansion of the oil and gas industries may not always be visible, but these activities are nonetheless reshaping the sea bed and the coasts and are heavily impacting land/water ecologies. The most important changes are driven primarily by juristic and economic decisions. To frame the viscous urbanisation of the sea, we need to extend the borders of the solid territory out to sea and at the same time redefine the concept of national borders—from solid to loose and liquid. This would enable the construct of a common Mediterranean to develop organically, linked to historical connections and cultural partnerships, but also including new shared concerns that do not yet make up a formal configuration or recognisable organisations. In "Liquid Traces: Investigating the Deaths of Migrants at the EU's Maritime Frontier," Charles Heller and Pezzani Lorenzo write that "the seas are in fact increasingly documented and divided, and inextricably so. A complex sensing apparatus is fundamental to a form of governance that combines the division of maritime spaces and the control of movement, and that instrumentalises the partial, overlapping, and 'elastic' nature of maritime jurisdictions and international law."(1) In order to avoid the exclusive segmentation of the sea, we need a conceptual shift from land to sea. We need to explore the sea with urban eyes and understand it as an extended territory of our urban environment.

"Mittelmeerland" is a research project that explores the sea's potential as a single territory of water, taking a sea-to-land perspective. This perspective allows a view beyond existing boundaries in areas fraught with division. Mittelmeerland questions what makes its cities Mediterranean. It envisions the Mediterranean as liquid territory and common ground with viscous borders governed by a network of cities tackling common issues pertaining to environment, climate, and trade independently of actions taken by nation-states.

In 2006, I started Mittelmeerland as a mapping project to visualise and explain economic, social, political, and spatial transformations of the Mediterranean as a whole, using present and future master plans of twenty-three industrial ports around the

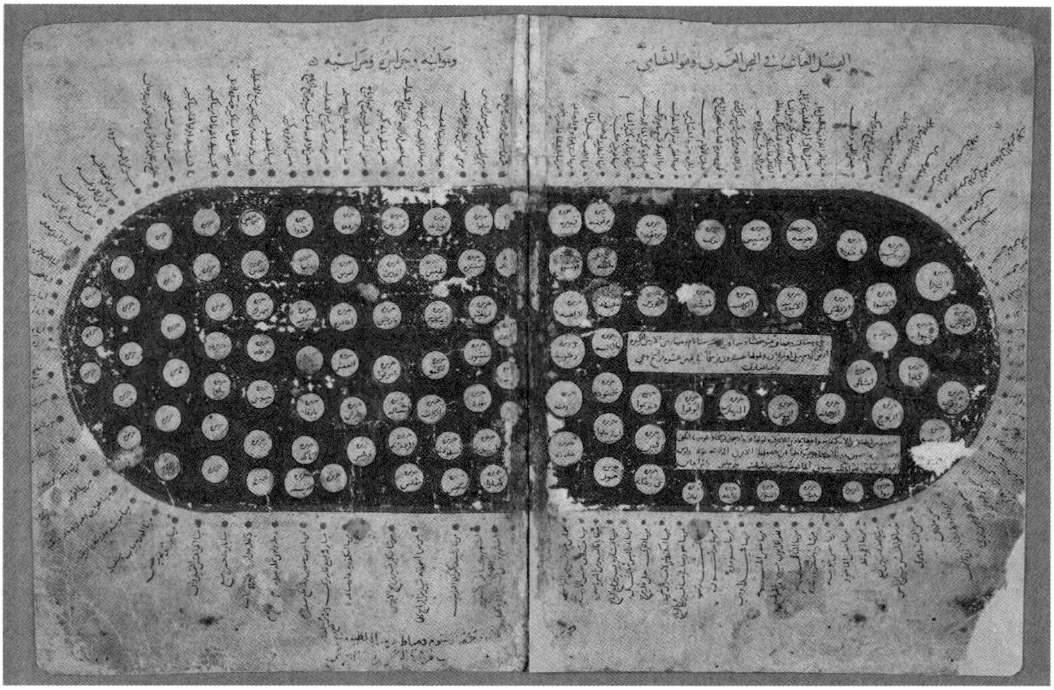

Fig. 1
Map of the Mediterranean Sea, in Medieval Islamic Views of the Cosmos.

Mediterranean coast. This work resulted in a book of cartographic drawings that considered three areas: the sea, port cities, and land. From 2011–2015, together with Stephanie Tunka I co-organised and co-directed a series of six ten-day workshops as part of the Visiting School Programme at the AA in London. The workshops took place in six Mediterranean metropolises: Dubrovnik, Tangier, Beirut, Algiers, Alexandria, and Izmir. We focused on how the urbanisation of the sea transforms the sea's shores. Participants were local and international students as well as teachers with their own students. The workshops were organised in collaboration with contributing local universities, institutions, architects and experts, and financed by the AA London, local universities, participation fees, and a variety of institutions.

THE ROLE OF CARTOGRAPHY AND NARRATIVE MAPPING

The workshops used cartography and narrative mapping as a primary tool. Since conventional ways of reading, mapping, and understanding the Mediterranean have limitations in describing viscous aspects and subjective observations, new maps were developed to provide additional layers of information, to combine knowledge of the sea and land, and to uncover additional aspects of urban coastal dynamics. In addition to developing our own mapping methods, we used historical maps as a source of inspiration; the unusual medieval map of the Mediterranean shows the contours of the Mediterranean Sea in a reduced oval shape and the harbours and islands represented

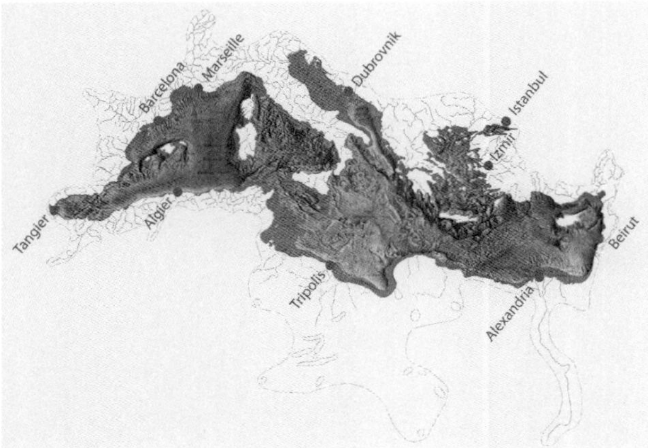

Fig. 2
Mittelmeerland
Territory defined by its watersheds and the topography of the sea floor, (Altiok, 2010)

as dots of the same size [Fig. 1]. Mittelmeerland also envisions Cities and Islands as equal entities sitting at a round table for a discussion, where Cities are seen as a family that are somehow connected. They differ in their urban character, identities, and geographies, but share many aspects of ecology and culture.

Coastal cities are partly independent from the land and are bound to the sea through their ports. They could be removed from their national context and shift into the liquid body of the Mediterranean Sea. Supported by cartographic maps that can represent territorial dimensions, this conceptual shift can assist in restoring a certain unity to this large, complex and contested sea. From this perspective, the sea is seen as a common territory defined by its watershed, similar climatic conditions, and a differentiated maritime scape [Fig. 2]. It is a shared resource within which port cities are interconnected through common shipping networks and economically can act independently of their nation-states. The economic strength of the ports could empower the sea as a territory even if the economy of its city or hinterland is weak. For example, in Tangier this independence allowed the port Tanger Med to become one of the Mediterranean's important container transshipment hubs.

Cartographic representations and narrative maps provoke wider geopolitical questions about the space of the sea and how the Mediterranean can be imagined, and possibly governed, as a unified territory shaped by its central body of water. Such representations can help communicate imaginative concepts on a territorial scale and bridge various scales. Narrative mapping in this project served as an important research tool that combined abstraction and different graphical representation techniques.

In urban studies, the coast is usually studied from the perspective of the land and in urban plans the sea appears as an empty blue, black, or white spot. In the Mittelmeerland workshops we aimed to develop narrative maps that combine different types of information and different scales, such as both the territorial and architectural scales, of a redrawn, unified Mediterrennean territory, one in which the port cities operate throughout and communicate with each other. We depicted different conditions such as land and sea, liquid and stable, both subjective as well as objective, qualitative as well as quantitative, and physical as well as phenomenological spatial observations (e.g., the sun's path, including light and shadow, wind direction to remind planners that climate should be incorporated in design and building solutions). Statistical and historical information was also consulted in order to gain a deeper understanding or to clarify questions. This method allowed us to compile diverse readings and understandings of the Mediterranean Sea and its relation to the cities. As well as historical maps, the map-making process drew on the contemporary maps of Atelier Bow Wow and ETH Studio Basel. We were inspired by ETH Studio Basel's working method and how they conducted and documented their study of cities, in particular their work on the Nile Delta, Beirut, and Casablanca.(2).

The 1375 Catalan Atlas of Europe and the Mediterranean is Abraham Cresques' "visual story" of the Mediterranean [Fig. 3, p. 271]. It consists of a compilation of trade routes, sites of raw materials and resources, dynasties, and places of all major cities along the coastline with only a few inland features. Religious references are illustrated as well as a synthesis of the medieval travel literature of the time in "an overlapping set of information that attempts to convey a broader meaning."(3)

HOW THE MITTELMEERLAND WORKSHOPS WORK

For the Mittelmeerland workshops, we developed a method that we applied to all the cities. We studied the urban patterns along the waterfront, agricultural areas connected to rivers, industrial harbours, historical centres, and geographically unique and run-down residential areas. We looked at informal interdependencies between water and land uses, transformation caused by migration and trade and problems caused by the construction of new ports or other infrastructural projects. The workshops were structured in four modules and resulted in different types of information, a set-up inspired by Raoul Bunschoten's "Urban Gallery" methodology, a specific architectural management methodology for looking at, managing, and proposing solutions on an urban and city scale.(4) We used four questions to introduce and formulate exercises, which built on each other:

1. How can we see? We drew urban portraits to analyse sea-land relations of public spaces.
2. How can we play? We made narrative maps to understand sea-land relations in a larger context.
3. How can we act? We explained the existing landscape ecology including climatic aspects and environmental issues and proposals.

4. How can we tell? We created imaginative collages to explain how an intervention would transform a situation and to communicate a possible improvement.

Beginning with a conventional black-and-white topographic and bathymetric base map, we added open source data from Google Maps, climatic aspects like shadows, sun and wind direction, and water depth. After doing fieldwork, we created narrative maps and added information including hand-measurements, scenarios, critical observations, informal spatial uses between sea and land, borders, historical traces, climatic issues, patterns of behaviour, routes, rumours, and interactions among local inhabitants. Typically, people in Mediterranean cities use the sea mostly for leisure and fishing and this relation to the sea is important to them. In all cities studied, the common climate results in similar uses of the outdoor spaces between houses, streets, and sea. We observed that any limitation of the access to the sea through privatisation, industry, a port area, an agricultural or military zone with restricted access, or environmental damage such as flooding, is experienced by people as a negative factor.

Finally, we created imaginative collages to discuss a critical statement about an existing spatial situation in the community and how this situation could be improved.

In each city, we observed more or less similar situations that need improvement: ecological imbalances, illegal migration, and trade, erasure of collective memory, poor infrastructure, and authoritarian politics.

DESCRIPTIONS OF PORTS AND SAMPLES

Before starting the workshops, we paired two relevant aspects, which became the main topic in each context: Tourism and Industrial Nature in Dubrovnik, Ecology and Politics in Beirut, Colonial Past and New Mega Projects in Algiers, Old and New Society in Alexandria, and Infrastructure and Politics in Tangier and Izmir. In general, we approached these aspects and phenomena in each city in a similar way, but for each city this pair of aspects describe the most prevailing and driving forces in urban transformation, which create spaces that damage the environment or are disconnecting or exclusive. By looking at the prevailing aspects we also hoped to find out how the cities differed from one another.

TOURISM AND INDUSTRIAL NATURE IN DUBROVNIK

We observed Croatia joining the EU with great effort. It was closing most of its military shipyards, which became redundant and would transform for other uses. Along the coastline from Dubrovnik to the port of Ploce, which extends more than 113 km, we found an amphibious context defined by ongoing conflict between the natural seascape, industry, and tourism. Due to the rapid growth of global shipping and cruising, the industrial port of Ploce and the touristic cruise port in the historic centre of Dubrovnik are expanding. The city urgently needs to guard the health of its environment as the rising number of container ships, cruise ships, and tourists are at risk of damaging the coastal ecology. We observed that post-war economic stagnation and current political conflicts have slowed down coastal investment and that negotiations between Croatia and Italy concerning how to define the borders of national and international waters are ongoing. The unstable economy and dependence on tourism are creating unsustainable communities.

In the Dubrovnik area, a critical topic is the ecological imbalance in the Neretva River Delta resulting from conflicting interests involving a protected natural area, industry, and agriculture. On one side of the Neretva River, the industrial port is expanding to connect a waterway that would allow larger container ships into the hinterland. On the other side, an orange plantation with small buildings and artificial irrigation channels is slowly disappearing due to decreased agricultural production. The sensitive river mouth is under protection and located between the port, infrastructural nodes, and agricultural fields. The narrative map describes how the clash of these four areas is causing environmental conflicts. It shows all major activities simultaneously and with equal importance. Physical elements such as ships, animals, farmhouses, and raw material stored at the port are all represented on the same scale.(5)

For the Dubrovnik historical centre, it would be interesting to attract new inhabitants by supporting and reinforcing unconventional year-round activities to achieve more diverse economies along the coast and more sustainable communities. One example would be to invest in the existing summer residences of various universities from Zagreb, making them year-round institutes that would encourage students and scientists to stay permanently in Dubrovnik and, in the long term, would create new economies through university spin-off companies serving commercial markets with innovative products.

POOR INFRASTRUCTURE AND ACTIVE POLITICS IN TANGIER

In Morocco, we observed the building of Africa's best-developed infrastructure leading to the new Port of Tanger Med, which is competing in container-shipping capacity with the Port Euro-Méditerranée in Marseille. The presence of many civilisations and the former Tangier International Zone (which operated from 1924–1956) has given Tangier a rich cultural history. Today the city is undergoing rapid development and modernisation, greatly benefiting from the new Port of Tanger Med. Once an urban wasteland, Tangier is turning into a cultural and commercial gateway between Africa and Europe. Tanger Med is part of the economic policy orienting

Fig. 4
Fall of
Canstantinople,
1455

Morocco toward exports, with particular emphasis on the free trade agreement with the European Union. Tanger Med is the largest port on the Mediterranean, situated on a once-empty site about 40 km from old Tangier, linked by a new highway along the coast. Just 14 km from Spain, it competes with other ports in the Strait of Gibraltar to attract shipping traffic passing through the Strait, considered the gateway to Europe. The success of the port has attracted many investors so that a new city is starting to develop behind the port. The border situation between Morocco and Spain, especially in the enclaves of Ceuta and Melilla, is a conflictual space, but also has the potential for sustainable common growth.

The miniature painting of the fall of Constantinople, when the Turkish army of Mehmet II attacked Constantinople in 1453, serves as a historical reference for a narrative perspective of the border between Ceuta and Tangier [Fig. 4]. Soldiers can be seen pointing canons at the city while others are pulling boats into the Golden Horn. The painting composes the story with the main spatial features of the land, water, hills, weapons, people, and ships using different scales and perspectives and exploiting both foreground and background.(6)

The spatial representation, especially of the topography, helps give an understanding of the strategy behind the position of the ships, soldiers, walls, tents, and so forth, and the reason behind the successful attack. The narrative map of Ceuta re-interpreted these techniques to illustrate the border condition and conflicts between Ceuta, Tangier, and the strategic position of Ceuta in the Straits of Gibraltar. Conflict has been increasing since a border fence was erected in 1993 to prevent illegal migration and trade. The narrative map shows the physical walls and the process of crossing the border, with the main activities of informal trade simplified and positioned to read from left to right [Fig. 5]. Moroccans who live in four towns close to the border do not need a visa to cross into Ceuta and they can take as many goods with them as they can manually carry. In order to trade without paying taxes, this agreement is exploited and the maximum allowance of goods is physically carried across the border by traders. The drawing identifies the informal occupation of public space by traders and migrants, who created specific types of spaces for waiting, hiding, and storage.(7) For future developments, it is important to ensure consideration of the potential loss of these local economies and that local inhabitants are compensated. Looking at the larger context of the coast, it would be important to place greater value on local heritage and culture. For example, a maritime and terrestrial (inter-) national park along the beautiful, wild border area between Morocco and Ceuta could help diffuse tensions.

Fig. 5
Crossing the border in Tangier: process and walls between Morocco and Ceuta (Mittelmeerland, 2010)

ECOLOGICAL IMBALANCE AND POLITICAL DECISIONS IN BEIRUT

Lebanon is culturally rich and home to different religions, but is still suffering from the instability of wartime. Beirut is situated at the meeting point of three continents—Europe, Asia, and Africa—and functions as a trading hub. Its port has been constantly extended to meet the demands of a growing population and economy. The port is considered a gateway for transporting freight to Syria, Jordan, Iraq, and the Gulf States but is in a vulnerable situation when political tensions rise. Once embedded in the urban fabric, it has now become a giant container port blocking one-third of the city's coastline. In August 2020, the tragic mega- explosion called attention to the dimensions of the political and infrastructural grievances in the port. Against this backdrop of diversity, conflict, unpredictability, and complexity, we considered how Beirut's coastline is changing in relation to the Mediterranean and the driving forces behind its reconstruction. The obvious environmental problems of sewage pollution, garbage, or non-climate conforming building systems, seem to be ignored. Beirut has explored all varieties of materialising difference from the very cosmopolitan and mixed to generic and less contextual neighbourhoods. For example, the reconstruction of the historical centre and construction of the new marina resulted in exclusive spaces that are controlled by signs, cameras, and gates and only the middle-class and very wealthy can afford them. These were areas that historically were socially mixed with a range of uses. When analysing recent property developments, one wonders about the relationship between speculative urbanism and the local geography. Regardless of their origins, the current urban projects seem not to even meet superficial social or environmental needs.(8)

THE COLONIAL PAST AND MEGA PROJECTS IN ALGIERS

Algeria is an ambitious North African country with a very strong economy. The city planning department of Algiers developed an extensive urban vision for 2030 to transform the coastline and the city, including the renewal of the current industrial port. Between 2015 and 2030, mega projects will transform the city of Algiers and its surroundings by equipping them with retail and leisure facilities. We observed that these projects almost seem to oppose a top-down urbanist's approach, since so many questions remain unanswered concerning the integration of people, connections to the existing urban tissue, and the enhancement of characteristic qualities and identities and the health of the environment. Currently, Algiers is disconnected from the sea, separated by the port in front of the city. Suburbs have developed differently than first planned. Both informal urbanisation and past colonial references can be found along the coast.

The agricultural area and nature resort around the lake and river of Reghaia is affected by the mega projects as they are creating impulses for urban developments that span to nearby neighbourhoods. Similar to the Neretva River Delta in Dubrovnik, the narrative map of Lake Reghaia in Algiers uncovers illegal activities and unplanned developments that take place in the surrounding area [Fig. 6, p. 272]. This is information that cannot be found in conventional maps. The lake is an important place for goats and migrating birds, but at the same time it is surrounded by tourist industry developments, settlements, and farmlands, both legal and illegal, that are expanding in an uncontrolled manner, pushing into the edge of the lake and polluting the water system. These developments are in conflict with the city's official plan to establish a protected nature resort, and the nearby farmlands and industries are illegally releasing chemicals into the lake's tributary rivers. The ecologically sensitive and vulnerable area between the lake and sea is illegally used as a car park, a football field, and by a hotel.(9) We found the current and projected relation between the city and the sea could be strengthened more and we perceived the chaos and beauty of current informal mutations as positive impulses that could be incorporated into the future plans for 2030.

OLD AND NEW SOCIETY IN ALEXANDRIA

Egypt is developing a gigantic global transportation route along the Suez Canal and struggling with sewage systems and waste management. Alexandria is located on the western extremity of the Nile Delta, an historical area with highly fertile and productive agricultural soil. In Alexandria, we investigated the transformation of both the old agricultural area and of society. In the Nile Delta, industrial activities have increased while agriculture and tourism have decreased, and the global significance of both has changed. Through industrialisation, the whole Nile Delta has became fragmented through new housing built on the fertile land, where 50 percent of the population is housed, resulting in a heavy loss of fertile agricultural soil. We observed new urban developments that are scattered as well as disconnected, and walled islands within old run-down areas. Here, the old and new societies hardly interact, and there are marked contrasts in the quality of the built environment. Located at the edge of the city, Sidi Kerir, for example, is an agricultural and rural neighbourhood, where luxurious walled tourist resorts and private houses have been recently built. In Sidi Kerir we were looking for urban proposals and ideas that could reinforce existing neighbourhoods and build bridges with the new areas and inhabitants. Adding common, transitional spaces such as public clubs, instead of walling and separation, could help connect old and new societies, making the area more diverse and initiating new economies.

Fig. 7
Connections on the sea could improve traffic problems. Izmir (Mittelmeerland, 2015)

POOR INFRASTRUCTURE AND POLITICAL RESISTANCE IN IZMIR

As the biggest container port in Turkey, the port of Izmir occupies an important position within the city. Centrally located between Western Europe and the Middle East, it is the agricultural and commercial centre of the Aegean region and plays a significant role in the export of Turkish products. The current container port, however, has reached its capacity, and the construction of a new port jeopardises the sensitive sea floor, which should be environmentally protected from deformation and the pollution generated by new building work. Both ends of the coast touch vulnerable areas. Northwest of Izmir`s coast are natural wetlands and the southwest contains agricultural lands. With its back to the hinterlands, Izmir has a fully Mediterranean spirit in terms of culture, trade, and politics. We discovered political resistance to the country's dominating party system: 46.8 percent voted for the opposition party CHP in 2015, compared to 31 percent for the AKP.(10) As a result, the AKP- dominated government cut financial support for urban development which slowed down Izmir's architectural and infrastructural modernisation. At the same time, this gives the municipality greater freedom to develop urban visions that are more holistic and driven not only by political and economic goals, but also by social and cultural ones. A fast public waterway connection could make public transport more attractive and could solve an important infrastructural problem during rush hours, as well as having environmental benefits [Fig. 7].

CONCLUSION

The Mittelmeerland investigation aimed to conceptualise a unified territory and to redraw the map of the Mediterrannean from the perspective of the sea. The narrative maps promote a better understanding of the complexity of port cities. They help detect locations where spatial improvements could be beneficial for the community. Combining both scientific and subjective information, they add urban layers and serve as a tool with which to tackle common environmental and societal issues and to gain a critical perspective on current urbanisation processes. Through the combination of scales and a playful composition of elements, the maps reveal conflict and hidden potentials, which may otherwise be intangible or located beyond the visual edges of the water basin.(11)

According to Christian Schmid, "the contemporary urbanising world cannot be adequately understood without systematically revising inherited concepts and representations of the urban. It is therefore first and foremost an invitation to adopt a different perspective, one that decentres the focus of analysis and looks from an ex-centric position on the urban world."(12) The case studies discussed above show examples where liquid urbanisation has a direct impact on the urban transformation taking place along the coast. They open up new and expanded dimensions of the relationship between water and society. Liquid urbanisation is directly linked to the land and is formed by maritime jurisdiction and maritime activities such as fishing, tourism, migration, trade, and the interconnections among these activities. Coastal cities share concerns regarding ecological imbalances, the loss of collective memory, and increasing migration and trade. As an additional source of knowledge, the narrative maps can communicate issues and proposals for a broad spectrum of citizens and serve as a basis for innovative and participatory planning processes, not only within local communities but also with the family of Mediterranean cities at a shared table.

ACKNOWLEDGEMENTS
I would like to thank following participants for their contributions: Marta Lozo, Iva Perucic, Lana Patrak, Janika Šlipulova for the drawing of Neretva Delta in Dubrovnik; Valentin Kunik, Nassim Bensedik, Iklyl Sari Mohammed, Esma Benkhelil for the drawing of Lake Raghaia in Algiers; Iva Jelinic, Morana Mazuran, Gunnar Ploner for the drawing of the border of Ceuta-Tanger; Aline Haddad, Mayssa Jallad, Karonline Liedtke, Yelta Köm for the drawing of Downtown-Normandy in Beirut.

(1) Charles Heller and Lorenzo Pezzani, "Traces liquides : enquête sur la mort de migrants dans la zone-frontière maritime de l'Union européenne," *Revue européenne des migrations internationales* 30, no. 3 (2014): 71-107. URL : https://www.cairn.info/revue-revue-europeenne-des-migrations-internationales-2014-3-page-71.htm
(2) ETH Studio Basel, *Territory: On the Development of Landscape and City (Zürich: Park Books, 2006)* and *The Inevitable Specificity of Cities (Zürich: Lars Mueller, 2015).*
(3) Mohamed Ballan, "Cartography, Maritime Expansion, and 'Imperial Reality': The Catalan Atlas of 1375 and the Aragonese-Catalan Thalassocracy in the Fourteenth Century." Ballandalus, August 27, 2014. Accessed September 6, 2019. https://ballandalus.wordpress.com/2014/08/27/cartography-maritime-expansion-and-imperial-reality-the-catalan-atlas-of-1375-and-the-aragonese-catalan-thalassocracy-in-the-fourteenth-century/.
(4) Hélène Binet, Raoul Bunschoten, and Takuro Hoshino, *Urban Flotsam: Stirirng the City* (Rotterdam: 010 Publishers, 2001).
(5) Nancy Couling, Paola Alfaro d'Alençon, and Medine Altiok "Narrative Cartography: Capturing a Holistic Perspective on Waterscapes," *European Journal of Creative Practices in Cities and Landscapes* 2, no. 1 (2019):11–36.
(6) Ibid.
(7) Ibid.
(8) For the Mitteelmeerland proposal for Beirut, see Couling, d'Alençon, and Altiok, "Narrative Cartography."
(9) Ibid.
(10) CHP is the Republican People's Party, AKP is the Justice & Development Party currently ed by Recep Tayyip Erdoğan. https://en.wikipedia.org/wiki/%C4%B0zmir_(electoral_districts) #June_2015
(11) Couling, d'Alençon, and Altiok, "Narrative Cartography."
(12) Christian Schmid, "Journeys through Planetary Urbanization: Decentering Perspectives on the Urban," *Society and Space* 36, no. 3 (2018): 591–610.
[Fig. 1] The Books of Curiosities, Book 2, Chapter 10: "On the Western Sea, that is the Syrian Sea, its harbours, islands and anchorages" (MS. Arab. c. 90, fols. 30b-31a); Source: Bodleian Library; http://cosmos.bodley.ox.ac.uk; Author: unknown.

Chapter 19 SINGAPORE STRAIT: AN URBAN PORTRAIT

Milica Topalović

Urbanisation processes driven by the Port of Singapore in combination with the city-state, exert a powerful influence on both Singapore's sea edge and the entire Strait. Milica Topalović shares the results of her ground-breaking study and stresses the urgency of addressing the sea from an urban design perspective.

Milica Topalović is an Associate Professor of Architecture and Territorial Planning at the ETH Zurich Department of Architecture. Her work is concerned with territories beyond-the-city and urgent transformation processes they are exposed to, through the movement of capital, social restructuring, and environmental change. She undertook a range of territorial studies around the world, in remote regions, resource hinterlands, and countrysides, in an effort to decenter and "ecologise" architect's approaches to the city, the urban, and urbanisation. In her recent work, she looks at regions whose social and environmental qualities have been degraded through unsustainable agriculture and resource harvesting practices, with intention to design their transitions toward territories organised around the principles of agroecology.

Singapore is one of the world's largest ports located on a strategic part of the global shipping belt. Every year, around 130,000 vessels pass through the Strait, translating into one every two minutes. In 2014, we estimated there were 1000 boats in the Strait at any given time, some of them 300–400 m long [Fig. 1, p. 273]. These vessels appear to dictate the architecture of the coastline and the sea bed—they determine water depth, the length of berths, and the arrangement of quays. Zoning and regulation further describe a hierarchy of use of the sea surface comparable to urban blocks separated by streets, with primary and secondary waterways, zones of activity, anchorages, and controlling infrastructures across all areas. The sheer occupation density, the frequency of movements, and the degree of control of the sea surface are astonishing.

Through the encounter with the Singapore Strait, the urbanisation of the sea became one of the crucial themes in our study. Carried out at the ETH Zurich and the Future Cities Laboratory Singapore from 2012 to 2015, the study was originally conceived as research on the hinterlands of Singapore.(1) The island city-state of Singapore, a city and a state ostensibly conceived in the mainstream political imagination as being "without a hinterland," actually mobilises a vast network of resource extraction, manufacturing, processing, and trade agents, across Asia and other parts of the world. The Singapore Strait continues to play a crucial role in these hinterland geographies and networks, a piece of sea with a unique geo-political advantage, which has afforded Singapore a role among the primary nodes in the global economic network. The sea came into the foreground as a central space within a cross-border metropolitan region formed around the Singapore Straits and encompassing Johor Bahru in Malaysia, Batam in Indonesia, and Singapore itself.(2)

Looking at the character of urban transformation across this tri-national territory, one of our research insights was that in recent history, a land-based logic of organisation of territory and the functioning of urban networks has replaced what would have been the historical experience of a sea-based or archipelagic logic underlying the organisation of settlements and connections among them. In the second half of the twentieth century, instead of connecting the region, the sea has become a divider, through hardened national borders. The older archipelagic experience of life with and by the sea has been largely lost.

In the same period, everyday life in Singapore has become removed from the port and the sea, with Batam and Johor following a similar path. Cast back inland behind reclaimed lands and heavy infrastructures, the centres of all three cities in the region have formed at a distance from the coast. Networks of car and rail transport have been pulled to the land, and as an echo, the sea has gradually exited the stage of consciousness to occupy a periphery of cultural interest. While it has become more urban—more occupied and controlled—due to stringent border regimes and automated port activities, the sea has also become less populated. Excluding the cruise ship industry, at a given moment only around 20,000 crewmembers serve ships on the Strait, many without permission to disembark. Over time, various technologies have enabled the profiling of this maritime space as grounds for logistics, trade, and economic globalisation, while everyday human interaction with the sea has been discouraged. The sea has become part of the extended territories of freight transport and industrial production—a space whose social significance has moved from a cultural to an economic medium, and its definition transforming from fluid to hard borders. The formation of borders emerges as a correlate or enabler of urbanisation processes, and as a result, the land-based territorial logic is consolidated, even at sea.

The maritime border along the Singapore Strait operates de facto as a wide borderzone territory that extends from the sea onto the land. Militarised and securitised, the borderzone has absorbed the techno-zones of industrial and logistical activities and is corroborated by them: military, industry, and cargo act as urban functions in synergy. As a result, the coastline of Singapore has become largely separated from the publicly accessible urban areas. Port operations are central to this change: although increasingly efficient and automated, they still exert ever-increasing spatial demands, and are thus pushed out of the city centre, into the borderzone. Historically a cosmopolitan site at the core of a growing city, the contemporary port is an autonomous entity, kept at a distance from urban quarters by an elaborate security system with special access regimes. Consumed by restrictions dictated by the port and the borderzone, the entire sea space of the Singapore Strait has become largely non-public, while still fully instrumentalised.

Together with military installations and the airport, the water-dependent urban functions of shipping and petrochemical industries have been major forces exerting physical pressure on the littoral zone; through land reclamation and dredging, they have sculpted the coastal topography to their needs.(3) Over the last century, more than a quarter of Singapore's land area has been artificially constructed and added to the "national territory"—a process which has escalated since the 1970s. Owned by the state, the port and the airport are motors for the production of wealth. We have calculated that 42 percent of Singapore's GDP is earned on reclaimed land. The coastline can be seen as an artificial structure, a spatial product of industrial modernisation, in which a condition of "flatness"—a tabula rasa, a surface of historical and cultural amnesia—is produced as a site of the modern city.

Compared to the first British topographic survey in 1924, Singapore's present-day land-sea topography shows a staggering difference. Land and water ecologies are not static, but are viscous, malleable, and interrelated. Today they are highly operationalized and exploited, with both human and non-human communities and ecosystems largely expelled from the coast. These processes are not neutral; they create friction and resistance in particular through the work of the younger generation of artists.

Our research was also concerned with a projective perspective —how to formulate a possible urban agenda for the sea and the Singapore Strait— based on the underlying ethos we have described. The maritime context, unfamiliar to an architect and an urban designer, presents the opportunity to rethink and recalibrate settled approaches. The case of Singapore Strait leaves no doubt that the relationship with the sea is crucial not only for the ports and shipping, but for the three cities, their quality of life, and their relationship with the environment. Yet, the urbanisation of the sea and coastal areas remains understudied, and is yet to be included in current urban planning and design discourses. Urban design for the sea will be concerned with the fact that the sea has been relegated as a territory of industrial urbanisation. A sea-centred view gives us the possibility to experience a cultural, historical, and ecological sense of this territory, as well as a more cosmopolitan perspective.

Buckminster Fuller developed his Dymaxion projection of the world in order to show, among other novel perspectives, that "the whole world is one ocean."(4) Just as the Mediterranean was one of the pools where civilizations brewed, the sea is the planetary figure that connects people and places. Today the sea is an historically unprecedented space of separation and has become an instrument for enforcing stronger geo-political demarcations of our world. This makes the sea the theatre of a different kind of violence, recently and dramatically wielded against refugees and migrants and against the EU in the case of the Brexit division of the North Sea. It is urgent that we as architects and urbanists develop local situated projects where, if we have the right perspective, we can work against these geopolitical forces.

(1) Milica Topalović, (ed.) *Hinterland: Singapore Beyond the Border* (Zurich: ETH Zurich and Singapore-ETH Centre, forthcoming 2021); Milica Topalović, "Beyond the Limits of the City: Urbanizing Territories", in *New Geograhies 08 Island*, New Geographies 08 (Cambridge, Mass: Harvard University Graduate School of Design, 2016), 164–75.
(2) Milica Topalović, Hans Hortig, and Stefanie Krautzig, eds., *Architecture of Territory. Sea Region* (Zürich: ETH Zürich DArch, FCL Singapore, 2015).
(3) Milica Topalović, "Land as Project: On Territorial Construction", in *Infrastructure Space*, ed. Andreas Ruby and Ilka Ruby (Berlin: Ruby Press, 2017).
(4) Richard Fuller Buckminster, "Fluid Geography", *American Neptune–A Quarterly Journal of Maritime History and Arts* IV, no. 2 (April 1944).

Chapter 20 AQUARIUM FOR THE ANTHROPOCENE*

Rania Ghosn & El Hadi Jazairy (DESIGN EARTH)

The ocean is inextricably linked to climate. While both are rapidly changing, these changes seem too vast and complex for everyday comprehension. Design Earth explores the aquarium as a device to enable public proximity and to develop a new mythology capable of reinstalling an aesthetic sense of wonder to the ocean world.

DESIGN EARTH is led by Rania Ghosn and El Hadi Jazairy (MIT; University of Michigan). Recipients of the Architectural League Prize for Young Architects and Designers, their work has also been supported by the Jacques Rougerie Foundation and Boghossian Foundation and it has been collected by the Museum of Modern Art. DESIGN EARTH has exhibited and published widely, at, for example, Venice Architecture Biennale (2018 and 2016); Seoul Biennale; Boston Design Biennale; Oslo Architecture Triennale; Times Museum, Guangzhou; and the Sursock Museum, Beirut. Ghosn and Jazairy are authors of *Geostories* (2018) and *Geographies of Trash* (2016) and editors of *New Geographies 2: Landscapes of Energy* (2009) and *New Geographies 4: Scales of the Earth* (2011).

*This essay was first published as "Leviathan in the Aquarium," *Journal of Architectural Education* 71, no. 2 (2017): 271–79. Reprinted with permission.

How do we make sense of the environment at a moment when human beings have declared themselves "geographic leviathans?" To live in an epoch that is shaped by extensive environmental transformations is to be confronted with uncertainties at the scale of the planet. Paradoxically, we remain so little mobilized in part because of our failures to represent the scales of a story that is difficult both to tell and to hear. The Pacific Aquarium project appropriates the object of the aquarium to take aim at the scalar dissonance between our selfish economic worries and the expansive scales of Earth.(1) The project constructs the future of the ocean in relation to anthropogenic dynamics—of gyres of marine debris, deep-sea mining plumes, and ocean acidification. Thus, the miniature channels our cultural enchantment with natural history and its propensity to make universal knowledge a personal experience and attempts to reclaim environmental externalities as an intimate part of the political constituency of Earth.

> Although I sometimes participate in these critiques of ideologies of nature, I am increasingly convinced that for all the merit of our deconstructive erudition, we are left with a rather antiseptic nature which has little if any political appeal. [...] Where the analytical practicality of left critiques is at all implemented, it is largely subordinated to a science-driven, policy-oriented, bureaucracy centered project of environmental management. [...] I want to insist that the re-enchantment of nature... be mobilized against establishment environmentalism.
> Neil Smith, "Nature at the Millennium: Production and Re-enchantment"

> There will be unexpected consequences. Taking care of unexpected country will be required—again and always. Reconciliation is not guaranteed; it is proffered, suggested, haltingly pictured. Any reconciliation will depend on descendants of settler worlds letting go of salvation history and instead learning to live in technoculture in something more like the time of Aboriginal country, facing ancestors of many kinds and responsible for those who come after. Technocultural people must study how to live in actual places, cultivate practices of care, and risk ongoing face-to-face encounters with unexpected partners. Donna Haraway, "Speculative Fabulations for Technoculture's Generations: Taking Care of Unexpected Country"

In 1853, Philip Henry Goosse, a self-taught naturalist and popularizer of natural science, created the first public aquarium at the London Zoo, and published *The Aquarium, An Unveiling of the Wonders of the Deep Sea*, the first manual on how to build and take care of a miniature ocean. An aquarium, he asserted, was "the perfect way to get acquainted with the peculiar creature of the ocean without having to descend into the depths."(2) Until mid-century, the bottom of what the sailors call "blue water" was "so unknown to us as is the interior of any of the planets of our system."(3) The first systematic efforts to sound the open sea date from the mid-nineteenth century. The growth of commercial and strategic opportunities, such as transoceanic shipping, whaling, and submarine telegraphy, attracted investigators to the ocean's third dimension. The aquarium genre quickly grew into a craze, first within the home then as a collective experience, comparable to funfairs, zoos, and natural history museums, which offered viewers the chance to contemplate aquatic creatures in miniatures of their environments, both for scientific study and popular pleasure.

Among the many early handbooks on aquarium care is *Ocean Gardens* by the British artist and naturalist Noel Humphreys. In his opening chapter, Humphreys admonished his reader: "To appreciate Nature, the mind requires a special education, without which the eye and the ear perceive but little of the miracles passing before them." He added, "the wonders of the ocean floor do not reveal themselves to vulgar eyes."(4) The aquarium was born out of such a desire to represent to the senses, or make sense of, the inaccessible, expansive, and mysterious deep sea. As the locus of an unprecedented form of knowledge production, the aquarium made visible a new site of knowledge. Here, scientific, socio-economic, technological, and political forces were manifested, entailing new modes and aesthetics for the production of evidence."(5) It is both an aquatic cabinet of curiosities that surveys the terra incognita of the submarine world, and a miniature ocean, which by framing a portion of the underwater world gestures toward an unframeable whole. Wild speculations and fantasies are subsequently woven around the unfathomable abyss and "compressed into an easily comprehended menagerie, an oceanic garden in miniature, a submarine chamber of wonders."(6)

Today, Humphreys' call to develop our "vulgar eyes" is very timely as humans make sense of the ocean at a moment in which they have declared themselves "geographic leviathans." The ocean is increasingly present in visualizations of Earth and of scientific accounts of the impact of industrial activities on the planet. Although the Blue Marble was a proto-environmentalist icon for a fragile ocean planet, for a few decades after the first space satellite images, the ocean remained a giant blank blue surface in web-based models of the planet. "We had this arbitrary distinction that if it was below sea level it didn't count," recalled John Hanke, the Internet entrepreneur who co-created the progenitor of Google Earth.(7) Until 2009, all of the existing features on Google Earth—mountains, valleys, cities, plains, ice sheets—were built through programming from an elevation of zero up. It was only in 2009 that representations of submarine topography and other ocean data began to figure in Google Earth, and even then only 5 percent of the ocean floor is mapped in detail.(8) The ocean is also an inseparable dimension of geographies of climate change. About 93 percent of the excess heat energy stored by Earth over the last fifty years is found in the ocean. A major resource for life on Earth, the ocean is undergoing significant anthropogenic transformations—of gyres of marine debris, deep-sea mining plumes, and ocean acidification. In 2014, the Intergovernmental Panel on Climate Change (IPCC), which was set up in 1988 to inform policymakers of the science of climate change, gathered all the scientific knowledge for the first time in a single document, which extended interest in the ocean beyond the surface concern of rising sea levels to engage the totality of the role of the ocean in the climate system and climate change impacts.(9) Several barriers impede the ability of the general public to think about and feel the impacts of deep-sea mining and climate change on the ocean. In general, complex systems are difficult to fathom, and the issue of climate change is particularly challenging because its effect involves vast scales of both time and space. While weather is both temporally and geographically closer and part of everyday life and experience, climate refers to patterns over time. Furthermore, an ocean is large, difficult to see all at once in its depths and extents, and requires a vast representational machine to comprehend. Its sheer size is overwhelming.

What is the affective agency of a cabinet of natural history in a post-natural world and within this ocean of uncertainties? If environmental issues are un-representable in their scale, their ubiquity, and their duration, then perhaps miniatures of Earth can present such scientific concerns to the senses. Miniaturization becomes a demonstration of the rule of containment: the microcosm encapsulates the scales of Earth, it is a *tableaux vivant* predicated on manipulation of crafted "props" in carefully defined technologies and landscapes. The reverie of the miniature is a pervasive feature of the human imagination, as Gaston Bachelard has shown in his explorations of the rich textures of the real. "Miniature is an exercise that has metaphysical freshness," notes Bachelard. "It allows us to be world conscious at slight risk," he adds, "and how restful this exercise on a dominated world can be! For miniature rests us without ever putting us to sleep. Here the imagination is both vigilant and content."(10) The microcosm renders the ocean visible, comprehensible and hence a possible domain of reflection and action. Beyond a symbolic surrogate of the totality, the microcosm is also world-building, which by channeling wonder and marvel, aspires to build a world beyond the strict values of the economy. Susan Stewart recognized such capacity of miniature objects. "The reduction in scale which the miniature presents skews the time and space relations of the everyday lifeworld, and as an object consumed the miniature finds its 'use value' transformed into the infinite time of reverie."(11) Within such a complex web of environmental relationships between facts, uncertainties, emotions, and actions, the aquarium brings remote scales, uncertain futures, and intangible science concepts, such as climate change, to the personal realm.

The Pacific Aquarium project was developed for and first exhibited at the Oslo Architecture Triennale "After Belonging."(12) The invitation to contribute to the section on "Markets and Territories of the Global Home" brought us to speculate on what it is to belong to Earth, and in particular to the Clarion-Clipperton Zone (CCZ) in the Pacific Ocean. The site of CCZ covers an area approximately the size of Europe and has the world's largest deposits of deep-seabed rare earth minerals, which are used in the production of batteries and alloys. The seabed outside of national jurisdictions, called the "Area" in the United Nations Convention on the Law of the Sea (UNCLOS), is legally part of the "common heritage of mankind," which following UN General Assembly Resolution 2749, should not be subject to national appropriation. The "Area" is under the legal mandate of the International Seabed Authority (ISA) that was created in 1982 with the mission to oversee exploration, mapping, and resource management in the High Seas. Since 2001 however, ISA has granted twelve exploration licenses for minerals on the CCZ deep seabed. The magnitude of the damage to the CCZ reserved for resource extraction cannot be fully anticipated, as the scale of mining is unprecedented and the ecosystems at this depth of the ocean are yet to be fully understood. Researchers have stated that "efforts to adapt to and/or mitigate the effects of climate change on marine ecosystems must operate in a framework characterized by uncertainty from multiple sources," and that "the scientific community has to rely on scenarios to consider complexity and irreducible uncertainty."(13)

Pacific Aquarium appropriates the object of the aquarium to take aim at the scalar distance between our selfish economic worries and the great scales of Earth. A series of nine aquariums, each addressing a particular economy-environment nexus, reclaim ocean space as public controversies by connecting political ecology with speculative design and a collective aesthetic experience. The Aquarium reckons as such with the cognitive and affective dissonance between what feels like minute individual concern and agency and a context of enormous collective impact. It also presents the following significant attributes:

1. The aquarium is a three-dimensional territory that materializes the vertical element of volume.(14) It is inherently sectional.

2. The aquarium is populated, a multi-species space. It counters images of the sea that present it as a "territory of emptiness,"(15) such as Lewis Carroll's evacuated *Ocean Chart* from *The Hunting of the Snark*.(16)

3. The aquarium is *now*. Rather than the vastly accelerated aesthetics of contemporary Anthropocene representations, of

exponential info-diagrams or disaster satellite images, the aquarium favors an immersive, enchanting experience that speaks directly to climate change. The aquarium slows down thought and grounds it in the immediacy and wonder of the present.

4. The aquarium is also *there*. It is both a model of the world and an object of wonder. It actually capitalizes on its distance from the real through its transparent, yet clearly defined, boundary condition. Its technologies of the spectacle draw on the perceptual logics and plots of the shop window, the theater, the panorama, and literal and fictive travels to become an amalgam of all.(17) With monsters, storms, a modern-day Noah, scientists, and jellyfish on stage, the aquarium is the setting in which the non-speaking and non-human entities operate as devices of estrangement. The aquarium's uncanny ability to draw on multiple, even competing, visual and textual logics is central to its work.

5. The aquarium holds vividly in tension the panorama and its details. It stages a slice of the ocean nesting a range of scales—from the micro to the macro—into one another, without ever fitting neatly.

The project drawings bring the attributes of the aquarium into a microcosm on a sheet of paper. They depict three-dimensional cross-sections of the ocean with a split view that shows the environments both above and below the water surface. This mode of representation, known popularly as the aquarium view, draws on illustrations in the biological sciences and geological sciences, such as the frontispiece from Charles Lyell's *Principles of Geology*, which depicts the rock cycle and Charles Darwin's illustration of coral reef formation,(18) or *Duria Antiquior*, a pictorial representation of a scene of prehistoric life based on evidence from fossil reconstructions. The drawings also appeal to a geographical project that predates the disciplinary schism of sciences of the earth, and in particular to Alexander von Humboldt's "portrait of nature," which presented a totality of the scales and sciences of the earth in an assemblage of astronomy, geography, botany, and geology. Although Humboldt's avowed purpose was that of "scientific traveller," his drawings assembled forms of knowledge, which, beyond the accumulation of information, engaged the aesthetic experience of the reader. They made commensurability possible. "People want to see," Humboldt noted, "and I show them a microcosm on a sheet of paper."(19)

The aquarium view is also an act of fantastic world-building, much like the task of science fiction (or what Donna Haraway prefers to call "SF: Science Fiction, Speculative Fabulation, String Figures, So Far").(20) This model of the ocean resonates with Haraway's concept of "worlding" as a process of actively reimagining a non-anthropocentric world. "These knowledge-making and world-making fields," Haraway observes, "inform a craft that for me is relentlessly replete with organic and inorganic critters and stories, in their thick material and narrative tissues."(21) The purpose of worlding is not to predict the future, let alone to fix it, but to raise questions about present relations between humans and the world they inhabit. The stories being told serve as such to explicate the here-and-now. They build on surrealism as the procedure of using violence to illustrate the present political-environmental-moral state of affairs.(22) "Sometimes the most direct way to tell the truth," Ursula Le Guin reminds us, "is to tell a totally implausible story, like myth. That way you avoid the muddle of pretending the story ever happened, or ever will happen."(23) The figures and events of myth also provide a medium through which universal environmental knowledge becomes personal experience and a common ground on which we can meet, not only rationally, but aesthetically and emotionally. Framed as such, their end is the assembly of a body that cares to speak to and with Earth.

Such fabulations are part of the process of developing a new mythology of the environment—a space for our fables, legends, and architectural precedents to be retold, rethought, and reenvisioned. Bruno Latour proposes that climate change calls for a new worldview that counters the objectification of Earth and its associated Promethean worldviews. In his view, the assumed divide between nature and society—and the accompanying focus on deanimate, disembodied, undisputed reason—has led directly to the current ecological crisis. We do not live on a "Blue Marble," insofar as that famous image of our planet symbolizes an objective, holistic, impersonal earth made visible by our own technological achievements. Such metaphysics of technological progress, Latour argues, should now be countered by a redefined assemblage of *values*, so as to extend beyond the critique of the modern objectification of the Earth to a new ecological belief-system in the embodiment of Gaïa. As its name evokes, the Greek goddess of Earth is an "odd, doubly composite figure… the Möbius strip of which we form both the inside and the outside, the truly global Globe that threatens us even as we threaten it."(24)

Each of the nine aquarium views below reckons with the uncertainties of environmental and technological futures in the Pacific Ocean.

CLASSIFIED SEDIMENTS [Fig. 1]

Nearly five centuries of marine discovery notwithstanding, the ocean remains largely unknown, unmeasured, and unmapped.(25) Those agencies and corporations that have invested the most in visualizing the CCZ are those that are only intent on gauging the value of the materials found in the seabed. The two-dimensional "floor plans" developed from their data clearly show the narrow scope of their interests. In Classified Sediments, an artificial landform camouflages the entrance to a sequence of vaults that extend deep into Earth's crust to house security and intelligence records on the deep sea. This icon of secrecy dissimulates itself by mimicking the cartographic resolution of the trigonometric projection of the deep sea. The territory of the deep sea hides in the map.

OVERMINING [Fig. 2]

With support from the ISA, a twenty-first-century gold rush is set to begin on the ocean floor, with likely consequences that may include changes to the geochemistry of the sediment and light and noise pollution from the machinery. The same ISA has also mandated a detailed procedure in order to conserve the flora and fauna of the mining area to facilitate an accelerated recovery of the ecosystem post-extraction. Each mining entity will be required to extract substrate samples along a geographically indexed system of transects on a 500 meter grid across its claim. Suspended by cables from a grid of surficial floats, the forest of linear striations is a Hanging Gardens of the Pacific, which similarly to its Babylonian namesake is subject of controversies on whether it is an actual construction or a poetic creation. Over a decade, the infrastructure incubates a benthic ecosystem that will be grafted onto the depleted seabed.

CYBORG FISH COLONY [Fig. 3]

The International Seabed Authority mandates the conservation of the flora and fauna in the mining area of the Clipperton fault. Deep-sea mining however produces plumes that smother near-bottom species away from their habitats. The project draws on the modernization of the fishing industry and the radical changes in capture techniques and in the fish themselves. With killing machines and robo-fishers ruling the oceans, the fish itself is transformed into

Fig. 1
Classified Segments (Design Earth, Pacific Aquarium, 2016)

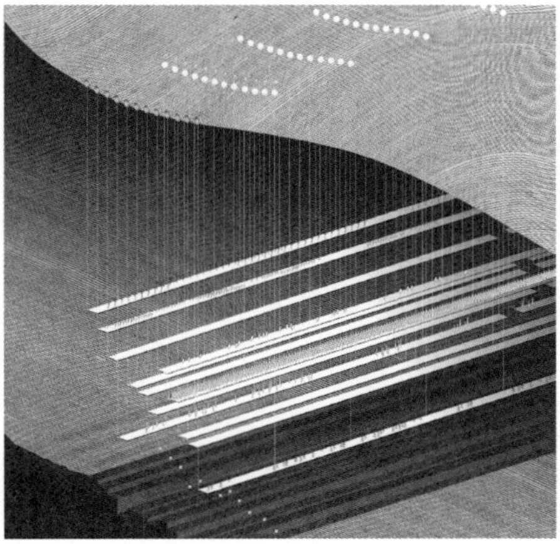

Fig. 2
Overmining
(Design Earth,
Pacific Aquarium,
2016)

a hybrid of machine and organism, a creature of social reality as well as a creature of fiction. A school of cyborg fish collects the plumes into a massive spherical sponge-like nest where the toxic particles are solidified and processed into energy. The fish subsequently decompose into organic sustenance for the returning species.

BELOW THE WATER TOWERS [Fig. 4, p. 274]

At the ocean floor the sharply toothed, combine-like suction machines will churn and rip the ocean surface into a sediment slurry, which if not contained would distribute widely through deep ocean currents. A catchment dome caps mining activities to contain sediment plumes. Polluted water is separated from surrounding water and transported into a series of inverted water towers just below the surface for processing. Purified water is gradually released back into the ocean. Under the Water Towers flips Manhattanism on its head. It displaces Buckminster Fuller's Dome over Manhattan, and rather than protecting the air of the city it processes the water of the deep sea.

MARINE LANDFILLS

Gyre plastic is matter in motion across the North Pacific Ocean connecting ocean ecosystems with cultures of consumption and waste.(26) It is estimated that without significant action, there may be more plastic than fish in the ocean, by weight, by 2050. Large-scale landfills capture floating waste, oil, fuel and detergents from the Pacific gyres. Seawater cascades into a landfill to be filtered by a one-way membrane surface. When a marine landfill site is filled, the inverted pyramid is sealed and becomes a floating island in the sea.

IRON TOWERS [Fig. 5, p. 274]

The uptake of carbon dioxide (CO2) from the atmosphere is decreasing the pH of Earth's oceans. A number of ocean scientists and businesses are exploring iron fertilization as a means to stimulate photosynthesis in plankton, converting dissolved carbon dioxide

Fig. 3
Cyborg Fish Colony (Design Earth, Pacific Aquarium, 2016)

into carbohydrates and oxygen. The vertical tensile structure, which contains high iron concentrations of water in its tubes, extends the habitat of phytoplankton to the deep ocean attracting corals and other sea creatures to the infrastructure.

MEDUSA MAZE

Jellies, which bloom seemingly wherever ocean environments are destabilized, are a visual index of a dying ocean. As coral reefs, cetaceans, sea turtles, and fish die off, jellyfish will take stage as the main animal protagonists of oceans. As the seas become distressed. "the jellyfish are there, like an eagle to an injured lamb or golden staph to a postoperative patient—more than just symptoms of weakness, more like the angel of death."(27) The Medusa Maze is a jellyfish Pac-Man, populated with planktons and sea turtles. The Maze is a jellyfish husbandry for an emerging cosmetic industry. It is also a *Damnatio ad bestias*,(28) an Anthropocene arena that pits the gelatinous beasts against their predators in a luminescent aquarium.

CLIMATE SANCTUARIES

A Small Island State (SIS) is a low-lying coastal country that is particularly vulnerable to sea level rise. When a SIS loses its land fully to the rising sea level, its defined territory ceases to exist, hence no longer meeting one of the four UN criteria for statehood.(29) The Climate Sanctuaries project reconstructs the territories of the first five submerged Pacific islands of Vanuatu, Marshalls, Fiji, Tuvalu, and Kiribati through their cultural landscapes: volcanic mountains, coastlines, highlands villages, cliffs, and water territories.

PARLIAMENT OF REFUGEES

The challenge of governing the ocean is that it lacks formal representation—both political and aesthetic—through which to think the new environments of climate change. The ocean hovers awkwardly outside the zone of national claims, like an uninvited guest without seats at the table. If politics, as Latour articulates, "is the art of cohabiting together in this immense greenhouse with species that have very different demands for survival,"(30) then what is the greenhouse, or should we say "blue-house" of climate change? What assemblies could stage a totality, especially when that whole is opaque, fragmented, contradictory?

The Parliament of Refugees contains within the same artificial envelope different things and species of the Anthropocene, such as sea turtles, CO32– molecules, scallops, bleached corals, drowning wetlands, hammerhead sharks, algae, *Homo sapiens*, *Brighamia rockii*, Nihoa finch. The Assembly is organized around a hollow pillar that connects it to the center of the earth through a submerged volcano.

CONCLUSION

To live in an epoch shaped by such anthropogenic transformations is to be confronted with risks at the scale of the planet. Paradoxically, we remain so little mobilized in part because of our failures to address uncertainties and to represent the scales of a story that is difficult both to tell and to hear. The current environmental condition seems to involve a crisis of the imagination, the amendment of which might depend on finding other forms and forums of eco-political engagement. Pacific Aquarium discloses its epoch's capacity to feel that there are other possible ways for the environment to consist.(31) The miniature of Earth explores an alternative mode of environmental narration in order to reclaim and cultivate response-ability. In the midst of spiraling ecological devastation, this speculative fabulation is "not interested in reconciliation or restoration," but is "deeply committed to the more modest possibilities of partial recuperation and getting on together. Call that staying with the trouble."(32) For speculative fabulation, Haraway reminds, "It matters what thoughts think thoughts. It matters what knowledges know knowledges. It matters what relations relate relations. It matters what worlds world worlds. It matters what stories tell stories."(33) Charged with wonder, such environmental fabulation might be the necessary storytelling for the geographic leviathan's earthly survival. It channels enchantment to reclaim territorial externalities within the political constituency of Earth.

(1) Pacific Aquarium Project Credits: Rania Ghosn and El Hadi Jazairy, with Reid Fellenbaum, Ya Suo, Jia Weng, Shuya Xu, Saswati, Rixt Woudstra, Alaa Quraishi, Namjoo Kim, Ammar Ahmed, Alexandra Chen.
(2) Bernd Brunner, *The Ocean at Home: An Illustrated History of the Aquarium* (Princeton: Princeton Architectural Press, 2005), 41.
(3) Quote by Matthew Fontaine Maury, in Helen M. Rozwadowski, *Fathoming the Ocean: The Discovery and Exploration of the Deep Sea* (Cambridge, MA: Harvard University Press, 2008), 33.
(4) Noel Humphreys, *Ocean Gardens* (London: Sampson Low & Sons, 1857), 3-9.
(5) Natascha Adamowsky, *The Mysterious Science of the Sea, 1775-1943* (London: Routledge, 2015), 103.
(6) Brunner, *Ocean at Home*, 126.
(7) Andrew C. Revkin, "Google Earth Fills its Watery Gaps," *New York Times* (February 2, 2009), http://www.nytimes.com/2009/02/03/science/earth/03oceans.html
(8) Stefan Helmreich, "From Spaceship Earth to Google Ocean: Planetary Icons, Indexes, and Infrastructures," *Social Research* 78, No. 4 (2011): 1211–42.
(9) IPCC, "Climate Change 2014: Synthesis Report," https://archive.ipcc.ch/report/ar5/syr/
(10) Gaston Bachelard, *The Poetics of Space*, trans. Maria Jolas (Boston: Beacon Press, 1994 [1958]), 161.
(11) Susan Stewart, *On Longing: Narratives of the Miniature, the Gigantic, the Souvenir, the Collection* (Durham, NC: Duke University Press, 1993), 65.
(12) For further information about the Triennale, visit http://www.afterbelonging.org
(13) M. R. Payne et al., "Uncertainties in projecting climate-change impacts in marine ecosystems," *ICES Journal of Marine Science* 73, no. 5 (2016): 1273,1278.
(14) Philip Steinberg, "Wet Ontologies, Fluid Spaces: Giving Depth to Volume through Oceanic Thinking," *Environment and Planning D: Society and Space* 33, (2015): 247–64. For more on recent literature on the sea in geographical research, see Kimberley Peters, *Water Worlds: Human Geographies of the Ocean* (London: Routledge, 2016).
(15) A term used by Alain Corbin to describe the seaside before its appropriation by nineteenth-century Europe. Alain Corbin, *Le Territoire du Vide: l'Occident et the Desire du Rivage 1750-1840* (Paris, 1988); *The Lure of the Sea: The Discovery of the Seaside in the Western World, 1750-1840*, trans. Jocelyn Phelps (Cambridge: Polity, 1994).
(16) Lewis Carroll, *The Hunting of the Snark*, 1876.
(17) Judith Hamera, *Parlor Ponds: The Cultural Work of the American Home Aquarium, 1850–1970* (Ann Arbor: University of Michigan Press, 2012), 2.
(18) Charles Lyell, *Principles of Geology* (London, 1930).
(19) J. M. Drouin, "Humboldt et la popularization des sciences," in Humboldt et Bonpland, 1799-1804: *une aventure savant aux Ameriques, Revue du Musée des Arts et Métiers* (2003): 54–63, 60.
(20) Donna Haraway, *SF, Speculative Fabulation and String Figures: 100 Notes, 100 Thoughts*, Documenta Series 033 (Berlin: Hatje Cantz, 2012).
(21) Donna Haraway, "SF: Science Fiction, Speculative Fabulation, String Figures, So Far," Pilgrim Award Acceptance (2011), http://people.ucsc.edu/~haraway/Files/PilgrimAcceptanceHaraway.pdf.
(22) Ursula Le Guin, *The Language of the Night: Essays on Fantasy and Science Fiction* (New York: G.P. Putnam's Sons, 1979), 159.
(23) http://www.swarthmore.edu/Humanities/pschmid1/engl5H/leguin.interv.html
(24) Bruno Latour, *An Inquiry into Modes of Existence: An Anthropology of the Moderns* (Cambridge, MA: Harvard University Press, 2013), 9f.
(25) Jeanne Gang, Claire Cahan, and Sarah Kramer, "Deep Mapping," *Climates: Architecture and the Planetary Imaginary* (Zürich: Lars Muller Publishers, 2016), 1.
(26) Kim De Wolff, "Gyre Plastic: Science, Circulation and the Matter of the Great Pacific Garbage Patch" (PhD dissertation, University of California, San Diego, 2014), 8–9.
(27) Lisa-Ann Gershwin, *Stung! On Jellyfish Blooms and the Future of the Ocean* (Chicago: University of Chicago Press, 2013), 2.
(28) *Damnatio ad bestias*, latin for "damnation to beasts," was a form of Roman capital punishment in which the condemned person was killed by wild animals. This form of execution was also a form of entertainment and part of the wider class of blood sports called Bestiarii.
(29) Erin Halstead, "Citizens of Sinking Islands: Early Victims of Climate Change," *Indiana Journal of Global Legal Studies* 23, no. 2 (2016): 819-37.
(30) Bruno Latour, "There is no Terrestrial Globe," in *Cosmograms*, ed. Melik Ohanian (New York: Lukas and Sternberg, 2005), 216.
(31) Isabelle Sengers, "Gaia, the Urgency to Think (and Feel)," https://osmilnomesdegaia.files.wordpress.com/2014/11/isabelle-stengers.pdf
(32) Donna Haraway, *Staying with the Trouble: Making Kin in the Chthulucene* (Durham, NC: Duke University Press, 2016), 10.
(33) Ibid., 35.